PRAISE FOR
The Tin Ticket

"A moving and fascinating story—both of forgotten people who were ruthlessly exploited and of a remarkable woman who did much to help them."
—Adam Hochschild, author of *King Leopold's Ghost* and
Bury the Chains; cofounder of *Mother Jones* magazine

"The Irish feature in disproportionate numbers among the convicts transported to Australia . . . Deborah J. Swiss brings new light and insight into the story."
—Máirtín Ó Fainín, Ambassador of Ireland

"Deborah J. Swiss eloquently and engagingly uncovers a buried and important piece of Australian 'herstory': convicted women who endured injustice, cruelty, and hardship. Even more than that, Swiss skillfully illuminates their essence in their extraordinary resilience, determination, and courage. An inspiration to all."
—Birute Regine, author of *Iron Butterflies: Women
Transforming Themselves and the World*

"The stories of the women in this book are not too different from those of the millions who are trafficked across continents even today for cheap labor or sex. And like these women, the founding mothers of Australia exemplify the same remarkable resilience and resourcefulness that women show to pull themselves and their families out of adversity."
—Ritu Sharma, cofounder and president, Women Thrive Worldwide

THE TIN TICKET

The Heroic Journey of Australia's Convict Women

Deborah J. Swiss

BERKLEY BOOKS, NEW YORK

THE BERKLEY PUBLISHING GROUP
Published by the Penguin Group
Penguin Group (USA) Inc.
375 Hudson Street, New York, New York 10014, USA
Penguin Group (Canada), 90 Eglinton Avenue East, Suite 700, Toronto, Ontario M4P 2Y3, Canada
(a division of Pearson Penguin Canada Inc.)
Penguin Books Ltd., 80 Strand, London WC2R 0RL, England
Penguin Group Ireland, 25 St. Stephen's Green, Dublin 2, Ireland (a division of Penguin Books Ltd.)
Penguin Group (Australia), 250 Camberwell Road, Camberwell, Victoria 3124, Australia
(a division of Pearson Australia Group Pty. Ltd.)
Penguin Books India Pvt. Ltd., 11 Community Centre, Panchsheel Park, New Delhi—110 017, India
Penguin Group (NZ), 67 Apollo Drive, Rosedale, Auckland 0632, New Zealand
(a division of Pearson New Zealand Ltd.)
Penguin Books (South Africa) (Pty.) Ltd., 24 Sturdee Avenue, Rosebank, Johannesburg 2196,
South Africa

Penguin Books Ltd., Registered Offices: 80 Strand, London WC2R 0RL, England

The publisher does not have any control over and does not assume responsibility for author or third-party websites or their content.

PRINTING HISTORY
Berkley hardcover edition / October 2010
Berkley trade paperback edition / November 2011

Berkley trade paperback ISBN:978-0-425-24307-7

The Library of Congress has catalogued the Berkley hardcover edition of this title as follows:

Swiss, Deborah J.
   The tin ticket / Deborah J. Swiss. — 1st ed.
     p.   cm.
   ISBN 978-0-425-23672-7
1. Penal transportation—Australia—Tasmania—History—19th century.   2. Women prisoners—
Australia—Tasmania—History—19th century.   3. Convict labor—Australia—Tasmania—
History—19th century.   4. Exiles—Australia—Tasmania—History—19th century.   I. Title.
   HV8950.T3S95   2010
   994.602092'2—dc22
   [B]
                              2010014357

PRINTED IN THE UNITED STATES OF AMERICA

10 9 8 7 6 5 4 3 2 1

To Digney Fignus

CONTENTS

Contents

ACKNOWLEDGMENTS

Like Agnes McMillan and Janet Houston, I'm blessed with true-blue mates. Digney Fignus patiently edited chapter draft after chapter draft, transcribed stacks of nineteenth-century newspaper accounts and convict records, and composed the beautiful song "All for Love," which honors the transported women. My children, Alex and Alison Rice-Swiss, cheered me through each deadline and across the finish.

Molly Lyons, my agent at Joelle Delbourgo Associates, is exceptional and believed in me from our first meeting. Berkley Books editor Natalee Rosenstein and associate editor Michelle Vega were outstanding at all the details that moved The Tin Ticket into production. A giant thank-you to Berkley publisher Leslie Gelbman, managing editor Jessica McDonnell, Richard Hasselberger and Andrea Tsurumi in the art department, and everyone in publicity, promotion, and sales.

An extraordinary team helped build this book. Anne Raisis provided excellent editorial expertise and moved mountains to gather photo permissions from around the world. Ames Halbreich added atmosphere and poetry as she edited chapters. Connie Hadley helped shape The Tin Ticket's tone by asking the right questions, and generously delivered healthy care packages for the final crunch. Audrey Block contributed brilliant edits through every phase of this project, along with humor at just the right moments. Shannon Hunt, Mary Kantor, Judy Noonan, and Judy Walker offered comments and suggestions that improved each chapter. Charlie Mitchell quickly answered several thorny research questions. Magnificent technical expertise came from Tom Coy and Yamil Suarez. Kay Coughlin, David Holzman, Jo Hannah Katz, Dari Paquette, and Wendy Tighe-Hendrickson also extended wonderful support.

Special thanks to Shirley McCarron, project manager for the Cascades Female Factory; Father Peter Rankin, parish priest in Kilmore, Victoria; and Rob Valentine, Lord Mayor of Hobart, Tasmania. Members of the Female Factory Research Group—Trudy Cowley and Fiona MacFarlane—provided superb transcription services for Tasmanian records. Cary Memorial Library staff Heather Vandermillen and Jean Williams located many obscure reference materials through interlibrary loan that, in turn, led me to other original sources.

My research journey began with inspiration from Tasmanian artist Christina Henri's poignant and thought-provoking work *900 Bonnets*, an installation that honors the children who perished at the Cascades Female Factory, and her recent *Roses from the Heart* project, for which people on many continents are sewing bonnets to honor each of the twenty-five thousand transported women.

I first fell in love with Tasmania and then with the convict women who helped shape a nation. Over the course of the past six years, I've been rewarded with the gift of friendship, wit, and wisdom from convict descendants and their families, including Mary and Chris Binks, Sherilyn Butler, Edna and Phil Cullen, Lisa and Denis Samin, Joy and Joe Sharpe, Kaye Williams, and Glad and Bob Wishart. Agnes, Bridget, Janet, and Ludlow would certainly smile at their legacy.

INTRODUCTION

Life's most interesting journeys often begin with a surprising coincidence. Sometimes a story finds you. In 2004, I traveled to Tasmania to join two wilderness treks. Challenging myself among a group of highly experienced trekkers, I completed the eighty-kilometer Overland Track in the Cradle Mountain–Lake St. Clair National Park and climbed Mt. Ossa, Tasmania's highest peak. I also explored the Bay of Fires in Mt. William National Park, where huge Aboriginal middens mark Musselroe Point.

During a break from hiking, I happened to meet Christina Henri, a Tasmanian commemorative artist whose work honors the twenty-five thousand women exiled from the British Isles to Australia. She was standing in line ahead of me in a post office in Launceston, Tasmania. Without knowing that I'm a writer, she turned to me and said: "I have a story I want to tell you."

I knew little about this chapter in history until that day I stood in the queue chatting with Christina. Out of the blue, she began to describe the piece of paper she held in her hand, a pattern for a christening bonnet. Christina was mailing one of nine hundred bonnet patterns to a volunteer helping her create a traveling memorial honoring the nine hundred infants and children who died at the Cascades Female Factory. Newspapers of the day had labeled the damp, converted distillery, hidden under the cliffs of Mt. Wellington, "the Valley of the Shadow of Death." This was the prison that housed the women featured in *The Tin Ticket*.

The backdrop for these women's lives exposes a time in history still unknown to many. The journey of the convict women began in slums all across the British Isles, where the destitute struggled to survive. Profit trumped morality as wigged and powdered Parliamentarians sold grain at inflated prices to other countries and ignored widespread hunger and homelessness among their own citizens.

High levels of unemployment, created by the Industrial Revolution and an exploding urban population, left a working-class girl with few options in the early 1800s. Even a woman fortunate enough to find work was always paid less than a man. When thousands of soldiers returned from the Napoleonic Wars, many female factory workers lost their jobs to the men. The *Glasgow Courier* suggested that if a woman was "not ugly," she might "find relief in prostitution" instead of a crippling life in the textile mills.[1] Many girls had no choice but to resort to selling their bodies, which was not a crime in nineteenth-century Britain. Others staved off starvation by collecting and selling bones, singing ballads for pennies, picking pockets, or pilfering small items that might be traded for food or a place to sleep. Petty theft was a way of life for women, men, and children desperate to make it through another day. As a result, prisons across the British Isles were packed far beyond capacity.

For nearly one hundred years, England had routinely disposed of its convict population in the American colonies, and built its rich empire on the backs of convict and slave labor. However, the American Revolution, followed by the abolition of slavery, eliminated this option. During the frenzied imperial land grab at the beginning of the nineteenth century, Great Britain could not persuade its "proper"

citizenry to homestead its new colonies in Van Diemen's Land and in
New South Wales. Few responded to ads in London newspapers seeking single women to populate a land where men outnumbered them
nine to one. Parliament's solution was to conscript a slave labor force
using the Transportation Act, an old law passed in 1718 that allowed
prisoners to be shipped anywhere in the world. Originally crafted to
be a humane substitute for the death penalty, it served a new purpose
at the close of the eighteenth century. Under the pretense of justice,
a greed-driven government expatriated the powerless. Ever since Captain James Cook's discovery of Australia in 1770, England resolved to
keep it for herself. The empire was especially concerned with France,
its longtime enemy, which had already laid claim to Tahiti.

Under the Transportation Act, 162,000 women, men, and children
were exiled to Australia from 1788 to 1868. The legislation resolved
several problems. It supplied cheap, disposable labor and removed the
"unsightly" poor from Britain's shores. Most important, it provided a
steady supply of young women who could serve as breeders for the
empire's newest crown jewel: Australia. Once the government shifted
the focus of the Transportation Act to include more women, constables targeted and arrested female petty thieves in droves. The
women were placed in irons, packed onto ships, and exiled to New
South Wales and Van Diemen's Land, known today as Tasmania. Of
the twenty-five thousand sent, fewer than 2 percent had committed a
violent crime, and 65 percent were first offenders.

The Tin Ticket focuses on the women and children shipped to Van
Diemen's Land, whose horrific journey and miraculous survival has
largely been overlooked in written history. The tale unfolds through
the eyes of the women themselves. Agnes McMillan was one of thousands of children cast into a system where the punishment far exceeded the scope of the crime. *The Tin Ticket* explores the background,
the daily life, the brutal choices, and the surprising destiny of this
struggling young girl who grew up in extraordinary times.

Wandering Glasgow's back alleys in 1832, abandoned by her parents at age twelve, Agnes McMillan could rely on no one but herself and her thirteen-year-old surrogate big sister, Janet Houston. Mates in the truest sense of the word, the two young lasses sacrificed neither loyalty nor hope as they traveled together to a land where even the stars in the sky seemed out of place and upside down. Friendship, ingenuity, and irreverent humor helped sustain Agnes and Janet as they came of age in the face of unimaginable hardship and humiliation. These same traits, their descendants suggest, permeate the Australian character today.

Ludlow Tedder represents another important part of the convict women's story. Like many mothers, she was transported with her youngest child. A widow who worked as a maid, the mother of four never earned enough to make ends meet. In 1838, she lost poverty's gamble, which thousands of others took every day, when she pilfered eleven spoons and a bread basket from her employer. Tried for petty theft in London's Central Criminal Court, Ludlow was sentenced to ten years in Van Diemen's Land with her nine-year-old daughter, Arabella. Innocent children suffered the same punishment as their mothers, and sometimes worse, yet their voices have been largely ignored, their existence buried in government reports. Ludlow and Arabella were forced to leave behind the rest of their family, and thus transport was a life sentence for them, because there was no way back.

Arrested for minor crimes, tagged and numbered as chattel for forced migration to Australia, women like Agnes McMillan, Janet Houston, and Ludlow Tedder were identified in Newgate Prison and on certain ships by a tiny tin ticket hung around their necks. Surprisingly, these women—more sinned against than sinning—found an ally in Elizabeth Gurney Fry, a Quaker reformer whose tireless labors proved how simple acts of compassion can change the fate of many. Her influence brightened hope for the female convicts and paralleled their harrowing journeys from Newgate Prison to the transport ships and finally to the Cascades Female Factory in Van Diemen's Land.

Fry's personal journal chronicles a deep understanding of what the convict women endured, including a description of the numbered tickets she placed around their necks on a red ribbon. The fateful tin tags are also mentioned in the second officer's report for the convict ship *Garland Grove* and in the diary of Lady Jane Franklin, the wife of the governor of Van Diemen's Land.[2]

A radical for her time, Elizabeth Fry was the first woman to speak before Parliament, lobbying on behalf of prison reform. Her diary reverberates with the power and the passion of her convictions, a revolutionary voice in the raging Victorian debate that deemed only men capable of reform and redemption. Believing that education and learning a skill could change the lives of the desperately poor, the forward-thinking Mrs. Fry set up a school for the children of convict women and taught their mothers how to sew while they awaited transport.

Fry and her volunteers met with nearly half of the female transports. They boarded the convict ships and gave each prisoner a packet containing patchwork pieces, needles, and thread for stitching quilts that could later be sold in Australia. One such quilt, assembled aboard the convict ship *Rajah* during its 105-day voyage in 1841, was found stored in an attic in Edinburgh, Scotland, in 1987. Today this treasure is housed in the National Gallery of Australia, stained with the blood and sweat of girls and women who would become colonial pioneers and founding mothers of modern Australia.

Primary sources for *The Tin Ticket* meticulously document comprehensive and often surprising facts about the women's lives. For example, Agnes McMillan's court transcripts reveal her occupation: "age 12, ballad singer." Even the fact that her fence, Daniel Campbell, carried his belongings in a red handkerchief is carefully noted.

Convict musters archived by the Tasmanian government describe each woman's physical characteristics: eye and hair color, height, shape of face, shade of complexion, freckles, dimples, pockmarks. They also describe her demeanor, acts of rebellion, marriage applications, and where she lived and worked once freed.

Details of time and place are drawn from original nineteenth-century documents, including ships' logs, newspaper accounts, letters, and diaries written by ship officers, ship surgeons, police magistrates, and religious reformers; trial and police transcripts; statements issued by the women; prison and orphan school records; and government publications, including select committee reports that investigated allegations of mistreatment and abuse.

After five years of research, I returned to Australia in 2009 to complete my work. My first stop was Tasmania's capital, Hobart, and the ruins of the Cascades Female Factory. Once I finished my research in Hobart, I set out across Tasmania and then went on to mainland Australia, following the journey of the freed convict women portrayed in *The Tin Ticket*. I walked along the docks on Macquarie Street, where the women were paraded through crowds of hooting colonists. Under the shadows of Mt. Wellington, I placed my hands on the prison's cold stone walls and viewed artifacts that offer a glimpse into the everyday lives of those who were transported: a tiny barred window that allowed only a sliver of light into the women's ward, the damp solitary cell remains lying next to the Hobart rivulet, a stone washtub from Yard Two, perhaps the very one at which Agnes, Janet, and Ludlow spent their punishments and scraped their hands and elbows. Standing in the yard at midnight, I felt the chill left behind by the women and children who could not survive Cascades.

My initial research led me to descendants of the women featured in *The Tin Ticket*. After corresponding with them for several years, I was graciously invited into their homes on my return trip to Australia. They shared extensive collections of family history, granting me access to information and secrets that, for some, had been suppressed for generations. In a remarkable coincidence, the three women whose lives I chose to study were at the Cascades Female Factory at the same time. Their lives intersected in ways that surprised me as well as their descendant families.

As the paper trail unfolded, I began to see through Agnes McMillan's eyes as her world changed from the black and white of the Glasgow woolen mills and Newgate Prison to the bright greens of untamed Tasmania, the Huon Forest, and later the dusty goldfields in Victoria.

In following the paths of the women and traveling with their descendants, we unearthed new facts about their lives that had been tucked away in used bookstores, small museum resource rooms, and the Archives Office of Tasmania. We discovered that Agnes McMillan's family had witnessed an event that shook the continent, the Eureka Rebellion. A former female convict helped sew the well-known blue and white Southern Cross flag raised during this workers' revolt. The rebellion would come to be known as the birth of Australian democracy, ignited by a furor over taxation without representation.

It is estimated that at least one in five Australians (and two million from the United Kingdom) share convict ancestry. This has recently become a source of pride for many. When I asked ten-year-old Keely Millikin what she knew about her great-great-great-great-great-grandmother Ludlow Tedder, she stood up very straight and replied: "She was a *very* strong woman." Father Peter Rankin, parish priest in Kilmore, Victoria, also expressed his admiration for the resourceful and enterprising women "who had nothing and yet had it all," and emerged "from the darkness of the ship's hold to become the light of Australia's future."

The legacy of the transported women, once referred to as the "convict stain," reveals new truths about a social engineering experiment that, for nearly a century, was covered up by both the British and the Australian governments. Not until the year 2000 was the practice of systematically destroying convict census records overturned by the Australian legislature. Fortunately, key records are intact for each woman featured in *The Tin Ticket*. In the final years of transportation, the aftermath of the Irish potato famine led to a marked increase in women and men from Ireland who were exiled for stealing food, livestock, and clothing. Often overlooked, the Irish had a profound effect on early colonial history. To help tell their story, I chose Bridget Mulligan. Had Bridget not survived the harsh sentence imposed because she was Irish, her great-granddaughter Mary Binks would not be running Gran's Van in 2010. Gran's Van is a mobile soup kitchen for the homeless and the needy in Devonport, Tasmania. Former mayor of Devonport and a finalist for Australia's Local Hero Award in 2009, Mary is a living legacy to the important role convicts played in helping found modern Australia.

During the nineteenth century, twenty-five thousand women were discarded by their homeland. For many, that journey began with the accident of being born poor and the crime of stealing food or an article of clothing. Yet by sheer force of will, those who survived forged a promising future and became the heart and soul of a new nation. In marked contrast to Britain's rigid class system, freed convicts built, in record time, a society that enjoyed a vibrant economy alongside easy mobility between classes. Women who were banished by their home country saved a new colony from collapse, accelerated social change, and were among the first in the world to gain the right to vote and to own property.

Their epic tale reveals universal themes involving the depths and heights of humanity, long-suppressed intergenerational secrets, and the potential for nobility that lies within us all. Though some historians paint women like Agnes, Janet, Ludlow, and Bridget as harlots and criminals of the worst order, they were among the most resourceful and resilient women of their generation. Every breath and every step was a choice to survive rather than succumb to their captors' cruelty. Theirs is a story of courage, transformation, and triumph.

The Grey-Eyed Girl

Bloody Christmas, Bloody Hell

The lush coastal hinterland offered a perfect day for Christmas 1869. The temperature was a lovely seventy-five degrees Fahrenheit. At the head of the table, Grandpa William rose from his seat, cleared his throat, and recited a prayer from the Bible. It was time to carve the traditional mutton and ham. Every December, the red flowers of the native Christmas bush came into bloom just in time for the holiday and filled the vases in the center of the handmade cedar table. On the sideboard, buttery cakes stacked with fresh fruit sat next to the cooling mince pie.

Grandmum Agnes hurried to the kitchen and took a plum pudding out of the wood-fired oven. She brought it straight to the table and, to the delight of the three-generation clan, set it aflame with brandy. Everyone knew what was coming next. A small silver sixpence had been surreptitiously placed inside. Whoever found it on his or her plate would enjoy good luck for the coming year.

Agnes McMillan Roberts already considered herself a lucky woman and counted her good fortune every single day. Just a year earlier, the British government had overturned the Transportation Act, a social engineering experiment that had exiled 162,000 women, men, and children from England, Ireland, Scotland, and Wales. Thirty-three years ago, at age fifteen, Agnes had been shipped from Glasgow to Van Diemen's Land (present-day Tasmania), the small island off the southern coast of Australia. It had proven to be both a curse and a blessing.

After the Christmas feast, Agnes moved to her favorite spot. Sitting on the sprawling porch, she looked out on her seven children and seven grandchildren, who came to visit Lismore every summer. Situated between the sea and the subtropical rain forest known as the "Big Scrub," Lismore, Australia, had been founded by a Scotsman who had honeymooned on an island of the same name in Agnes's home country. The family matriarch had grown accustomed to seasons turned upside down from the land of lochs and northern lights where she was born forty-nine years ago. Although she still maintained a hint of the Scottish brogue, her secret past lay securely cloistered in the confidence of her husband, William, and her longtime childhood friend, Janet Houston.

As her grandchildren played hide-and-seek along the banks of the Richmond River, Agnes chuckled at the skinny legs that peeked out from their short pants. She reached for a cup of hot India tea, freshly brewed to wash down the midday feast. Wisps of silver hair blew gently in the seasonable breeze, framing grey eyes the color of steel and a gaze that seemed to go on forever. The same rare color of the eyes of Athena, the Greek warrior goddess known for her strength and wisdom, Agnes's eyes mirrored these traits. Her Scottish eyes had witnessed the births and deaths of people and nations. Today they sparkled in December's summer sun.

The content matron, just over five feet tall, rocked back in her chair and considered how far she had traveled. Neither her children nor her grandchildren knew anything about Grandmum's early Christmases, including the one thirty-seven years before that changed the course of her life and made theirs possible. She started to hum. It was an old melody, one her mother had taught her, one she had sung on the streets of Glasgow so many years ago.

It was December 27, 1832. The gas lamps glowed in icy orbs that ran in crooked rows throughout the sleepy town. Even by Scotland's standards, the weather was horrid. Gale-force winds from the west pelted heavy downpours onto the small faces that bobbed in and out from the protective doorways in the wynds by the Green. It had been raining for days and days. Temperatures hovered just above freezing. "Bloody Christmas, bloody hell," muttered the street people.

In a dense alleyway along the River Clyde, twelve-year-old Agnes McMillan shivered and huddled close to her friend Janet. Her breath billowed white and frosty, and she pulled what was left of a scarf over her nose. The two girls had eaten nothing for days but "Irish apricots" and had a taste for something other than potatoes. Some nights, even in the wettest winter months, they slept in a doorway, other nights in an outhouse. Pilfering a slice of bread from a street vendor was commonplace, but that didn't pay for lodging. For homeless waifs like Agnes and Janet, sleeping in a bed, typically with several others, was a luxury they could seldom afford.

At this time of year, there were only seven hours of daylight, and nightfall arrived by four in the afternoon. Under the cover of Glasgow's darkest recesses, the fated duo hatched a plan to celebrate the holidays with clean clothes and fresh lamb. Theft had become their lifeline. Four friends from the streets were in on the plan, and together they targeted a gabled mansion in the rich part of town, where for several days not a single candle had flickered. The owner, a widow named Elizabeth Barbour, had likely traveled from her Fife Place home for holiday merrymaking at a country estate.[1] After all, it was bloody Christmas.

As the clocks marked midnight, every ounce of Agnes's cunning centered on the task at hand. It was time to accomplish something more than mere survival in Scotland's toughest town. Since her father had disappeared and her mother had basically abandoned her, Agnes had managed to get by and make a few coins singing ballads near the Glasgow Green. Although she could neither read nor write, she'd remembered the songs her mother taught her and put together a repertoire for impromptu street performances. At twelve, the lithe lassie with a bit of a voice often attracted a small crowd of passersby, but the day had been too miserable to sing.

Friend and protector Janet Houston had taken the ever-hopeful ballad singer under her wing because she knew firsthand what it took to survive in Glasgow's unforgiving alleys. Both Janet's mother and father had passed away. The thirteen-year-old sometimes slept at her aunt Gibson's flat, but that was not always an option; Janet also relied on a network of small-time neighborhood thieves who managed to steal enough to pay for food and shelter. They often banded together to pilfer food from street vendors, but tonight they gathered around the Glasgow Green to gamble on the higher stakes of a house break.

Creeping along the ghostly edges of the tightly built stone structures, the co-conspirators made their way through the wynds, the winding passages that would deliver them to the city's upscale West End. The girls approached the mansion's iron gate and gave a quick glance up and down the lane. This was the moment when they would make their move. The neatly swept neighborhood seemed nearly deserted. Looking skyward toward the graceful lancet windows, Agnes paced nervously and pulled her wet shawl tighter. This had to be easier work than picking the pockets of a "groggified" pedestrian or pilfering meat from a sharp-eyed butcher. It seemed simple enough. Breaking a rear kitchen window provided the typical point of entry for small-time burglars. A quick smash of the pane and they'd be in, out, and gone. The scraggly housebreakers held their breath as the sound of shattering glass settled into the night. They waited for a moment, ears tuned, hearts pounding, ready to flee at the first sound of a footstep.

The older, more street-savvy Janet reached through the jagged glass. She lifted the bolt and unlatched the door. Ever so carefully she leaned her shoulder into the heavy ash frame and cracked it open, sending the smoky smell of mutton into the damp night air. The well-stocked larder was bolted shut to prevent the maids from stealing. Hunger, all too familiar, would need to wait. Out of the wind in the still of the mansion, fully charged with adrenaline, the girls set to work. Gold watches, silver spoons, silk scarves, and fashionable gloves were the prime targets for young thieves. There was no time to ponder how much the wealthy could afford to lose. The gang of six quickly snatched up items they could hide inside their shawls and sell unquestioned at the pawnshop. They had ten minutes, at most, to complete the heist.

Mission completed, the nervous trespassers darted through the swinging back gate, confident that this was going to be a holiday they would enjoy. They were wrong, terribly wrong. Agnes McMillan, Janet Houston, and the rest of the troop charged straight into the grasp of a waiting constable, who knew all too well what the sound of breaking glass meant. They must have been novices. Experienced thieves took the time to learn the regular route for police patrols and took advantage of a force too lean to keep up with the rising tide of Glasgow crime.

Flushed and gasping for air, Agnes "lied with a latchet," the Scottish term for telling a big fib. She did her best to talk her way out of being trapped with the others, but there was no escape. According to Glasgow court records, the grey-eyed waif told the officer that her name was Agnes Reddie, perhaps out of shame, or out of naïve desire that a different name would protect her from wearing the chains that rattled in his pocket. This was the first arrest for the pink-cheeked street urchin, but she had already faced off against bad tidings more times than she could count. She would confront this latest predicament with Janet at her side.

Goosedubbs Street

Agnes McMillan was born to an age of extremes in social class, politics, and physical environment. The years leading to her parents' marriage had been tangled in one national disaster after another. As Mary Henderson and Michael McMillan moved into adulthood, climate, political upheaval, and geography conspired against their future.

The year 1815 opened with the promise of peace when Britain ended its three-year war with America on February 18. Any euphoria, however, was short-lived. That March, Napoleon returned to power and terrorized Europe yet again. Michael McMillan, like thousands of young Scots, was conscripted under the command of the Duke of Wellington and the Seventh Coalition. Thankfully, by June the coalition had defeated Napoleon at Waterloo. Unfortunately, as one war ended, a battle of a different sort exploded.

On a remote Indonesian island called Sumbawa, the jungle grew silent and the ground began to shudder as Mt. Tambora spewed its molten heart into the atmosphere. Though it occurred five years before Agnes's birth, the most powerful eruption in ten thousand years, and the largest ever recorded, changed the world's climate and magnified the struggle her parents would face to put bread on the table. The massive surge of volcanic ash circling the globe could be neither stopped nor controlled. When Michael McMillan returned to Glasgow from the Belgium battlefields in 1816, brown snow fell throughout Europe. It was "the year without a summer." Birds fell frozen from the sky. Crops failed all across the British Isles, and families went to bed hungry night after night. "Bread or blood" became their battle cry as food riots broke out, protesting the skyrocketing price of wheat.

Amid this chaos and uncertainty, Mary Henderson fell in love with Michael McMillan. Many young women, including Mary, married after the return of the soldiers, prompting a baby boom. This population explosion was ill-timed to coincide with an implosion of the British economy, but Michael was lucky and found a steady job working for the railroad.

Scottish citizens were part of Great Britain's kingdom, joined by the Act of Union in 1707 and subject to the laws of Parliament. Mary and Michael McMillan would certainly have despaired over their daughter's future had they known how people like themselves were described in a report to Parliament on administration of the Poor Laws in Scotland: "The people who dwell in those quarters of the city are sunk to the lowest possible state of personal degradation in whom no elevated idea can be expected to arise, and who regard themselves, from the hopelessness of their condition, as doomed to a life of wretchedness and crime. . . . They nightly issue to disseminate disease and to pour upon the town every species of abomination and crime."[2] Agnes's parents were likely spared this prediction because nearly all the poor were illiterate.

Agnes was born on September 11, 1820, in a tenement flat on Goosedubbs Street, a narrow lane in the center of Glasgow's worst slum. It was a gruesome affair, assisted by a midwife who would not have washed her hands nor cleaned the dingy muslin in which Agnes was wrapped. A woman's strength in surviving childbirth bode well for a baby born in the pre-Victorian era. Twenty percent of mothers died in labor.

In stark contrast to most new citizens, the future Queen Victoria was birthed with the assistance of a female obstetrician and several attending doctors. Baby Victoria entered the world "as plump as a partridge"[3] the year before Agnes was born and held the honor of being the first member of the royal family vaccinated against smallpox.

As a parent, Mary McMillan carried the additional responsibilities of a factory laborer and was expected to be on her feet for fourteen-hour shifts throughout her pregnancy. A woman who worked in a mill since childhood commonly paid the price of a narrow and deformed pelvis, which made labor difficult and increased infant mortality. This deformity was caused by the stress of standing without movement coupled with malnutrition. As Mary stumbled toward what she hoped would be a better future, the only work available endangered her health and the life of her unborn child.

Like her co-workers, Mary McMillan returned to work two weeks after giving birth, fearful of losing a prized job. Some mothers were allowed to bring their infants to the mill, tied in a sling and quieted with a pacifier made from a dirty rag soaked in milk and water. Agnes may have been cared for by an elderly neighbor or by a youngster unable to find employment. Reliable child care was rare and unaffordable for most parents, but the poor looked out for one another and invited their young neighbors in for porridge or bread whenever they had an extra morsel to share.

From an early age, "weans," as children were called, often spent their days alone inside a one-room flat while their parents worked. Toddlers were given "pap" to eat, a watery paste made from bread and water. Some mothers used laudanum, a cheap and readily available derivative of opium, to drug their children during the day. An ounce cost the same as a pint of beer and suppressed hunger as it fueled an addiction. Others silenced crying babies with Godfrey's Cordial, a mixture of opium, sassafras, brandy, caraway seeds, and treacle. Gin was another widely used comforter, an all-purpose soother from cradle to grave, as cheap as beer and sold on every street corner to young and old alike. Not until the twentieth century was the purchase of alcohol limited to adults. Liquor often provided the main source of calories for entire families, and it was safer to drink than the tainted water from the river.

Peeking out onto Goosedubbs Street as a five-year-old on her own, Agnes saw a world of cobblestone and brick, full of misery and manure. Coal particles stung her eyes at every blink. Each sip of water she drank from the brackish public well carried the risk of dysentery or typhoid fever. She and everyone else who lived near the mills coughed out pieces of black grit breathed in from Glasgow's raging industrial fires. Neighbors overhead tossed their garbage out the window onto the walkway. Most had witnessed some unfortunate soul drop dead in the street or on the job. The grey-eyed five-year-old had already proven to be lucky, since half the Scottish children born in 1820 had already been laid in the ground by their parents. In the slums, dunghills and raw sewage blanketed the crowded space with a sticky black glaze. This was Agnes's playground and schoolyard.

Children dashed around the wynds playing tag, hide-and-seek, and peever—the Scottish version of hopscotch. Boys picked up sticks to bat whatever they could hit in the air. An old barrel hoop started a contest for who could spin it the farthest. Street waste offered an abundance of possibilities for games and entertainment. Clever mothers sewed dolls from scraps of cloth. Discarded shoe heels, hammered with nails resembling eyes and a mouth, formed the perfect face for the doll. Pieces of rope were snatched up for skipping along the bank of the River Clyde. Nothing went unused, and nearly everything was used again and again with renewed purpose.

Among the laboring class, a child's role included the duty of earning a living. By age seven, Agnes would have been expected to contribute to the McMillan household income. Every penny mattered. Children her age, and younger, worked full time as chimney sweeps or factory workers, hired for the ability to reach small crevices and machine parts. Weans sometimes earned more than their parents because of the market value attached to their small size. Mine owners employed five- and six-year-olds to crawl through muddy scum deep inside the shafts and scurry back with a heavy load tied over their shoulders.

Hunger and hopelessness incited families to commit unthinkable acts. Some parents relied on punishment to make their children earn money or commit a crime, whatever it took to keep the family afloat.

Five-year-olds were forced to stitch gloves until the midnight hour. Six-year-olds were booted into the streets and ordered to steal a pocketbook or grab a loaf of bread. Small bodies with fast legs made good criminals. Other parents made valiant attempts to protect their sons and daughters from miscreant street influences, sometimes hiding their clothing so they could not venture outside.

Most Glasgow families lived in poverty. Even with two incomes, subsistence wages were not enough to lift a family out of destitution. Absent the availability of homegrown meat or vegetables, the average city dweller spent at least 60 percent of earnings on food, some spending up to 90 percent. Members of the laboring class, like the McMillans, lived on oatmeal for breakfast and potatoes for dinner. Bread, beer, and lard rounded out their diet. Luxury items like milk, butter, cheese, or a piece of pork were rarely purchased. The largest meal portions were reserved for Michael McMillan, the primary breadwinner, especially when he could afford meat. When food ran short, mothers and children were expected to go without and sacrifice for the survival of the household.

A Glasgow father spent very little time in the home. When his shift ended late into the evening, he generally headed straight for the flash house to "swallow a hare" at the pub. Workmates in tow, he drank heartily into the wee hours. Glasgow taverns, one for every fourteen people, guaranteed escape from the bleakness of a one-room flat. "Drunken statistics" published in the *Scotsman* revealed that Glasgow residents drank more than five times the amount of their London counterparts because of worse housing and less assistance for Scotland's poor. Like their parents, the young took solace under alcohol's haze, as described by a fourteen-year-old stonecutter: "Usquebaugh (whisky) was simply happiness doled out by the glass and sold by the gill."[4]

The comfort of the bottle expanded Glasgow's generation of abandoned children. Police commissions investigating the cause of juvenile delinquency in the early nineteenth century linked alcoholic parents to criminal children. "It is likely that drunkenness was often the result of indigence rather than simply bacchanalian pleasures. Many families of juvenile delinquents seem to have been engaged in a fight between destitution and respectability in the struggle to keep their heads above water from day to day."[5]

Among the poor and middle class, it was a woman's duty to try to protect the family from the lure of the bottle, to ensure that a man's paycheck wasn't spent entirely at the pub. On payday, she would wait, children in hand, along the rail tracks or outside the factory exit. Money spent on prostitutes was another problem. Marriage in the Regency era was a loose concept at best, fidelity an uncommon one. As unemployment rose, so, too, did wife beating. If a woman found the courage to take her mate to court, he claimed that she had been drinking, fully aware that drunken wives could be gaoled by their husbands' testimony. Desertion was commonplace among men. Without warning, many ran away from the Glasgow tenements in search of better employment or an easier life.

These were the stresses that robbed childhoods from the thousands of Scottish children who ended up on the street or in a factory. Agnes McMillan was no different. Her father abandoned the family early in her life. She never learned why he left, but there are many possible explanations. Railway men worked fifteen-hour shifts, seven days a week, with only one holiday a year. Michael McMillan's job of coal porter entailed lugging a wheelbarrow back and forth, loading and unloading mound upon mound of dusty fuel. So pitiful was the pay for this backbreaking work that many resorted to larceny. Men Michael's age often surrendered to arrest, alcoholism, or the grave. The average life expectancy for a Glasgow native was just under thirty-one years.

Nearly 30 percent of Glasgow households were headed by a woman. Some were widows and others abandoned wives like Mary. Many Scottish lasses had never married because of the availability of jobs in the mills coupled with a shortage of men. If a woman lost her job or her mate, her options for employment were severely more limited than a man's. If the sole breadwinner didn't work, she ended up on Glasgow's streets. There were no alternatives, no safety nets. If a woman was poor, it was considered her fault. If her children went hungry, it was blamed on her flawed character.

Poverty was treated as a crime, conveniently alleviating the conscience of the upper classes. Poorhouses were designed to be as miserable as possible to discourage use by people who needed help most. When Agnes was born, local counties couldn't handle the swelling number of women, men, and children who were without food, a place to sleep, or prospects for employment. The few admitted to a workhouse were called "inmates" and were required to wear uniforms. Each inmate performed hard labor. Men worked breaking stones with axes. Women and children pulled apart old hemp rope that would be reused on ships, tearing their flesh as they teased dirt and tar from the rough fibers. In *The Borough*, British poet George Crabbe described this "pauper-palace":[6]

> *Those gates and locks, and all those signs of power:*
> *It is a prison, with a milder name,*
> *Which few inhabit without dread or shame.*

If Mary McMillan had lost her job and been forced into a poorhouse, the overseer would have separated her from Agnes. He would have shorn Agnes's hair to three inches, thereby reinforcing her beggar rank and discouraging a return to "poor relief." Mother and child would have gone to sleep hungry. Food rations, deemed "an efficient test of poverty," were half the amount served in prisons, just enough to keep the worker inmates on their feet.[7] In gaol, hard labor was generally not required, so, in effect, poverty was punished more harshly than stealing. The workhouse was a death sentence for 23 percent of those who entered, a mortality rate more than double that for the homeless.

The End of Eden

For a time, Mary McMillan was able to provide for Agnes by laboring at the nearby woolen manufactory, as the mill was called. The work was stifling and dangerous, but because she was paid based on her productivity, she trudged on. There was no ventilation, nor privies, nor provisions for water. Agnes's mother considered herself fortunate to have a job, but toxic tedium and twelve years on her feet had finally ground her down. In theory, the Industrial Revolution offered women the potential for economic freedom. In reality, most earned between one-third and one-half of what a man brought home.

No matter how Mary scrimped and saved, she was always behind. With wages on the order of four shillings per week, there was little chance to make ends meet. Her basic expenses required at least five shillings, exceeding her earnings in spite of working overtime. In neighborhoods like Goosedubbs Street, weekly rent cost one shilling, six-pence; oatmeal and flour, one shilling, ten pence; potatoes, five pence for a large sack; candles and fuel, one shilling, two pence.

Facing the numbing struggle to make it through the next day, Mary McMillan found optimism beyond her grasp. Whether it was despair, drink, or a different reason, Mary ultimately gave up on motherhood. Unable to cope with work and parenting, she often left Agnes to fend for herself. By age twelve, Agnes was left entirely to her own resources. Her mother still allowed her to sleep at the flat, but Agnes spent many a night wandering the wynds. Luckily, she made friends easily, thanks to "a spirited demeanor," as described by her descendants. Deserted by her family and consigned to wretchedness by her government's grim prediction in Parliament's Poor Laws report, the Goosedubbs Street girl found protection in what would be called a street gang today.

Janet Houston, a year older, adopted the abandoned little song-stress. Agnes's alliance with a surrogate big sister provided a sense of belonging and a semblance of a family, at least for a while. Agnes sang to whoever would listen, and Janet collected coins from passersby. Together the best friends looked out for each other as they managed a lean existence along the River Clyde. Life on the dingy streets was certainly hard, yet these two independent souls had decided that sleeping in an alleyway was preferable to the workhouse or the factory. Now, however, the sunken-cheeked twelve-year-old was under arrest, chains shackled to her wrists. As the iron door closed, leaving her and Janet in the damp silence of the holding cell, Agnes cursed her bad luck. She knew what justice meant for the poor. Bloody Christmas, bloody hell.

If a society is judged on how it treats children and the downtrodden, the British Empire failed on all fronts during Agnes's lifetime. Voices of reason were few and rare, even among leading intellectuals. Francis Hutcheson, one of the founders of the eighteenth-century Scottish Enlightenment, suggested that benevolence arose from the instinctive human commitment toward "the greatest happiness for the greatest numbers." Man's morality, he believed, would inspire "a determination to be pleased with the happiness of others and to be uneasy at their misery."[8]

Enlightened optimism like Hutcheson's faded in favor of luminaries voicing more cynical views about the future of humanity. In his famous *Essay on the Principle of Population*, published in 1798, Thomas Robert Malthus argued that in accordance with the laws of nature, famine and starvation would weed out the poor, thus alleviating the strain of population growth on modern civilization. He recommended that the underprivileged be prevented from marrying and having children.[9] A father of three, he felt exempt from this proclamation because of his wealth. Following his logic, Agnes McMillan should not have been born.

A controversial celebrity of his time, Malthus advocated against the Poor Laws and any assistance that might help sustain the struggling. This was the brand of popular thinking that permitted the abuses of power under the Transportation Act, including shipping twenty-five thousand girls and women to the other side of the world, Agnes and Janet among them.

Throughout the British Isles, madness and hypocrisy permeated politics and everyday life. In 1820, a child who stole clothing could be banished and worked to death in Australia, but George IV, a known bigamist and suspected murderer, would be crowned king. King George IV humiliated Queen Caroline when he continued his relationship with a commoner to whom he'd been secretly married years earlier. Her Highness, too, engaged in scandalous behavior, including dressing in see-through gowns during alleged affairs with her servants. Her death in 1821 was widely attributed to poisoning by His Majesty.

The Industrial Revolution heightened society's imbalances. It fattened the prosperous and starved the weak, widening the chasm between classes and creating an incubator for juvenile criminals like Agnes and Janet. In earlier decades, parish schools in rural villages welcomed children during the slower farming cycles and fostered a relatively high literacy rate. Had Agnes been born into an agrarian family, hard labor would still have been her fate, but she would have eaten better food, grown up in healthier surroundings, and perhaps learned to read. Though farmhands labored long and hard, there were changes in pace and a variety in chores, unlike the perpetual monotony that poisoned the factory floor. Farm children were valued by their parents, if for no other reason than their ability to work the fields. This bond helped keep rural families intact.

Factories, on the other hand, demanded labor every day of the week, every month of the year. As industry enhanced technology, it stunted education for the poor, and literacy declined. There were simply not enough hours in the day for children to learn to read and write. The lowest classes, following the lure of progress, traded a self-sufficient agrarian lifestyle for enslavement in an urban jungle. From 1780 to 1830, child labor grew exponentially, largely due to the end of a family-centered economy.

Well on its way to becoming one of the largest cities in Europe and already Scotland's most congested, Glasgow had grown to a population of two hundred thousand. As daylight broke, low-lying smog erased the city's color. Ashen figures wandered hopelessly through a black-and-white world. By Christmas 1832, Agnes's hometown, unrivaled in squalor, was dirtier and more dangerous than any city in the empire.

This was a far cry from the pristine paradise enjoyed by Glasgow's seventy thousand inhabitants just thirty years earlier. The city's name came from the Gaelic *Glaschu*, or "clean green place." English writer Daniel Defoe described eighteenth-century Glasgow as "one of the cleanliest, most beautiful and best cities in Great Britain."[10] Built along the River Clyde, this peaceful enclave was protected by steep rolling hills. Children played in the water, and men fished in the streams by tree-lined meadows. This was an urban oasis defined by nature's beauty, resplendent in its orchards, cornfields, and terraced flower gardens.

Agnes and Janet never knew the green, open spaces of a more serene Glasgow. The tobacco and linen trade had set the Garden of Eden on fire. Seldom did the close companions see the magical northern lights, hidden under a murky haze that rarely lifted from their city's sky. The lazy River Clyde was widened and violated to make room for noisy steam-powered ships bringing sugar and raw cotton to fuel Glasgow's new industries. The fragrance of buds in bloom was replaced by the stench of the slum. A once-glistening metropolis had lost its luster by the time the Goosedubbs Street girls sat before the sheriff.

Glasgow residents lived on average twelve years less than their rural counterparts, a fact attributed to urban housing: "damp earthen, muddy floors, walls saturated with moisture . . . small closed windows admitting of no perflation of air, crowded apartments, thatched roofs saturated like a sponge with water."[11] The physical toll on the tenement dweller was devastatingly obvious. The rich were almost always taller than the poor by four inches or more.[12] One-third of

Glasgow's children hobbled along with a disfiguring gait caused by malnutrition and rickets.[13] More were maimed by their work in factories or mines.

Laborers were pitted against one another for every job, every day. A person willing to work for less landed the job only until someone more desperate arrived at the factory door. Glasgow shipping companies imported starving Irish citizens who eagerly accepted cheap wages, thereby putting Scottish citizens out of work. To make matters worse, peasants from the highlands crowded the city in search of a better life that did not exist. In addition, the shift from hand to power looms destroyed a large cottage industry and left thousands of traditional weavers without employment and their families without food. Bleakness clung to the land like mold on an old loaf of bread.

The Glasgow wynds did not suffer fools. Like feral dogs, children on the streets learned to live according to their wits and a well-developed talent for exploiting opportunity. Alley dwellers worked their way up the street society according to a criminal hierarchy. Agnes and Janet would have started at the bottom, lifting an apple or two from a vendor cart. With small successes, the novice progressed to stealing items from stores and passersby. The proceeds could be bartered for money through any number of fences who lurked under the cover of candle shops, street stalls, and public houses. Many lodging-house owners offered thieves a bed for the night in return for an item that could be pawned easily. Other proprietors, fences themselves, encouraged crime as they made their boardinghouses a safe haven for gangs and a thriving underground economy from which they, too, profited.

Impoverished girls, Agnes and Janet included, faced three basic paths to survival: mill slave, thief, or "fallen woman." An article in the *Glasgow Courier* appeared to sanction the third option. Accounts of fifteen-hour days and floggings by mill overseers led the *Courier* writer to this conclusion: "If the females when grown up are not ugly they may find relief in prostitution."[14]

Even though she was only twelve, Agnes had been offered the job of trollop many times. Part tomboy, part rebel, Agnes rejected the "loose habits" that would have branded her a strumpet. Stealing carried the risk of gaol, but prostitution was legal. Still, she refused to sell her body, an all-too-common fate for abandoned children.

Street-smart Agnes and Janet often felt more at ease roaming the wynds, where they at least knew what to expect and where to hide. The boardinghouse might have offered the pair some relief from the worst of the Scottish weather. However, there was no safety in numbers in the rented rooms they could afford. "In the lower lodging houses, ten, twelve, and sometimes twenty persons, of both sexes and all ages, sleep promiscuously on the floor in different degrees of nakedness. These places are generally as regards dirt, damp, and decay, such as no person of common humanity would stable his horse in."[15]

Glasgow's slums devoured the innocent every hour of the day. Yet even alley life was not all gloom and doom. A piece of fresh bread tossed from a street vendor, an onlooker who applauded her singing, a penny pressed into her hand; Agnes was grateful for such moments of simple compassion.

And then there was laughter, considered indecent among the upper crust, a necessity among those missing life's most basic comforts. From the bosom of misery, the ridiculous and sophomoric permeated everyday activities. Humor found gleeful abundance when a carriage driver stepped deep in horse droppings or a passing pedestrian looked up at a window just as garbage was dumped on his head. Even the dark comedy of a staggering drunk created a welcome catharsis with hearty guffaws and waves of falling-over giggles. An organ grinder with a monkey on his shoulder regularly carried a traveling circus to Agnes, Janet, and all the street urchins.

The pleasure palace of the poor was located in the smoke-filled pub, which could suddenly transform to a theater. Clowning, rowdy song, ribald humor, and parodies that poked fun at political figures took center stage as spectators, standing shoulder to shoulder, packed this den of amusement. Such bawdy acts later gave birth to vaudeville and the music hall. The pub's enthusiastic audience, most arriving with empty stomachs and dirty clothes, cherished distraction in the wisecracking, dancing, and drunken choruses. The precocious twelve-year-old and her red-haired chum sometimes joined in the animated merriment. This was a precious penny well spent, whether earned, stolen, borrowed, or begged.

These brief respites for fun were one of the anchors for Agnes's exuberant spirit, creating some small consolation in a world where every step, every breath, every sip of water, carried the risk of catastrophe. Life was usually short and cheap. Any mistake Agnes made among the street people might be her last.

Some dangers weren't visible, though they were no less treacherous for the ragamuffins of Goosedubbs Street. As she and Janet meandered through the wynds that fateful night in December 1832, the tough twosome had already avoided a cholera outbreak that killed ten thousand Scots earlier in the year. Scarlet fever, measles, smallpox, tuberculosis, and whooping cough ravaged thousands more.

From a haughty distance, the mighty rich blamed these epidemics on the struggling masses. They believed that the lower classes brought disease onto themselves because they failed to practice religion. Succumbing to typhoid fever was seen as a sign of God's wrath, a fitting retribution for moral corruption. Local papers like the *Scotsman* declared that the wealthy caught diseases from "the ragged, the starved, and the degraded."[16] While the Church recommended humiliation and prayer to purge afflictions from the poverty stricken, the radical press began to focus on sanitation, or the lack thereof, as the primary cause for contagious illness.

Agnes proved sturdy enough to resist air- and waterborne disease. But now the grey-eyed girl could hear the heavy footsteps of the gaoler and the rattle of his keys. The holding cell swung open, and a gruff hand reached inside. As she was dragged off to face the sheriff for sentencing, Agnes knew that her life was about to change forever.

Mr. Green's Mill

Across the British Empire, children age seven and older were sub-
jected to the same punishment as adults but were exempted from the
death penalty. The last hanging of a child took place in 1708, when a
seven-year-old boy and his eleven-year-old sister were convicted of
theft and sentenced to death. Agnes was considered an adult at age
twelve, and in Scotland adults were hanged as late as 1963. Once accused, she had no right to counsel in court even if her neck was about
to be strung up. Thankfully, the wayward waif escaped the gallows,
though she couldn't elude Glasgow's mandate to crack down firmly
on young offenders. Thomas Johnston, Scotland's secretary of state in
1941, described justice during the times in which Agnes lived: "Theft
was the great crime; a man guilty of culpable homicide got only half
the sentence of the man who stole the 23s. [shillings] in silver."[17] Essentially, a person's life was worth less than the cost of a teapot.

Organized police were a new concept in the early nineteenth
century, allowing for arbitrary sentencing, widespread bribery, and
wholesale corruption. When it came to standards of behavior, there
was a fine line between the uniformed officer and the common criminal. The police generally came from the same tough neighborhoods
as those they arrested. Many supplemented their income by extorting
bribes from the shopkeepers they were paid to protect. Others were
quick on the take for thieves willing to pay them for a reduced sentence. Local authorities wielded tremendous discretionary power
over the punishment of girls like Agnes and Janet. Some simply gave
a stern warning delivered with a thrashing to their backs. More than
a few hid behind their officer's badge to get away with the sexual
abuse of girls whose word would not hold up before a jury.

For their bungled burglary at the mansion, Agnes McMillan and
Janet Houston stood before the Glasgow sheriff, from the streets himself and now a hard-nosed bureaucrat. He certainly understood that

the two dispirited petty thieves presented no possibility of paying a bribe. At least they could be parceled out to the mill for a few pence. Lawbreakers were sentenced according to the severity of their crime. A juryless police court could impose an imprisonment of up to sixty days, whereas the sheriff held jurisdiction for sentences ranging from three to eighteen months. Fortunately, the feisty pair had yet to land in circuit court, where immediate deportation to Van Diemen's Land was guaranteed. Unfortunately, the local sheriff was not in a holiday mood nor was he feeling the least bit generous, considering that Agnes had lied about her name to the arresting officer. He sentenced the two to the maximum sentence he could enforce: eighteen months at Mr. Green's woolen mill along the Kelvin Docks. The four neighbors who assisted with the house break-in also received a sentence of a year and a half.

Forced labor was considered a form of apprenticeship. When Agnes and Janet were sentenced, 43 percent of Scotland's woolen mill workers were under age eighteen. Had the sheriff sentenced Agnes to gaol, she would have avoided hard labor yet faced the perils of imprisonment with violent felons, the untreated insane, and corrupt prison wardens.

A police officer hustled the best friends, now in irons, into a waiting black carriage along with the other children sentenced to the mill. In the cold early morning light, Agnes knew exactly where she was headed. Every street urchin had heard stories about all forms of punishment, real and imagined. She looked down at the chains around her wrists.

As the buggy neared the factory, the giant mill wheels came into view, the machinery that powered the mill's innards by pulling energy from the flowing River Clyde. After having her irons removed, each apprentice was inspected and logged into the mill journal. An unsympathetic matron issued their coarse grey uniforms. Marched across the factory yard, the new arrivals were indistinguishable from the veteran workers save for the short-lived cleanliness of their ill-fitting shifts.

Despite the eighteen-month sentence before her, her lack of a home, and no parent to rely on, Agnes hadn't lost Janet. Records don't indicate whether the factory overseer separated the two or if they were assigned the same room, but they worked together on the factory floor. Most mill owners were also the landlords for the "bothies," the buildings that warehoused child labor: "Doors were all locked, both with check and turnkey; they slept on the premises, which had iron-staunched windows and were guarded all night; they had no chance of escaping till the morning, when he (the manager) released them for their next day's employment."[18] At least two workers and often a third shared the beds in the bothy.

The sheriff had warned Agnes and Janet not to be late for their labor assignments. Oversleeping and tardiness were severely punished. Some latecomers were hung by the wrists and flogged. Others were plunged half-naked into a well.

Clang, clang, clang: The wake-up sounded at four thirty A.M. sharp. The bell went on and on until each child climbed out of bed into the sleepy darkness. It was a requirement to be alert and on the floor for the five A.M. whistle call. The half-hour spent from dreaming to drudgery was barely enough time for the girls to throw on their uniforms and gulp down a scoop of gruel. Their next meal was in eight hours.

As they entered the millworks the first time, Agnes and Janet were directed toward the overseer, also called an "overlooker." Standing above the fray on a small platform, he ordered each girl to tie her hair in a bun and pull her sleeves above her elbows. Anything not tethered tightly was an accident waiting to happen. A strand of hair caught in machines scalped some girls on the job. There were no shutoff valves for a sleeve or a finger that caught in the looms. Each child was responsible for her own safety. If she hurt herself, the overseer blamed her stupidity.

The mill was a notorious breeding ground for abuse and perversion. If a child fell asleep on her feet, the overseer dipped her head into an iron vat filled with water. "Some adult operatives and overlookers did not look beyond themselves for tools of abuse. They kicked children, struck them with clenched fist, and yanked children's hair and ears."[19]

Disaster loomed ominously over the wide-eyed apprentices, imprisoned in a maze of spindles, tangled threads, swaying metal bars, and exposed wire teeth. Agnes, Janet, and the other young thieves stood before the spinning machines like flies examining a spider's web. From every corner, gas lamps sputtered and hissed. The swinging rods crisscrossing the sunless tomb clanked noisy warnings. Strange sounds bombarded the new arrivals from every direction as they strained to hear the overseer. Stone walls reverberated and amplified the auditory assault: the whir of spinning bobbins, the slapping of the looms' reeds, the hypnotic drone of leather belts and pulleys, the spastic flapping of the newly woven wool.

By the time Agnes and Janet were sent to Mr. Green's, conditions of child labor had become so appalling that several government investigations were taking place. Evidence for an 1832 House of Commons Committee on the Factories Labour Regulation Bill described "one girl so bow-legg'd that you could put a chair between her legs."[20] Page after page of testimony described the fate for those conscripted as weans. A man about thirty years old "does not stand, with his deformity, above 4 feet 6 inches high, and had he grown to his proper height I think he would have been about 5 feet 8 or 9 inches. He has been in the mills since he was 5 years old, and he is reduced to that state that he slides along on a stool to do his work."[21]

Another investigation, by a committee on the Employment of Children in Manufactories, interviewed adults about their experience as child workers. Robert Blincoe offered testimony that could not be challenged. He hobbled forward on his crooked legs, the deformity most common from youthful years spent in a mill. The committee asked Blincoe, now a father of three, if he would send his children to work in a factory. Without hesitation, he responded: "No; I would rather have them transported to Australia."[22] Robert had watched ten-year-old Mary Richards being torn to pieces when her apron caught on a shaft that turned a drawing frame, the device used to straighten fibers. "In an instant the poor girl was drawn by an irresistible force and dashed on the floor . . . the bones of her arms, legs, thighs . . . crushed, seemingly, to atoms, as the machinery whirled her round, and drew tighter and tighter her body within the works."[23]

At the forefront of the Industrial Revolution, the same risks stalked Agnes. Seasoned mill laborers soon figured out that keeping pace with the frames and spindles meant staying alive. They developed rhythmic movements that mimicked the millworks; their motions turned mechanical, their gait robotic. Speech, too, took on a short staccato cadence to compete with the mill's deafening cacophony.

Wool production was a labor-intensive business. It took ten girls to prepare the yarn for one weaver. Older lasses like thirteen-year-old Janet were assigned sorting, according to the wool's texture. "Picking" the wool, the mill's most unpleasant task, was primarily assigned to younger workers with smaller hands. Agnes was led past the looms and spinners and brought to the picking bin, where she would stand for the next eighteen months, fifteen hours at a time. Grabbing one piece of wool from the monumental stack before her, strand by strand, she pulled out fatty wool grease infused with dirt, animal skin, sweat, and sheep dung. Tearing the grime out of the bristly fibers, Agnes picked the matted wool clean with her fingers and a large needle. Her lack of experience punctured her skin as she clumsily pulled out thistles, thorns, and burs. Within the first hour, her hands began to cramp and to coil like talons around prey.

The factory was without ventilation. As the shift dragged on, the air grew heavier and thicker. Endless grey filth, never fully cleaned from the sheep's wool, joined flying fibers, creating hazy smog that covered workers and gears in a grainy veneer. Agnes and Janet were quickly layered in sweat and dust from head to toe. With no place to wash, the children were coated with sticky particles that lodged in their eyelids and their hair for months at a time.

Amid the whir and clang of the machines, Agnes heard the distinctive sound of the overlooker tapping a wooden rod against his palm. The iron tip on the rod's end threatened a rap on the head for those with rebellious dispositions. Rule breakers were flogged with the same straps that drove the pulleys. Failure to obey the overseer could bring a trip to the "throttle room," where a girl was tied to a harness and forced to walk back and forth with weights on her back. The most severe punishment of all was reserved for lasses who spoke to the lads on the factory floor. The smallest flirtation took away what was considered a woman's most prized possession: Her head was shaved bald. The rest of the girls would soon wear the crown of thieves with telltale short haircuts.

After eight hours on the floor, the new recruits felt their stomachs shrink and growl. The piercing sound of the supper bell arrived not a moment too soon. Agnes had only a half hour to shove hot boiled potatoes into her mouth and stand in line at the outhouse. Plunking down on the straw with Janet, this was her one chance to stretch her arms and set aside the stress of trying to keep up the pace. The workers "held up their . . . aprons that were saturated with grease and dirt, and having received their allowance, scampered off as hard as they could to their respective places, where, with a keen appetite, each apprentice devoured her allowance, and seemed anxiously to look about for more."[24]

By twelve hours into the shift, Agnes and her co-workers were reduced to a zombie-like state. Speechless, detached, and numb, they prayed for the peal of the nine o'clock release bell. When it finally rang, sighs of relief followed the scuffling sound of several hundred bare feet. The exhausted twelve-year-old dragged her leaden legs down the mill's path back to the sleep room, ears ringing, thankful for Janet at her side. Half deaf from the din of the mill, the girls soon became immune to the commotion caused by street brawls and hooligans just outside the bothy. Nightfall brought a fitful peace, silence being an experience foreign to a child of the factories and the streets. So, too, was clean air. With no ventilation in the room, Agnes and Janet breathed blackened air even during the five hours they slept.

This was day one of Agnes's 548-day sentence of wool picking. Her hands would never be the same.

While Agnes and Janet toiled in Mr. Green's factory, young Princess Victoria was touring cotton mills throughout England in an effort to introduce the future monarch to her subjects and improve the Crown's image. Like that of most Glasgow girls, Agnes's coming of age reflected none of the leisure or revelry savored by the empire's future queen. On September 11, 1833, Agnes turned thirteen. There would be no party. Birthdays were celebrated only among the upper crust.

There was little dignity in becoming a woman on the factory floor. The lower classes could barely afford a single layer of clothing and had no undergarments of any sort. Agnes's entire wardrobe consisted of one coarse shift. When a lass became an adult with the onset of menstruation, everyone in the mill knew. A trail of public blood marked this rite of passage. Straw spread on the floor absorbed the fluids. Mercifully, one effect of malnutrition was that a girl's cycle was lighter and shorter than those of the well fed, thus sparing her greater embarrassment.

As she crossed into adolescence, the grey-eyed girl met few adults who were able to rise above the despair and drudgery that overran the slums. On the days she sang on the streets, Agnes had been propositioned by smelly sailors, cursed by pawnbrokers who bristled at her bargaining, and scammed by the bitter crone who owned the boardinghouse. A few of the older women in the mill offered the new apprentices snippets of motherly advice, though they had walked no easy path themselves.

A factory owner held full rein over the daily life of his indentured "street vermin." Under his authority, sexual abuse was tolerated and even encouraged. After all, he owned these young women for eighteen months or longer. It was not uncommon for owners to offer sons and friends their choice among the mill girls.

Nineteenth-century law provided protections for industry, while labor had none. Parliamentary legislation lavished loving care on its principal source of wealth in the hundreds of laws covering the wool trade, ranging from the correct clipping of sheep to the length and weight of the wool. As for child protection, there wasn't any. Humanitarianism was in the thoughts of very few. In 1816, utopian socialist Robert Owen first proposed day care for working mothers, free medical care, and comprehensive education. In his mind, a humane government was necessary to temper technology's rising cruelty, spawned by the Industrial Revolution. A mill owner himself, Owen tried to set an example by providing schools for his workers and allowing children to work no more than ten hours a day. He was considered idealistic for his time, and his forward thinking was widely ignored in an era when greed was the order of the day.

Owen prompted Sir Robert Peel, home secretary and later Britain's prime minister, to form a Committee of Investigation into the textile factories. Heavily lobbied by the wool industry over fine wine and lavish dinners, the committee examined whether fifteen-hour days were harmful to girls like Agnes and Janet. When mill owners produced long lists of witnesses to testify on their behalf, Owens's efforts produced exactly the opposite of his intentions. He wanted to expose the abuse of children and ignite social reform. Instead, expert witnesses like Dr. Holmes and Dr. Wilson used medical evidence, provided by the factory owners, to conclude that industrial exploitation brought children no harm.

The committee posed the following question to the physicians it had chosen as experts: "Suppose I were to ask you whether you thought it injurious to a child to be kept standing three and twenty hours out of the four and twenty, should you not think it must be necessarily injurious to the health?" Dr. Holmes replied: "If there were such an extravagant thing to take place and it should appear that the person was not injured by having stood three and twenty hours, I should then say it was not inconsistent with the health of the person so employed." Dr. Wilson agreed with his colleague, adding that it is "not necessary for young children to have recreation."[25]

One way or another, most people born poor ended up in a mill or a coal mine before age ten. Factory owners could buy a child for about five pounds from a workhouse or orphanage. Children signed with an X contracts that bound them to the factory owner until age twenty-one. A lad about the same age as Agnes described his feelings about working in a mill: "I think that if the devil had a particular enemy whom he wished to unmercifully torture the best thing for him to do would be . . . keep him as a child in a factory for the rest of his days."[26]

Sir Robert Peel's committee never heard the testimony that mattered most. Joseph Rayner Stephens, owner of the *Ashton Chronicle*, wrote it years later. He documented firsthand accounts of factory children who had labored during the same years as Agnes. Sarah Carpenter, a young adult in 1849, described to Stephens her experiences as a mill girl, including an account of a supervisor known to the children as Tom the Devil: "I have often seen him pull up the clothes of big girls, seventeen or eighteen years of age, and throw them across his knee, and then flog them with his hand in the sight of both men and boys. Everybody was frightened of him."[27] "Tom the Devil" had pummeled one girl into insanity and beaten two others to death. Another young mill slave by the name of Samuel Davy described the suffering he had witnessed: "Irons were used as with felons in gaols, and these were often fastened on young women, in the most indecent manner, by keeping them nearly in a state of nudity, in the depth of winter, for several days together."[28]

The powerful in Parliament turned a blind eye toward these abuses because the textile trade helped feed their fortunes as it spurred the empire's economy. Forced apprenticeship was ideal for the factory owner because the purchased children were paid substantially less than adults. Men earned about seven shillings a week, boys and girls just one or two. Juvenile thieves like Agnes and Janet were a bargain. They weren't paid at all except for a small contribution to the local "parish," the county government under the sheriff's jurisdiction.

By the summer of 1834, the child who had entered Mr. Green's mill eighteen months before was now a woman of almost fourteen. In a blur of yesterdays and tomorrows that all looked the same, Agnes completed her sentence. With stupefying repetition, 548 days, 8,222 hours of picking wool, had somehow passed. Strand by strand, the fifteen-hour days toughened her hands and fingers. She'd had enough of Glasgow. Agnes and Janet launched a new plan the day they left the mill. They would save their coins for lodging in Kilmarnock, a lovely town where Agnes's mother Mary had once lived.

~ 2 ~

Crown of Thieves

Glasgow Green

Agnes felt light-headed as she stepped across the threshold defining the boundary between the mill and the street. Over and done at last; the sooner forgotten, the better. Eagerly she took in Glasgow's June breeze, a welcome relief from the stale air in Mr. Green's bothy. Today even a whiff of coal dust smelled like freedom. Her shabby shift felt comfortable and familiar compared to the coarse factory uniform she had tossed behind her. Relief, however, was fleeting. Her newly found liberty was sweet, yet it quickly left a bitter aftertaste.

Agnes's hair was a dead giveaway to her status as thief. The thirteen-year-old was marked, and there was little she could do about it. Her closely shorn locks invited suspicious looks from shopkeepers and street vendors alike, who knew all too well what such short hair meant. It would be months before it grew back to a length that allowed her to blend into her surroundings. Even a bonnet was only a temporary disguise. Her workhouse haircut effectively barred her from any honest occupation. Nobody had any interest in listening to an ex–mill girl sing. What's more, her spot by the Glasgow Green had been taken over by another anonymous young balladeer, and it would take a tussle to get it back. Everything had changed, and nothing had changed.

In 1834, a young girl came of age when her "crowning glory" grew long enough for an updo, complete with layers and layers of cascading ringlets. So valued was a woman's hair that the wealthy saved every strand to weave into ornamental bracelets, hair adornments, and watch fobs. Agnes, however, wore the crown of thieves, branded for as long as it took her hair to grow back. The shorter a lass's locks were, the more recent her gaol time.

During her eighteen months at the mill, Agnes had, in the eyes of society, graduated from ragtag orphan to reprehensible thief. Gone were the days when a concerned mother offered a cup of milk or a kindly shopkeeper tossed a penny her way. Begging was a lost cause for a young adult. She would only be swatted away with an angry "Gae straecht to hell, ye sneak!" Besides, the blind, the crippled, and the infirm staked out the prime street corners for donations from passersby.

In *Sketches by Boz*, published in 1836, Charles Dickens observes the tragic drama of two London girls the same ages as Agnes and Janet: "These things pass before our eyes, day after day, and hour after hour—they have become such matters of course, that they are utterly disregarded. The progress of these girls in crime will be as rapid as the flight of a pestilence, resembling it too in its baneful influence and wide-spreading infection. Step by step, how many wretched females, within the sphere of every man's observation, have become involved in a career of vice, frightful to contemplate; hopeless at its commencement, loathsome and repulsive in its course; friendless, forlorn, and un-pitied, at its miserable conclusion!"[1]

Meandering through the morning's damp mist in search of Janet, Agnes considered her options—though certainly with a bit more optimism than Dickens, or she might have given up entirely. Fortunately, she'd been blessed with a bit of talent, and her singing brought in a few shillings every now and again. Yet her days as a street performer were dwindling. Though there was nothing cuter than a wean belting out a lively tune from a doorway, she was a betwixt-and-between awkward adolescent, emaciated like everyone else but not nearly as pathetic as young mothers crooning with babes in arms.

Agnes could not return to the mill. She'd rather die in the alley. Nearly fourteen, she was old enough to work as a housemaid or cook, but she needed references to be considered. Moreover, why would anyone risk hiring a convicted criminal with so many others in line for a job? From an economic perspective, it made sense to be a thief. For girls her age, the rewards of theft were higher than those of millwork—and the hours much shorter. Thieving was also preferable to prostitution.

Nineteenth-century British social reformer Mary Carpenter echoed this reality as she lobbied for the education of children like Agnes: "If a helping hand be not extended to raise them . . . these form the perishing classes . . . who unblushingly acknowledge that they can gain more for the support of themselves and their parents by stealing than by working."[2]

Agnes understood, and followed, Carpenter's conclusion. With true-blue friend Janet Houston, she returned to the life she knew best. Her first heist was for newer clothes. Pawnshops and secondhand stores thrived in abundance around the Glasgow Green. Many residents operated cellar shops located underneath their homes. Entered from a flight of steps off the alley, they were the cheapest places to find used shoes and boots. The prize selection for a girl like Agnes was a sturdy pair of low-heeled half boots that tied just above the ankle. Well broken in by several previous owners, the leather was a soft and pliable shabby brown. Cellar shoppers also hunted for thick wool socks, practical and warm albeit thoroughly dingy. Homeless youngsters either bartered for clothing with freshly pilfered booty or purchased it with coins received from stolen merchandise they sold to fences.

For some, the instinct to survive fueled the unseemly practice of literally stealing clothes off the backs of the weak and gullible. According to Henry Mayhew, a journalist of the time: "This is generally done by females, old debauched drunken hags who watch their opportunity to accost children passing in the streets, tidily dressed with good boots and clothes. They entice them away to a low or quiet neighbourhood for the purpose, as they say, of buying them sweets. . . . When they get into a convenient place, they give them a halfpenny or some sweets, and take off the articles of dress, and tell them to remain till they return, when they go away with the booty."[3]

Known as "child stripping" and performed by those hardened from decades on the street, this lowly act of desperation bode ill promise for both Agnes's and Janet's future. The two youngsters, however, spent little time worrying about what might lay ahead. What they dreaded most about winter—the fear of freezing to death during the night—was on temporary hiatus. Now that Scotland's warmest season had arrived, the closely knit pair felt as though huge boulders had rolled from their backs. They would only need to pilfer food for the day and not bother about buying a bed for the night.

Agnes hadn't seen her mother since she'd been in the mill and didn't feel welcome on Goosedubbs Street anymore. Some summer evenings, the grey-eyed lass and the spirited redhead hunkered down in a familiar doorway inside the East End wynds. Other nights they crawled into a sheltered hideaway along the River Clyde. Hours before industry's stirrings shook Glasgow from restless slumber, the clear sweet song of the lark awakened the girls.

Soon after dawn, their idyllic river retreat lost its luster. Once the winds picked up, an inescapable stench arose from the raw sewage and industrial waste being dumped directly into the River Clyde. Pollution killed the fish, whose corpses then lay along the shore, adding to the fetid odor. It was time to move on.

Careful to avoid the stinging bristles of nettle plants that had taken over the muddy river's edge, Agnes and Janet watched glossy blackbirds dive and swoop along the banks. Atlantic winds warmed by the Gulf Stream brought an unusual lightness to the air, and Agnes found a bounce in her step. She felt like singing again. This was going to be the best summer ever.

The fair on the Glasgow Green was a week away. This working-class holiday was a bonnie break from the press of sixteen-hour days on the docks or in the tannery. For street waifs, it was a celebration of unlimited possibilities. Young thieves like Agnes and Janet were known as "sneaks." Lacking the skill for picking pockets and the tools for clean house breaks, they sneaked about seeking ready targets for theft.

Although a good friend, Janet was not an ideal partner. Her russet tresses stood out like a flashing beacon in a crowd. On July 2, 1834, two days after Agnes's release, a constable caught Janet carrying off a bolt of blue-and-white fabric from a shop owned by James Fraser on High Street. A judge sent the sassy redhead straight back to Mr. Green's mill for sixty days. Only half the pair was arrested because the lookout did not get caught. Out of the officer's direct sight, Agnes must have blended into the crowd and made her getaway. It was Janet's turn to take the fall. Theirs was a friendship but also a business partnership that helped them through another day. The fair wouldn't be the same without her trusted confidante. Bad luck and bloody hell. Now she was a gang of one.

On her own for two months, Agnes knew enough street people to get by. The summer of 1834 lumbered on as she drifted through the alleys, counting the days until Janet's release. She had big news to share. No sooner had Janet been freed from Mr. Green's than Agnes grabbed her hand and dragged her to the corner of Saltmarket and Greendyke Streets. Ta-da! Englishman William Mumford had opened a theater in a ramshackle shed next to the Glasgow Green.

Listening for the sound of musicians who signaled the lifting of a canvas flap, the laboring class and the homeless gathered around and watched a new form of entertainment in a neighborhood rife with brothels and unlicensed taverns. Sword in hand, Mr. Mumford played the lead in *Rob Roy*, a play about the romantic Scottish outlaw born in the seventeenth century. As he poured glass after glass of gin down his throat, he lectured his patrons on the evils of drink.[4] Mr. Mumford might have been rather surprised to learn that his primitive theater would become Scotland's most famous penny *geggy*, a Scottish term for "show."

Boxing matches, cockfights, fortune-tellers, jugglers, and players of the "mouth organ" (harmonica) brought a kaleidoscope of entertainment to Glasgow's teeming East End. These spontaneous, frequently ribald, and sometimes bizarre performances diverted attention from the daily real-life dramas of the weary and abandoned playing throughout the tenement slums.

Agnes turned fourteen during the second week in September, when the deep purple heather burst into full bloom. Her hair had grown long enough to be less conspicuous as she roamed the wynds around the Green. Janet had completed her sentence just in time for Agnes's birthday and the lingering remnants of summer warmth.

The days were soon shorter as autumn approached and October's heavy rains returned. By November, the sun all but disappeared. The first snowflakes fell in December and posted a stark reminder of the holiday celebration that had gone so terribly, terribly wrong nearly two years ago, when Agnes was involved with the gang of burglars. This year, Agnes and her blue-eyed chum managed to sing holiday songs and pilfer their way through the season without getting caught.

On December 31, Glasgow came alive in holiday celebration. Agnes and Janet brought 1834 to a close as they bellowed out a chorus of "Auld Lang Syne," written by national poet and favorite son Robert Burns. Church bells across the city chimed at the stroke of midnight. This was Hogmanay night, Scotland's most important holiday, elevated in importance because of a long-standing ban on Christmas. Beginning in the seventeenth century, the Presbyterian Church forbade Christmas celebrations, fearing pagan origins among its traditions.

Hogmanay traditions, practiced continually since the 1600s, marked the season of rebirth as days became longer and nights shorter. Scots cleaned their homes thoroughly, paid off their debts, and burned juniper branches to ward off evil spirits for the coming year. Inside Glasgow's west-side mansions, holiday merrymakers feasted on whisky and steak pie. This was followed by traditional black buns, a type of fruitcake filled with raisins and currants, covered with pastry. If Agnes and Janet were quick enough on their feet, they'd lift a bun or two from a delivery basket left unattended. After all, Hogmanay was a high holiday for thieves. An abundance of revelers carried bottles of whisky from door to door, and as midnight approached, inebriated celebrants provided easy picking for their watches and their money.

The upper crust exchanged gifts on Hogmanay and practiced a custom called "first-footing." Depending on who it was, the first guest to enter a home after midnight brought either good or bad fortune for the new year. Visitors delivered coins and packages of coal, signaling the wish for security and warmth. According to folklore, the preferred first guest was a tall, dark, handsome man, because he was more likely a "true" Scotsman than someone fair-haired, perhaps descended from Viking invaders who terrorized Scotland for three hundred years. A redheaded first-footer was considered bad luck, a redheaded woman the worst of all.

Janet's bright hair caused her own bad luck, as she stood out in Glasgow's wynds. She was arrested again for petty theft on February 16, 1835. While Janet plodded through another mill sentence, Agnes took Helen Fulton, a kimmer (young girl) from the Goosedubbs neighborhood, under her wing.

Then, shortly after Janet's return, Agnes was arrested for petty theft. On April 14, 1835, the comely fourteen-year-old was sentenced to another sixty days in Mr. Green's mill. The grey-eyed lass fingered the locks that would be mercilessly shorn. Her hair had just started to grow out, and now she was back in chains. Back to the bothy again, bloody bad luck.

Agnes took her place in the cart with the other prisoners. The wagon creaked forward as the workhorse headed down the familiar path toward the mill. Yellow marsh marigolds and white hawthorn buds marked Agnes's trail of frustration.

Frolic o' the Fair

Agnes spent the spring in the mill, but was happily released from picking wool before temperatures reached 120 degrees inside the building. Through a stroke of good luck, the fourteen-year-old stepped out of the factory in time for the 1835 Glasgow Fair. It was the one holiday she could happily celebrate without a home. Established by William the Lion in 1190, the fair opened on the second Monday in July and lasted a full week. Everyone in Glasgow was in a better mood, even the shifty-eyed fences who turned stolen goods into a few coins. A halfpenny admission transported the youngsters through a rainbow of fluttering flags. "The air resounded to the strains of bagpipes, trumpets, trombones, cymbals, bass drums, and touters' horns. Sideshow touters, dressed in threadbare stage clothes of many and soiled colours, were doing their shouting and cavorting best to attract people with pennies in their pockets."[5]

Like all adolescents, Agnes and Janet primped a bit for special occasions, though their clothing was never laundered and was worn until it fell apart. As temperatures rose to a comfortable sixty-five degrees, Agnes and Janet joined the many poor who washed their faces, arms, and feet in the River Clyde, even though the water was polluted and nearly toxic. Bathing from head to toe was a rarity for every class, not just the homeless.

With their new friend, Helen Fulton, in tow, the girls linked arms and headed straight to the Glasgow Green, just steps from where Agnes had been born. Early summer harvests brought a temporary freshness to the city's dingy wynds. Flower hawkers brightened the morning fog, their wagons bursting through the muddy lanes. The sun peeked playfully in and out through the dispersing afternoon clouds as the Gulf Stream warmed the Atlantic winds.

Coal-dust-covered streets surrendered to dazzling yellow and red banners hung across the fairgrounds. "Tumblers performed miraculous feats of gymnastics, bears danced, jugglers juggled and clowns wandered about with fixed smiles painted on tired faces, among pressing crowds of eager urchins, grown-ups and the young men and women-about [sic] town."[6] Before the annual celebration began, the wealthy left town and headed "doun the watter" to summer resorts along the Clyde, deftly avoiding this lower-class festival.

Agnes, Janet, and Helen had been around long enough to know how to sneak into one of the tented shows or beg coins from the older gents leisurely smoking clay pipes. A crowd of thousands from both the city and the countryside pushed and shoved to gain a closer look at conjurers, Punch and Judy puppets, sword swallowers, and fire eaters. The boisterous festivities offered prime pickings for thieves and pickpockets, with hundreds of stalls to be stalked, watches to be stolen, and handkerchiefs to be snatched.

For a ballad singer of any age, it was peak musical season. Agnes had been born with the talent and desire to perform, and her singing often kept her out of trouble. Listening to the competition, she'd be able to pick up a few new songs and expand her repertoire. At the festival, she could get away with wearing a floppy felt hat that covered her convict hair. Laborers came to the fair ready to spend a bit on entertainment and cheerfully pressed a coin into the hand of a pretty grey-eyed girl who belted out favorite tunes like "Rob Roy," "The Maid Freed from the Gallows," "Glasgow Peggie," and "My 'Art's in the 'Ighlands." There was also a popular ballad about the fair:

> Glasgow fair on the banks of the Clyde,
> That pure winding stream of the City,
> Where all sorts of fun doth preside.
> Which help to arouse up my ditty;

Large Booths are arrang'd to the eye.
There's Horsemanship, Theatres, and Tumbling;
With all sorts of games to rely.
Where losers are always a Grumbling.[7]

A ten-year-old boy whose family owned a grocery store next to the fairgrounds described what he saw in a book he later published: "the Savages from Africa, the Armless Lady from Newfoundland who could sew and cut watch-papers using her toes, the Fire-Proof Lady who pranced about on a hot iron, the Hercules who could bear tons of weight on his body and toss immense weights around like balls of wool, the Smallest Married Man in the World and sundry pairings of giants and dwarves."[8]

All was not as exotic as it appeared. The street-savvy Goosedubbs girls soon figured out that the native African tribesmen were actually Irish laborers paid to dance in rabbit skins and feathers, but it didn't matter. Children of the street grew comfortable with illusions that allowed them to view the world through rose-colored glasses every now and again. During this week of fantasy, they collected enough tall tales and adventures to last through the wintry weather, when laughter alone soothed the chill in their bones and the pangs in their stomachs.

Agnes, Janet, and Helen each managed to avoid arrest through the remainder of the year and into the winter, but it was getting harder and harder to get by in Glasgow. Agnes's voice was beginning to change, too, and she hadn't quite figured out how to stay in tune. She and her two mates decided on a fresh start. Shortly after Hogmanay, the trio would head south toward Kilmarnock.

The Castles of Kilmarnock

Before sunrise on Monday, January 25, 1836, Agnes cinched her boots tight, tucked the laces inside her droopy socks, and walked purposefully through the neighborhood where she was born. The days were short and the sun set early, but today it wasn't snowing or spitting sleet, and it was high time she got out of town. She had become too well known on these sinful streets, more for her nimble fingers than her lilting ballads. With each passing hour, her means for survival were diminishing.

As a wean, Agnes remembered her mother reminiscing about a charming little village called Kilmarnock, where her cousins lived. She couldn't recall their names or addresses, but the promise of finding family members gave her the kick she needed to start walking south. Trudging down Goosedubbs Street for what would be the last time, she touched the few pennies and the stale bread she had squirreled away in a handkerchief and fixed her gaze on the low hills that circled the River Clyde.

Kilmarnock lies about twenty-two miles southwest of Glasgow. If she kept up a brisk pace, Agnes could make it in a day. It was much too dangerous for a lass so young to walk the sparsely populated glens and moors alone. Fortunately, Janet and Helen had eagerly agreed to make the journey. The motley troupe looked forward to a great adventure and made haste past the gritty tenement slums in the Gorbals village, home to Irish immigrants and Glasgow's growing Jewish population.

The ragged damsels hugged the south banks of the River Clyde and followed Pollokshaws Road toward Kilmarnock Road. Out of the city proper, one hour and three miles later, the view turned magical. Barely visible under grey camouflaging shingles, a pointed turret poked through the morning mist, heralding the first castle along their route. It was Haggs Castle, the fortress named for the bogs, or "haggs," on which it was built in 1585. Upon closer inspection, the castle, one of Scotland's oldest secular buildings, didn't look as grand as it had appeared from a distance. Nearly deserted since 1752, the fortress's rubble walls, once five feet thick, had fallen to ruin. Elaborate carvings around the doors and windows, uniquely squared gun loops, and round shot holes for explosives belied its current use. Agnes saw a castle occupied once again and converted to a blacksmith's shop that serviced a nearby coal pit.

Ancient remnants of history lay prostrate across the Scottish hillsides, where feudal lords had built fortunes by subjugating peasants. For generation after generation, the poor worked the land they could not own. Never far from reminders of Scotland's past, Agnes understood her dictated fate. No matter where she lived or what she did, the rich reminded her of opportunities that lay completely beyond her reach. There were the lords; there were the lowly. Scottish society had never allowed for social mobility. For Scotland's bottom rung, the promising economic freedom of the Industrial Revolution offered few differences from the old feudal system. Throughout the centuries since Scotland's founding, little had changed for its poor.

Over the farm-studded hills into miles and miles of wide-open country, the girl from Goosedubbs walked the fields where peasants had long toiled. But out here, Agnes was no peon repressed by a greedy baron. Step by step, she made her way across the timeless landscape, experiencing what it meant to feel free, if only for a day.

A toll road constructed in 1820 eased travel in and out of Glasgow and was built according to the broken-stone "macadam" method developed by Scotsman John Loudon McAdam. Perhaps Agnes and her ragtag team hitched a ride on the back of a farmer's cart or with a benevolent mail-coach driver. Though advantageous to wagon wheels, the crushed rocks were not so kind to tired feet and skinny ankles.

Seven miles into the journey, it was time for a rest. Crossing into Newton Mearns, Agnes spotted a "halfway house," as roadside taverns were called. Here horses were fed and watered or changed if the travel was long, creating an ideal spot to catch a ride. Vagabonds, locals, and travelers stopped for a smoke and a drink. In the city, women were generally not seen in saloons, but in the country, all paying customers were welcome. A few pennies would buy Agnes, Janet, and Helen a steaming bowl of soup and a soft piece of bread. Weary foot travelers, they huddled near the warm fire, removed their boots, and rubbed the bottoms of their feet. The three lasses dared not dawdle because nightfall approached by half past four and they had fourteen miles yet to go.

Over the braes and past sheep that grazed the gentle grasslands, the city girls arrived in real farm country. Unlike drab January in Glasgow, this landscape was bursting with winter wildlife. Geese, ducks, blackbird-sized woodpeckers, and bright blue-and-orange king-fishers kept the wooded lochs alive with activity. Giant whooper swans migrating from Iceland were everywhere. Their silly honking, echoing through the hollows, would have cracked a grin on the face of even the gloomiest adolescent.

As the city disappeared, it was like walking through a looking glass and emerging into an enchanted countryside of glistening lakes, streams gurgling pristine water, and cozy thatched-roof cottages. The determined damsels tramped down the track toward Kilmarnock, lapsing into silence. The only sound was from the footfalls of their rough-worn boots. The lonely road dragged on and on. Four hours of majestic beauty had become tedious and exhausting.

Five miles outside Kilmarnock, Agnes, Janet, and Helen happened upon another inviting halfway house, its pristine whitewashed stucco and shiny black shutters unlike anything they'd seen in Glasgow. Amid the merriment inside of gin drinkers and tobacco puffers, the girls made a beeline for the coal-burning stove. Toasting her feet before the fire, Agnes rubbed her aching toes. Janet, knowing that daylight was in short supply, soon pulled her younger charges onto their feet and back into the January cold. Lengthening shadows signaled the final leg of their trek. The sun's quick descent had begun to dull the soft green palette cast across rolling farmland.

In the thick of gnarled sycamores tinged pink, turrets rose from the horizon. This late in the day, nearly twenty miles on the road, Agnes, Janet, and Helen probably didn't care much about abandoned castles, but the Rowallan estate commanded attention from the most road-weary traveler. Located in a sheltered hollow, it is "environed with trees, many of which have braved the blast for centuries, and still wave their branches as majestically as they did in days of yore, when knights and ladies gay walked beneath their shadows."[9]

Rowallan was, in fact, the birthplace of scandalous Scottish royalty. Countess Elizabeth Mure was born on its marshy grounds in 1315. Longtime mistress to Robert II, High Steward of Scotland, she married him after giving birth to nine children. Because they had violated forbidden degrees of kinship, approval to marry required a papal dispensation. Had she not died before Robert ascended the throne, Elizabeth would have been crowned Scotland's queen.

The three untamed princesses carried less regal concerns. As shadows fell, questions arose. Where would they sleep this night? Would they be able to locate Agnes's cousins? Could they prosper as thieves in a new town?

One mile from Kilmarnock, the girls turned onto Glasgow Road and walked straight toward Dean Castle, built by Lord Boyd in 1457 and situated in a wooded glen, or "dean," for which the palace was named. Two square towers, unequal in height, loomed over the enclosed courtyards and three-story palace. Barren orchards, weedy gardens, and overgrown rhododendron bushes blanketed the deserted estate.

Nineteenth-century Kilmarnock historian Archibald M'Kay offers this view of the castle: "Though grey and rent with years, it looks as if conscious of its strength, and as if frowning defiance down the valley that stretches before it. From the same eminences we have a glimpse of the town, with its towers and spires, which give it an air of importance; and the eye, ranging still farther, rests delighted on the beautiful green hills of Craigie."[10] A fairy-tale panorama welcomed three hungry, grumbling lasses. Kilmarnock's grand entrance was nothing like Glasgow's.

The Best-Laid Plans

The turn toward Kilmarnock revealed handsome villas adorned by wooded grounds and well-groomed shrubbery. Spires from eight churches poked their silhouettes through the waning afternoon light. Situated in a valley through which the rivers Kilmarnock and Irvine flow, the village was just two miles long and a half mile wide. It would be easy to find the heart of what the girls hoped was their new home. Glasgow Road merged with Wellington, then Portland, bringing the girls directly to the town's center. Seven streets branched off Kilmarnock's spacious and open town square, known as the Cross. Chimes rang from the Laigh Kirk (low church) tower clock that anchored the commercial center.

Agnes, Janet, and Helen had been on the road for more than ten hours. By chance they arrived in Kilmarnock on Robert Burns's birthday, a celebration that had become a national holiday. Born two miles south of Kilmarnock on January 25, 1759, Scotland's favorite bard had frequented the Cross on market days. Like Agnes, Burns had been born to the labor class, but he was fortunate to have lived in the country and received an education. A schoolmaster who visited farms in return for room and board taught Burns to read and write and introduced him to Shakespeare.

In July 1786, Burns, the impoverished farmer who wrote in his free time, shuffled into John Wilson's print shop in Kilmarnock. After negotiating a good price for six hundred copies of *Poems, chiefly in the Scottish dialect*, Burns published his first edition. The village had offered a struggling writer the break he needed. Perhaps Agnes would find good luck here as well.

On this holiday night, traditional Burns suppers all across Scotland featured haggis, "tatties" (potatoes), and "neeps" (turnips), each course garnished with humorous toasts to the poet. A dessert course of sherry trifle or Caledonian cream was washed down with *uisge beatha*, Gaelic for "water of life," or whisky. After dinner, inebriated men in kilts roamed the alleyways and belted out Burns's "Auld Lang Syne." The Glasgow girls must have felt right at home and thought: *Lord, we've gone to heaven. The town is crawling with rich drunks making for easy targets.*

More pressing matters, however, consumed their attention. Sleeping in alleyways was not so easy in a small town. The charming red stone buildings on King Street, the main thoroughfare, offered no alcoves or doorways where they wouldn't be noticed. On the lookout for a neighborhood not so posh, the girls followed King Street to a somewhat shabby lane called Croft. A sign outside Mr. Cairns's lodginghouse advertised rooms for rent.[11] For a good night's rest, it was worth spending the few coins they had left.

Shortly after daybreak on Tuesday, January 26, Agnes hauled herself out of bed and set out to find her cousins. The trio needed to survey Kilmarnock and figure out if they could afford to stay, ideally with Agnes's relatives. The girls began by exploring the confusing maze of streets and intersections. Winemakers, hairdressers, coffee rooms, and candy shops lined its elegant center, casting an air of refinement.[12]

Agnes's mother, Mary, must have loved living here as a young girl. How different Agnes's story could have been had Mary wed a chap from Kilmarnock. Most residents enjoyed a prosperous, peaceful life. Bankers sported double-breasted wool suits and white shirts with starched high collars. Ladies strolled the freshly swept shopping district, casting demure glances from under bonnets tied with lavish loops of satin ribbon.

In startling contrast, three city girls with unruly hair and dirty frocks clomped heavy-footed over the cobblestones. The harsh sound of Glasgow street dialect screamed trouble times three and drew vigilant, if discreet, stares. Agnes, Janet, and Helen were probably unaware of how out of place they appeared. Every newcomer to Kilmarnock was noticed.

While Agnes searched for her cousins, whom no one seemed to know, she discovered rows and rows of shops fully stocked and brimming over with capes, calico, and richly toned plaid woolens. Hatters and hosiers advertised their specialties on neatly painted signs wrapped across the front of each building. The town was filled with beautiful things. More than thirty bootmakers and shoemakers displayed hand-stitched footwear, much of it for export but with samples available for retail sale.[13]

The twenty-two-mile trek seemed worth it. This fashion paradise was enough to make a little thief's head spin. Where to begin? What to choose? Tuesday was market day, and the Cross bustled with vendors and shoppers. It was an opportunity that seemed too good to be true.

Among the well-dressed shoppers, the girls noticed someone who looked familiar. His belongings were tied in a red napkin, a style that was typical for a vagabond. Agnes recognized him to be Daniel Campbell, an acquaintance from the back streets of Glasgow.[14] Daniel boasted about his fencing connections in Kilmarnock, professing to know who would pay quick cash for stolen merchandise without asking questions. He convinced the three that he was exactly the fence they needed, a trusted accomplice who would generate a stack of shillings to pay the boardinghouse, buy food, and purchase finery from the shops. Everything was falling into place.

Each member of the quartet signed on for a specific role. The dance of the robbers was about to begin, a well-choreographed ballet that depended on a flawless performance by every member of the ensemble. One misstep, the curtain dropped, and the matinee turned to melodrama.

Agnes, Janet, and Helen had already targeted several merchants for the sting. The first hit was a clothing shop run by Hugh Young. The girls memorized their parts. In the lead role, one girl walked in with a group of customers. The supporting cast assumed a post on the opposite side of the street, poised to whistle at the first sight of a constable. A second lookout positioned herself just outside the shop's entrance. Her job was to trip the shopkeeper should he spot the thief and attempt her capture.[15]

Once inside the busy store, a member of the Glasgow gang slipped two men's cotton shirts off their hangers, opened a drawer to remove two women's cotton shifts, and on the way out lifted a cloak from the counter.[16] Mission accomplished. It had been fast and easy. They handed over the goods to Daniel Campbell so that he would have their cash by nightfall.

Next stop was a visit to 63 King Street and tailor John Granger, where the gang lifted twenty-four "braces," the elastic garters worn by both men and women to hold up stockings. Just three buildings away at 57 King, Janet Rankin ran a lovely hosiery boutique filled with stockings for day and evening wear. Her merchandise was especially inviting now that the girls had braces to hold them in place. The moment Mrs. Rankin turned her back, the thief stuffed stockings in her pockets, seven pairs in all.

A quick trip to the boardinghouse gave the Glasgow girls a place to stash their latest plunder. Before heading back to King Street, Agnes couldn't help herself and succumbed to temptation. She tore off her smelly socks and pulled on a pair of the sinfully soft wool stockings. In her hurried excitement, she forgot to remove Janet Rankin's hosiery label.

It was now four o'clock and time for one final stunt before the shops closed for the day. The seller of sundries looked particularly inviting, with draped fabric displays and trimmings of ribbon and lace. Now it was Agnes's turn to shoplift. It was also her misfortune to get caught exiting the shop with stolen beads pressed into her palm.[17]

It didn't take long before the full ensemble, the trio plus one, was hauled down to the police station, where the officer immediately focused on Agnes's new hosiery. The clean stockings looked unusually bright in contrast to her shift's fraying hem. Upon questioning, Agnes told the officer they were a gift from her sister. Her lie was naïvely transparent. When she was ordered to remove the stockings, damning evidence immediately identified them as stolen. The Rankin's tag was still attached.[18]

Kilmarnock's low crime rate had skyrocketed overnight, the charm of the village interrupted by the rustle of rogues from the north. Agnes, Janet, and Helen had blown into town like a gale-force wind, joining forces with the hapless Daniel Campbell. With the troublemakers arrested, calm returned to the township.

The book Robert Burns published in Kilmarnock included the poem "To a Mouse" and the line, "The best laid schemes o' mice an' men/Gang aft agley." This translates to "The best-laid plans of mice and men often go awry," prophetic words for fifteen-year-old Agnes McMillan, arrested just a block from where Burns's poem was published. Errors of desperation had lowered the curtain on the daring troupe. Their case would be tried on the first of the month in Ayr, the county's capital at the time.

The four scoundrels spent the next five days in the dusty little holding cells underneath Kilmarnock's council chambers. Built on the arch of a bridge, the government offices also housed a few lockup cells in "the most objectionable parts of the building, being low-roofed, almost without light or air."[19] At sunrise on February 1, 1836, the youngsters crept from the cramped holding cell, heads bent down like trolls emerging from a subterranean dwelling. Chained together at the wrists, the band was put in the back of a wagon for the thirteen-mile ride to Ayr.

The prisoner cart crossed the arched Auld Brig over the River Ayr, built in the fifteenth century and immortalized in Burns's poem "The Brigs of Ayr." Only wide enough for one vehicle to pass at a time, the stone bridge had been financed by two maiden sisters whose fiancés drowned when they attempted to ford the brackish water.[20]

Auld Brig converged with Weavers Street, where the cart of captives turned down the capital's Main Street. Ayr's town hall, erected eight years earlier, stood under "perhaps the finest spire in Scotland," rising two hundred twenty-five feet toward a cloudless sky.[21] A short ride from Newmarket Street to Sandgate brought Agnes and friends to the Wellington Square courthouse, where their tomorrows would soon be decided. The rhythm of the horses' hooves began to slow as the driver pulled on the reins and townspeople peered at the young prisoners in chains. Because of its coastal location along the Firth of Clyde, rarely is Ayr covered in fog. The view was crystal clear from the sprawling fenced lawn. A huge courthouse with eleven bays and a "scowling four-columned Ionic portico" housed the heavy hammer of British law.[22]

As the gaol wagon rolled away, Agnes, Janet, Helen, and Daniel bore the gravity of an impending county court trial. They scuffled against the marble floor in small steps, the sound of their leg irons echoing off two semicircular staircases that rose off the entrance hall. Large stained-glass windows, casting bands of red and blue from the county's coat of arms, lit each stairwell. Flashes of colored light ran across the deeply shaded fumed oak that decorated the entrance.[23]

Intimidating in both its beauty and its function, the Sheriff Court was adorned with highly polished Borneo cedar. The shining waxed mahogany benches reflected the dark silhouettes of the Glasgow hooligans, who would be tried as a group before Sheriff Substitute of

Ayrshire William Eaton. John Archibald Murray, Esquire, Advocate for His Majesty's Interest, read the prisoners' statements before the court. He droned on in the bored monotone expected from a civil servant, his words reverberating off the walls and perishing quickly. Nobody cared what he had to say, save the four prisoners at the bar.

Agnes dictated her statement because she could neither read nor write. In her arrest report, she admitted to having met Daniel Campbell in Kilmarnock. She pretended not to know Janet and Helen in a desperate attempt to protect her friends, but the die was already cast. Sheriff Eaton announced his judgment for "crimes of an heinous nature and severely punishable." Barely looking up, he declared that Agnes McMillan, Janet Houston, and Helen Fulton did "wickedly and feloniously steal and theftuously take away" from Kilmarnock merchants two men's cotton shirts, two women's cotton shifts, twenty-four braces, a cloak, and seven pairs of woolen stockings. Furthermore, he declared that Daniel Campbell had "wickedly and feloniously" and knowingly received the stolen goods.[24]

The four were scheduled for sentencing on May 3, 1836, before the Circuit Court of Judiciary. They would spend the next three months locked inside the Ayr County Gaol, an overcrowded holding area that adjoined the rear of the court. With a backlog of cases, it was a long wait for everyone.

Deep inside the cavernous passages, Agnes had ninety long days to contemplate her past and her future. The present looked very black. Agnes would not have known that a Quaker social reformer named Elizabeth Gurney Fry had labored fervently since 1816 to spearhead prison reform for the burgeoning population flooding into gaols. William Crawford, a Quaker who traveled in the same circles as Mrs. Fry, was, in 1835, appointed one of the first inspectors general of prisons for Great Britain. His words had explained Agnes's situation: "It is very easy . . . to blame these poor children, and to ascribe their misconduct to an innate propensity to vice; but I much question whether any human being, circumstanced as many of them are, can reasonably be expected to act otherwise."[25] Crawford was ahead of his time, yet too late to make a difference for Agnes. Rather than condemning her, he understood that parental neglect, lack of education, poverty, and just plain hunger propelled too many children into a life of crime.

When Elizabeth Fry and her brother Joseph John Gurney inspected prisons in Scotland, they witnessed the practice of housing the mentally ill, violent felons, and petty thieves together. In overcrowded gaols, they were packed into unheated cells, furnished with only a handful of straw and a single tub for every purpose. As was her custom, Elizabeth knelt down on the straw to pray with the incarcerated and encourage them to turn from crime to wage-paying work. During a visit to Glasgow, one prisoner, in particular, conveyed the raw hopelessness that led to thievery and the regret that lingered still. In her journal, Fry describes the "old woman, with the appearance of a menial servant and hardened features, [who] said, 'No! no use work!' But these rugged lines were at length relaxed, and I saw a tear fall over the brown visage."[26] She had worked her whole life, and here she was in gaol.

Age mattered hardly at all when it came to being poor. Realities and regrets were embedded in nearly every decision it took to survive. At fifteen, barely a woman, Agnes appeared to have reached the same conclusion. She'd seen what the mills had done to her mother—"no use work." Little did she know that in a London gaol four hundred miles away, the well-heeled and well-known Mrs. Fry had already woven herself into Agnes's destiny. The worst thing that had ever happened to the worried youngster was going to open up opportunities she'd never thought possible.

Four Hundred Miles

On Tuesday, May 3, 1836, true-blue mates Agnes McMillan and Janet Houston were refitted with irons and yanked out of their cells to appear before the Ayr Court of Judiciary. Helen Fulton and Daniel Campbell appeared as well. Records from the Glasgow Police Court were called into evidence, listing Agnes's prior arrests for housebreaking at age twelve in December 1832 and for theft in April 1835. The record included Janet's arrest for "a conviction of the crime of theft" on July 2, 1834, and the following February.[27]

Lord Justice General Charles Hope, head of Scotland's highest court, read aloud the report that deemed Agnes "habite and repute a thief," guilty of "crimes of an heinous nature and severely punishable."[28] It took all of five minutes. There were too many poor to be sentenced to spend much time pondering the merits of justice for one grey-eyed girl. From under his dusty wig, he sentenced the fifteen-year-old petty thief to seven years' transportation to "parts beyond the seas." Janet fared no better and in short order was condemned to the same punishment. Because the Kilmarnock heist was Helen's first offense, she was sentenced to eighteen months' imprisonment. Daniel, like Agnes and Janet, received seven years' transport, but he managed an escape and turned outlaw and fugitive.[29]

Wrestling away fear, wrists and ankles in chains, Agnes shuffled back to her holding cell to await she knew not what. While the young women were summarily dismissed, they were also meticulously numbered and documented for the authorities in Van Diemen's Land. As dawn broke on May 4, 1836, Agnes was rousted from her cell, where she and Janet lay in restless sleep on the clay floor. Gaol keeper John Kennedy attached black iron manacles across Agnes's wrists.[30] He chained her legs to Janet's and led the two girls to the front of the courthouse, where a commercial coach was waiting. Shoulder to shoulder, attached at their ankles, the duo was careful not to act too chummy. After everything they'd been through, these stoic soul sisters from Glasgow's streets dared not risk separation.

Their destination was Newgate Prison, where they awaited shipment to Britain's most distant colony. Men were marched in chain gangs, while convict women were transported on the outside of commercial stagecoaches. Getting up on the carriage required the agility of an acrobat for the two wrongdoers handcuffed at the wrists and chained at the ankles. With a hearty boost from gaoler Kennedy, Agnes and Janet were secured to the coach and plunked onto the wooden plank serving as a seat. The sooner such riffraff was removed from his jurisdiction, the better. As was typical for the times, a crowd of onlookers gathered for the send-off and watched with disgust and amusement as the two lasses tried to keep their skirts from flying above their knees. Small fingers poked through the manacles as the driver picked up his whip and prepared for departure.

Drawn by four horses, the stagecoach was cheerfully painted, belying the unpleasant bumping, bruising ride ahead. Travel by coach frequently included getting stuck in the mud or losing a wheel and crashing off the road. The carriage held up to eight passengers on the top and six inside. A guard armed with blunderbuss, pistols, and cutlass was perched next to the coachman. Dressed in signature scarlet livery, he watched the prisoners, protected the carriage from highway robbery, and secured the mailbags.

The coach company received a small stipend from the Crown for prisoner transport. Now that their cargo was secured, it was time to pick up the paying passengers booked for Preston, Birmingham, or London. The driver snapped his whip, and the carriage jolted forward, knocking Agnes and Janet against the iron rail.

Stagecoach travelers were bundled up in bonnets, scarves, and shawls and carried baskets of provisions on board. Like the upstairs-downstairs hierarchy inside fine homes, paying customers pretended not to see their traveling companions. For the duration of the four-hundred-mile, four-day trip to London, insiders were held captive themselves, sharing company with smelly, drunk, or overly talkative passengers.

The stagecoach traveled at a speed of seven or eight miles an hour. In May, it crossed the moors at their greenest, with the bluebells in full color. Every twenty miles or so, the driver made comfort stops, primarily for the horses' benefit. Coaching inns were open twenty-four hours a day and provided stables where the horses were groomed, fed, and changed when necessary.

Sounding his bugle, the driver alerted the innkeeper to their approach. Passengers could buy a rushed meal consisting of "scalding soup-stained warm water . . . underdone boiled leg of mutton, . . . potatoes hot without and hard within."[31] Unscrupulous innkeepers delayed serving meals until just before the carriage was scheduled for departure. Travelers barely had time to inhale a few mouthfuls. As they hurried out of the inn, the food was scraped from their plates and served to the next customer. Businesses stole from customers, and customers stole from businesses. Nearly everyone pursued a criminal pursuit of one sort or another. It was merely a question of who got caught.

The stagecoach driver scheduled a stop for the night before darkness fell. In early May, that meant close to nine o'clock. Most prisoners were ill-equipped for evening temperatures that plummeted close to freezing. "Sometimes they had insufficient clothing to even properly cover themselves and it was not unknown for women to arrive frost-bitten and suffering from other physical disabilities brought on by the ravages of exposure and hypothermia."[32]

For a convict lass, the ease or difficulty of her transport depended on the weather and the driver's disposition. Some of the prisoners had families who gave them a cloak and a hat for warmth. Most, like Agnes, wore one thin layer of clothing. If the coachman felt kindly, he might have offered Agnes and Janet a spare blanket on the road. If generous, he might have shared a piece or two of bread and sips of warming brandy. If not, his charges went cold and hungry for four or five days. After three years on the streets, the girl with the glint in her eyes had learned how to draw on the sympathies of those who might help her. It was one additional survival tool in her growing reserve.

Years earlier, Elizabeth Fry, whom the Glasgow pair would soon meet in London, followed a similar route during her inspection of Scotland's prisons. Although she traveled by private coach, her diary recorded an arduous journey, traversing bogs and streams in weather similarly damp and chilly. Fry's nights were spent inside the warm homes of fellow Quakers, while for three nights in May, Agnes and Janet slept in stables with the horses. It was, however, a step up from their typical alleyway dwelling, and it would be their best housing for some time to come.

When she awakened from her bed of stable straw on Saturday, May 7, 1836, Agnes had already traveled more than three hundred miles. Tethered to Janet, she sloshed through the mud in her crinkled and droopy brown boots, her skinny ankles raw from the irons. The driver hoisted the youngsters back atop the stagecoach and reattached the shackles that tethered them to the seats. Over the past few days Agnes had figured out how to brace herself, pulling her knees tight against the seat and balancing against the carriage's unpredictable drop and sway.

As evening drew near, the petite Scot watched her dreaded destination come slowly into view. Built on London's highest point, the blackened dome of St. Paul's Cathedral rose 365 feet in the air and dominated the skyline. To the west of the cathedral lurked the grim façade of Newgate Prison, known to Londoners as "the Stone Jug."[33] The granite vault for the poor sat across from St. Sepulchre, the church whose bells tolled on execution days.

The two friends linked by heavy chains and iron loyalty had never traveled more than twenty-five miles from home, so London must have seemed like the end of the world. The city proper grew ever more congested. Children taunted the girls and threw stones at the coach. Janet's bright red hair made for a fine target. This was not the performance Agnes had imagined in her dreams of singing on a London stage.

3

The Angel of Newgate

Nighthawks

All roads for the desperate poor eventually led to Newgate Prison. Righteous reformer Elizabeth Gurney Fry, in an act of selfless determination, shocked the nation when she founded a Quaker ministry inside London's chapel of the damned. By the time Agnes and Janet were headed to Newgate, Fry was already a London celebrity.

Elizabeth's husband, Joseph Fry, accepted his wife's commitment to a higher purpose. He also tolerated her blatant defiance toward how London ladies were *supposed* to behave. In return, every day of the week except Sunday, Mrs. Fry rousted Joseph out of a deeply stuffed parlor chair, rallying the ambition that too often escaped him. On workdays, the dutiful Mr. Fry opened their front door and headed out to his bank's countinghouse, conveniently located just below their living quarters at Mildred's Court. In the morning fog, Joseph sometimes tripped over the skirts of women and children who waited patiently on the front stoop. Word had spread on the streets near

Bishopsgate, Poultry, and Cheapside about a Mrs. Fry who helped destitute women, offering them fresh food and clean clothing. "In very hard winters she had soup boiled in an out-house in such quantities as to supply hundreds of people with a nourishing meal."[1]

Between the births of her children, eleven in all, Elizabeth expanded her humanitarian projects. Determined to stop the spread of smallpox, she vaccinated families who lived in remote villages and in London's darkest slums. She established a girls' school in Plashet for the children of laborers and servants, set up libraries for men stationed at remote coast-guard locations, and founded a nursing school that provided free care for those without funds. Years later, Florence Nightingale, a distant cousin, would take some of Fry's well-trained nurses to the Crimean War front. Still, this was not enough.

In a coincidental turn of fate, just as Elizabeth was searching for her own spiritual purpose, a French aristocrat turned American Quaker minister knocked on her door at Mildred's Court. On a cold, rainy afternoon in January 1813, Stephen Grellet was shown into the Frys' drawing room, the well-known British Quaker William Forster at his side. A striking figure with ragged silver hair, dark bushy eyebrows, and a prominent nose, the pockmarked but graceful Grellet could barely contain the fullness of his heart.

Grellet was an outspoken reformer, who devoutly followed the tradition of Quaker empathy and compassion for society's outcasts. Drawn to the cause of London's forgotten poor, Grellet was appalled to learn that nearly a million faced imminent starvation. As the New Year approached, Parliament refused imports of wheat and oats in an effort to maintain the high price of British-grown grain. Artificially inflating the price of grain backfired. It undermined the farmer and caused a dramatic spike in crime as thousands fled the fields and flocked to the city for work that did not yet exist. Bread had become a luxury item in London. The poor either suffered starvation or took desperate measures to feed themselves, resorting to theft and prostitution. Some abandoned their children. Others blinded reality with London's cheap and plentiful gin.

Stephen Grellet rejected the ruling class's prevailing belief that the destitute deserved their suffering. In January 1813, he called a meeting for thieves, pickpockets, and prostitutes at the St. Martin's Lane Quaker house. It was an unprecedented request, and no one knew what to expect. The meeting was called for seven P.M. because most among this group were considered "nighthawks." Surprisingly, thousands attended, most barely twenty and nearly all homeless. Grellet understood the depths of their misery and wrote: "I wept bitterly over them. The lofty heads, the proud looks were brought down. I have seldom known such brokenness and so general as it was that evening."[2] The police chief magistrate who watched as the crowd exited deemed Grellet foolish and offered to collect *all* the scum in London for his guardianship. Grellet declined his taunting offer but used the opportunity to ask for permission to visit London's prisons, where he had heard that even young children were housed.

Grellet quickly filed the required petitions to visit Newgate Prison, "having religious opportunities in the many separate apartments, where the miserable inmates are confined."[3] Once inside, he tried to comfort the boys and men who awaited hanging. When he asked to visit the women's quarters: "The gaoler endeavoured to prevent my going there, representing them as so unruly and desperate a set that they would surely do me some mischief . . . concluding that the very least I might expect was to have my clothes torn off."[4] Grellet refused to be turned away.

On that auspicious January afternoon, over a glass of brandy to chase away the biting winter chill, Stephen Grellet told Elizabeth Fry, rather breathlessly, what he'd just seen. About three hundred half-naked women and children lived in a cell about forty by forty-two feet in size, allowing each inmate a space about two feet by two feet, barely enough to sit down. A few among them had committed murder or arson. Most were chained and imprisoned for stealing a watch, a dress, a piece of cloth, or a cloak. For minor misdemeanors, prisoners waited up to six months to be assigned a ship that would transport them to Van Diemen's Land, known today as Tasmania.

Grellet found the women gaoled in conditions much worse than those he had witnessed for Newgate's men. His aristocratic ease became completely unhinged upon visiting the women's sick ward. "On going up, I was astonished beyond description at the mass of woe and misery I beheld. I found many very sick, lying on the bare floor or some old straw, having very scanty covering over them, though it was quite cold; and there were several children born in the prison among them, almost naked."[5]

Grellet never had to ask Elizabeth for her assistance. Fry immediately volunteered to visit Newgate to see for herself. As it happened, her friend Anna Buxton was visiting when Grellet arrived. Within hours of his departure, the Fry household grew alive with activity. In the twinkling light of the silver candelabras, Elizabeth and Anna immediately began making flannel clothes for the infants at Newgate. Throughout the night, a small parade of Quaker neighbors arrived at Mildred's Court to assist with the sewing.

The very next day, Mrs. Fry awoke with a fire in her belly as she pulled back the curtains around her four-poster bed. Turning down the cotton sheet underneath several wool blankets and a silk coverlet, Elizabeth felt none of the malaise and depression that had plagued her so often since her mother's death twenty-one years ago. She was on a mission.

As mistress of Mildred's Court, Elizabeth's first order of the day was to attend to her household duties and give the staff their orders. Technically, her address was St. Mildred's Court, but Quakers do not believe in saints, so the Fry clan simply shortened the name to suit them. Hustling her husband, Joseph, out of bed and into his dark grey waistcoat was a daily ritual. They were served their breakfast in the parlor before Joseph headed downstairs to his office at the family bank. For Elizabeth, getting dressed was somewhat of an ordeal. Her lady's maid had already laid out a corset and five starched white petticoats. After a quick curtsy, she applied the ornate silver hook and cinched tight Elizabeth's corset, stiffened with whalebones and not at all comfortable. Then she layered one petticoat at a time, pulling and tugging each into place. As a final adjustment, she fluffed Fry's billowing skirt and pulled on the creases of the puffed beret sleeves. Decorative but impractical, they added to the illusion of an hourglass. Together, they accentuated the feminine waist, even if it was a bit round like Elizabeth's.

Fry's maid drew back the heavy, deep crimson silk damask curtains, fastened with fringed tiebacks, that protected Mildred's Court from London's boisterous streets and blackened air. Elizabeth looked out her bedroom window and watched a relentless drizzle fall across the slick black slate roof of the family's teahouse. She walked to her dressing room, opened the enormous ceiling-high carved mahogany wardrobe, deliberately chose a simple black wool cloak, and then reached for another. Mrs. Fry would need a second shawl to protect her from the penetrating dampness.

Before heading downstairs, Elizabeth looked in on the eight children she had given birth to during the first twelve years of her marriage. They were currently under the watch of her housekeeper, Jane King. Efficient, albeit haughty and distant, Miss King ensured that Elizabeth's children had fine care, but still Mother Fry worried about her absences from home. Entries in her diary reveal an emotional struggle over her responsibilities as a mother and her ordained purpose: "May I not be hurt in it, but enabled quietly to perform that which ought to be done; and may it all be done so heartily unto the Lord, and through the assistance of His grace."[6]

The clocks in the house began to chime, first the large grandfather clock in the hallway, seconds later the mantel clock kept under glass to protect its delicate works from persistent, penetrating coal residue. Eight o'clock; the day was well underway. Elizabeth expected Anna

Buxton at any moment. Hours before, the downstairs maid had lit a fire to warm the breakfast parlor, replenishing the hand-carved coal scuttle at the base of the fireplace. With no central heating, Mildred's Court was filled with thickly stuffed lounging chairs and velvet couches that helped insulate the rooms from the blustery cold outside. Typical upper-class taste in décor was characterized by excessive detail in which elaborate wallpaper met floral-scrolled carpets beneath embossed, patterned ceilings. Ostrich feathers in painted vases accented shelves of cluttered bric-a-brac that required endless dusting. Crowning this visual carnival, treasured family portraits covered virtually every available space.

Long before sunrise, the downstairs maid had filled several bucket loads with about thirty pounds of coal. The work was not easy, but employment as a housemaid offered the coveted benefits of a reasonably warm room, just off the kitchen, and three hearty meals a day. Leftovers were plentiful in this grand home. A typical breakfast included porridge and salt, eggs and potted beef, toast, and butter. This cornucopia was presented on the finest translucent china covered by monogrammed silver domes. The feast filled the Frys' mahogany sideboard to overflowing. On this gloomy London morning, the starched white linen tablecloth brightened the dark English oak that paneled the breakfast room. Logs crackled in the marble fireplace. A sliver of steam rose from the gleaming silver teapot while Elizabeth silently sipped from the gold-rimmed cup she held between her fingers.

From outside, Elizabeth heard the chains rattling as Anna Buxton's coach delivered her just in time for morning tea. Anna and Elizabeth had been friends since childhood. Anna's brother Thomas Fowell Buxton was a fervent Quaker abolitionist, and later Member of Parliament, who was married to Elizabeth's sister Hannah. He would soon join Elizabeth and his sister in their work to save the women who awaited exile inside Newgate Prison, including Agnes McMillan and Janet Houston.

The Bone Gatherers

Mrs. Fry, anxious to head straightaway to the prison, tied her bonnet securely under her chin and fastened a satin shawl at her bosom with a rose pin made of wool. Her carriage soon arrived, and the footman obediently draped Elizabeth's outer cape over her shoulders. He held her elbow to steady her as she climbed into the small black buggy that creaked under the weight of its new cargo. Sitting bolt upright just as her mother had taught her, she directed the coachman to Newgate without delay.

The horses tensed, steam blowing out of their nostrils as they shifted nervously against the leather harnesses. Elizabeth and Anna heard the crack of the whip, the wheels began to roll, and with a lurch they were on their way. The Fry horses had their own groomsman, who fed them a steady diet of fresh oats and barley, a feast worthy of envy by most of London's poor. Although Mrs. Fry erred on the side of modesty in public displays of status, even riding in an open carriage in the winter, her horses' smooth coats glistened with impeccable care and signaled her family's wealth. Elizabeth liked to keep pretense at bay. In conspicuous contrast, her sisters, Louisa and Hannah, preferred the comfort of a glass coach for their leisurely excursions to the fashionable St. James Park. Her older siblings never fully understood Elizabeth's affinity for helping the unfortunate. Louisa felt supremely annoyed by the intrusion of London's downtrodden on their family visits, remarking: "We have had a regular Mildred Court day, poor people coming one after another till twelve o'clock, and then no quiet."[7]

Distanced and detached from the true city, the well-to-do often carried pampering to heights of the absurd, taking extreme measures to avoid contact with the world inhabited by most Londoners in 1813. When a woman of means shopped for a dress in the upscale West End, she expected to be carried from the carriage across the shop's threshold, her dutiful servant careful not to soil her satin slippers or the bottom of her gown. With a well-positioned ivory-handled fan, she need not look upon the paupers that were nearly everywhere. More than seven hundred thousand people, 85 percent of the city's population, lived in tenement slums or in the alleyways. Hay carts, sheep, pigs, beggars, street dwellers, and pickpockets all jostled for survival in the constant commotion pulsating through London's dark heart. Children battled with rats over scraps of rotting food.

For many, adults and children alike, prison offered more comfort than life on the street, including the certainty of a free piece of bread. Purposely committing a crime was a gamble on their future the desperate were willing to take. Depending on the judge, they either gained food and shelter inside a gaol or risked transport to Van Diemen's Land.

As Elizabeth's coachman turned onto the notoriously bad Cheapside, tiny figures scampered around the carriage in a slippery blend of horse manure, dead rats, human waste, and rotting refuse. These were the bone gatherers. Ragged six- and seven-year-olds grabbed at the prime bone pickings, their barefoot toes bleeding into the gutter's muddy winter sludge. Bone ash was mixed with clay to strengthen the ceramic that lined the shelves of the wealthy. If the bone grubbers were lucky in foraging for a key ingredient to delicate bone china, they earned enough to pay for a meal.

If one of these street urchins had parents, his mother probably worked as either a laundress or a prostitute. Perhaps his father was one of the few who hadn't been drafted and was able to find work in the winter of 1813, when jobs were hard to come by. Gin, however, was cheap and all too easy to find, so there was a good chance that father, mother, or both were drunks. Even children stumbled through the byways in an alcoholic stupor, fed beer to fill their stomachs.

While the Fry children fancied pony rides and tea parties, the poor were chained to their lot in life like donkeys to a cart. Some crawled through the alleys, stuffing into their pockets the dog dung they could sell to tanneries, where it was used to cure fine leather. From baby to toddler to drone, as soon as a child could carry a bucket or hold a tool, he or she was put to work. Physical aging arrived early, stealing youth and health. As in Glasgow, half of London's children died before age five, poverty's only blessing offering them an early grave and an end to their suffering.

Mrs. Fry's carriage rolled through the cobbled streets now bustling with activity. As the morning fog lifted, dead horses, drunks, and sometimes infants were found decomposing, stiff, mouths agape, and covered with flies. Despite the handkerchief pressed to her nose to block the cold and filter the soot, Elizabeth could not help but gag on the noxious vapor of raw sewage and decay that clung to everything, and everyone, on the streets of London.

"I Come as a Thief"

The street grew noisier as the Frys' driver arrived at the corner of Newgate Street and the Old Bailey. The coachman began to slow the horses when the carriage approached the gaol entrance. In the flesh-chilling morning rain, Elizabeth and Anna came face-to-face with Newgate's stoic presence. The prison had been rebuilt after a fire in 1780; creator George Dance's design drew on the school of *architecture terrible*, a style intended to evoke terror in those on both sides of its walls. London's Lord Mayor William Domville eagerly and enthusiastically promoted Newgate's sinister reputation, believing that fear deterred crime.

The very structure of the building was designed to undermine the prisoner's spirit in every possible way. Female statues depicting Liberty and Plenty interrupted the harsh masonry blocks under the protection of sheltered niches in the wall. The cornucopia of plenty taunted those for whom there would be no feast of abundance. A French-capped Liberty mocked the freedom lost by those within the granite walls.

Newgate's ominous exterior characterized what novelist Henry Fielding described as a "prototype of hell."[8] Iron chains carved above the main entrance offered a stern warning as newcomers were admitted into this human-made purgatory. A façade of windows composed of stone, rather than glass, reinforced the prison's impenetrability and purposeful claustrophobia. Bricks filled in framed indentations where light should have entered, suggesting a cruel joke by designer George Dance. Newgate's real windows faced inward and delivered a ridiculing message to the damned: This hell hath no escape. His design allowed the prisoner not a single glimpse of the outside world. Instead, the windows faced the inner yard, where fellow inmates were marched in circles for exercise.

Elizabeth and Anna looked up at the chains and shackles carved over each doorway, representations of the leg irons worn by prisoners inside who could not afford to pay an "easement." Inscribed on a sundial just above the menacing iron door were the words "Venio sicut fur" (I come as a thief). The two Quakers had passed Newgate many times but had never considered entering.

The horses came to a stop. Newgate's center gate opened, and the driver helped the ladies down from the carriage. John Addison Newman, the gaol's governor, greeted them personally. Bundles of flannel baby gowns tucked under her arm, Elizabeth explained the reason for their visit. They wanted to attend to the physical neglect of the infants and the spiritual deprivation of their mothers. This was a highly unusual request, and Governor Newman planned to dissuade the ladies from their folly. Seldom did outsiders find the courage to enter this dreary enclave. Fewer still dared visit the Newgate females, a place where no male risked entry by himself, fearful of assault by the unruly creatures.

The governor had no choice before a determined Elizabeth Gurney Fry. He grudgingly acquiesced to her request and unlocked the inner gates to the gaol. The ladies were led to the infirmary, housed in a small room on the prison's second level. At first, Elizabeth and Anna stood motionless outside the tiny quarters. Gagging from the reek of death, the two needed a moment to regain their composure. Nothing in their serene souls could prepare them for the scene before them: A woman was in the process of removing clothing from a dead child to put on her own suffering baby. Without saying a word, Elizabeth and Anna untied the flannel bundle and passed out the gowns to women too ill to react. They had not brought enough clothes to outfit every infant and would need to sew more gowns for another day's visit.

Mindful of her promise to Stephen Grellet, Mrs. Fry asked to be taken to the common criminal ward. Governor Newman reluctantly escorted the women to the turnkey station that guarded the women's wing. An agitated turnkey, responsible for keeping the cells locked, issued a stern warning to the two ladies, just as he had cautioned Stephen Grellet. The gaoler was certain that the caged women would injure the do-gooders and that he alone would be held responsible. He pleaded with the surely misguided women, imploring their retreat from the gaol's dark recesses and its subhuman population.

There would be no turning back. The tall Quaker stood her ground, refusing to leave. The turnkey saw the answer in her eyes and shook his head. If he could not spare foolish Mrs. Fry from the vile and the violent, he could at least protect her material possessions. Fearing that within minutes her gold watch would be stolen, he beseeched her good sense to remove it. Once again, Elizabeth stood her ground. Shrugging his shoulders in resignation, the turnkey plunged the iron key into the gate's lock, and the bars swung open.

Bibles in hand, Elizabeth and Anna entered the cavernous tunnels that connected Newgate's wings. The gas lanterns that lit the passageway to the women's ward seemed to whisper a warning to the two intruders, like the sound of the wind before a storm. The gate slammed shut, and the outside lock fell against the latch. Its impact reverberated down the stone hallways with a sorrowful shudder. The two were undeterred, though a terrified Anna relied on her friend to lead the way. A painting by Henrietta Ward depicts a later Newgate visit and shows another volunteer hiding behind Elizabeth's ample frame, eyes wide with trepidation, hands clutched tightly to Fry's. In the same painting, Elizabeth appears at ease, her countenance calm and saintly.

The ladies began to walk hand in hand. Their footsteps reverberating through the long hallway made a sound as though there were many people walking with them. Reluctantly, the turnkey led the two ladies toward the deafening outburst of bellows, screams, sobs, and cries that emanated from the hallway's end. Bony, blackened hands grasped at the cell's iron grating, begging for notice. Unbolting the barred door, lifting the heavy latch that creaked under its own weight, the turnkey took one more look at these silly women before ushering them across the cell's threshold. He sighed, then retreated quickly and snapped the gate shut.

Three hundred women and children began to claw their way forward, moving as a teeming mass of misery, fascinated by the two ladies who wore clean clothes. The scraggly group deduced their upper-class status immediately by their polished fingernails and clear skin. Elizabeth stepped forward to meet her audience, revealing her "tall, large figure . . . with eyes small but of sweet and commanding expression— a striking appearance, not plain, but grand rather than handsome."[9]

A frenzied jumble of the innocent, the mad, and the condemned greeted them. Anna's brother, Thomas Fowell Buxton, described what confronted another Quaker upon visiting Newgate for the first time: "The railing was crowded with half-naked women, struggling together for the front situations, with the most boisterous violence, and begging with the utmost vociferation. She felt as if she were going into a den of wild beasts, and she well recollects quite shuddering when the door closed upon her, and she was locked in with such a herd of novel and desperate companions."[10]

In this communal cage, young girls who had stolen small items to fight off starvation and get through another day were trapped with murderers, violent felons, shivering babies, and the feeble-minded. Lurking in the shadows, tormented souls would explode at the slightest provocation with rage so overwhelming that it oozed from their every pore. Mayhem and madness were the order of the day. Pelting the air with foul language and encouraging fights among the inmates helped the condemned pass the time and release their seething frustration. The crowd surged forward again, tearing at the ragged clothing on the silhouetted figures closest to the entry. The rowdiest prisoners called out to the two well-dressed Quakers in a chorus of competing voices begging for money.

A few pence went a long way in gaol, where everything was available for the right price. Bribes to the guards could buy a pint of beer from Newgate's prison tap, an extra source of income for the wardens. The tap flowed continuously, even when food ran out. Cheap gin was also for sale. Consequently, many prisoners were drunk day and night.

Still adjusting to the dim haze of near darkness, Elizabeth and Anna looked toward the blurry outlines surrounding them. They were the ghostlike remains of women whose stooped frames clung tenuously to the remnants of existence. As the two Quakers moved closer, they were greeted by vacant stares, many too numbed from life's weariness to speak.

Heavy-lidded eyes crusted thick with grit and infection opened slowly as women from all corners squinted to focus on their unexpected visitors. Their matted hair ran wild with lice and fleas. Most had learned to ignore the live vermin that continually ravaged their tired bodies. Rats brushed against their flimsy clothing, skittering around their legs. Beetles and cockroaches moved in a constant parade across the floor, where the women lived, ate, and slept. Lying on the stone floor, scratching halfheartedly at scabies and other itchy rashes born of filth, scores of women and children lay covered in oozing sores raw with infection and neglect. Most were pockmarked.

Some stank from the rotting odor of syphilis. Others squatted along the cell's perimeter to relieve themselves.

The two finely dressed ladies had no choice but to breathe in the cell's stagnant air, thick with the taste and smell of urine, unwashed bodies, and rotting afterbirth from infants born in prison. Unshaken by the stench, Elizabeth stood straight up to her full height and stepped forward. Immediately, her heels sank deeply into the muck of mud, menstrual blood, rotting straw, and human excrement carpeting the entire cell. Never once did Elizabeth look down, her blue eyes level with the curious mass that pressed closer to examine her. Not for a moment did the Quaker minister avert her glance in the manner expected from a woman of her stature.

Captivated by the three hundred pairs of eyes riveted on her face, Elizabeth felt drawn to a young mother who cowered against the stone, anxiously cradling a tiny infant to her breasts. Eyes lit with compassion, so many times a parent herself, Fry reached forward to comfort the mother and child, unfazed by the lice as she stroked the baby's fine hair. This gesture of touch, pure in intent and unmarked by judgment, composed the chaos and hushed the room to an eerie silence. The Quaker's gentle manner shocked the condemned as it drew them yet closer.

Compassion was a rare commodity at the turn of the nineteenth century. The wealthy rarely spoke to those outside their class, save to bark orders at their servants. Neither Elizabeth nor Anna carried the slightest hint of moral condescension into Newgate's dungeon. Three hundred women immediately connected with the two Quakers, the lines of caste erased by an act of human decency. In this grey mildewed pen, the boundary between England's black-and-white social orders dissolved for an instant. Dignity entered a setting where it seemed out of place but where it took hold in its purest form.

As the crowd pressed against her, Elizabeth seized the moment to introduce herself and her friend Anna: "I am Mrs. Fry and this is Miss Buxton." Even among the condemned, etiquette demanded certain polite customs. Fry spoke plainly in the Quaker style, addressing royalty and prisoners alike as "thee" and "thou," well-mannered references that would have sounded quite strange to her Newgate audience. It was unlikely that a lady of Elizabeth's pedigree had ever addressed these petty thieves and prostitutes with this courtesy. Acknowledging them as one woman to another, the Quaker minister asked: "Tell me. What doest thou need?" This question, luxurious in its directness and simplicity, kindled a bond between Mrs. Fry and London's forgotten that lasted many decades. The answer to her question would also ignite social change and prison reform across Europe and around the globe.

Minds numbed by the January cold, the mob paused to consider the Quaker's request. A momentary reprieve of silence reverted to Newgate's cacophony: the hollow cough of tuberculosis, the whimper of a sick baby, moaning, bickering, and the occasional piercing wail of the insane. The women with the sunken eyes and yellowed teeth searched to understand Mrs. Fry's intention. It was puzzling to receive an offer of hope, but the initial shock soon dissipated, and the throng began to speak all at once.

Quickly the group reached consensus and despair dissolved into eager anticipation of the touch and scent of clean cotton against the skin. This was the first wish for the half-dressed women in torn and filthy rags. The indignity of near nakedness tugged at them in a way that an empty stomach did not. If Mrs. Fry could do anything, their first request would be for clean clothes. A simple shift would suffice.

Mrs. Fry promised the women she would return with a dress for each of them. Anna, silent throughout the visit, spontaneously fell to her knees and began to pray. Elizabeth joined her friend in divine supplication. Several of the prisoners followed, kneeling rather awkwardly on the wet floor. In the eerie darkness, the embossed gold lettering on Fry's Quaker Bible flashed through Newgate's shadows. Stillness enveloped the cell in a dreamlike state of heavenly quiet. Elizabeth described it in her diary: "I heard weeping, and I thought they appeared much tendered; a very solemn quiet was observed; it was a striking scene, the poor people on their knees around us, in their deplorable condition."[11]

In the early nineteenth century, Quaker views of the poor differed radically from those of other Christians. It was every Friend's challenge to lift people up, whereas the prevailing Church of England view considered poverty a condition of sin resulting from the indigent's own wickedness and self-damnation. Early Quakers had been persecuted vigorously throughout Europe. In England alone, fourteen thousand were imprisoned during the reign of Charles II, the "merry monarch" who ascended the throne in 1660. During that time, members of the Society of Friends were stripped naked, placed in stocks, publicly whipped, and gaoled for refusing to take an oath of allegiance to the Church of England. At the same time, its members in the American colonies were executed for practicing their religion. The most famous Quaker of all, founder George Fox, had been imprisoned at London's Newgate Prison, as had William Penn, the Quaker who established the state of Pennsylvania.

Swept into a rising crest of evangelism that defied the traditional British view, Elizabeth and Anna felt obligated to help "the wretched" heal both body and soul. Although Mrs. Fry believed that words from her Bible brought the gaoled closer to the Lord and to redemption, she might well have recited Shakespeare and achieved a similar reaction. For most Newgate women, religion played no part in their lives. Still, they were drawn to the Quaker minister who read to them, enthralled by stories strange and new. A few dared to ask aloud, "Who is Christ?"[12] Never before had they heard this name. Even so, the ragged souls found themselves inspired by Fry's kindness. Seduced by the rhythmic cadence in her voice and the serene softness in her eyes, the female prisoners found momentary escape in the soothing beauty of her words. No sooner had the women begun to feel comfortable than the visit was over. The turnkey swung open the gate and beckoned the two do-gooders to retreat. Mrs. Fry promised the women she would return, although few believed it.

Elizabeth had much to ponder as her carriage slowed to a jolting halt. It had been a short, cold ride back to Mildred's Court after they'd dropped off Anna. As the coachman helped her from the buggy, a liveried butler swung open the town house's grand door to greet the mistress as she approached the steps. Before crossing the threshold, she first removed Newgate's muck from the soles of her shoes using the wrought-iron boot scraper located just outside every upper-crust home. Elizabeth immediately requested that hot water be brought upstairs for a bath. Her house servants hurriedly set up the bathtub and prepared several steaming buckets of hot water to be carried from the kitchen stove. Mrs. Fry's personal maid assisted her mistress in the complicated process of unhooking and unbuttoning her contaminated clothing. Like a rancid onion, every layer was permeated by Newgate's putrid presence. Her clothes were in ruins, but her soul was on fire.

A Promise Fulfilled

For the next three days, Mrs. Fry lobbied her network of Quaker friends to assist in sewing garments. As promised, she collected and delivered clean clothing to everyone in Newgate's congregation of the forgotten. The women she first visited left a lasting impression on Elizabeth, but after a week of prison visits, life events prevented her return to their stony tomb until four years had passed.

Mrs. Fry's Newgate work was put on hold as she gave birth to two more children and suffered the loss of her beloved daughter Betsy at age four. The Tambora volcano eruption led to the "year without a summer" in 1816, causing the tea crop to fail and bankrupting her husband, Joseph, who was heavily invested in it. While they dealt with their financial crisis, they sent their six oldest children to live with wealthy relatives.

Although Elizabeth and Joseph were in debt, the Gurney family still owned a successful banking business. Elizabeth's mother had died when she was twelve, so she had been responsible for helping raise the younger children, including her brother Joseph John Gurney, who was now an influential lobbyist. He was inspired by "Betsy's" work to the point of bailing out the Fry bank and joining her mission of prison reform.

When Elizabeth turned to Newgate again, just after Christmas in 1816, it was with renewed purpose. She organized regular visits and opened a schoolroom for the children who were imprisoned with their mothers. She taught the women to sew and to read the Bible. In 1817, she founded the Association for the Improvement of Female Prisoners in Newgate. All of this activity occurred at a time when the public's sordid interest was turning toward the plight of the poor. A female reverend was strange enough, but the image of her reading the Bible to the Newgate "beasts" was sensational. Stories and drawings of these encounters began to appear in London newspapers, which were now widely available to the general public.

In 1818, Thomas Fowell Buxton, who had married Elizabeth's sister Hannah, was elected to Parliament and began to promote Elizabeth's causes. Mrs. Fry had become a figurehead for a prison reform movement and was now backed by powerful allies in Parliament. Little did she know how her widely publicized visits would expose the empire's secret plan to replace its slave labor pool with poor young Londoners, starving Irish, and other undesirables. Designed by effete Parliamentarians, the scheme hinged on a belief that outcast girls like Agnes McMillan would never be missed. These exiled citizens included the twenty-five thousand girls and women whose unfortunate fate included transport to an isolated island on the other side of the world. In the years to come, Elizabeth would meet many of these women as they passed through Newgate Prison on their way to the convict ships.

Mrs. Fry and her Association for the Improvement of Female Prisoners could not be ignored. She became one of the few advocates for treating the female inmates humanely. This plain and proper revolu-

tionary broke nearly every rule for how a respectable lady was supposed to behave.

On the afternoon of April 28, 1818, Elizabeth prepared for her call
at Mansion House, the Lord Mayor's residence. Queen Charlotte was
this day's honored guest for a charity event at the mayor's palace. Mrs.
Fry could not possibly leave her brownstone without the layers and
layers of attire required for a woman of her social standing. Fashion
dictated that multiples of crinoline and lace measured pedigree. Abundant petticoats signaled affluence for a middle-class lady, although
Elizabeth's were modest and unfussy in the tradition of her Quaker upbringing. Her dark silk gown, light silk cloak, and unadorned Friends'
cotton cap stood out from the brocaded gowns and jeweled tiaras of
her contemporaries.

Elizabeth was among the last to arrive at Mansion House, delayed
by a bitter dispute with Britain's home secretary, Lord Sidmouth, over
a young woman's execution outside Newgate. As she entered the Egyptian Hall, filled with princesses, lords, and bishops, "A buzz of 'Mrs. Fry,'
Mrs. Fry,' ran through the room."[13] While the guests strained for a
closer look, their exclamations were muted ever so slightly in the thick
carpet fibers and sumptuous satin curtains surrounding the hall.

At Windsor Castle, a rather miserable, cold, and distant Queen
Charlotte prepared for another state function, donning in melancholy
silence the sumptuous regalia demanded by her position. At public
pageants, her well-practiced detachment helped perpetuate the royal
mystique for those outside the inner circle. Quaker daughters in the
prominent Barclay family who observed the Queen wrote: "She is
vastly genteel with airs . . . truly majestic. . . . Her clothes, which were
as rich as gold and silver and silk could make them, were a suit from
which fell a train supported by a little page in scarlet and silver."[14]

Now a well-publicized humanitarian, Elizabeth Fry was more
widely admired within British society than Queen Charlotte and her
mad King George. Elizabeth spent her days on the unfashionable
tasks of soliciting funds for soup kitchens, setting up schools for

impoverished children, and lobbying to change Britain's tradition of punishing petty thieves with death. Her work at Newgate Prison had become a public spectacle, part of the Dickensian melodrama that ran in the daily newspapers. "The American Ambassador wrote home to say that he had now seen the two greatest sights in London—St. Paul's Cathedral, and Mrs. Fry reading to the prisoners in Newgate."[15]

It was appalling for an upper-crust lady to consider any of the Newgate women worth saving, so shocking that the warden issued tickets for admission to view the fearless missionary who read to the prisoners. Each day, the idle rich flocked to the grey fortress to watch in awe as the gentle voice of hope transformed the "wretched creatures." A schoolmaster who visited Newgate observed that the features of prisoners were "strongly marked with animal propensities" with "an approximation to the face of a monkey."[16] Newgate had become a zoo of sorts, with the full range of human suffering on display and safely locked behind its iron bars.

On a much loftier stage, the royal family, too, was part of this theater of the absurd. At age seventy-four, Queen Charlotte often focused her attention on her husband, the mentally unstable George III. The king had recently taken to running naked through the palace as his dressers chased him, tackling him to put on his pants. He is today believed to have suffered from porphyria, a genetic disorder with symptoms that include mental disturbance. This may have been triggered by arsenic contained in a medication he was given. Queen Charlotte served as his "regency of the person," his surrogate. In this capacity, she dispensed funds for the Queen's Lying-In Hospital and for various orphanages. The queen's concern for these causes, whether genuine or feigned, was an attempt to promote a favorable image for a monarchy whose political influence was in ruins.

Today, in the center of the Egyptian Hall from her platform three steps up, the aging queen had come to view the children who attended Mrs. Fry's basement school and London's charity orphanages. It was highly unusual for anyone save nobility to share this opulent space, but

Queen Charlotte required a comfortable venue from which to inspect the little waifs, examining them like the exotic bird-of-paradise flowers she grew in her botanical gardens.

The queen watched over the banquet with cultivated regal detachment. The sound of sterling silver knives, tapping ever so lightly against the patterned bone china, pleased the queen in a way that the voices of Mrs. Fry's young students never could. The royal family's practiced opulence shone in full display under the Corinthian columns that lined the mayor's palace. Jewels glittered in the candlelight. The refrains of Johann Christian Bach, formerly court musician and music teacher for the queen, wafted through the air while ushers guided distinguished guests to their seats. From her dais above the fray, Queen Charlotte overlooked the well-adorned hall, complete with the Union Jack and crests symbolizing the Crown's expanding empire. Attendants wearing golden brocade robes, lined with beaver fur, moved in military precision and filled five hundred crystal glasses with Moët's finest champagne. In anticipation of the royal toast, the court's choir sang "God Save the King" from the hall's inner balcony.

Teetering stacks of puffy white rolls surrounded silver trays luxuriously garnished with fresh fruit and dense buttery cheese. Shimmering sterling platters featured collared veal and rump steak pie smothered in thick gravies. The battalion of cooks it took to prepare the feast, the creamy custards, and cakes dripping with icing, included a chef de cuisine, two attending yeomen, and twenty-four chefs from Windsor Castle.[17] Between courses, forty or fifty in all, ladies in feathered head-dresses and men in shiny topcoats sipped wine or sherry. With each course, plate after plate was sent back uneaten. Even the most gluttonous lord left heaps of delicacies on his plate as he began unbuttoning his leather braces to make room for more butter and cream. By the time dessert was served, portly men with red noses and fat ankles leaned back in their chairs, unable to cross their legs, many suffering from gout—a malady that affected only the overindulgent upper class. Meanwhile, Fry's unappetizing waifs were kept out of sight.

The bishop of Gloucester ushered Mrs. Fry to her seat alongside a bench full of bishops. When Queen Charlotte rose from her chair and walked to greet Newgate's heroine, every pair of eyes in the room followed the diminutive queen, as the rustle of ten crinolines announced her every step. Earlier in the day, men in grand uniforms had laid down yards and yards of scarlet cloth to ensure that the Queen's slippers would not be soiled. The starch in the translucent lace that framed her face, thick with white powder, crinkled ever so slightly as she moved down the dais to begin her audience with a few carefully selected attendees. Her Majesty's voluminous skirts, designed for perching atop a throne, created the effect of her floating across the hall.

While Her Majesty reviewed the guests, Elizabeth sat serenely amid the silk and lace. Queen Charlotte shocked the hall when she stopped before the properly plain Quaker wearing a simple white cap and practical shoes. Her daughter, Katherine Fry, recounted to her aunt, Hannah Buxton, how she saw her mother in this moment: "her light flaxen hair, a little flush on her face from the bustle and noise she had passed through, and her sweet, lovely, placid smile."[18] When Mrs. Fry rose with the row of bishops, Queen Charlotte extended an arm, her elbow-length gloves adorned by her beloved pearl bracelets, etched with a miniature portrait of King George from his healthy days.

The two women looked an odd pair. Elizabeth was almost a foot taller than the queen. Despite this inelegance, she began the rote ritual etiquette demanded in the presence of royalty. Barely recognizing the unexpected honor of the queen rising to meet her and careful not to speak before being spoken to, Elizabeth leaned forward to greet the elderly monarch. Onlookers strained to listen as the queen asked: "How large is your family?" "Where is your home?" "Are you not afraid when you visit those terrible prisons?"[19]

"Why, the queen is talking to Mrs. Fry," whispered astonished guests across the room.[20] Being on the queen's guest list was in itself quite a social coup for even a well-connected commoner like Elizabeth. Being addressed by royalty was an honor of stunning proportions. A mounting murmur erupted into a thunderous clapping, acknowledging Her Majesty's salute to the plain-clothed Mrs. Fry. Like any devout Quaker, Elizabeth bowed only to the King of Kings. Her faith prevented her from following expected protocol of genuflection before the queen. To worship a mere mortal would have been, in her eyes, heresy. Elizabeth's young daughter observed this first meeting as a study in contrasts: "The Queen, who is so short, courtesying [sic], and our mother, who is so tall, not courtesying, was very awkward."[21]

As the pageantry unfolded, Elizabeth could think of nothing but the plight of Harriet Skelton, executed at Newgate prison that very day. She had begged Lord Sidmouth to seek a pardon for the poor girl, whose husband had persuaded her to pass a forged banknote. Elizabeth's urgency to express outrage grew louder each time a life was extinguished for a minor crime. Searching for answers about how she might have saved Harriet Skelton, Elizabeth surmised that perhaps she had annoyed Lord Sidmouth by calling upon influential friends to lobby her cause. The Duke of Gloucester, a former dance partner now married to the daughter of King George III, had spoken to Lord Sidmouth personally on her behalf. The paranoid Sidmouth refused to budge, fearing that the end of capital punishment would lead to the sort of uprisings that had sparked the French Revolution. Elizabeth berated herself for exerting too much political pressure, writing in her diary: "In the efforts made to save her life, I too incautiously spoke of some in power."[22]

A realist, Mrs. Fry quickly recognized that philanthropic work came at a price. As her list of charities grew, Elizabeth became increasingly dependent on other people's money and power for support, especially with the collapse of the Fry bank. In moments of uneasy self-reflection, she focused on her own contradictions, worrying how her popularity might impede her hands-on social work. When newspapers began to write about her, she blamed the conflict on herself: "I have felt of late, fears, whether my being made so much of, so much respect paid me by the people in power in the city, and also being so publicly brought forward, may not prove a temptation, and lead to something of self-exaltation, or worldly pride."[23]

Pulled from her musings back to her regal surroundings in Mansion House, Mrs. Fry heard the heralds as Queen Charlotte bid her leave. Later that night, reflecting on her introduction to the queen, Elizabeth felt unimpressed. In her diary, she wrote: "I think I may say, this hardly raised me at all, I was so very low from what had occurred before, and indeed in so remarkably flat a state, even nervous."[24]

On this day in 1818, Elizabeth Gurney Fry could not know that her good work had thrown her unwittingly into the gears of the empire's grand plan for social engineering. It was a scheme birthed by greed and nurtured on corruption. Because so many of the Newgate women were bound for transport, Mrs. Fry and her Quaker friends began to regularly visit the convict ships that anchored on the docks along Woolwich by Bony off the Butt for weeks at a time.[25] A simple act of kindness became Elizabeth's legacy. She made it her mission to save the souls of the female cargo bound for Van Diemen's Land. As fate would have it, in giving them hope, Mrs. Fry freed them.

4

Sweet Sixteen

Enterprising Women

In about AD 47, the Romans settled the town Londinium and surrounded it with a defensive wall. Built on one of the six original gates of this wall in 1188, Newgate Prison protected Londoners from a different type of invader. In the nineteenth century, nearly half of the 162,000 men, women, and children transported to Van Diemen's Land and mainland Australia passed through the prison.

On Saturday, May 7, 1836, the names Agnes McMillan and Janet Houston were added to the Newgate roster. They'd danced with the devil before. This time, however, they were about to enter Satan's private ballroom. They'd endured the mills, been in and out of gaol, but Newgate was the end of the line in Great Britain. Women did not return from Van Diemen's Land.

Scotland's weary transports toppled from the stagecoach, and two pairs of small feet searched for steadiness on solid ground. Their legs buckled beneath them and refused to work after the long, jostling ride. Leaning against each other, they caught their balance as their chains clanked against the cobblestones. This familiar rattling of irons announced the duo's arrival to a gathering crowd of onlookers. London's everyday seekers of the macabre were thrilled to see the latest unfortunates delivered to Newgate. Tonight's bill of fare included two bonnie birds from the courthouse in Ayr. As they made their way from the coach, the gaggle of misery mongers closed in on the two young waifs in dirty shifts and muddy boots. Leers, jeers, and whistles announced the newest spectacle in nighttime street entertainment.

There was nothing to sing about. Discouraged footsteps followed the sheriff into Newgate as Agnes and Janet filed through the first of many bolted doorways. The gaoler slammed it shut and locked it behind them with a clang. Agnes's boots fell ploddingly on the stone stairs as she made her way through the dimly lit maze. Two flights up, a winding passage led to the matron's quarters, secured behind another heavy door. After a quick rap on the wood, the turnkey thrust first one key, and then another, into the oversized locks. Hammer in hand, another gaoler stood ready to remove manacles and fetters that the comely lasses were more than happy to shed.

A matron wearing a gathered white nightcap looked over the two newcomers and jotted down a few notes about eye and hair color. Names didn't always ensure accurate records, as evidenced by the number of "Smiths" listed in the prison roster, so wardens recorded facial characteristics and bodily marks, such as moles or scars. Agnes and Janet were unusual in that neither had pockmarks on her face.

The matron was in a foul mood. It was well past her bedtime and she was anxious to hurry back to her room, situated next to the female quadrangle. These girls had no personal property to surrender, so her only duty was to search them for contraband. Instinctively, Agnes pulled away from the unwelcome touch of rough hands patting her down, but it wouldn't pay to be sassy at this hour. There was little the warden could do to make her stay worse. However, there were many favors she could extend to make it slightly less miserable. Some fresh straw for the floor, a taste of beer, or extra time in the courtyard sometimes rewarded an inmate's good behavior. At least it wasn't a man examining her. Elizabeth Fry had successfully lobbied Parliament to replace male wardens with female matrons, whose salary her volunteer association paid. In the past, guards had treated the women's ward like a private brothel, a sin Elizabeth would not tolerate.

The sleepy matron issued her new charges a tin, a wooden spoon, and two pieces of sturdy brown sackcloth, one to lie on and one to use as a cover. The "rugs," as they were called, reflected improvements in the women's ward since Mrs. Fry's first visit in 1813, when she found women sleeping on straw atop the squalid stone floor. Candlestick in hand, the matron motioned Agnes and Janet back into the hall. Her lecture about rules and regulations would wait until morning. A flickering candle cleared a hazy path to a giant oak door reinforced with 117 iron rivets. The disinterested turnkey released two deadbolts and inserted the key into the first lock, then the other. As the heavy portal groaned open, it unleashed waves of stirring across the large, communal group locked inside. The girls blinked their eyes, adjusting to the smoky darkness, and squinted to make out the shadowy figures lodged in the low-ceilinged cell.

The instant the door swung open, Agnes and her redheaded friend could feel eyes from all corners of the room peering at them. Faces shone in the candlelight, looking like startled creatures in the forest— some ready to pounce, others merely frightened. Shoved into darkness thick with sighs and swearing, the two tried to hold their breath against a stench far worse than the River Clyde on a steamy summer day. Although they benefited from Mrs. Fry's work at Newgate, the sounds and smells that assaulted the girls had changed little since the Quaker's first visit twenty-three years earlier.

Bodily functions were still taken care of in the cell, although chamber pots replaced the bare floor as the primary receptacle. The dreadful marinade had been there for so long that it seeped into the stones and became part of Newgate's surroundings—a mix of human waste and decay that never washed away no matter how many times it was disinfected. Without delay, the matron ordered the girls to drop their rugs by the door and settle in for the night. The Glasgow pair had arrived too late to be fed, but neither felt much like eating.

The gaoler secured the double locks and slid the bolts across the door. Agnes held fast to Janet as they listened to the sounds of their new mates in the darkness: snoring, muffled weeping, the cry of a baby struggling in her mother's arms, the tapping of wooden spoons from those descended into madness. The two friends barely closed their eyes that first night in Newgate. Both the gaoler and the gaoled preyed on newcomers. On guard until the first sign of daylight, Janet and Agnes each felt grateful they had arrived as a pair. A county gaol was small and predictable, with some drunks and many pickpockets, but a city prison housed highway robbers, murderers, and other violent felons. This was unfamiliar and dangerous territory.

Shaken into full consciousness at the sound of the matron's bell at seven A.M., the girls watched as a huge pot of gruel was shoved into the cell. With no hesitation whatsoever, they joined the mad dash for a scoop in their tin cups. Toughened from the wynds of Glasgow near the Green, Agnes and Janet were fully attuned to the unwritten rules for how things worked. They used the closest chamber pot and, without being asked, helped empty it into Newgate's sewer. First impressions counted.

The ward's only source of light filtered through one small barred window. Even on sunny days, its milky darkness never brightened beyond twilight. By nine o'clock, cheerful members of Fry's Association for the Improvement of Female Prisoners arrived armed with Bibles and a supply of soft green cotton dresses. The new inmates were not yet wearing the women's uniform. With their customary gentle greeting, Fry's volunteers introduced themselves and unwrapped two dresses. The Glasgow girls turned their backs, pulled their mud-encrusted clothes over their heads, and straightened the neatly pressed uniform in place. The Quaker-inspired design wasn't exactly their style, but it felt good to put on clothes that smelled fresh.

Following Mrs. Fry's recommendations, the prisoners were divided into groups of twelve, with a monitor elected from each group. This was part of her plan for order amid chaos. At the morning Bible reading, prisoners dutifully agreed to renounce swearing, drinking, gambling, and card playing, although these halfhearted promises were generally broken as soon as the Quakers left. The mission for the association was clear and practical: "To provide for the clothing, instruction and employment of the women; to introduce them to knowledge of the Holy Scriptures; and to form in them, as much as possible, those habits of order, sobriety and industry, which may render them docile and peaceable while in prison, and respectable when they leave it."[1] Volunteers never spoke to the women about their crimes, choosing instead to help them prepare for a future. Agnes and Janet didn't know what to make of the pious do-gooders, but at least they weren't picking oakum in a workhouse or pulling wool in the mill.

Defying contemporary beliefs, Mrs. Fry perceived shades of grey in trying to understand the plight of the convict women. The popular view cast by the upper class considered girls like Agnes either "good" or "bad." For the bad, there was no turning back from a destiny of damnation. Yet a male criminal, they believed, held the capacity for reform and redemption. Typical of the Victorian era, one code of morality applied to men and another to women. Members of a Committee Inquiring into Female Convict Discipline explained the duality this way: "Society . . . fixed the standard of the average moral excellence required of women much higher than that which it had erected for men, and that crime was regarded with less allowance when committed by a woman . . . because the offender was deemed to have receded further from the average proprieties of her sex."[2]

Just one year before Agnes and Janet entered Newgate, the stately Quaker had testified before the House of Lords on the condition of British prisons and admitted: "We are doing the best we can with a very bad system."[3] A prison inspector for the government also testified and criticized her mission as meddling and naïve. Undaunted, she continued to blatantly defy the City Corporation, which had concluded it was "useless to attempt to reform such untamed and turbulent spirits except by punishment."[4]

Mrs. Fry held high hopes that girls like Agnes and Janet could become enterprising women if guided by example and training. Her volunteers assigned them to groups gathered around tables, where they were taught to sew clothing, knit socks, and make patchwork quilts. Elizabeth persuaded local merchants to donate materials and negotiated agreements to market the finished products in both England and Australia. Prisoners produced more than one hundred thousand articles over a five-year period,[5] shared the profits, and purchased "small extra indulgences," like fresh food, soap, and beer.[6]

The girls put down their needles and thread at three o'clock to consume their main meal of bread and soup. Boiled beef from the lower part of the quarters, known as "mouse buttock," was served several times a week unless the gaolers stole it. With good intentions, Fry advocated serving the Newgate girls white bread rather than the cheaper brown loaves, which were actually more nutritious. Believing their diet too meager, Fry's association hired a woman to run a prison shop that sold tea, coffee, butter, and sugar, although the prison inspector looked askance at what he considered the sale of luxuries.[7]

At six o'clock, the Quaker ladies bid farewell with another scripture reading in the prison chapel. The number of names carved into the pews recorded a high degree of boredom among prisoners. Still skeptical about the do-gooders, the two friends rolled their eyes as the well-dressed women exited. At the very least, the Quakers provided diversion from their caged routine. Once Mrs. Fry and her volunteers were out of sight, it was business as usual. Drinking resumed, hidden card decks magically appeared, and fights ensued until the Quakers returned the next day.

While their cell mates sized up the petite lasses with thick Scottish brogues, Agnes and Janet were busy figuring out whom they might trust. Their search for allies commenced without delay. The sooner they discovered who was dangerous, the better their chances of leaving Newgate unharmed. Having had some experience in gangs and in gaol, the girls had an easier time adapting than most. They quickly found out who played the roles of "fixer" and "scrounger." At the top of the convict hierarchy, these were the inmates who knew how to get special treatment and what it might cost. Under Fry's system, the prisoners elected monitors who essentially managed the ward, distributing food rations and reporting unruly inmates. They, too, extorted favors and payoffs from the women in their charge.

Entering this motley pack as a team afforded influence, particularly in a fluctuating prison society like Newgate. A duo could cover two places at once. Agnes ran for the food while Janet guarded the spot staked out for bedding. Two sets of eyes were more attentive to scams, schemes, and allegiances, which often incited unpleasant initiations. Bullies and troublemakers targeted the weak. Appearances mattered. In such close confinement, emotions escalated and mutated when the intoxicated or the deranged lashed out with pent-up fury and frustration, pulling hair or indiscriminately attacking with teeth and dirty fingernails. Insanity and the unpredictability of madness proved intimidating to even the most street-hardened. One careless move might provoke a deadly attack from someone possessed with what seemed like superhuman strength.

Elizabeth Fry spent thirty-five years devoted to prison reform, but even divine prayer and activism couldn't purify this den of disease and corruption. Newgate seemed beyond God's reach. Outbreaks of typhus, or "gaol fever," spread by fleas and lice, killed countless women and children awaiting transport in the filthy, overcrowded cells. Seemingly contrary to common sense, prisoners were allowed to drink as much liquor as they could afford. Two taprooms conveniently adjoined the prison. Gaol keepers earned a hefty bonus keeping their charges drunk, docile, and "quite free from rioting."[8] The guards were often drunk themselves. Like hungry wolves in charge of sheep, some gaolers also turned a profit by smuggling prostitutes into the male ward.

Mrs. Fry and her association were disgusted to learn that even Newgate's governor made a habit of selecting female prisoners as domestic servants whom he moved into his home. The high-principled Quakers were particularly taken aback when he handpicked one "young rosy-cheeked girl" to work in his kitchen and then overturned her transport sentence without bothering to consult the judge.[9]

A bustling economy, regulated by favors and bribery, thrived where justice lay inert. "Extortion was practised right and left."[10] Word traveled quickly about which guards could be bribed. Shillings or spirits paid for visits with loved ones and for contraband from the outside. Money bought better food and a cleaner cell. Gaolers sold hungry prisoners bread far above cost, collecting two pence halfpenny for a loaf.[11] Entrepreneurial prisoners charged cell mates who awaited trial a few shillings to prepare their slipshod version of a legal brief. As a ruse to visit the women's ward on Sundays and Wednesdays, male inmates claimed to be relatives and fraternized inappropriately.

Rather fluid contact with the outside world fueled an illicit, albeit tolerated, black market. Sellers of tobacco, playing cards, newspapers, and scandalous books wandered freely about the prison and hawked their wares. There was profit to be made in every part of Newgate, even the chapel. Gaolers charged the public a fee to attend the final sermon delivered to those awaiting execution. Some of the chaplains sold sad tales, confessed by the condemned, to broadsheet publishers, who marketed them to the crowds gathered on execution day.

Amid the madness and mayhem of Newgate, renegades quickly gained admiration. Prisoners took great joy in taunting their captors, and in defiance, mateship blossomed. Any girl who thumbed her nose at the authorities became a welcome addition to this pack of rabble-rousers and malcontents. Being a ballad singer, Agnes McMillan made the perfect rebel and certainly expanded her repertoire with new tunes from the bawdy company she now kept. To pass the long nights, the women often entertained one another and turned captivity into theater featuring inspired and risqué performances.

The talented Scottish lass sang fearlessly at the top of her lungs. Well-worn melodies were often parodied with original words belted out in heartfelt disdain toward the guards and the turnkeys. Denied light and air, the rebellious escaped in song and solidarity. Dancing, gambling, palm readings, and dressing in men's clothing rounded out spirited entertainment that erupted nightly inside the fortress. Like Agnes, Janet, and their cell mates, English poet Richard Lovelace celebrated moments of freedom even inside gaol. In 1642, he wrote from a London prison: "Stone walls do not a prison make / Nor iron bars a cage."

Black Carriages

Between public executions outside Newgate and pandemonium within, "the day" finally arrived in the full heat of summer. After nearly two months in prison, it was Agnes's turn to depart. The cost for the British government to transport her to Van Diemen's Land was less than that to keep her in gaol, but the ships typically ran only twice a year.[12]

It was early morning on July 3, 1836. Two restless cell mates lay close together in the pitch-black cell. Agnes opened her eyes to the screeching sound of the metal locks in the door. Through the darkness she watched three gaolers enter with lanterns. As she tried to focus, a light flew in her face and blinded her for an instant. With that, a rough hand grabbed her arm, snapped her upright, and walked the sleepy girl on tiptoe toward the cell door. Janet was close behind. The guards shoved them down the narrow hallway to the matron's desk, and she promptly crossed off two names from the Newgate roster.

Reluctantly, they inched toward a smith who stood ready to rivet them into manacles and leg irons for the trip to the Woolwich docks. They all knew this day was coming, but it arrived without warning.

During Agnes's time, Mrs. Fry and her volunteers visited the girls and women awaiting transport. Before this, the gaol had been notorious for riots and violence, which erupted when fear of the unknown loomed largest. As women learned of their impending departure, they broke windows and smashed chamber pots in fits of anger, often fueled by drunken rage. These days, although rumors always ran rampant, the actual date of departure was kept secret.

The compassionate Quaker approached redemption in a manner totally opposite that of most of her contemporaries. Convinced that humiliation and undue punishment snuffed out inherent worth, Fry wrote: "The good principle in the hearts of many abandoned persons may be compared to the few remaining sparks of a nearly extinguished fire. By means of the utmost care and attention united with the most gentle treatment, these may yet be fanned into a flame, but under the operation of a rough or violent hand, they will presently disappear and be lost forever."[13]

Fry sought to soothe the soul and the spirit as she held the girls' hands, touched their faces, and read the Bible. In meeting nearly half the transported women, she helped many find peace in accepting what they could not control. Elizabeth was not about to give up on girls like Agnes and Janet.

Properly secured in irons, the two friends stumbled down two flights of stone stairs and out of the gaol. Dawn began to break into full light, and London's Old Bailey Street came alive with traffic, including a black carriage with boarded windows that stopped at Newgate's entrance. A guard abruptly hoisted the prisoners into the waiting wagon, slammed the door shut, and left them in a black vacuum. Janet sat silently, chained beside Agnes, deprived of sight. In the darkness, both sets of ears became acutely aware, straining to listen for clues about what would happen next: the grating of hinges as the guard bolted the carriage closed, the horse snorting and clomping its hooves in readiness, the sound of the springs as the driver mounted the carriage and the guard jumped aboard.

This same scene occurred in gaols across the British Isles as the roundup of "notorious strumpets" continued for the next six weeks. Their transport ship, the *Westmoreland*, awaited their arrival with stoic patience along the Woolwich docks. Had Agnes been banished a few years earlier, she'd have made the trip through London in an open wagon. Elizabeth Fry had lobbied Parliament to end the practice of transferring the women in exposed carts, where onlookers stoned and heckled them. Still, everyone knew what the covered hearses carried. To make certain spectators didn't attack the transport wagons, Mrs. Fry often followed them in her private buggy.

Agnes's eyes rolled back in her head as she fought the pitch and toss of the carriage. She struggled against the manacles, trying to ignore her matted hair and fingernails layered in grime. Composing herself long enough to let out a sigh, she thought about Goosedubbs Street. It seemed so long ago, but barely four years had passed since her twelfth birthday, when she last saw her mother, Mary. The grey-eyed girl knew little about geography but was perceptive enough to know that her life was about to change in ways she'd never imagined. At fifteen, she may have grown wise enough to deny herself the luxury of self-pity. Regrets and what-ifs would only distract her from figuring out how to stay safe and alive. Agnes had decided not to give up.

In the midsummer heat and humidity, most of the journey was spent in dumbfounded silence, baking inside the black carriage. It was a rolling, jostling, hypnotic mix of sound, heat, and darkness. More than one girl lost consciousness as she fell against the prisoner chained beside her. As the horse-drawn cart approached Woolwich, a confusing cacophony exploded in a mix of swearing, catcalls, and stone throwing, which stopped only when Mrs. Fry stepped out of her carriage.

Nearing the dock, Agnes smelled the river and heard the unmistakable screech of seabirds. Tense with anticipation as the cart shuddered to a halt, Agnes felt weighted down by the heavy irons on her hands and feet. The wagon strained and leaned to the left when the driver stepped off. His whips rattled against the seat. Muttering, grunts, and heavy breathing alerted the girls that a group of men had surrounded the carriage, poised to inspect the latest female freight. The bolted latch creaked open and interrupted the lascivious chatter all around them. A sudden, blinding light illuminated the carriage. In a flash, the bulky guard yanked first Janet and then her chum from their temporary womb. Struggling to regain her focus and balance, Agnes tripped over her leg irons and followed Janet's clumsy steps toward the small boat waiting to take them to the *Westmoreland*.

The boarded carriage had drawn a crowd of hecklers, gossipmongers, and curious passersby. Some looked on the girls with pity, some with scorn, and others with a smirk that sent chills down Agnes's spine. Once the carriage was emptied, the guard pushed the girls in chains toward a skiff at the edge of the dock. In hobbled steps, they shuffled down the gangway and crawled into the launch. The boat gave way under the weight and rocked in the river as the other women in irons were ushered aboard. Agnes could hardly breathe. The coxswain pushed off from the dock, and it hit her hard. There would be no coming back. Her feet had touched English soil for the last time.

Puffs of morning fog clung to the river as the oars slipped in and out of the water and propelled the small boat forward. The *Westmoreland* loomed like a specter in the Thames, mastheads eerily luminous in the early sun. Its overhanging gangplank seemed to poke a warning through the morning mist. Agnes wished she might awaken from this bad dream, but the rhythmic splash of the oars only reinforced the finality of her journey into heaven knew what.

As the ship strained and shifted in its mooring, a breeze blew the fog away, and morning sunlight transformed the scene from shades of soupy grey into brilliant color. In the clear light of day, Agnes looked up and realized she had an audience. Lining the starboard side, the crew leaned against the rail and ogled the new cargo about to board.

She was on display like a prize cow at a farmers' market, and she didn't like it one bit. The waiting sailors whistled, licked their lips, and made the rudest of gestures with their tongues. Many of these "Lord Mayor's men" were themselves conscripted during sweeps in pubs and prisons. Because the Navy charged enlistees for clothing, these men made their own roughly stitched tunics and tied them in place with a rope. The scraggly apprentices dressed in a motley assortment of wide trousers, which could be rolled above the knees for swabbing the deck. In contrast, the British naval officers, charged with navigation and discipline, wore tailored dark-blue uniforms sporting white collars and gold braiding. They were expected to remain above the fray but did little to restrain the crew from "a bit of fun."

The oars were raised and the small launch bumped gently against the *Westmoreland*. The coxswain steadied the boat as his cargo of exiles made their way up the gangplank onto the ship's main deck. The Officer of the Guard adjusted his brimmed wool hat and directed Agnes and the others on board. Still in manacles, making her way forward to the poop deck, Agnes was plunked down on a short three-legged stool. A shirtless sailor greeted her with a large hammer, puffing up his barrel chest to show off a tattoo. The deckhands, many mere lads themselves, watched in amusement as the sweaty smith leaned against Agnes's belly, smiling his gap-toothed grin. Harassment of the young girls aboard ship was legendary and, for the most part, ignored by the authorities. So long as the prisoners arrived in one piece, anything the crew did was more or less forgivable. If they arrived pregnant, it was all the better. The Crown's plan to populate Van Diemen's Land moved forward ahead of schedule.

Agnes was young and pretty, and her good looks often made life more difficult. Undoubtedly a target of taunting by crew members, she held her shift tight against her legs as the smith put on a performance for each manacle he unfastened. Given her street scrappiness, the tiny girl faced off against a crowd of staring sailors, grasping the stool with a death grip, determined to shed not a single tear. A loud

clang reverberated as her irons fell to the deck, and the raucous winking sailors let out a cheer. With a vulgar chuckle, the smith freed
Agnes to go aft for inspection by the ship's surgeon. Eyes full though
not yet overflowing, she stood up straight as a bolt and willed herself
not to trip over the heavy rigging, coiled like snakes all over the deck.

A Boatful of Bonnets

Surgeon Superintendent James Ellis, the man responsible for delivering Agnes to Van Diemen's Land, leaned against the wood railing,
black logbook in hand. As the first boatful of girls came alongside the
Westmoreland, he shot an admonishing glance toward the leering crew.
Straightening the brim on his cocked hat and squaring his shoulders
under gleaming gold epaulets, the surgeon made his way toward the
gangplank. He was dressed in a double-breasted blue uniform with
brass buttons and a short silk necktie pinned neatly under his shirt
collar.

Prior to 1814, there was no government supervision monitoring
how women were treated during the average four months at sea.
Transport companies received twenty to thirty pounds sterling per
head and packed women and men in such close confinement that
disease killed up to one-third of the human cargo. Payment was collected for the convicts whether or not they arrived alive. That practice
changed in 1815 when the Royal Navy appointed a surgeon superintendent to every ship. He allocated food servings, delivered infants,
and treated illnesses such as alcohol withdrawal, typhus, and syphilis.

Surgeon Superintendent Ellis opened his leather-bound ledger to
begin the tedious task of recording the names, ages, and physical characteristics of the newly arrived prisoners: Agnes McMillan, age sixteen,
fresh complexion, grey eyes, light brown hair, oval visage, no pockmarks or scars.[14] Although still only fifteen, she must have wanted to
appear more adult, and without birth records on hand, the surgeon

took her word for it. Names and dates were sometimes approximated in the records. Misspellings and inconsistencies were all too common.

While being measured—five feet, one and one-quarter inches—Agnes tried not to look at Mr. Ellis. Like all prisoners, she didn't trust the authorities. While she was the one being measured, the grey-eyed girl was most certainly sizing up the opposition, not liking in the least what she saw. The surgeon superintendent was wearing his full Navy regalia, and Agnes had never had good experiences with men in uniform. His white collar was so full of starch that the skin on his neck hung over it like a turkey wattle. It screamed of rules and regulations.

Janet Houston was next in line: age seventeen, fresh complexion, hazel eyes, red hair, oval visage, and no facial marks. She took off her shoes and was measured at five feet, three-quarters inches tall. Stern yet unexpectedly polite, Surgeon Superintendent Ellis handed the girls a sponge and a hunk of soap. The fully clothed sponge bath took place right on deck next to a cask of water. Among the first to embark on the *Westmoreland*, Janet and Agnes treasured the luxury of relatively clean water and fresh soap made from lard and lye. For the first time in months, Agnes scrubbed her hair and fingernails and used the sponge to clean her ankles and feet. She was happy to remove Newgate's grime, but her elation ceased when Mr. Ellis picked up her fashionable brown leather boots. He looked them over and handed them back to a relieved Agnes.

In earlier transports, the ship's supply list included "clothing for use during the voyage." But by 1836, this no longer appeared, and the allowance was enforced sporadically.[15] Many prisoners arrived with only the clothes on their backs, and with no means of repairing items that would be worn threadbare on slippery decks, in driving rain, and through frigid temperatures. Agnes's sturdy boots would come in handy in Van Diemen's Land, but she learned quickly that bare feet served her better on the ship.

Drawing a simple "X," the fifteen-year-old signed the convict record list that bound her as official property of the Crown for the next seven years. Agnes's 113-day journey had just begun. Her new world measured 28 feet between the scuppers and 133 feet stem to stern. The *Westmoreland*, built four years earlier, was a three-masted barque, registered at 404 tons, under the command of Captain Brigstock. The ship had spent the last month at Deptford, where it was fitted with guns and munitions for protection against pirates and mutineers. After the convict hulk had passed inspection by the Government Agent for Transports, a steamer towed it to Woolwich for mooring at a spot known as "the Bony off the Butt."[16] Here she lay ready to accept her human cargo. The vessel would eventually carry 185 female prisoners, their children, and a crew of 28 boys and men.

Surgeon Superintendent Ellis handed Agnes and Janet a wooden bowl and spoon, a blanket, and a bed tick of heavy cotton filled with straw. Primitive mattresses in hand, the Glasgow girls followed a waiting officer through a bulkhead, down a cramped ladder, then through another hatchway to the orlop deck. This was the ship's lowest deck. Two tiers of berths filled the tight space designed to pack in as many bodies as would fit head to toe, like tins of sardines tucked into His Majesty's larder. Once in the ship's bowels, Agnes was assigned a berth. Her bed and refuge aboard the *Westmoreland* was eighteen inches wide and four feet long, an elevated plank a foot and a half above Janet's berth. Across the aisle, another two prisoners would be squeezed into the stuffy passage.

While Agnes leaned over to lay out her bedding, she took in a deep breath and began choking on fumes emanating from beneath her feet. The *Westmoreland* was only a few years old but had already developed a distinct odor. Prisoners slept on the lowest deck right above the bilge, distinguished by a rotting stench from accumulating human waste and dead rats. Accustomed to the open air in the wynds, Agnes couldn't escape soon enough. The officer ushered her back to the main hatch and pointed to two tiny water closets in the center of the ship. Feeling a bit woozy in this floating cesspool, she stumbled toward the hatch ladder. Janet remembered to duck under the beams and pushed Agnes's head down to help her avoid a nasty gash.

Back on deck, the two friends watched a line of women, some pregnant and others holding children in their arms, waiting to sign the surgeon's ledger. Once topside, Agnes and Janet were immediately put to work scrubbing the deck. They soon learned that cleaning the ship was a never-ending task rotated among the prisoners. At midafternoon, they were assigned to a mess of six women and fed salted beef, cabbage soup, and a biscuit. This meal needed to last them until breakfast the next morning. Under the auspices of the Royal Navy, the girls were allotted two-thirds the naval ration.[17] This might have been adequate were it not for widespread corruption among the crew. "Rascally masters and their stewards did not hesitate to employ false weights and measures, and more than one ships' captain was accused of having set up store on arrival and retailed, at an exorbitant profit, the rations withheld from the convicts."[18]

The night watch came on deck as the ship's bell rang eight times. After the final prisoner inspection at eight o'clock, the girls were locked inside their berth and secured under two decks of hatches bolted shut. Gossiping about their new companions, the duo spoke in hushed tones through velvety black claustrophobia until the lapping of the waves against the hull lulled them to sleep.

The ship's bell sounded again: six bells, morning watch. Agnes looked up. She was only half awake. Perhaps she was dreaming. The fifteen-year-old tumbled out of her berth. Her neck hurt. She was only five feet tall, but her narrow bed, only slightly wider than her petite frame, didn't allow her to turn over without a delicate balancing act. As she untangled her arms, coarse wool scratched against her skin. At least she had a blanket. Her eyes lingered on the drops of water that slipped between the ship's seams and reappeared as a stain on the lower planks. Anchor chains strained against the river's current, and creaking beams oozed a rush of bitter smells from the *West-*

moreland's bowels. It was six o'clock in the morning, and she was already feeling queasy.

As the Officer of the Guard whistled through his pipe, Agnes scampered toward the newly opened hatch. She tossed her blanket over her shoulder, grabbed her bowl and spoon, and scurried up the narrow hatch opening, around the corner to a steep ladder for the final climb to the upper deck. Being young and fast moved Agnes to the front of the line for breakfast, but first she would have to pass daily inspection by Surgeon Superintendent Ellis.

Up on deck, a big barrel of water greeted a sleepy Agnes just as she rounded the main mast. Bending over the open cask under the watchful eyes of an officer, one of the swabbies scooped a sloppy cupful of the greyish liquid and shoved it into Agnes's hands. The water was drinkable by the standards of the day, light grey and murky, and the surgeon told the girls it would lessen seasickness. Accustomed to drinking beer rather than dirty water, Agnes took a few sips and splashed the rest on her face and tangled hair, just enough to jolt into full consciousness. Mr. Ellis took a glance inside her mouth, checked for fever, and administered the daily allotment of lime juice.

A wisp of fog clung to the river, but the sky was cloudless and ideal for Agnes to air her blanket on deck. Agnes wanted to keep the wool fresh for as long as possible. No one seemed to know how long the upcoming sea voyage would take, but she had heard rumblings from the crew about a previous trip taking four months. For now, she was stuck on a floating prison, tantalizingly close to but irrevocably separated from the land that had exiled her.

The longest time Agnes had spent on a boat was the fifteen minutes it took to ferry across the River Clyde in Scotland with Janet and Helen. Perhaps a bowl of the slimy gruel served for breakfast would help settle the young Scot's stomach. Worse yet, she had to contend with those bloody bells, clanging every half hour, bringing a perpetual headache.

Within four weeks of being stuck on the river in summer's heat,

Agnes hated the *Westmoreland*, the ship that never lay still in its mooring. When the ship swayed one way, she leaned the other, but nothing she tried could prevent her seasickness. Janet held on to her mate as she leaned over the railing and spit up the gruel. On August 1, Surgeon Superintendent Ellis admitted Agnes to his hospital for "obstinate costiveness," constipation typically caused by dehydration from seasickness and the animal fat in a new diet.[19] For her treatment, the petite lass was forced to endure generous doses of calomel, a mercury compound used for intestinal purging. Instead of helping patients, this nineteenth-century remedy caused bleeding gums, mouth sores, and more dehydration. After three days in the infirmary, Mr. Ellis released Agnes. She wondered if she would ever get used to the constant rocking.

It was a very humid August, and Agnes felt a bit better back on deck in the river's breeze. The morning sun had burned off the fog from the river. Agnes closed her eyes for a moment, leaned on the rail, and felt the warm light on her face. For a second she felt free. The fantasy soon passed, and with a gentle sigh she opened her eyes to a most curious sight. As the young prisoner glanced over the bulkhead, she spotted a boatful of bonnets headed toward the ship.

Elizabeth Fry sat prim and proper in an approaching skiff, filled with members of the Society for the Reformation of Female Prisoners. She founded this group in 1821 to address conditions on the convict ships and to include groups that had been founded across Europe and modeled after her Association for the Improvement of Female Prisoners in Newgate.

Captain Brigstock spied the visitors, buttoned his waistcoat, and barked orders at his crew. In an instant, sailors appeared out of nowhere, jumping around like wild monkeys. Barefoot to reduce slipping, the young mariners laid out the gangplank while the officers and mates prepared a proper reception for the arriving dignitaries.

Surgeon Superintendent Ellis straightened his silk tie and brushed his epaulets into place as sailors marched all the convict girls and women onto the main deck. The *Westmoreland* had taken on prisoners for the last five weeks and was nearly filled to capacity. Among the youngest on board, Agnes pushed forward with her trademark curiosity. She couldn't see over the rail, but she could hear rich people exchanging pleasantries, talking in the unmistakable accent of the upper class. Amid the shouts and confusion, one sound stood out from the rest. Agnes stood mesmerized by the approaching rustle of skirts—big full skirts with lots of crisp, white petticoats. Her thief's awareness suddenly tuned to high. Oh, to possess such finery, someday, someday.

The bonnet appeared first, capping the rest of the simply coiffed, impeccably dressed Elizabeth Gurney Fry. Serene and radiant with purpose, the Quaker reformer projected a powerful presence. Bound by a whalebone corset, pale, powdered, and stately, she stepped on board ready to battle for the reformation of "the poor creatures." Over the course of twenty years, Mrs. Fry visited 106 ships that carried nearly half the women transported, at times even risking her life to make the trip in terrible storms.

Today, Mrs. Fry had enlisted some of London's more prominent women to help "save" Agnes and the others awaiting transport. As the well-to-do ladies boarded the *Westmoreland*, Agnes could think of nothing but their dresses, how dear they were, each one a masterwork of delicate stitching across layers of soft silk, just like the ones she had coveted on the Cross at Kilmarnock. She snapped out of her daydream as Mrs. Fry began to speak, greeting Captain Brigstock and Surgeon Superintendent Ellis first.

After reading a short prayer, the earnest Quaker lectured her captive female audience about "abandoning their evil ways, and becoming Useful Members of Society."[20] Opening her Bible to the twentieth chapter of Matthew, she read the parable of the lord of the vineyard and explained its passages.[21] Although Agnes and Janet stood in polite deference to the woman who had been so kind inside Newgate's hell, the angel of gaols rambled on, as she spoke with "thys," "thees," and "thous." The friends who didn't need to speak to know what the other was thinking suppressed simultaneous yawns. Finishing the sermon at last, Mrs. Fry moved closer to her audience and asked if anyone wanted a message delivered to a parent or loved one. This was Agnes's last chance to communicate with her mother, Mary.

Mr. Ellis called for quiet and motioned the prisoners forward one at a time. Soon, the Scottish lassie stood face-to-face with the celebrated reformer. Drawing a deep breath of Mrs. Fry's starched lace and perfume, Agnes curtsied and bowed her head. First, Mrs. Fry handed her a Bible, paving the way for redemption of her soul. Next, she pressed into Agnes's hands a small burlap bag filled with precisely measured patchwork pieces, a thimble, colored thread, and needles. From the depths of her soul, Elizabeth believed that industry paved the path toward reform and an ultimately productive return to society. In the meantime, sewing hundreds and hundreds of tiny stitches gave the confined women something to do, keeping their minds off rebellion and other wicked enterprises. A finished quilt sometimes served as a political statement. When presented to a member of high society in Van Diemen's Land, it offered tangible evidence of Elizabeth's successful association.

Finally, the tall Quaker looked serenely upon the simply dressed grey-eyed girl and hung a small tin ticket, stamped with #253, around her neck. It became a symbol of her punishment for stealing a warm pair of stockings. It was also her voucher for travel to the Cascades Female Factory on the other side of the world. For the remainder of her exile, Agnes would be referred to as #253. Janet would soon be rechristened #284, as the two were initiated into an ever-growing sisterhood of sorrow.[22]

Fry's system of numbering and ordering seemed contradictory to her compassionate understanding of why Agnes had become a thief. A complicated woman, Mrs. Fry fervently believed that discipline hastened the road to redemption. With some reluctance, the British government adopted most of the recommendations outlined in her 1827 *Observations on the Visiting, Superintendence, and Government of Female Prisoners*, including her system of numbering:

"Every individual . . . may wear a ticket inscribed with a number by which she shall be distinguished. . . . Especially in convict-ships, the plan of *numbering* the prisoners will never fail to be advantageous. . . . This number must not only be found in the class-list connected with a register of her conduct, but must be inscribed on all the principal articles which belong to her—especially her seat at table, her clothing, her bed and bedding, and her books. Such a system is found by experience to be very effectual in preventing disputes among the prisoners, and in promoting that strictness of discipline which is essential to the order and regularity of the whole machine."[23]

Numbers documented every movement in the transportation system: first a convict number, then a probationary Ticket of Leave, and finally the welcome stamp on a numbered Certificate of Freedom. Aboard ship, the captain and the surgeon superintendent found it easier to keep track of numbers than names, particularly with so many Marys, Anns, and Sarahs in their charge. Counting the cargo lined up by the numbers minimized confusion and saved time. Surgeon Superintendent Roberts, who served on the ship *Royal Admiral*, took note of Fry's impact on the prisoners: "Those women who had for any time been under prison discipline, and had received the attention and care of Ladies Societies, more definitely those of Newgate and Edinburgh, were decidedly the best behaved and orderly . . . and their grateful recollections of such kindness and care was deeply implanted and cherished by them."[24]

Agnes stared at the red cord and tin marker that had been placed around her neck. The gentle Quaker gave the little lass in her well-worn green dress a reassuring smile and reached forward with a small bundle. These final parting gifts to the newly christened #253 included a practical black cotton cap, a burlap apron to protect her one dress, and a sack in which to store beloved trinkets. Agnes fingered the small tin ticket that hung between her breasts, lingering to grasp its significance until the first mate jerked her back into line for the closing prayer. The Quaker minister and her friends adjusted their full skirts. They knelt on the nearly spotless deck that the female prisoners had dry-holystoned earlier to scrub off the dangerously slick grime constantly deposited by wind and rain.

The service went on and on, and the sun blazed down over the unprotected audience. It was well past two before the proselytizing ended. Agnes could barely keep her eyes open. By the time the ship's bell rang for lunch, her Scottish nose glowed with a fine case of sunburn, a sensation quite foreign to a lass accustomed to Glasgow's overcast skies.

The Society for the Reformation of Female Prisoners continued to come aboard every few days for the remainder of the *Westmoreland*'s stay in Woolwich. By the time the ship lay ready to sail, a few of the older girls had gamely mastered vivid impressions of the upper-class philanthropists. The rowdy thespians performed their one-act play nightly, belowdecks, to rave reviews of muffled laughter. Four months from now, laughter could bring the punishment of shorn hair. Presently, the girls could savor a quiet giggle at the expense of the women in white petticoats.

Lying in her berth, Agnes opened and shut the Bible Mrs. Fry had slipped into her arms. It was of little use for spiritual solace, full of words on pages she could not read, but it was comforting to have something of her own. As she quickly leafed through the volume, she watched her berth mates put the Good Book to more practical purposes. Women accustomed to having nothing let nothing go to waste. Their God was a God of utility. One used the Bible for primping, tearing pages for curling papers in her hair.[25] Another folded its sheets into even squares and made a deck of playing cards.

In the logbooks above deck, Agnes's namelessness reinforced her baptism into anonymity under Britain's Transportation Act. It belied her true function as breeder and tamer for a motley aggregation of felons, freemen, and adventurers currently wandering the wilds of Van Diemen's Land. Belowdecks, the name Mary and Michael McMillan had given their daughter in 1820 grew ever more precious. Four years before, Agnes had concocted the fake name "Agnes Reddie," hoping to hide her identity from the judge and the gavel. Her clumsy lie had only made him more determined to deport her. Now her real name had never seemed more important. She wasn't going to give it up that easily. As #253 drifted off to restless sleep, she whispered five defiant words into the *Westmoreland*'s darksome hold: "My name is Agnes McMillan."

King Neptune's Visit

The ship's routine changed abruptly at dawn on August 12, 1836, when the mooring was released and the *Westmoreland* started its journey down the Thames under the tow of a steamer and pilot. It carried 185 convicts and their 18 children. An Australian folk song titled "Convict Maid" conveys what many must have felt that fateful morning:

> To you that hear my mournful tale
> I cannot half my grief reveal
> No sorrow yet has been portrayed
> Like that of the poor Convict Maid
>
> Far from my friends and home so dear
> My punishment is most severe
> My woe is great and I'm afraid
> That I shall die a Convict Maid[26]

The *Westmoreland* had to travel nearly thirty miles down the Thames to reach the mouth of the river. As the prisoners bid farewell to their native shore, the good fortune of favorable weather was not with them. As they sailed east, strong headwinds slowed the ship to a crawl. The river gradually widened and disappeared into the frosty North Sea whitecaps. Belowdecks, the women and children were tossed about while the barque pitched back and forth in the open waters. A strong wind carried the ship beyond Margate, around the North Foreland, and past the white cliffs of Dover. After thirteen days of seasick misery, the *Westmoreland* finally cleared the channel and headed into the Atlantic Ocean.

Surgeon Superintendent Ellis made this entry in his diary: "On putting to sea, we were so unfortunate as to encounter strong westerly winds, and it was not until the 24th of the month that we had cleared the channel; during this period the prisoners suffered very much from sea sickness more so inclined than I had ever seen on any former occasion, and which as is usually the case, was followed by obstinate costiveness, requiring the most active purgative medicine to subdue it. . . ."[27] For the second time, the surgeon admitted #253 to the infirmary, administered calomel for her constipation, and released her two days later on August 26. After two treatments, no matter how sick she felt or how much she vomited, Agnes vowed she would never ask Mr. Ellis for one more spoonful of his bilious medicine.

Allowed back on deck, Agnes squinted in the sunlight and watched young sailors scramble up rope ladders forty feet in the air to the mast platforms, then to the top of the yardarms, where they swayed like tiny dolls suspended by threads. Sails unfurled, the *Westmoreland* cruised full speed ahead, heading west with the wind at her back.

Agnes stared long and hard at the horizon that day, watching England fall into the sea, knowing in her heart she'd never see it again. Once the ship reached the open Atlantic, it sailed quickly, soon rounding Spain and heading south off the coast of Portugal. Favorable winds carried them past the mouth of the Mediterranean toward Madeira and Cape Verde, traveling more than a thousand miles the first week. Crashing through the waves, they entered the Tropic of Cancer and its sticky weather, rendering sleep on the lowest deck nearly impossible.

Agnes listened through the steamy blackness. Like clockwork, after the surgeon retired to his berth at nine o'clock, the crew reopened the orlop's hatch. Officers hushed the group of waiting women who had hardened themselves to the harshness of survival. The will to live trumped all matters of the heart. To be taken as a "wife" by a sailor sometimes offered protection from rape by the other men.

The laws of land dissolved at sea. While the *Westmoreland* stayed within sight of England, the crew maintained some degree of decorum. Once the shore dropped out of sight, new rules took hold. Each transport ship became a society unto itself. A few, particularly those that carried clergymen, functioned with relative harmony and order. They were the exception. Most captains permitted free rein over how the sailors treated their female cargo. None of this was new to Agnes and Janet, who had seen it all in Glasgow's alleyways.

Days turned to weeks, and the blues of sky and ocean merged into what seemed an infinite horizon. Time seemed to warp and come unhinged in the floating society. On September 11, 1836, Agnes turned sixteen somewhere off the west coast of Africa. It was a world away from Goosedubbs Street; she'd been at sea for nearly a month. Older women often adopted the younger transports, offering motherly protection against ever-eager advances from the crew. The streetwise girls were well accustomed to propositions from stinky old men who offered gin in return for sexual favors. Still, each proposition carried danger and disgust.

In their time aboard ship, Agnes and Janet witnessed things few people see in a lifetime. The Transportation Policy, in its haste to develop Australia, indiscriminately rounded up prisoners who were violent criminals, alcoholics, mentally ill, and mothers with infants. It also accepted outcasts from higher society—children born of scandal—including the rumored illegitimate daughter of a prime minister.

The long trip to Van Diemen's Land had the curious effect of landing Agnes and Janet in a second season of summer. They cast off in August, at the height of London's summertime heat, and arrived in December, again at summer's peak in the Southern Hemisphere.

Chasing the ships across the tropics and down to the bottom of the world, the sun unleashed merciless, unrelenting heat, day in and day out. The atmosphere dripped with humidity. As the girls baked in the stifling heat and were suffocated by the ship's lack of ventilation, the compounded stench of decay and disease hit them like a blunt instrument. Belowdecks, the reek of vomit followed Agnes everywhere. The ship's privies and bilges coalesced in noxious vapors from which there was no escape. Of course, there was no actual bathing because fresh water was at a premium.

At least when the weather was fair, most everyone found relief on deck, watching the horizon rise and fall into endless shades of green and blue. Topside for a luxurious breath of fresh air, Agnes startled and nearly jumped over the rail as the sound of gunfire thundered through the ship. Sailors fired pistols belowdecks, believing that gunpowder purged infectious vapors from the air. The lower decks were also fumigated by burning brimstone (sulfur) and sprinkling everything that didn't breathe with chloride of lime. The bleaching powder covered Agnes's bedding, her clothing, and her light brown hair.

In order to reach Australia, the *Westmoreland* had to sail a long way west to round Africa's coast. As the ship crossed the tropics, Captain Brigstock watched the sky for weather that changed in a flash. Schooners fell into the path of many a rising hurricane blowing off the Sahara and Serengeti. Like Agnes, most of the female prisoners had never been on a boat before, even under the best of conditions. During storms, the wet pitching deck turned into a rolling death trap. Everyone on board, except the most experienced crew, became violently seasick as the heaving waves rose in angry chaos. The screaming wind drowned out any sound save the most frantic orders shouted through a megaphone.

The scent of the sea air changed as a storm advanced. Agnes smelled the ozone in the atmosphere as lightning crackled in billowing thunderheads and the sky thickened with charged electricity. Turbulent clouds off Africa's west coast erupted like enraged hordes, blotting out the sun and swallowing the ship in their fury. The seas heaved, the crew tensed, and the captain screamed directions to keep the sailors focused and alive.

With little warning, a wall of wind and water approached the ship, poised to knock it over with a deadly strike. Barefooted sailors clung desperately to the rigging, frantically trying to reef the sails as thirty-foot waves submerged the ship's bow. The beams of the *Westmoreland* sprang to life, creaking and wailing under the pounding surge. Mary Talbot, an Irish convict, recorded this account of a storm while aboard ship: "During every moment of its continuance we expected to perish, and were washed out of our beds between decks, while the seasickness and groans and shrieks of so many unhappy wretches made the situation we were in truly distressing. . . ."[28]

For the orlop girls, there was nothing to do but cling to one another and wait it out. The roar of howling winds, the explosion of thunder, and the crash of broken rigging assaulted the prisoners who shivered belowdecks. Bodies, Bibles, and everything else not secured flew about the cabin. Surgeon Superintendent Ellis lashed the sick to their beds with the coarse ropes used on deck. The insane cried out in agony while the intensity of the tempest swallowed all but the loudest screams. Two hundred three terrified women and children had no choice but to huddle together in the soaking darkness until the storm subsided or the ship broke asunder.

Force-five gales tore some convict ships to pieces. Passengers who were hit by a falling mast or spar died instantly. Most didn't know how to swim and expired in panicked drowning amid the raging upheaval in the open sea. At least six convict ships sank in ocean storms, taking the lives of 246 women.[29] The year before Agnes's transport, the *Neva* departed Cork filled to capacity with transports. After five months at sea, it hit a reef and crashed on the rocks off King Island, located at the northwestern tip of Van Diemen's Land. The wreck claimed the lives of 151 women, 55 children, and 18 crew members.[30]

Fortunately, the *Westmoreland* survived. Between episodes of frightening intensity, Agnes's saga unfolded with monotonous regularity, marked by the maddening toll of the bells every half hour. On some days, #253 gave thanks for having a place to sleep, recalling the nights she'd spent wandering the streets of Glasgow with Janet and Helen. Every morning at sunrise, she heard the heavy hatch creak open as the Officer of the Guard unchained the locks. A burst of light in her face signaled that it was time, once again, to put her bare feet on the slippery floor.

Temperatures rose with a vengeance as the *Westmoreland* navigated the tropics. A month at sea, not a bed lay empty in the one-room hospital. On September 19, seventeen-year-old Jane Thompson stumbled into the infirmary, coughing up blood. Surgeon Ellis treated her for hemoptysis, a severe lung infection that surgeons addressed with bloodletting or purging. The girl who had been transported for stealing a purse spent the rest of the journey wasting away in sick bay.

Within six weeks of leaving Woolwich, the *Westmoreland* reached the equator. It was September 24, and she was headed southeast into the Gulf of Guinea off Africa's coast. The winds were steady and the sky beautifully clear that morning, as Janet and Agnes rose to muster with the banging of pots and pans. The ship had crossed the equator during the first morning watch, and now that the sun was up, the crew prepared for a special visit from King Neptune. A rambunctious din exploded on the main deck when the strong door sprung open and two sailors—dressed in grass skirts, painted in blackface, and adorned with strange sigils—enthusiastically motioned the women on deck. The fully intoxicated boys were amusing, particularly because the sun had just risen above the horizon. A much grander spectacle grabbed Agnes's immediate attention. It was King Neptune, the ruler of all oceans, incarnated by a tattooed sailor wearing the skin of a porpoise and a crown of seaweed in his hair, and holding a trident.

Blindfolded and stripped to the waist, two cabin boys and one young mate, Neptune's pollywogs, stood ready to be initiated into this ancient mariners' tradition. This was their first venture across the equator. Once initiated, they were allowed to pierce their ears and call themselves sailors of the Seven Seas. First, one of the "old salts" shaved their heads. Then the boys were ordered to kneel on deck and kiss Neptune's belly, conveniently covered with a combination of grease and bilge residue. As a final insult, the initiates were forced to drink from Neptune's cup, a disgusting concoction prepared by the crew and laced with the surgeon's strongest laxatives. The tribute to the ruler of all oceans unfolded with elaborate and exaggerated pomp and circumstance, much to the prisoners' shock and delight. As children of the streets, the girls found humor in the most unlikely places. Appreciating such absurdity, Agnes enjoyed it to the fullest. It felt good to giggle, arm in arm with Janet, laughing at the hapless initiates, releasing tension, and feeling for a moment like a carefree young girl.

Some captains banned the King Neptune ritual altogether, fearing a breakdown in discipline among the crew. Fortunately, Captain Brigstock maintained a fairly tight ship. He tolerated drunkenness to a point but had a hand ready to take up the lash if necessary. The captain stood at the helm, observing the festivities with detached amusement, taking advantage of the good weather, and allowing the crew and the women some levity before the final stretch of their transit.

By now, everything and everyone was for sale. When fresh food ran low, cooks sometimes sold precious remnants to the highest bidder, trading a piece of maggot-free beef for sexual favors in the galley. At this point in the journey, Agnes and her shipmates had fallen into biological synchrony and began sharing the same menstrual cycle. Everyone knew when a woman had missed her period. This was the time when pregnancies, begot by the crew, were discovered and seasickness merged into morning sickness. Birth control was primitive at best. Women douched with their daily allowance of dirty water. Some found protection using a cup made of beeswax. Even back in England, only the wealthy could afford "British overcoats," a condom made from sheep membranes. Crew members made many promises to their shipboard "wives," but even if they wanted to marry the mother of their child, the captain rarely allowed them to leave his service. Their sons and daughters would be delivered under different skies and different stars in another hemisphere.

The ship continued south, and even the night skies began to change. No longer could Agnes see the North Star that shone above Glasgow. A new constellation, the Southern Cross, began to rise above the horizon as the heat remained oppressive. Seasickness assaulted all but a very few as raging seas pounded the ship. Passage through the tropics continued into early October, while "inflammatory fever," dysentery, and pleurisy swept through the lowest deck. Elevating the girls' misery to a new plateau, common symptoms for dysentery were described as follows: "Violent griping and purging, great pain in the abdomen with great thirst, stools consist almost entirely of blood and are very offensive; tongue is coated with a brown fur."[31]

Now nearly two months at sea, Surgeon Ellis had treated 160 of the 185 prisoners, many requiring multiple infirmary stays. Two women presented the classic symptoms for scurvy—bleeding gums and bleeding under the skin—and were promptly administered extra doses of lime juice and sugar. Women who were pregnant when they boarded ship began to require medical treatment. On October 6, the day the *Westmoreland* entered the Tropic of Capricorn, Sarah Slow was admitted to sick bay for disability and pregnancy. The thirty-one-year-old fresh-faced governess had received a life sentence for forgery.

In the ninth week at sea, on strong steady winds, the ship finally headed due east again, recrossing the Greenwich meridian just west of the Cape of Good Hope. The irony of passing the Cape of Good Hope was not lost on the women. The voyage lapsed into an eternity. As they crossed the opposite side of the earth, propelled by the powerful winds along the Roaring Forties, the waters of the Atlantic merged into the Indian Ocean. The brutal sun, nearing its zenith, chased them all the way around the globe. Temperatures belowdecks often exceeded 120 degrees Fahrenheit. Tempers erupted in the stinky, cramped quarters. The nonstop use of two water closets provoked daily fights. There was no singing belowdecks, not even for Agnes.

Somewhere mid-ocean, after weeks of suffering from seasickness and constipation, Agnes lost her humor and good spirits, turning rambunctious and angry. Surgeon Ellis recorded #253's behavior in a word: "Bad."[32] Janet, on the other hand, he described as "orderly."[33] Agnes was lucky to hang on to her hair as she walked a fine line trying the patience of the surgeon, the man responsible for disciplining the prisoners. Thankfully, Mr. Ellis was progressive for his time and disputed the effectiveness of head shaving. Many women dreaded losing their hair more than any other punishment, but there would be no shearing on his watch. In 1833, Ellis wrote: "when this is once done, in place of bringing about a better conduct it renders them still more incorrigible, fancying as they do, that they have suffered the last and worse degradation. . . ."[34]

On some transport ships, the surgeon superintendent flogged misbehaving girls with pieces of rope whipped across their arms and the backs of their legs. Others locked offenders inside a narrow box on the upper deck. Although this punishment generally quieted male convicts, "women wailed so loudly, and used their tongues so freely, that it was found necessary to place a cistern of water on top of the box."[35] A fiery diatribe from inside the box was quenched immediately by this soaking punishment.

The *Westmoreland* was a world unto itself, where lives began and ended between the masts. As the ship made her way through the Indian Ocean, Sarah Robinson gave birth in a water closet to her second child. The twenty-six-year-old had stolen clothing and received a sentence of seven years' transport. She had attempted to conceal her pregnancy, although her berth mates knew the truth and kept a close eye on her condition. About midnight on October 18, another prisoner heard the cries of an infant. Surgeon Superintendent Ellis recorded what happened next: "The woman who had suspected her state immediately ran to the closet and actually drew out of the pan a female child apparently arrived at the full period. The miserable mother was found in a state from which she was, with difficulty, aroused. On the removal of the placenta which it was found necessary to do by the introduction of the hands, hemorrhage followed and for two days to an alarming extent, but which was eventually controlled.[36]

Dawn broke and the *Westmoreland* rocked the newborn and her exhausted mother in its oaken arms. Sarah and her namesake baby were safe and alive for today, but Elizabeth Booth became the first casualty of the journey. The forty-year-old died from apoplexy the day after little Sarah was born.

Burial at sea was one of the few traditions in British society that class did not govern. Captain Brigstock commanded Surgeon Superintendent Ellis, the entire crew, and every able prisoner onto the upper deck for a somber ceremony. In life, the British captors treated their chattel like animals. In death, they extended dignity. The crew carried Elizabeth Booth on a plank, inside a plain sack weighted with ballast and covered by the Union Jack. The captain read from the standard burial service: "We . . . commit her body to the deep, to be surrendered into corruption, looking for the resurrection of the body when the sea shall give up her dead."[37] The plank was lifted, and Elizabeth's body slipped from beneath the flag into the sea, where it quickly vanished from sight. The ship never stopped moving, not even for the dead. Agnes looked over the railing at the retreating wake and felt the closeness of death. Sharks began following the *Westmoreland*, waiting for more corpses to be dropped overboard.

The strange land was still a long way away, but at least the heat abated when the ship left the tropics. On the twenty-seventh of October, Surgeon Ellis made this entry in his log: "We soon began to experience a more congenial climate, the temperature had much downwards [*sic*], the weather was moderate and clear, and its beneficial effects were soon observable in the increased activity and improved looks of the prisoners."[38]

Tranquility, however, was short-lived. On November 11, twenty-one-year-old Anne Sergeantson went into labor. The redhead from Hull gave birth to a baby girl in the infirmary, delivered about one month prematurely. Six days later, the infant passed away after suffering from diarrhea and convulsions.[39] Once again, Captain Brigstock mustered the women and crew on deck. The baby girl, wrapped in white muslin from the surgeon's supplies, lay on the lee gangway until her mother pressed a final kiss and witnessed her quick descent into a watery grave.

The last two weeks of the voyage were spent in relative calm as the ship neared the shores of Van Diemen's Land. Agnes and Janet had been at sea for more than three months, and signs of the journey's end began to manifest. First there were the birds. As the *Westmoreland* approached the confluence of the Indian and Pacific Oceans, curious Pacific gulls flew overhead from rocky islands sculpted into odd formations by the tempestuous sea. Dolphins dove alongside the ship, riding its wake and bidding a welcome to the southern seas.

The crew anticipated landfall when the smell of the ocean changed to the musky odor of the earth and the scent of green intermingling with the brine. Finally, off the vessel's port side, a sailor spotted the shore. The call went out from high on the mast: "Land! Land! Van Diemen's Land!" Captain Brigstock focused the quarterdeck telescope and peered to the north at a dot on the horizon.

The sight of land ignited the ship with excitement. Agnes and Janet leaned over the rail, straining to see for themselves a shore that showed no signs of civilization. The ship stayed its course along the southern part of Van Diemen's Land into the Tasman Sea, turning northeast and sailing past Bruny Island. Rugged dolerite cliffs towered two hundred meters above the sea and sheltered coastal caves marked by gushing sprays of water. Australian fur seals with their massive grey necks fed on squid and octopus and sunned on island ledges. Tiny fairy penguins waddled along the shore rocks. Big black-faced cormorants, sporting white breasts just like the penguins, dove for fish along the coast. Mutton birds glided above at high speeds and floated on rafting logs between feedings. Giant albatross flew over the spindly eucalyptus trees that poked above the cliffs. This was a very bizarre place for two city girls from Glasgow.

Once again sailing through heavy rains, they turned north through Storm Bay and into the mouth of the River Derwent. The ship encountered whalers and store ships as it moved closer to the busy port of Hobart Town, the capital of Van Diemen's Land. When the barque entered the head of the river, Captain Brigstock alerted the town to the ship's arrival. The crew hoisted a square flag, half red and half white, which signaled that women prisoners were its cargo.[40]

On the third of December 1836, the captain anchored the *Westmoreland* in Sullivans Cove. It was seven months to the day since Agnes and Janet had been convicted of their crimes in Ayr. The two naïvely optimistic lasses had faith that they would brave this strange and mysterious destination together. It was not to be so.

∼ 5 ∼

More Sinned Against
Than Sinning

Birds of a Feather

The stormy heavens exploded in driving rain and spectacular lightning displays over Sullivans Cove. Blustering westerly winds pelted hailstones across the *Westmoreland*'s wooden deck. Surgeon Superintendent Ellis ordered all the prisoners belowdecks. If this was supposed to be summer, Agnes couldn't begin to fathom what winter might bring. The *Hobart Town Courier* recorded weather so awful in December 1836 that migrating birds failed to stop on the island: "The unusual inclemency of the present season is doubtless the cause of this phenomenon. No inhabitant of the island has any recollection of so long a continuance of cold fluctuating weather, which appears to have affected many other objects of nature besides the swallows, the absence of which our correspondent has so well remarked."[1] Even the raucous yellow-tailed black cockatoos avoided Van Diemen's Land the year Agnes arrived.

The *Westmoreland* anchored off Hunter Island in the River Derwent. Mr. Ellis was immediately rowed ashore to meet with local officials and turn over his now-dog-eared leather ledger along with court records for each prisoner. Because it was Saturday and government offices were closed on Sunday, the transfer of paperwork would take four full days. The gravely ill couldn't wait that long and were moved to the Hobart Town Colonial Hospital.

Seventeen-year-old Jane Thompson, who'd spent most of the sea journey inside the *Westmoreland*'s infirmary, was lowered into the waiting skiff lashed to a stretcher. After being transported around the world, she died seven days later in a ward full of strangers. Sarah Robinson was also sent to the hospital, suffering from complications after giving birth to her baby girl in the water closet a few weeks earlier. Mary Ring and Sarah Slow, both in the final stages of pregnancy, found comfort in the prospect of giving birth on dry land.[2]

Quarantined in limbo on the orlop deck, Agnes and Janet lay in their berths, not daring to contemplate where they'd sleep next. At the unexpected hour of six A.M., shouting blasted from the forecastle. "Rouse out there! Turn out! Turn out! Huzzah for the shore!" screamed the Officer of the Guard.[3] A drowsy Agnes opened her eyes and sat up with a start. She grabbed the little burlap bag given her by Mrs. Fry and tied it tight to protect her small comb and a few stray pieces of colored thread. The remnants of her Bible had turned grey and mildewed, so she left it on the straw mattress and headed under the hatch toward the main deck.

It was Tuesday the sixth of December, and Captain Brigstock awaited the arrival of Josiah Spode, Principal Superintendent of Convicts. He arrived accompanied by Muster Master William Thomas Napier Champ, a British soldier previously charged with the government mission to hunt down Aborigines. The two stern men were rowed from Hobart Town to the *Westmoreland* by male convicts who'd been conscripted into the police force because of a shortage of both funding and able men.

Spode, now a naval officer, had once worked in his grandfather's famous pottery business in England. He had little tolerance for the women, deeming them "worse in every respect to manage than male convicts. . . . They all feel they are working under compulsion which renders it almost a continual warfare between their employers and themselves."[4] Champ, who later became the first premier of Tasmania, was the record keeper for all convicts and also served as assistant police magistrate in Hobart Town.

Called in numerical order, Agnes and Janet were hurried on deck for inspection. Eyeing the grey-eyed lass up and down, Muster Master Champ compared the surgeon superintendent's descriptions against the sixteen-year-old standing before him. As he evaluated Agnes's health and ability to work, Champ considered her skills for assignment to a local colonist. Agnes confirmed that she could neither read nor write. According to indent records, when Muster Master Champ asked, "What is your trade?" she responded, "House servant."[5] Janet gave the same answer when it was her turn.

It took nearly two days to examine and interview the prisoners. Neither Mr. Spode nor Mr. Champ wanted to be blamed for disembarking contagiously ill transports. The whole colony had recently suffered from an outbreak of influenza, probably carried by a ship's passenger from London.[6] After consulting with Surgeon Superintendent Ellis, the two bureaucrats finally cleared his charges for landing. The women and their children were rowed ashore to Hunter Island and walked over a muddy convict-built causeway, connecting the isle to Hobart Town. The girls from Glasgow finally heard the annoying toll of the *Westmoreland* bells for the last time. Catcalls from the wharf soon replaced the harsh clanging from the ship. A crowd of scruffy-looking creatures raced toward the waterfront to inspect the Crown's latest chattel.

While the *Westmoreland* lay at anchor, Agnes had taken a good look at where she was headed. The busy little port of fourteen thousand sat on the river below soft green hills that lay dominated by the cliffs of an enormous mountain. The strangest creatures Agnes had ever seen bounced over the slopes on their huge hind legs and disappeared into the lush countryside. Black swans with bright red beaks floated at river's edge. Seagulls flying overhead appeared like the ones seen in the British Isles, but their calls were sharply different.[7] Everything, even the scavenger birds, seemed topsy-turvy.

Journalist Minister John West offers a clue about how Agnes felt on the day she set foot on the other side of the earth. Eleven years her senior, he lived in Tasmania in 1836 and wrote about the convicts who were among the first transported: "The letters they addressed to their friends . . . were filled with lamentations. They deeply deplored that the distance of their exile cut off the hope of return . . . they expected to be destroyed by savages, or to pine away in want. The females seemed least to fear their banishment; and while several of the men were deeply moved, a spectator, who curiously remarked the mental influence of their prospects, saw only one woman weep."[8]

Convict men outnumbered the female prisoners by nearly nine to one, creating an imbalance of uncivilized proportions. The arrival of a boatload of women quickly drew most Hobart Town men toward the wharves. "All kinds of men, except apparently decent ones, would gather round the waterfront and form an almost impossible mob, through which the girls had to make their way, the while insults, lewd suggestions, and all kind of horrible offers were hurled at them to the intense amusement of the crowd and the horror of those who were good among the girls. . . ."[9]

These days, men queued up at the quayside were still rambunctious, but less barbaric than in the early days of transport, when a man could buy a bonnie lass right on the spot in exchange for a bottle of rum. During the first twenty years of transport, female prisoners were left to fend for themselves. If a settler didn't choose a woman, she was forced to find lodging on her own.[10] "There was little delicacy of choice: they landed, and vanished; and some carried into the bush, changed their destination before they reached their homes."[11]

Fortunately, the two Scottish birds in forced exile arrived as a pair. Janet held tight to her friend's hand, and they both looked straight ahead, ignoring the screaming men who waved hats in their faces. Back on solid ground for the first time in 117 days, Agnes's not-so-steady land legs took their first rubbery steps onto the shores of Van Diemen's Land. A contingent of soldiers, dressed in scarlet uniforms, stood stiffly as Muster Master Champ directed the girls to wait for the next group. Under his watchful gaze, Agnes smelled the mudflats and took in the ramshackle riverfront wooden cottages and stone water-mills, which created little waterfalls as they turned.[12] Wharfside pubs filled with sailors, a bond store, and warehouses for importers and exporters signaled the importance of this shipping port. The *Westmoreland*'s cargo was bound for a warehouse of a different sort, a fortress known as the Cascades Female Factory.

Like livestock on the way to market, the 182 women and 18 children were paraded up Macquarie Street from the turn at the Old Wharf. Several women, in various stages of pregnancy, lumbered up the muddy hill a bit slower than the rest. Lagging as far behind as the soldiers allowed was Anne Sergeantson, the red-haired nursemaid who'd lost her six-day-old infant a few weeks earlier.

When clouds thundered down the valley and let loose a drenching rain, the leering welcome party began to disperse. The shift given to Agnes by Mrs. Fry's volunteers in Newgate had worn quite thin, and she shivered under the soaking onslaught. Giant leafy ferns trembled in the wind gusts, like another group of mocking spectators along the route.

The well-guarded entourage marched past Government House, the courthouse, and St. David's Church. The stucco and painted brick cathedral was crowned by a black lead-covered dome known as the "pepper pot." When the pepper pot's three-faced clock chimed the hour, it resounded all across the valley.[13] If Agnes thought she had heard the last of ringing bells, she was sadly mistaken.

St. David's was one of several churches where settlers, soldiers, and convicts gathered Sunday morning, the prisoners seated separately. Sometimes blurred but never forgotten, lines of class distinction followed Agnes to Van Diemen's Land. Few settlers could avoid mingling with the transports who kept the economy afloat, but the "convicts sometimes appeared like a pariah caste rather than a lower class."[14] Under his scruffy hair and unkempt beard, Muster Master Champ sat proudly in a front pew. Slayer of Aborigines in the Black War, the future premier condemned the petty thieves, who were more sinned against than sinning.

An 1838 Report from the Select Committee of the House of Commons on Transportation summarized the welcome extended for Agnes and Janet: "For want of servants a settler must apply to Government for convicts. He then becomes a slave-owner, not like the planters of the West Indies, or of the southern states of America, whose slaves, if not by nature, by education in bondage at least, are an inferior race, and having from youth been ignorant of freedom, consider it almost an honour to serve the white. On the other hand, the Australian settler has a property in men of his own race, hardened, desperate, and profligate ruffians, who have been nurtured in vice and crime, and have given way to the vilest passions."[15]

Conditions were even worse before Cascades opened. Women were imprisoned in an overcrowded holding area tacked onto the Hobart Town male prison and overlooking the execution yard, loosely guarded by male convicts; "trafficking," or contact with the outside world, was all too easy. In 1827, a concerned citizen wrote a letter to the local paper expressing his consternation over the "immorality of the lower class of people in Van Diemen's Land." He offered the following details: "I remember one night walking by the building . . . at the time the females were confined there; when I saw the place surrounded by many fellows, who were feeing the constables and sentries to gain admission, while language and imprecations the most disgusting and appalling issued from within. The next day I mentioned the circumstances to several persons, who said it was useless to kick up a stir about it, for no notice would be taken of it."[16]

As the demand for female servants grew and transport numbers rose, Lieutenant Governor Arthur responded in December 1828 by opening a new gaol in a converted rum distillery well outside the town. It was christened the Cascades Female Factory, belying its true purpose. Five years prior, Elizabeth Fry had approached Britain's Under Secretary of State for the Colonies with recommendations that he passed on to the governor. Her ideas for prison reform included specific plans for a new women's gaol, and Governor Arthur adopted most of them. Once again, the timely intervention of the Angel of Newgate saved Agnes, Janet, and many others from a fate even worse than the frightening scene they now faced.

In 1830, the gaoled women had witnessed the hanging of Mary McLauchlan, who had been transported from Glasgow for theft by housebreaking. Forced to leave her husband and two young daughters behind, she found herself pregnant by a man in Hobart Town who refused to recognize his paternity. As was often the case for convict maids with child, the father was likely her master. The baby either was stillborn or died soon after birth, and Mary was convicted of killing him. A large crowd gathered to witness the hanging of the woman who wore a white dress tied with a black ribbon.[17] Mary McLauchlan was the first woman executed in Van Diemen's Land.

Agnes stared at the tall gaol barricade along Macquarie Street, a monument of the penal colony's history and the first transport of three women in 1803. By the year the *Westmoreland* disembarked, public spectacles in Hobart Town were less gruesome. Freed convicts and settlers who were arrested for drunk and disorderly conduct spent a few hours in the town stocks, located prominently in front of the Macquarie Street Treasury. Female prisoners who acted out were punished away from town, unseen behind the thick stone walls of Cascades.

Well-to-do settlers, getting rich on whale oil and wool, resented both convicts and the Crown. A year before Agnes landed, many signed a petition to His Majesty requesting the removal of "unspeakable evils": "We, the undersigned, feeling that the measures adopted by the British Government, of increasing the penal character of the Colony . . . affix a moral degradation upon us, and our children . . . request you will convene a Public Meeting of the Colonists, for the purpose of addressing the King thereon."[18]

Reminders of the Crown's rule were everywhere on display. British soldiers, pressing muskets against their shoulders, guarded government buildings constructed in soft-brown sandstone and built by the hands of male convicts. Sentries posted at the gates outside George's Square stood locked at attention under leather shako hats topped with white woolen pom-poms, utterly impractical under the driving rain.[19] Scarlet-coated soldiers even guarded a makeshift zoo located behind the governor's mansion, lest the island's wildlife forget who was in charge of Van Diemen's Land. As the prisoner's parade filed past the governor's mansion, wild creatures on exhibit in the old paddock came into view. Emus strutted about, standing six feet high on spindly legs and swathed in swirls of soft brown feathers. Agnes looked across the street in amazement at the huge gawky birds and brown-eyed wallabies. If the island's chickens and rats were this big, what else might be wandering the forests?

The soldier in charge of the human prisoners tolerated not a moment of dawdling. The group of two hundred transports still had a two-mile march uphill before they reached the Female Factory. Agnes and Janet followed a muddy path toward the towering mountain, whose highest elevations were hidden under cloud cover. Shopkeepers leaned out their doorsills to inspect the latest shipment of new maids and helpers. Tucked behind white picket fences, neatly kept brick cottages lined upper Macquarie Street. Summer gardens were lush with raspberries, scarlet geraniums, and the rosy pink blossoms of sweetbriar plants. Ripe apricots and nectarines hung temptingly close along the track.[20] The new and distinctive scent of eucalyptus wafted through a valley thick with trees bearing the bluish-green leaves. Here Agnes saw shades of green she had never seen in Scotland. Even the air smelled green.

Agnes's knees were still shaky from months of walking unsteadily across the ship's rocking decks. As the bedraggled prisoner approached the Hobart Rivulet, the steady incline grew steeper, and her legs started to ache. The sounds of running water and birds in the bush intermingled with the tramping of feet as her troop made its way along the bank of the tiny river. On the outskirts of town, scattered wooden shanties teetered along the water's edge. Entrepreneurial settlers built breweries and sawmills next to the rivulet. Rats scurrying through the muddy gully were one of the few familiar reminders of home.

The stream meandered up the valley to the base of the cliff. Gradually the weather cleared, and the features of the summit came into view. The soldiers called it Mt. Wellington, named to reinforce Britain's claim on the island after the Duke of Wellington defeated Napoleon at Waterloo. It replaced the Aboriginal names—Unghbanyahletta and Poorawetter—given to the mountain layered in dense green forests and rising more than four thousand feet.[21]

Beneath this towering giant, Agnes shivered as the temperature dropped some ten degrees in the secluded hollow where her group was headed. After nearly an hour of stomping through the mud, a two-story stone fortress revealed itself at the soggy base of Mt. Wellington. Tucked away two miles beyond town, the prison lay hidden from the rising middle-class gentry. The building now used for the Cascades Female Factory began as a rum distillery and was hardly suited to house women and children. Raw sewage drained into the rivulet running next to the prison. Foothills cast long shadows over the institution, rendering it nearly sunless much of the year and damply cold in every season.

The largest of five female factories in Van Diemen's Land, Cascades opened in 1828. Agnes and Janet waited outside a large wooden gate secured shut with heavy irons. From behind the guard wall, which was at least twice Agnes's height, they heard the sounds of chopping wood and clanging pots bouncing off the face of the valley.[22]

As the rest of the tired troop caught up, red-coated soldiers nodded to the constable on duty and lined up the women and children in double file at the yard's entrance. Stone barricades inside stone walls reinforced the austere greeting that awaited them. Walking under the tunneled entrance, not knowing if they would be separated, Agnes allowed her hand a brush against Janet's.

At the soldier's command, a gatekeeper unlatched the weighty entrance door. Unlike the boisterous clamor inside London's Newgate Prison, the compound seemed eerily devoid of human voices. A rather imposing figure hurried toward the transports. White bonnet tied in a crisp bow under her wide chin, Matron Mary Hutchinson curtsied and greeted the British officers. A bundle of efficiency at twenty-six, she knew the factory system well, having grown up inside Sydney's Parramatta Female Factory, run by her father. She was the no-nonsense woman in charge, heavy black dress buttoned tight to the neck. Shuffling behind was her husband, John, with his gaunt face, high cheekbones, and scraggly little whiskers hanging over his neck.

John Hutchinson, a Methodist minister, was seventeen years her senior. He was named superintendent in 1832, but Mary essentially ran Cascades, particularly when her husband's health began to fail. Elizabeth Cato, who had arrived in 1831, assisted the Hutchinsons as deputy matron and midwife. Her husband, William, served as prison overseer.

The officer in charge of the soldiers observed the brief formality of handing over the women and children in his possession. Superintendent Hutchinson, an efficient bureaucrat, had already organized the conduct records and physical description for each prisoner. A porter opened a small, heavily reinforced door and led the weary transports into a paved yard. Agnes and Janet scanned the enclosure, filled with women busy at work but mum as mutes. They would soon learn the reason for silence. No one spoke, but their eyes told many stories. The two Glasgow lasses stared at the women in dingy uniforms coughing and running their tongues over sore gums and missing teeth. Surely they couldn't have looked this bad upon arrival.

Gradually, Agnes moved to the front of the line for processing. Surgeon Superintendent Ellis had classified the grey-eyed lass as a troublemaker. She and Janet were listed as accomplices in crime, so Mr. Hutchinson considered it his duty to separate the pair immediately.

Clothes Don't Make the Woman

Assistant Matron Cato brought one girl at a time into a small reception room, where Mrs. Hutchinson stood next to a tall stack of ugly dresses. Hairstyling was not allowed at the Female Factory, so Agnes was forced to hand over the comb Mrs. Fry had tucked inside her sturdy burlap bag. Mrs. Cato told Agnes she would put it in storage for safekeeping and gave her a nudge toward the washtub. Every prisoner was required to disrobe and bathe upon arrival.

Splashing the cold water over herself was a shock, though Agnes experienced some relief in removing salt and dirt accumulated from nearly four months aboard the *Westmoreland*. Most clothing worn at sea was beyond repair and thrown in a pile for burning. After checking Agnes's head for lice, Mrs. Hutchinson issued the prison uniform, sewn from low-grade wool and chosen for its coarseness. It would be a constant reminder of the transgressions that brought the grey-eyed rebel to Van Diemen's Land. Pulling the wool shift over her head, Agnes recalled many unpleasant memories of the days spent in Mr. Green's Glasgow mill. The fabric was scratchy and the shift had no shape, but at least it was clean. New stockings were a pleasant surprise and, in spite of everything else, felt refreshing on her feet. Agnes received the remainder of the unfashionably dreary wardrobe for her seven-year sentence: a second shift for when she washed the first, two aprons, two caps, two handkerchiefs for her monthly flow, and a second pair of stockings.

Convict dress was meant to be a marker for the wearer, a warning that she was an untrustworthy outcast. The clothes Agnes and Janet wore were so unbecoming as to elicit derision from the highly decorated Colonel Mundy when he visited the Female Factory. After an initial observation that the prisoners appeared deaf and dumb performing their work in silence, he added: "There must be a good deal in dress as an element of beauty—for I scarcely saw a tolerably pretty woman."[23]

Ugly attire in tow, Agnes held on to her familiar brown boots now stiffened with salt from the sea, the last remnants of her life in the Glasgow wynds. Officially a member of the Assignment Class, one of three Cascades ranks based on conduct, she joined a group of twelve. Bad behavior carried punishment in the Crime Class, followed by a sentence in Probation Class for those whose conduct improved, and finally return to the rank from which prisoners were assigned to settlers.

Janet underwent the same processing as Agnes, but the Hutchinsons directed her to a different mess. It was noon, and Mrs. Cato rang the bell for dinner, as the midday meal was called. Straggling at the back of the line, Agnes lifted her eyebrows the moment she caught Janet's eyes. *What in the bloody hell have we gotten ourselves into?*

Prisoners rotated the duty of serving the meal to those seated on wooden benches at long tables. The menu remained the same, every day, every week. The two Glasgow lasses sipped their first taste of watery ox-head soup, garnished with a big hunk of brown bread. Prepared without regard for nutritional value, the recipe called for twenty-five pounds of meat for every one hundred quarts of broth. When the ox head wasn't all bone, each girl received about four ounces of gristly protein a day.[24]

After the meal, Agnes and Janet milled about aimlessly until everyone was bathed and checked off the roster list. With a clap of her hands, Matron Hutchinson corralled the assembly of newly uniformed women and shushed their restless children. It was time for the first of many lectures by Superintendent Hutchinson. He opened his black leather book to the page inscribed "Rules and Regulations for the Management of the House of Correction for Females." Rule Number One: No talking, no laughing, no whistling, no singing. No singing? The ballad crooner was appalled. Even London's Newgate allowed song and conversation.

The governor of Van Diemen's Land from 1824 to 1836, Colonel George Arthur, was a consummate bureaucrat. He wrote the Cascades rules and regulations himself. With military precision he demanded of "all the Female Convicts on their admission . . . the utmost cleanliness— the greatest quietness—perfect regularity—and entire submission. . . . If these be observed . . . patient industry will appear, and reformation of character must be the result."[25] The rules were printed everywhere, including in the *Hobart Town Courier* because "so many of our readers having expressed a desire that they should be printed. . . ."[26] Yet most of the women at Cascades couldn't read a word.

The Female Factory's strict regulations relied on the presumption that if prisoners weren't allowed to converse, disruptions and bad influences could be controlled. What the authorities never anticipated was how quickly creative measures arose among women who were told they couldn't talk.

Not surprisingly, Reverend Hutchinson warned the *Westmoreland* transports about punishments suffered for smoking tobacco and using profanities. When the straight-laced superintendent read the rule that forbade bringing poultry, pigeons, or pigs into Cascades, several of the youngest prisoners let out a giggle. How in the bloody blazes could a girl get a pig over the top of these thick stone walls? Their merriment was quickly extinguished when Mrs. Cato hustled over to the troublemakers and hissed a stern warning from behind their shoulders.

Standing himself a bit taller, Superintendent Hutchinson concluded his monologue with a review of the daily routine, including mandatory chapel attendance twice a day, after breakfast at half past eight and after supper at eight P.M. The little church was designed to double as a school between services and provide space for quiet study. Although superintendents were supposed to teach prisoners to read, it rarely happened. The reality of managing more than three hundred women and their infants allowed Mr. Hutchinson little time to do anything beyond managing the paperwork it took to run the institution. Though Mrs. Fry argued fervently for a school within the female factories, Governor Arthur had largely ignored her recommendation, concentrating instead on bureaucratic details, such as the degree of roughness in the fabric for convict garb.

Indoctrination complete, Agnes and Janet followed the line of two hundred back into the main yard. The twenty-foot-high walls of the Female Factory cast long shadows across the interior yard when the sun dropped behind Mt. Wellington. Light faded quickly in the valley, and the temperature dipped yet again. Time took on another dimension inside the unforgiving fortress encased in double stone walls. The women who had arrived on earlier ships appeared to move in slow motion, looking more like chalky zombies than industrious workers. For some, Cascades chipped away humanity piece by piece.

At half past seven o'clock, Mrs. Cato clanged the supper bell. It was a repeat of the noontime repast: brown bread and a pint of oxhead soup. At five minutes to eight, the new congregation was ushered into the chapel, lit by two small candles on the altar. Mothers tried in vain to quiet their children until a distraction, entering from the back of the chapel, caught their attention. The Reverend William Bedford had arrived. Fancying himself a regal figure as chaplain for the Female Factory, he strutted by the pews filled with potential converts. His beak of a nose and protruding lower lip grew more prominent as his fire-and-brimstone preaching rose to a crescendo. By the end of the reverend's half-hour rant, Agnes had a stiff neck from trying to hold her head up. At last, it was over.

Mrs. Hutchinson announced the roll call for the night's bed check.

Following factory regulations, Mrs. Cato designated an overseer for each mess, choosing one of the older women from the *Westmoreland* whom Surgeon Superintendent Ellis had reported as "orderly." The convict overseer was responsible for the conduct of her eleven peer inmates, a daunting assignment under the best of circumstances.[27]

There was never enough space to accommodate the rising numbers of transported girls and women. Sleeping rooms were filled to capacity with hammocks slung in tight rows, leaving no room to walk unless the suspended beds were tipped to the side. It took more than a little spontaneous choreography to get four rows of women in place without tipping someone else to the floor. A single chamber pot sat in the far corner and was very difficult to reach in the darkness. Its distant location explained the dreadful stench beneath Agnes's boots. She kept them tied close by and pulled both knees to her chest, trying to get comfortable. From time to time, she could still feel the rhythmic rocking of the ship.

Inside her low-slung hammock as she started to doze off, Agnes considered violating the first rule of silence. She knew her eleven bunkmates well from nearly four months together aboard the ship, but could they really be trusted? What she really needed was to talk with Janet. Her canvas bedding smelled of mildew and crawled with fleas. At least there were no rules against dreaming.

By sunrise, the odor of human waste dominated the cramped space that had no ventilation and no windows. At five thirty A.M. the bells rang, and Agnes was rousted from her hammock for morning muster in the yard. Matron Hutchinson walked the long rows of women and children for morning inspection, making certain they looked somewhat clean and tidy. Today was the day most would be assigned to local settlers who would wield complete control over their lives. Mrs. Hutchinson, herself a parent and descendant of a convict grandmother, informed the mothers what would become of their children. Those younger than three would be housed in a nursery inside the factory. The rest would soon be transferred to the Queen's Orphanage, where well-behaved mothers could visit them on Sundays if their masters issued a pass.

One mess at a time, Mrs. Hutchinson directed the new arrivals to a very large yard on the other side of the complex. Her purpose was abundantly clear as she showed Agnes and her group what happened to girls who disobeyed rules and were sent to the Crime Class. It was only six A.M., and several hundred girls and women were busy at work. Most were scrubbing clothing inside stone washtubs, while others hung the laundry to dry across wooden rails. Mrs. Hutchinson issued a stern warning as she pointed to the cells for solitary confinement. Pretending to pay attention, Agnes covertly studied a woman with yellow "C"s emblazoned all over her clothing. Before long, she and Janet would learn the meaning of the yellow "C."

The breakfast bell was ringing by the time Matron Hutchinson finished the Crime Class prison tour, which she hoped sent a warning. Agnes and Janet sat down in their separate groups to a pint of watered-down gruel and a piece of brown bread. Before they were done, each was summoned to Mr. Hutchinson's office.

A string of settlers made the long walk up the valley and lined up outside Cascades to retrieve their free labor. Turning the transports over to colonists spared the government the expense of funding their food and lodging. The Female Factory was essentially a hiring depot for girls like Agnes. Her fate fell into a lottery. The luck of the draw determined for whom #253 worked and what she might be forced to endure at the hands of her master.

Treatment ran the gauntlet from kindness to torture. Plum assignments went to women with special skills, such as dressmaking or baking. Some girls were allowed to sit at their master's dining table and were welcomed into a family. More commonly, they were treated like slaves, and many suffered sexual abuse, as evidenced by the number of women who returned pregnant to the factory.

The Assignment Board consisted of the chief police magistrate, the local treasurer, and the superintendent of prisoners. The bureau-cracy ran rife with favoritism, which played a major role in their deci-sions. Military officers and wealthy businessmen were often rewarded with the cream of the transported crop. Women who could read to the colonists' children or prepare a banquet were most desirable, and a pretty face was also coveted.

There was high demand for domestic help in the colony, so the women of the *Westmoreland* were not expected to stay at Cascades for long. Everyone from the *Westmoreland*, except women showing signs of pregnancy, was automatically "eligible for service." One by one, they disappeared into Hobart Town, Sandy Bay, or one of the other nearby settlements, each at the mercy of an unregulated, indiscrimi-nate assignment.

Young and healthy, #253 was immediately turned over to a Mr. Donahoo, who lived in Hobart Town. She stole a quick hug from Janet, who stood outside the superintendent's door, and the two parted ways. Without question, they would find each other, some way, some-how. Taking her by the arm, Mr. Donahoo escorted his new servant back down the hillside she'd trudged all the way up just one day earlier.

Working as a housemaid for the Donahoos was nothing like being a servant in a fine Scottish home, a home like the one she and Janet had burglarized four years earlier. Doing laundry, ironing, scouring pots, scrubbing floors on her hands and knees, and endlessly chop-ping wood for the stove filled every waking hour of Agnes's day. Lug-ging water up and down the Hobart Town hills was the worst of all chores. A pipeline from the Hobart Rivulet connected to a storage tower on Macquarie Street, where a brigade of servants with buckets waited their turn.

Agnes soon discovered an advantage to the work that nearly pulled her skinny arms from their sockets. For a precious few moments, she could sit and gossip with Janet on the Macquarie Street benches and plot their next rendezvous. Church services also provided a divine opportunity to see her friend. Many abusive masters, unrepentant sinners themselves, dragged their young servants to Sunday service under the guise of promoting their salvation. Relegated to the back of the church, the convict maids devised elaborate schemes to pass contraband in the form of tea and tobacco, often hidden under the mob caps issued at the Female Factory.

Most days, the girl from Glasgow was isolated and lonely. Walking through town, Agnes could sense dirty looks and not-so-furtive head shaking from citizens who resented her presence. Not every settler could afford the expense of feeding another mouth in return for free labor. Hobart's struggling poor deemed the gruel and ox-head soup served at Cascades an unfair government handout. The convicts were perceived as taking their jobs. "Far better it is to arrive in this colony as a Prisoner of the Crown, than as a poor Free Settler!" blared a headline in the *Colonial Times*.[28] This angry, rising sentiment ignited the beginnings of an anti-transportation movement.

On her feet, worked to exhaustion six days a week and half the day on Sunday, Agnes had lots of time to think about the seven years ahead. Out on legitimate errands, she'd been down nearly every street and alley in Hobart Town. There was nowhere to run and nowhere to hide on this upside-down island surrounded by sharks. But without a doubt, she would find an easier way to do her bloody time.

Nearing the last day of December, Agnes hummed "Auld Lang Syne" under her breath, thinking about the Hogmanay celebration back in Scotland. The steady rain and stormy grey heavens sometimes reminded her of home, though there was a frightening unpredictability to the weather here. As the squalls reached gale force rumbling through the valley, Agnes put down her chopping ax and bolted inside for cover.

It was evening on Friday, December 30, when multihued streaks of lightning crashed across Mt. Wellington, with wind gusts reaching sixty miles an hour. The "hurricane" was described in the *Hobart Town Courier* as "a most awful storm unprecedented in the memory of the oldest settler"; chimneys crashed down on Macquarie Street, windows blew to bits, and several roofs collapsed. "The weightiest articles of timber were lifted up and blown about like straws. . . . Large, gigantic trees in all directions were thrown down, their power of withstanding the blast being weakened, from the unusually moist season having relaxed the roots."[29] The storm's course of destruction rivaled the worst winter blizzard back in Glasgow. This was certainly no way to welcome in the new year.

Holy Willie

Shortly after the worst storm on record, another event dominated the *Hobart Town Courier*'s feature page. The island's new governor and his wife had arrived. It was the same day the *Westmoreland* departed for Calcutta to pick up its return cargo of raw materials for London's factories. On January 5, 1837, Sir John and Lady Franklin stepped off the passenger ship *Fairlie* onto the shores of Van Diemen's Land. A naval officer known for his Arctic expeditions, Sir John was nicknamed "the man who ate his boots." While mapping the Northwest Passage, his poor planning led his crew toward starvation along with reported cannibalism and eating of the leather from their boots. Knighted by George IV in 1818 despite his failings in the Arctic, Sir John was hailed as a hero by the London elite and given the assignment he wanted in the new British colony.

Van Diemen's Land welcomed its new governor with a twenty-one-gun salute and cheering crowds along Macquarie Street. Later in the evening, the entire capital lit up for him. The *Hobart Town Courier* reported: "It was really amusing to witness the preparations, which even the humblest Hobartonian was busily making for the occasion: those who could not obtain lamps procured candles. . . . Almost every house . . . displayed its loyalty in some shape, and a general feeling of good will and amity seemed universally to prevail." The newspaper also announced that "His Excellency . . . appeared in good health."[30]

A male convict sentenced for being a political activist saw Governor Franklin quite differently, as he later wrote in a book: "Clad in his official garb, adorned with his star, and covered with his cocked cap and feather, no nabob of India could affect more dignity and importance. He appeared to feel, as he strutted about, that he was the only man on earth. His height was . . . about five feet nine inches; his circumference quite out of proportion, and clearly indicating, that however starved he might have been as 'Captain Franklin,' in his northern expedition . . . that here there was no scarcity of grease and good foraging."[31]

Standing beside her portly husband, Lady Jane, the governor's second wife, drew notice for the tight ringlets around her face and her custom-made lavender Burmese silk dress. Back in London, she had already met some of the convict women. A politically ambitious social climber, Jane Franklin visited Newgate Prison to observe Elizabeth Fry as one of London's revered celebrities. After seeing the prisoners, Lady Jane wrote in her journal, judging almost all of them as "strapping ugly women with the most low-life air and impudent expression of countenance."[32]

In London, Elizabeth thought she'd found an ally in asking the newly appointed governor's wife to write about conditions in the Female Factory and to visit the women. It would be four and a half years before Lady Jane found the time to send her first letter to Mrs. Fry. In the meantime, Fry had received news from some of the many thousands of women she had comforted inside Newgate. One letter from a mistress in Hobart Town was written on behalf of a convict maid assigned her: "She begs I will offer her grateful recollection of your kindness, and that of the other Ladies, and hopes never to forfeit the good opinion you have been pleased to bestow upon her."[33] Reassured that her work made a difference, Mrs. Fry wanted Lady Jane to take up her cause.

Elizabeth had asserted hands-on influence in mainland Australia, which she planned to extend to Van Diemen's Land. Earlier in 1836, she sent Charlotte Anley, one of her volunteers, to inspect the conditions at the Parramatta Female Factory in New South Wales. The conditions she witnessed represented the more common experience for convict maids: "They told me of wrongs which no one heeded, or seemed to care for: that bad masters and cruel mistresses, often made them worse than they were; that in service they were treated 'like dogs,' and seldom spoken to without an oath, or 'as devils,' more than human beings."[34]

A convict lass couldn't escape an assignment unless she acted up. Three and a half months into her seven-year sentence, Agnes couldn't take her indentured servitude any longer. On March 22, 1837, Mr. Donahoo dragged #253 before the Hobart Town magistrate for being "absent without leave and insolent."[35] Immediately declared guilty, Agnes was returned to Cascades, the punishment factory. She was sentenced to three months in the Crime Class.

The most dreaded punishment came first. Mrs. Cato went to her drawer for a pair of scissors. The deputy matron's mood was stern when she approached the girl, whose grey eyes looked straight into hers. Not a word was spoken. The shears clipped across the nape of Agnes's neck and above her ear, cropping her hair like a boy's. Donning the cap of humiliation, Agnes would soon wear the color of disgrace. Mrs. Cato handed her a needle, thread, and yellow fabric cut in the shape of a "C," for "Crime Class."

Having seen the woman in the washing yard, Agnes knew what was coming next. Forced to confirm her degraded status stitch by stitch, she sewed three large yellow "C"s: one on her right jacket sleeve, another on the back, and a third on the hem of her petticoat. Displaying yellow, recognized as a color of infamy throughout Europe, she was meant to suffer shame and humiliation.

Dressed for the Crime Class, Agnes lumbered toward the washing yard, her assigned workstation for the next three months. Deputy Matron Cato delivered an armful of dirty clothes. The laundry she scrubbed from townspeople generated income for the prison and punished her for acting out. The hard stone tubs scraped her knuckles, the harsh soap stung bruises, and her bent shoulders and neck ached all the time. Agnes stood ankle-deep in water that seeped through her boots and her stockings. Beneath her boots, groundwater overflowed and formed deep pools in the yard. Agnes shivered in the shadows. Because Cascades was built on a rain-forest bog, drainage presented a chronic problem. Dampness crept over the floors and encased the stone walls, seeming to add yet another layer of impenetrability.

March's days began to shorten and confused the Scottish transport, unaccustomed to seasons that fell opposite to the ones she had always known. Early autumn had arrived in the Southern Hemisphere, condensing a thick layer of dew over the complex and delivering a chilling wind down the valley. As the days blurred one into another, the Goosedubbs Street girl began to look forward to the warmth of the Female Factory's ox-head soup. Dunking the brown bread up and down to soften the crust, she leaned on her elbow and held up her chin. The broth, reheated from the noon meal, tasted surprisingly good. Following the overseer appointed for her new group of twelve, Agnes sat on a hard chapel pew through another interminable sermon by the lisping and hissing Reverend Bedford. Back in the sleeping room, she settled into her hammock and pulled a thin blanket up around her chin. She tucked her legs in a fetal position trying to warm herself. Would she ever see Janet again?

It seemed like she had just closed her eyes when Agnes heard the ringing of the muster bell at six A.M., providing an extra half hour for sleep because of the autumn schedule. On her feet in the washing yard from sunrise until sunset, Agnes labored three months in Crime Class according to its rules and regulations. Back in the British Isles, King William IV had died on June 20, 1837, and Queen Victoria ascended the throne. Word of the colony's new queen did not reach Hobart Town until late October, the middle of spring in Van Diemen's Land.

While Victoria became accustomed to her new throne, Agnes

found herself in a cart riding away from Hobart and into the bush. In late June, Mr. Hutchinson decided to send the troublesome #253 out to Mr. Parker's farm, ordering that she was "not to be assigned to a town again."[36] Her red-haired friend was not faring much better. On August 12, 1837, a Mrs. Ray brought Janet before the magistrate for "disobedience of orders." After serving her sentence of three days in solitary confinement, on only bread and water, the eighteen-year-old maid was retrieved by her mistress.

Agnes's second assignment proved very rustic. While the eighteen-year-old Queen Victoria attended sumptuous state banquets, the grey-eyed Scot dined on what she deemed vermin. Her master called it kangaroo. The "roo" meat tasted gamy and tough, and she had to skin it before roasting. Cooking and cleaning, however, were the least of her worries. Never-ending wood chopping required her to brush away webs built by a wild assortment of spiders colored in red, green, and silver. At least their brilliant markings made them easy to spot. Lizards and frogs, on the other hand, blended into the forest and startled her every time she turned around. And the bloody serpents drove her mad.

Agnes had been warned about the poisonous snakes that killed horses, cattle, and sheep.[37] She found the hissing creatures coiled inside the cupboard, under the dining table, and inside the outhouse she was required to clean. Her disgust for reptiles was probably the only passion the Scottish rebel shared with the governor's wife. In her quest to civilize Van Diemen's Land, Lady Jane Franklin had offered a reward of one shilling for every snake killed. Over the course of a year, she soon discovered that the fourteen thousand bounties she paid made little impact on the quickly reproducing snake population.

Out in the pastoral rolling hills, Agnes lost track of days except for the monthly wagon ride into Hobart Town to attend Sunday services. She turned seventeen on September 11, 1837, with neither notice nor celebration. The grey-eyed girl had no privacy and rarely a day off. People made fun of her short hair and her accent. Lugging the mistress's chamber pots into the woods to be emptied, battling snakes, and fighting off loneliness, all of it was more than Agnes could tolerate. Once again, she walked off the job.

On November 3, Mr. Parker delivered his misbehaving servant to the Hobart Town court building. The magistrate pronounced Agnes guilty of "disobedience" and sentenced her to two months in the Cascades Crime Class. Trudging back up the hill toward the shaded morass, Agnes couldn't help but notice how beautiful Hobart Town looked in the spring, outfitted in lush shades of purple and green.

New residences, built by convict labor, had sprung up throughout the valley, each red brick labeled and numbered to confirm the prisoner's assigned quota. Imported roses, now in full bloom, tumbled over the painted white fences. Magpies and brightly feathered lorikeets fluttered over her path, and Agnes felt a warm breeze blowing up from the River Derwent. If her presence in Van Diemen's Land had not been born of punishment, she might have relished this beautiful island, where she breathed the cleanest air on earth. For today, she was assaulted with the stink of the sewers as she approached the top of the town, along with the stone washtubs she knew were waiting for her.

The routine at Cascades was familiar, though no less humiliating, for the troublemaker known as #253. Brow furrowed, Mrs. Cato produced her scissors, clipped Agnes's hair once again, and handed her more yellow "C"s. Bloody hell, back to the washtubs she lumbered. Highly attuned to her surroundings from years on city streets, Agnes spotted a young woman whose eyes sparkled with fiery passion. It was the legendary Ellen Scott, the queen of troublemakers. Queen Victoria ruled the empire, but Ellen Scott ruled the Crime Class.

A native of Limerick, Ireland, Ellen was sentenced to transport for life because she had stolen a watch chain and had been arrested before on vagrancy charges. A hero among the Female Factory women, she affronted and provoked the Reverend William Bedford when he least expected it. Nicknamed "Holy Willie" by the prisoners, Bedford was charged with raising moral standards for the colony. Perhaps the biggest hypocrite ever to step foot inside Cascades, he was despised bitterly by the women for forcing himself on many of them. An impostor of all sorts, he had no theological training, though he'd received an honorary degree. Holy Willie was a married man, the father of two sons and a daughter, but that didn't stop him from taking advantage of the women he was supposed to guide and protect. The self-important hypocrite was the first voice they heard in the morning and the last at night.

In October 1833, Ellen delivered her own message to the lecherous, grinning, always supercilious preacher. Her cheeky response to another condescending lecture was the ultimate working-class insult. The petite Irish prisoner turned around in her pew, lifted her skirt, and, wearing no undergarments, loudly slapped her bare behind. She was charged with "indecent behavior during the performance of divine service" and sentenced to an additional two months in Crime Class, commencing with thirty days in solitary confinement.[38]

Ellen was a charter member of the Flash Mob, a Crime Class subculture named for "flash" language, or the jargon of thieves. The now notorious Flash Mob reveled in tormenting their captors at every opportunity. They took special pride in "debagging" Holy Willie as he waddled down the chapel steps, where "some dozen or twenty women seized upon him, took off his trousers and deliberately endeavoured to deprive him of his manhood. They were, however, unable to effect their purpose in consequence of the opportune arrival of a few constables who seized the fair ladies."[39]

The wash yard was a school of sorts. Under the corrupt tutelage of the cleverest, most resourceful women she'd ever met, #253 learned many tricks that undermined their captors' control. With the help of their mates, prisoners retrieved locks of shorn hair from the trash. Weaving the strands together and placing them strategically under the gathered prison caps, the crafty lasses created the illusion of a full head of hair.

In the dark of the night, the Flash Mob dressed for merriment, silk scarves saucily tied over their heads, earrings dangling fashionably, sparkling rings displayed on their fingers. Thriving underground trade provided the means to decorate their bland uniforms with forbidden ornaments. After the Hutchinsons retired for the evening, a new society took hold, and the Mob set the rules. Sneaking out the front entrance posed little challenge. Cascades guards, easily bribed with rum or coins, let the women slip into town, where they danced with abandon at a rowdy tavern of their choice. According to a male convict who arrived shortly after Agnes, "the 'tip,' it was said, was taken by every government officer in the colony, from the governor down to scavenger, and was what, in civilian countries is called bribery."[40]

Trafficking and illicit commerce between turnkeys and prisoners enabled the women to purchase food, tea, tobacco, sugar, and liquor. The Mob broke even the unwritten rules, defying strict Victorian notions concerning sexuality. Some, including Ellen Scott, were punished for an "unnatural connexion" with another woman, although Ellen later married a freed male convict.

Both fearful of and fascinated by the Flash Mob, the local press described "women, who, by a simple process of initiation, are admitted into a series of unhallowed mysteries, similar, in many respects, to those which are described by Göethe, in his unrivalled Drama of *Faust*. . . . Like those abominable *Saturnalia*, they are performed in the dark and silent hour of night, but, unlike those, they are performed in solitude and secrecy, amongst only the duly initiated. With the fiendish fondness for sin, every effort, both in the Factory, and out of it, is made by these wretches, to acquire proselytes to their infamous practices . . ."[41]

The advantages amassed by members of the Flash Mob were later revealed in testimony by a Cascades prisoner assigned work as a guard: "I was once turnkey over the Crime Class and used to sell and buy on my own account Tobacco, Tea, Sugar, Meat etc. Two women after Muster were released, by me or by Mrs. Hutchinson's servants, from the Cells as I managed to abstract the keys I wanted and we were supplied from over the Wall with what we wanted."[42]

This sturdy Crime Class subculture, founded on rebellion and solidarity, managed better food, new clothing, and more merriment. The Cascades rebels drank, smoked, talked all night, played cards, exchanged ribald jokes, and put on elaborate theatrics that mocked the authorities. They danced in the moonlight, pretending to be goddesses at the base of Mt. Wellington, and they belted out bawdy songs night after night.

Many were punished for singing obscene lyrics. Others found protection in this rebellious sisterhood of solidarity and devised a myriad of schemes to try the pious patience of Matron Hutchinson. In one well-practiced stunt, the rebels sang at the top of their lungs. The minute they heard the matron's heavy steps, their chorus fell silent. By the time Mrs. Hutchinson returned to her housing on the second floor of Cascades, the musical entertainment commenced all over again. Testifying before an inquiry into convict discipline, Mrs. Hutchinson admitted: "Their songs are sometimes very disgusting. They leave off when they know I am coming. When they do not (which is sometimes the case in a wet night when they do not hear my foot on the pavement) I turn out the whole ward till I get at the woman whom I send to a cell."[43]

Agnes met members of the Flash Mob as she toiled along the washtubs. As a new arrival to the Crime Class, she may have been recruited into their fold, because the Mob would have welcomed the young Scot's musical talent and her feisty disposition. After serving the second of her eventual twelve trips back to the Crime Class, Agnes was released in early January 1838 at summer's peak in Van Diemen's Land.

For eight months, she dutifully fulfilled her sentence until returned by her new master on September 8 for "refusing to return to her service."[44] She was sentenced to ten days on bread and water.

Three days later, Agnes spent her eighteenth birthday in solitary confinement, branded yet again with yellow letters on her clothing. Recalling her days in the mill, she'd spent the morning picking oakum, pulling apart coarse rope so that the recycled fibers could be used to caulk ships like the *Westmoreland*. Handed a hunk of bread and a bowl of water for dipping, she eagerly put aside the work assignment that had already bloodied her hands.

As she sat in a cell barely bigger than a coffin, Agnes cursed the captors who could never extinguish her spunk. Surprisingly, she found a small benefit in solitary confinement. The tiny opening to the outside was covered with iron grates but was wide enough to let in shades of light and shadows. Deprived of human contact, her senses became acute. She listened for the yellow wattlebirds and the kookaburra's laughing call. She fingered the greyish-brown stone that never warmed to the touch. Assaulted by the disgusting stench from waste flowing next to her cell and into the rivulet, Agnes vowed to make it through the night. There was no other choice as she closed her eyes. Like heavy shadows in a jungle, blackness arrived in layers and lulled her into sleep.

Upon release from her solitary cell, Mr. Hutchinson assigned Agnes to a Mr. Harvey. The untamable lass was soon found "out after hours" and returned to Cascades for six additional days on bread and water. When Superintendent Hutchinson sent her back to Mr. Harvey, she immediately escalated her behavior, taking his two children on an excursion without permission. Agnes didn't hurt the wee ones, who seemed to enjoy her company, but the magistrate was not amused. He sentenced her to one month in Crime Class, beginning with six more days on bread and water.

When Governor Arthur set the rules for solitary confinement, he had assumed that hunger would tame and temper a rebel like Agnes. In fact, malnutrition produced the opposite effect, rendering emotions more difficult to contain and increasing the likelihood that she would lash out with hostile confusion. Many girls and women imprisoned at

Cascades broke under the stress and fell prey to the ills of depression, alcoholism, or madness.

Agnes turned more defiant with every return to the Female Factory. She and many of her cohorts quickly figured out the loopholes created by a high demand for maids and laborers. When she needed a break from service, she acted out, a pattern she would follow for her entire sentence. Seizing the upper hand and shifting the balance of power in her favor, she turned the tables on her captors. With every scrub of dirty drawers in the washtub, every mouthful of watery gruel, every chopping of her hair, Agnes McMillan willed herself to live for the day she walked free. Rather than breaking her, her captors made her stronger. Never remorseful yet ever hopeful, she remained open to what tomorrow would bring. At this point, there was little more they could take from her.

Agnes walked away from the assignment that followed Mr. Harvey's. On December 7, 1838, she appeared before a now-familiar magistrate. He sentenced her to two months' hard labor at the washtub and solitary confinement at night. Agnes would soon discover what a holiday blessing this proved to be. And her future would hold a series of surprising coincidences. As she glanced back toward the hills around Hobart Town, she had no way of knowing that, half a world away, someone she'd never met would influence both her life and Janet's at the prison nursery on Liverpool Street.

⋙ 6 ⋘

Ludlow's Choice

The Widow and the Barrister

Clickety-click, clickety-click. A slight matron, just over five feet tall, scurried across the cobblestone lane in the well-groomed residential neighborhood known as Bloomsbury.

On the first day of December 1838, Ludlow Tedder's pursed lips bore her trademark press of determination. As London's morning sun filtered through the "pea soup" fog, her wooden heels echoed off the tiny lane she now called home. The woman with hazel eyes and dark brown hair quickened her steps down Keppel Street and lifted her skirt, trying to avoid the gooey sludge splashing over her boots whenever a carriage passed. One hundred tons of horse manure dropped in the streets each day, and Mrs. Tedder didn't want to clean one more thing.[1] It was but nine o'clock in the morning, and she'd already scrubbed floors, cleaned grates, and polished furniture. The widow worked as a servant in the city's chic center, where middle-class professionals lived in terraced Georgian town houses adorned with lacy grillwork.

Hours before sunup, the forty-five-year-old had swept soot from the front steps, lit the fireplaces, and prepared the daily soup for Fitzowen Skinner and his wife, Laura. At five thirty in the morning, the mother of four shook her nineteen-year-old awake from dreams of silk dresses and handsome suitors, pulling her sleepy frame upright onto the damp basement floor. Eliza, her adopted daughter from her husband's unmarried sister, had been hired as a maid-of-all-work in the Skinner residence. Ludlow's youngest, eight-year-old Arabella, could sleep a bit longer. It was best for her not to be underfoot with so much to be done. Besides, talking was not allowed below stairs, and sometimes Arabella needed reminding that they were to speak only in their "under voices."

Already Arabella had been taught her place. There was no laughing permitted for those who lived belowground in the servants' quarters. She and her mother shared a straw-stuffed mattress in the scullery adjoining the kitchen. Eliza slept on a quilt atop a wooden pallet, where mildew was a chronic problem. It invaded the tiny room in a constant assault on Ludlow's bedding, on her hairbrush, and on the cotton apron tied around her waist. Yesterday's grease clung to the stone walls like a sticky veneer. A single tallow candle shed a band of light, illuminating the relentless patrol of black beetles and cockroaches crawling over the walls and across the kitchen floor. Smoky coal fumes crept down the narrow stairs from the dining room, where Ludlow lit the first fire of the day.

The essence of Ludlow's station was captured in the words of Eliza Lynn Linton, who also lived in nineteenth-century London and was among the first women to earn a living as a journalist: "When harshly spoken to she must have only the soft answers which are said to turn away wrath. When fretted, nervous, ill, in trouble, she must wear the same smooth manner, the same placid face. . . . She must abandon every personal affection and the outward show of all personal desires when she enters this cold stranger's house."[2]

The moment Ludlow accepted the position in the thirty-year-old barrister's household, she surrendered her private life. The no-nonsense widow had grown accustomed to the strict demarcation drawn between employer and maid. Practical and clever, she quickly honed the skills required for the part of obedient servant, exhibiting just the right calibration of deference and devotion. Careful not to wake the master and mistress, mother and daughter plunged into their sixteen-hour day. As senior housekeeper, Ludlow was also Eliza's supervisor and didn't hesitate to remind her about lighting the kitchen stove and heating water for the barrister's shave.

Ludlow attacked the early-morning tasks in earnest. Down on all fours, she brushed the carpets by hand, cleaning a few inches at a time. Then it was back to the kitchen to awaken Arabella before kneading dough for the breakfast rolls she would later serve with jam and tea. Since Ludlow's arrival in London nine months ago, the diligent head servant had acquired a knack for anticipating her twenty-nine-year-old mistress's every need. From the second floor, a steady jingle of the bell alerted Ludlow to the family's imminent arrival in the dining room.

While the Skinners sipped tea, Eliza toted hot water up two flights of stairs to their bedrooms. She retrieved their chamber pots and emptied them in a cesspit next to the garden. During the day, the pots were stored in a dining room sideboard. For the middle class, this was eminently superior to the single privy shared by more than a hundred people in London's working-class neighborhoods.

Cleaning box tucked under her arm, Eliza trundled upstairs to scrub the barrister's bedroom fireplace. After sweeping out ashes and cinders from the spent fire, any coal residue stuck to the grates had to be rubbed off with brick dust or sanded smooth with scouring paper. Finally, the fireplace was polished with oily black lead to prevent rust. Only after the hearth was properly prepared was Eliza allowed to run back down the stairs to the basement, fill the coal scuttle, and lug it up the two flights to the master's bedroom. She would repeat this grungy process at the dining room hearth.

Arabella, too, was expected to pitch in with the interminable chores. Among other duties, she polished silverware, broke the lump sugar into small pieces, and folded the laundry. While living in Chelmsford, Ludlow had taught each of her children to read and write. Knowing her letters had proved an invaluable asset when her husband died. Her ability to read and keep household accounts had spared her the fate of millwork. Still, even a literate widow had few options for employment. She certainly wanted more for Arabella.

Monday through Friday, the eight-year-old could attend a "Dame School." Typically run by an elderly woman at a cost of three or four pennies a week, it was the cheapest education available to the working class. Students age two to fifteen were taught reading and writing in a crowded parlor. The youngest were enrolled primarily for child care while their parents worked, making for a rather disruptive classroom. Amid the chaos, Arabella could keep up with her reading as well as learn to sew and knit. Girls were taught these useful skills to make them employable by the time they turned nine or ten.

Ludlow considered little else than trying to make ends meet while she dusted rows and rows of porcelain bric-a-brac calling for her attention from their mahogany shelves. Next on the list was the boiling of the barrister's shirts, pants, and drawers. Stinging lye soap had to be applied by hand, as scrubbing clothes in hot water was the only way to get them clean. On the heels of wringing out her master's wool flannel drawers, she climbed up on a stool to wash coal grime from the stained-glass fanlight above the front door. The cleaning never seemed to end.

Ludlow did her best to maintain a tidy appearance, just as she had in her country home in Chelmsford. The prim matron washed her uniform in the kitchen sink at least once a week. She removed the heavy apron that protected her print dress and allowed herself a quick glance in the oversized mirror above the mantel. Eight months on the job and the maid's collar still scratched annoyingly at her neck. The overstarched white doily stuck at permanent attention, tickling her chin as she finished with breakfast and prepared to go to market. For the sake of her youngest child, Mrs. Tedder tolerated the ridiculous rules of etiquette a proper maid was expected to obey. Thankfully, on this day she needn't suffer the indignity of walking several paces behind her mistress or delivering misplaced items on a silver salver, the type of tray used to present objects before royalty.

Looking neat and clean wasn't enough to disguise Ludlow's station, despite her contrast to the unwashed figures skulking about in London's underbelly. She was missing the accoutrements that would adorn an upper-class lady, including a feather-trimmed bonnet, satin muff, pink silk flounce sleeves, and fringed parasol. Furthermore, women of a certain means rarely wandered the metropolis unless accompanied by a gentleman chaperone.

The hardworking mother threw a shawl over her shoulders and ventured out into the December cold. With hair parted in the middle and pulled back in a severe bun, her high forehead and long face carried the imprint of family tragedy. Still, she looked much younger than her forty-five years. Her mahogany hair showed not a touch of grey, and her cheeks were covered with freckles. On this busy Saturday, she planned to squeeze in an additional stop. Ludlow needed to finish the Skinners' shopping with all possible speed so that nothing would seem amiss.

The Bells of Chelmsford

Ludlow's slim frame carefully maneuvered the mist as she made her way through London's yellowish haze. This infamous soup came from coal fires mixed with the stinging residue from paper mills, tanneries, and breweries. Everyone around her was coughing, and no matter how tightly she held her breath, she could not stop herself from hacking up the coal dust lodged in her throat. Water might have soothed her were it not for its brown tinge and rancid taste from overflowing privies and factory waste. Her mob cap, the small gathered muslin hat worn by servants, would not stay white for long. On the streets of London, anything light-colored turned shades of grey within minutes. At this time of year, the thick pollution caused such low visibility that lamps were lit inside homes during the day.

With barely an hour to complete her errands, Ludlow slipped through the fog. Visibility was often so poor that she could stretch her arms out and not see her fingertips.[3] She kept close to the stone buildings and counted the gas lamps, making her way toward the butcher shop to purchase a mutton chop, sweetbreads, bacon, and beef. Despite an increased availability of fruits and vegetables, meat was the preferred food for most Victorians and filled several courses for the evening meal.

Though she had no time off, save two or three hours on Sunday, errands allowed the dedicated mother to steal a few moments for herself. These past five years, she'd done little more than scrimp and save, trying to preserve a semblance of her former family life. After her husband, John, died, she'd worked in vain to hold on to their little cottage on Slades Lane in Chelmsford, just thirty-two miles northeast of London. Now it seemed a world away.

Ludlow and John had married twenty-five years before on May 14, 1813, at the All Saints Church in Maldon, a small town ten miles east of Chelmsford. Just twenty on her wedding day, the young bride walked through the church's arched stone entrance and stood beside her future husband. John's siblings had sprinkled the tiles with spring blossoms to ensure a happy union. Ribbons of gold, sapphire, purple, and deep green shone through the stained-glass window in the Friday morning light. As Ludlow and John joined hands under the ornately carved oak choir screen, five bells tolled from the church's seven-hundred-year-old unique triangular tower.

Rather than spending earnings on elaborate nuptials, the working class put aside funds for proper funerals. A bride did not always wear white, choosing instead a Sunday frock in pastel pink or blue, crowned with a wreath of wildflowers. Grooms wore a frock coat of mulberry or claret, often borrowed, with a flower in the lapel. Following the ceremony, family members served the couple a breakfast of fruitcake covered in white frosting. After the celebratory repast, the groom usually went to work to avoid losing a day's pay.

There was a pressing reason the young couple had decided to marry. Four months later on September 22, John and Ludlow returned to the All Saints Church to baptize a son, John Bulley. Daughter Frances was born in 1816, followed by namesake baby Ludlow in 1818. The Tedders expanded their brood to four when they adopted their niece Eliza from John's sister, who had fallen on hard times. Life was about as stable as it could be for a working-class family. They'd moved to Chelmsford, a prosperous market town, situated on two transport rivers, with well-stocked shops and busy taverns. Like Ludlow, John was literate and held a steady job as an ostler who groomed horses at an inn. His wife, born Ludlow Stammers on July 28, 1793, grew up in a working-class family in Southminster, Essex. Her parents were ahead of their time and ensured that their daughter was literate. Ludlow, in turn, did her best to pass this skill on to each of her children.

After ten years of comfortable family life, tragedy struck the Tedder clan. At age seven, oldest daughter Frances fell ill. She likely suffered from measles or scarlet fever. The illness quickly overwhelmed the little girl, who passed away on August 10, 1823. The grieving parents prepared to bury their daughter in the village plot. On a warm August Sunday, the bells in the All Saints Church tolled thirteen times for their beloved Frances. In rural communities, "passing bells" were rung for those close to death, six times for females and nine for men, with an additional peal for each year lived. The hollow sound of the death knell reverberated across the village green. As people started to count, the brevity of peals alerted the town that it had lost another child.[4] During the first half of the nineteenth century, nearly half of Britain's children died before their tenth birthday.

Nothing was more important than a proper church burial, even if it depleted a family's savings. As was tradition, their daughter's body was kept at home until it was time to bury her. The Tedders drew their curtains closed, and family members gathered around for an informal wake and prayer. A neighbor's wagon slowed to a stop by their front door, and the family tied white "love ribbons" along its sides.[5] John held Frances's coffin steady for the solemn ride to the cemetery. Frances would be laid to rest in an elm casket painted white. She wore a white dress and was covered in a white shroud. The family, too, dressed in white, including ten-year-old John Bulley, five-year-old Ludlow, and four-year-old Eliza. At the end of the service, the church bells tolled one last time for Frances, alerting the parish that she had been laid safely to rest.

The day after the funeral, Ludlow, like so many grieving mothers, brought the tailor a light-colored dress to be dyed black. John wore a simple black armband. All but the destitute followed a prescribed period of mourning, one year for a child, two for a husband. Ludlow wore her black mourning dress every day well into 1824.

Six more years passed as the Tedders raised eleven-year-old Eliza and their two biological children: John Bulley, now seventeen, and Ludlow, now twelve. In September 1830, they were all quite surprised when new life entered the cottage with the birth of Arabella. Sadly, the youngest Tedder barely had a chance to know her father. She had just turned three when John passed away in November 1833. He was forty-two years old, about the average life expectancy for a man living in the country. Working-class city dwellers generally died even younger, before turning forty, many felled by epidemics. John passed away at a time when Chelmsford suffered a cholera outbreak, and that may well have killed him. Ludlow, a new widow and mother of four, buried her husband next to their departed daughter as the bells in the churchyard tolled a final farewell. They had been married for twenty years.

For the next two years, Arabella saw her mother dress only in black. Ludlow, like most widows, wore a bracelet she made from plaited strands of her husband's hair. Gradually the recovering widow began to don a light-colored bonnet or scarf until she felt comfortable enough to put on a dress of grey or purple. Living in the country, Ludlow was offered more support than those in the city, who had fallen upon hard times. Villagers often took up collections to help widows who needed time to find work and figure out how to survive on their own. The mother of four rejected the prospect of moving into a workhouse. There she would be separated from her children, and they, too, would be conscripted into hard labor. As for the future, widows rarely remarried because of a shortage of eligible men, most of whom died earlier than their female counterparts.

Widow Tedder continued to pay her rent with the help of her two oldest children. Later on, when John Bulley and daughter Ludlow approached their twenties and started their own families, the widow had no choice but to move. Like nearly half of Britain's population, she chose London, believing it offered the best prospects for steady work. Her ability to read job listings in a newspaper offered Ludlow a supreme advantage. Servants were hired by ads in the paper, through a servants' registry office, or by word of mouth.

Ludlow had worked as a cook before her marriage, and in March 1838 she arrived at 25 Keppel Street with references in hand. Although well beyond the average age for new staff, the widow was hired because she could write a grocery list and maintain household accounts. Barrister Skinner compensated her with room and board along with a small allowance, from which he deducted the cost of feeding Arabella. Ludlow might not be able to get ahead on her wages, but she could at least count on food and shelter for herself and her two youngest children.

Despite working seven days a week, Ludlow's pay was not enough to make ends meet. Even as an experienced cook, she earned only forty pence for every one hundred that a man took home, even though the work of female servants was often more physical. Like most cooks, Ludlow supplemented her earnings by selling leftover fat drippings. Tenement families spread it on bread or used it to flavor potatoes and provide extra calories for their children. Today she delivered a small tin to a stall vendor, who handed her a few pence in return. Still, Mrs. Tedder was caught short. Candles and soap, along with clothing and milk for Arabella, cost more than she earned.

Arabella needed leather shoes and a wool cap for the walk to school. She wore a pinafore to keep her one dress clean and a wool cloak that doubled as her blanket at night. Adherence to unwritten rules of modesty was expected from all classes save the homeless. Young girls were required to cover their legs with pantalettes should a gust of wind lift the skirt that fell just below her knees. Arabella's were sewn from simple white linen, unlike the frilly silk versions worn by wealthy girls under dresses of velvet and lace.

Ludlow consistently practiced the eleventh commandment: Do whatever it takes to provide for your child. As her situation grew more desperate, she resorted to small dishonesties just to get by. Never had she expected to be a thief, and she convinced herself it was only temporary until she could get back on her feet. Like any mother, she had fears about her children's future, alongside dreams of advancing their station. For the present, such dreams were cast aside in favor of the barrister's needs.

Because there was no refrigeration in 1838, Mrs. Tedder shopped for fresh provisions every day of the week. Today was no different. The din of the marketplace rose ever louder as Ludlow distanced herself farther from Keppel Street and entered the gritty world where most Londoners dwelled. She jostled her way through the hanging carcasses of cattle, sheep, and pigs to make her purchases. Dogs barked and hawkers argued over the price of beef. Beggars pleaded for a copper halfpenny. Fishmonger carts rattled through the alley, clearing the path of pigeons, rats, and flies.

After selecting a mutton leg, beef filet, and larded sweetbreads for the Skinners, she purchased eggs, milk, and butter for the rice pudding she often served with dinner. In a few weeks, she'd be buying figs, almonds, and ribbon candy for the Skinners' holiday guests and preparing the goose and the brandy pudding. On this Saturday, vendors hawked Christmas wares, especially the Advent candle wreaths families lit beginning the first Sunday in December. The wreaths were displayed on dining tables and illuminated with four candles, three purple and one pink, signifying the season's hope and glory.

For the thrifty Ludlow, a fresh tallow candle might do. Gifts were rarely exchanged among the poor unless handmade. Children like Arabella didn't expect a Christmas package and were delighted if they received a handknit scarf or a pair of gloves.

Even though it was only December 1, the pawnshops were already decorated with boughs of evergreen garland tied with red ribbon. Blurry images behind dingy glass displayed valuables from the rich, abandoned through bad luck or filched by the ragged. Silver boxes, gold watches, lace handkerchiefs, jeweled brooches, and silk scarves lay in loose disorder and out of place inside the musty storefront. Among the scattered finery lay treasures less grand, which had been given up by the laboring poor: a pair of children's boots, a plain wedding ring, a man's threadbare overcoat, a family Bible, and housewares of every sort. All matter of irretrievable ill fortune stocked the overfull shelves.

The economics of shop trade were painfully simple, as described in signs above the door: "Money advanced on plate, jewels, wearing apparel, and every description of property."[6] London's underground economy pulsed through the heavily trafficked pawnshops that marked the edge of a deep chasm between abundance and struggle.

Earlier that week, Ludlow had pocketed a few pence advanced for some spoons she'd left at John Wentworth's pawnshop. Over the past few months, she supplemented her income by occasionally slipping a piece of silverware into her dress pocket. The petite cook didn't expect to make much from the items she'd "borrowed" from the house on this Saturday morning. But it might be enough to cover family expenses, with perhaps a little left for a small bottle of gin for herself. Surely Barrister Skinner could do without a few spoons when there were so many he barely touched.

Mrs. Tedder was well familiar with the doorway marked by three hanging balls. She popped in from the fog and headed straight to the counter. Mr. Wentworth barely looked up to see what misfortune had blown through his door. He'd seen it all and never asked questions. Stepping up to the dusty display case, the determined widow pulled a little bundle from under her cape and unwrapped two spoons and a bread basket. Mr. Wentworth leaned over the countertop and examined what was brought to him. After a bit of polite bargaining, in contrast to transactions typically more heated or pleading, they settled on payment of a few shillings. Mr. Wentworth made out numbered tickets and issued her "duplicates," as pawn slips were called. Lifting her chin in the air, Mrs. Tedder straightened her skirt, pivoted on her heels, and headed back toward Keppel Street.

Back in the smoky cellar kitchen, Ludlow set down her groceries and put the receipts in a glass storage jar, where they would stay dry for the weekly accounting. The position of cook offered tempting opportunities to skim a bit off household accounts. Tenuous loyalty offered ready justification for stealing from what was viewed as a master's cornucopia of riches. An article in *Nineteenth Century* described the perspective of those who lived below stairs: "They are connected with the wealthier classes principally as ministering to their material well-being. . . . No people contemplate so frequently and so strikingly the unequal distribution of wealth: they fold up dresses whose price contains double the amount of their year's wages; they pour out at dinner wine whose cost would have kept a poor family for weeks."[7]

For the present, Ludlow concentrated on carving gristle off the meats, peeling potatoes, and beating eggs for the boiled rice pudding. Pounding spices and stoning raisins were the next tasks awaiting her attention. Already eight hours on her feet, she was halfway through her shift. Not a minute was left idle. She mended linens and scrubbed the sheets white while pots simmered on the coal-fired stove.

As the maid-of-all-work, daughter Eliza was charged with emptying Master Skinner's spittoon and polishing his boots. Mixing turpentine and wax, she made her own polishes. After her mother served the meals, she plunged her arms into hot greasy water and scoured the pots and dishes piled high from lunch and dinner. Harsh washing soda stung her hands and reddened them beyond their nineteen years. Arabella was tasked with wiping the dinnerware dry and stacking it neatly in the china closet.

In London, one-third of young women between fifteen and twenty worked in domestic service.[8] Marriage offered the preferred route of escape from the basement servant quarters. Officially excluded from social interaction, other than opening the door for the occasional delivery, Eliza faced scant opportunity to meet potential suitors. Servants were allowed no visitors and were rarely given a day off. If a young lass somehow managed an admirer, she would have met him in secret, slipping out of the house as the others slept.

In her magazine article "On the Side of the Maids," Eliza Lynn Linton describes the lonely frustration girls like Eliza Tedder experienced: "No friends in the kitchen, no laughing to be heard above stairs, no romping for young girls to whom romping is an instinct all the same as with lambs and kittens . . . moping in the dreary kitchen on the afternoon of her Sunday in. All grinding work claustral monotony, with the world seen only through the gratings of the area window as the holiday folks flock to and fro . . ."[9]

The end of the day was finally nearing for the downstairs staff. On her hands and knees, an exhausted Eliza scoured the sticky mix of grease and soot stuck to the kitchen floor. When the upstairs hall clock chimed eleven, mother and daughter bedded down next to the scullery sink, where Arabella lay fast asleep. Ludlow recounted the coins received from Mr. Wentworth and tucked them into a small pouch pinned to the inside of her bodice.

The Case of the Missing Plate

After his three-course dinner Saturday evening, Master Skinner walked to the sideboard and poured himself a glass of port. Perhaps he was suspicious of his staff, because it was not uncommon for servants to pilfer from their employers. For whatever reason, this was the night he noticed forks and spoons missing from his silver drawer. In the household hierarchy, the maid-of-all-work was responsible for care of utensils and plates. Early Sunday morning, the agitated Barrister rang for Eliza and asked the whereabouts of the missing silverware. At this time, the nineteen-year-old may not have known her mother was the culprit.

Eliza must have felt desperate. She knew that a conviction for theft meant gaol at best and more probably transport to the other side of the world. When pressed by the barrister, she didn't even try to cover for the mother who had adopted her and who had unintentionally put her in great peril. Perhaps she felt frustration over her lot in life and miserable job, or anger with her mother for drawing her into this entanglement. Given her daunting workload, she might have lost hold of reason and simply lashed out at a supervisor who was also her parent. Whatever Eliza's motivation for informing on her mother, a furious Fitzowen Skinner confronted his cook. Ludlow immediately confessed her transgression, handed him the duplicates, and offered to retrieve the pawned cutlery from Mr. Wentworth first thing Monday morning. The barrister's response was clear as he uttered the words, "Justice must take its course."[10] A sense of dread permeated the remainder of the Sabbath.

When she found free moments, Ludlow had scanned the barrister's discarded newspapers that lay scattered across the upstairs parlor. The *Times* and the *Morning Herald* posted accounts about women convicted of stealing household items who were punished with transport to Van Diemen's Land. The worried mother knew it wasn't just her own future at stake. She shuddered at the thought of Arabella in a London orphanage. Who would care for her? But staying together meant gaol for her little girl, or possibly transport. Could they even survive the sea voyage?

Ludlow had lost her gamble, and she couldn't blame Eliza. At least the poor girl was old enough to be on her own. Sometime during the morning of Monday, December 3, 1838, a distraught Ludlow crept out of the maid's quarters at 25 Keppel Street, fearing an imminent arrest. With Arabella in tow, she hustled through the gardens in fashionable Russell Square. With Christmas barely three weeks away, Bloomsbury town houses were adorned with spruce boughs draped above the doorway and around the railings. Pinecone wreaths, decorated with scarlet holly berries and dried fruit, hung from ribbons on the front doors.

Holiday merriment was the last thing on Ludlow's mind. On the run with her eight-year-old, she lacked the street skills Agnes and Janet had relied on for food and shelter those many nights in Glasgow. With little money in her possession, choices were few. Perhaps they stayed with friends or relatives, moving from place to place every night or two so as not to get caught. Mother and daughter couldn't stay in one location very long because harboring a fugitive might endanger those who, out of kindness, had provided a temporary safe haven.

For nine days, the pair somehow managed to remain in hiding and elude arrest by London's bobbies. The widow from the country had lived in the city only nine months and rarely navigated London's seamy street circus. Options for a bed for the night quickly wore thin. As what little money she had started to run out, Ludlow pondered the prospect of begging on the street in the midst of one of the coldest winters on record.

She was probably searching for a boardinghouse when a bobby wearing an oilskin cape grabbed her by the arm. On Tuesday, December 11, 1838, he delivered the still neatly dressed servant for processing at the Bow Street station house. This was the first stop for prisoners who would be tried in London's Central Criminal Court, also known as the Old Bailey, for the street on which it is located. Mrs. Tedder was ordered to appear before Judge Baron Parke the week before Christmas. There would be no cooking of the holiday goose this year. For the next eight days, she awaited trial in a Newgate holding cell with Arabella as well as dozens of women accused of various crimes.

The following Wednesday, the nineteenth of December, police officer Richard Lesley ushered mother and child into a packed Central Criminal Court. The wind whistled across the courtroom. Although it was the middle of winter, the windows were wide open because officials feared catching diseases from the prisoners. As the accused approached the bench, jurisprudence seldom smelled sweet. "Juries, counsel and judges chewed on garlic, citrus peel, cardamom and caraway to prevent infection from the prisoners' breath."[11]

Property owners, all men, formed the grand jury that would decide Ludlow's fate. After swearing them in, Judge Parke rambled on about the common law of England, liberty, and morality under the reign of Her Majesty Queen Victoria. It was the kind of public spectacle that appealed to sordid sensibilities. The court's galleries were filled with the curious, who paid a small fee to catch a view of the upper-crust jury, but "what they were really waiting for was the thrill of seeing felons in irons stumble up from the gaol and tell their stories."[12] It was all a rather tedious affair until the accused entered the front of the courtroom to stand behind the bar of a raised platform known as "the dock." Once the court officer motioned the gallery into silence, the sound of light footsteps resonated through the drafty hall. Unless a female spectator attended the session, Ludlow would have been the only woman in the room.

The accused stood alone under a sounding board used to amplify her voice from the prisoner's dock.[13] Herbs lay strewn across the ledge before her as a means of disinfecting whatever the prisoners touched. There were no public defenders, so only the affluent were guaranteed legal counsel.

Mrs. Tedder stepped forward to raise her manacled hand before the clerk, who asked: "How will you be tried?" She replied as she'd been told at the police station: "By God and by my country."[14] As was tradition, a visibly bored Judge Baron Parke inquired, "Have you any witnesses that will speak to your character?" The only answer that might have conveyed a lighter sentence was: "Yes, sir, I have a letter from my vicar speaking to my good character." Without that, there was no hope for her acquittal. Ludlow was doomed.

The prisoner stood directly before her accuser. Barrister Skinner was the first to rise from the witness box. With well-practiced intonation and outrage, the professional member of the bar testified: "The prisoner was in my service as cook since March last. I missed fourteen forks and eleven silver spoons, on Saturday night, the 1st of December, after the prisoner and her daughter were gone to bed. Her daughter had the charge of the plate, but she had access to it. On the Sunday night her daughter came to me, and said her mother would drive her mad. I went down into the kitchen, and asked the prisoner what was the matter. She [Ludlow] said it was about the plate that was missing. I asked her where it was. She said she had pawned it, but she would get it back on Monday morning. I had said nothing to induce her to confess."[15]

When pawnbroker Wentworth took the stand, Ludlow knew she was done for. His testimony was short and damning: "I have a bread basket, pawned on the first of December by the prisoner. This is the duplicate I gave for it. I have also eleven spoons, pawned by her at different times."[16]

As Christmas approached, judges were sometimes inspired by the season of giving and imposed lighter sentences. The majority administered "justice" with casual indifference and were not held to consistency in punishment guidelines. Ludlow's luck had run out. Judge Parke was not inclined to be merciful. Neither was the jury. The Crown demanded efficiency, so trials were conducted at lightning speed. Most sentences were preordained. On average, it took eight and a half minutes to go from accused to condemned.[17] Once the evidence was presented, the all-male jury didn't even bother to leave the courtroom. They huddled together and went through the motions of conferring from their box. In truth, many jurors cared very little about the law and simply followed the foreman's judgment. Some read newspapers during the proceedings, while others dozed politely, with their chins resting on stiffened shirt collars.

The foreman for the third jury announced a swift verdict for Ludlow Tedder: "Guilty. Stealing on the first of December two spoons, value one shilling, and one bread basket, value ten shillings, the goods of Fitzowen Skinner, her master."[18] With a resounding thump of his gavel, Judge Parke pronounced the sentence: "Transported for Ten Years." Amid the public buzz from the galleries, he took a moment and adjusted the great white wig that fell clumsily over his shoulders. But what was to be done with the child? Perhaps because it was nearly Christmas, Judge Parke informed Ludlow she would be allowed to take Arabella with her. She looked at her little girl and signed her name on the Sessions Papers. At least they would be together.

A Newgate Christmas

British justice was a hodgepodge of haphazard sentencing that thrived on corruption, prejudice, incompetence, and bribery. On the streets, the police were commonly in cahoots with the criminals. A cash payoff or sexual favor often bought a look in the other direction instead of an arrest. Judges were observed giving preferential treatment to the police and the pretty girls on trial. Inside the courtroom, gaolers, clerks, ushers, police sergeants, and barristers greased one another's palms to get what they wanted. If a policeman didn't like a certain lawyer, he could have him blacklisted and barred from entry to court. Barristers were busy bribing court clerks, who solicited business for them from the prisoners' loved ones. Families with no savings were encouraged to pay the lawyer with wedding rings or family heirlooms, which could be pawned. Many attorneys barely understood the law and entered the profession as a way of earning easy money. Onetime barrister Sir William Gilbert, who became a famous nineteenth-century playwright, made this observation about the Central Criminal Court: "There are, among the thieves' lawyers, men of acute intelligence and honourable repute, and who do their work extremely well; but the majority of them are sneaking, underhand, grovelling practitioners, who are utterly unrecognized by men of good standing."[19]

Sir William went on to write: "Probably the first impression on the mind of a man who visits the Old Bailey for the first time is that he never saw so many ugly people collected in any one place before. . . . The jury have a bull-headed look about them that suggests that they have been designedly selected from the most stupid of their class; the reporters are usually dirty, and of evil savour; the understrappers have a bloated, overfed, Bumble-like look about them, which is always a particularly annoying thing to a sensitive mind; and the prisoner, of course, looks (whether guilty or innocent) the most ruffianly of mankind, for he stands in the dock."[20]

Dressed in a velvet cape held by gold chains, the Lord Mayor Samuel Wilson was driven to the Old Bailey from his town palace a few blocks away. He attended the court proceedings in his role as chief magistrate for the city, but his primary focus attended to pomp and circumstance. Common thieves like Ludlow were simply another London nuisance to be disposed of in the most expeditious fashion. At three o'clock precisely, the Lord Mayor paused the session and retired to consume a lavish banquet in his private dining room inside the courthouse. Seated on leather chairs around a mahogany table, mayor and judges were served foie gras, turtle soup, haunch of venison, and filet of pheasant.

As his guests relaxed next to the mosaic-tiled fireplace, their feet resting on the sumptuous Turkish carpet, they sipped wine from the Lord Mayor's private vault and smoked cigars. In less grand settings, jurors, barristers, and witnesses drank heavily in nearby pubs. British writer, lawyer, and chaplain Martin Madan noted that it often took an hour for a judge to bring order to the court when so many returned drunk. In the summer, it was even worse: "The heat of the court, joined to the fumes of the liquor, has laid many an honest juryman into a calm and profound sleep, and sometimes it has been no small trouble for his fellows to jog him into the verdict—even where the wretch's life has depended on the event!"[21]

Ludlow's trial took place late in the day amid this drunken chaos. Such timing undoubtedly worked to her disadvantage. For the judges weighted down by heavy wigs and thick robes, it was just another boring day, as a blur of humanity briefly stood before them. Sleepy from their ample meals, they prepared for the grind of the afternoon session. Beneath the courtroom's four brass chandeliers, 155 trials took place that week. Ludlow's was just one of many.

During this week, glaring inconsistencies were recorded, typical for the Old Bailey. Depending on the judge, the jury, and who the prisoner might know, people convicted of similar crimes received radically different punishments. Policeman Henry Jones stole a goose. He was pronounced not guilty despite being caught with the bird in his kitchen. Young Benjamin Lambden pleaded hunger for his crime of stealing a sheep: "being determined to have a turnip, or something to eat, but did not get it, and found the sheep. . . ."[22] He was punished with ten years' transport.

Twelve-year-old David Barry stole six knives from a shop. The judge sentenced him to a whipping and one month imprisonment in Newgate. William Singleton, fifteen, was also whipped and confined six days for stealing a few pieces of beef and pork. Stripped to the waist, the boys were flogged up to fifty strokes with a leather whip. Husband and wife Francis and Ellen Morris, both twenty-two, stole a watch from a man who had fallen asleep on a bench. Ellen pleaded not guilty and was set free, but the judge imposed a sentence of ten years' transport on Francis. He would never see his wife again.

Londoner George Bird picked a handkerchief from the pocket of an ironmonger. Once in custody, he lashed out at the officer who arrested him. Sealing his fate, George's indictment record was marked by an obelisk (†), indicating "that a prisoner is known to be the associate of bad characters."[23] Guilt by association carried a heavy burden for those on trial. At thirteen, it was his good fortune not to be hanged and instead sentenced to ten years' transport. Under the "Bloody Code," earlier judges had sentenced pickpockets to death.

When eighteen-year-old Princess Victoria became Queen of England in 1837, the royal duty of presiding over executions was transferred immediately to the House Secretary for the sole reason that he was a man. She was considered too delicate for the task. By 1838, execution was limited to those who committed murder, arson, or violent crime. Still, every Monday morning a crowd gathered in front of Newgate to watch the spectacle of death. "Publicity was traditionally an essential feature of this punishment, serving to shame the offender and deter others from committing the crime."[24]

On the Sunday before execution day, the condemned listened to a long sermon in the prison chapel and gathered around the very coffins that would lower them into the ground. "The Old Bailey, although extremely inconvenient, is beautifully compact. You can be detained there between the time of your committal and your trial—you can be tried there, sentenced there, condemned-celled there, and comfortably hanged and buried there, without having to leave the building, except for the purpose of going on to the scaffold."[25]

Most of those tried at the Old Bailey had committed petty theft, adding hundreds daily to the 162,000 convicts ultimately transported to Australia. Detailed records kept by the British government indicate that youthful boys were more likely to be transported for minor crimes than older prisoners who committed similar offenses.[26]

Seventeen-year-old Frederick Osborn had stolen his dinner and three plates on which to serve it. His beggar's banquet of beef, cheese, and butter brought a seven-year sentence. Charles Griffin stole two loaves of bread while his mother waited outside the market. The fourteen-year-old was punished with transport for seven years because he had been in custody before. Charles's defense fell on callous ears: "I took the loaves because I was hungry. I did not touch the till." The Transportation Policy specifically targeted healthy young boys like Frederick and Charles, who could best serve a new colony.[27]

It seems the plea of poverty was heard only when a lawyer was paid. Indicted for house robbery at sixteen, John Sherwin admitted the crime and somehow afforded counsel. In pleading his case, his lawyer stated "that poverty had led him to commit the offence, and that he threw himself on the mercy of the Court." The jury "recommended to mercy in consequence of his destitute state," and the judge imposed two months' confinement.[28]

The inventory of goods stolen by those on trial during Ludlow's day in court reads like a list of family necessities. Henry Brown, age twenty-two, pinched two pots valued at three shillings. He pleaded his own case, stating: "I was out of work. These two pots were in the street, and I picked them up."[29] Thomas Saunders, just sixteen, stole a pair of trousers. Seventeen-year-old Thomas Cook purloined a pair of boots from a display in a shop doorway. For these crimes, each received seven years' transport.

Whether sentenced to seven or ten years, this was the era when only a tiny percentage of those transported would ever make their way back to England. Convicts who completed their sentences rarely returned to their homeland. The only way back was through a daring escape at the Cape of Good Hope or by paying a large fee for ship's passage.

Five other women were among those convicted the same week Widow Tedder was exiled to Van Diemen's Land. Like Ludlow, forty-seven-year-old Amy Wilson stole from her master and was sentenced to ten years. Twenty-five-year-old Ann Price, with friend Mary Grady, had taken two pairs of stays, the boning used in corsets. Valued at eight shillings, their small heist brought seven years' transport for each. Mary Sullivan also received a seven-year punishment. At forty-six, she was caught stealing clothes and a bedcover. Hannah Herbert stood trial just before Ludlow. She had committed forgery, an offense that typically carried a life sentence. Somehow the thirty-four-year-old convinced the court that the laudanum she had taken the day of the crime impaired her judgment and was "Recommended to mercy by the Jury" with a seven-year sentence.[30]

The Central Criminal Court adjoined Newgate Prison and made for the convenient transfer of Ludlow, Arabella, and the five other women, all new chattel for the Crown's colonies. They were convicted during peak years for the transport of women, a period that spanned 1826 to 1840.[31] The gaoler led them back through the underground passage that ran between the Old Bailey and Newgate's female ward, the sound of dragging chains wailing through the tunnel with hollow despair. When they approached the ward, the clanking of iron intermingled with the screams and shouts of prisoners from behind the great wooden door.

Arabella clung to her mother and followed the turnkey's silent instructions. He pulled the creaking entrance open and motioned the pair inside. Mother and daughter reentered the icy darkness that had been their home over the past six days. If they huddled with the other newly convicted, they might stay warm. For the next 141 days, the future shipmates waited for the black carriages that would transfer them to the docks to begin their journey to Van Diemen's Land.

At first, time passed quickly. In a week it would be Christmas, the first holiday Ludlow would observe without Eliza, John Bulley, and the younger Ludlow. Instead of delighting in Arabella opening a small trinket from the pawnshop, she watched her nine-year-old struggle to get comfortable on a dirt floor crawling with cockroaches and rats. Yet it might have been worse. Some judges separated children from their mothers. Youngsters older than twelve were rarely allowed to accompany their mothers.[32]

As Ludlow shared her daily bread ration with Arabella, bells pealed from across the street, calling parishioners to St. Sepulchre for services on Christmas morning. For the wealthy, Yule logs burned in fireplaces as families dined on goose, plum pudding, and steaming wassail flavored with cloves and cinnamon.

This was one holiday that inspired philanthropy among the well-to-do. Some brought mince pies, cakes, and a few precious oranges into the gaol, although such treats rarely made it beyond the guards. Elizabeth Fry, however, delivered her kindness directly. Her schoolroom for prisoners' children had been in place since 1817. Since then, at least one member of her Association for the Improvement of Female Prisoners visited Newgate every day. The dedicated Quaker continued to comfort women and children awaiting transport until 1843. She delivered clean clothes for Arabella and sewing materials for Ludlow and her new companions. She helped them sell the clothing and quilts they made as a group, enabling them to purchase tea and meat from their gaolers.

As days passed more slowly and winter turned to spring, Newgate's hell began a slow thaw. The lives of Ludlow, the two Marys, Amy, Ann, and Hannah were soon intertwined. With no such intention, Old Bailey's Judge Parke unknowingly set in motion the foundation for kinship, solidarity, and protection among unlikely allies. Over the next seven years, friendships born from fear and uncertainty began to thrive, as overturned futures unfolded. First cell mates and then shipmates, these six women were bound together for whatever fate might offer beyond the seas in Van Diemen's Land.

⌒ 7 ⌒

Liverpool Street

Two Hearts and Two Doves

Not wanting to worry Arabella, Ludlow straightened up in her irons, composed herself, and willed serenity into her limpid hazel eyes. The two stood quietly on the wooden pier, waiting for Fate to tip its hand. Abruptly, a scarlet-jacketed guard from Newgate brushed the prisoners and children away from the black carriage toward a waiting launch tied to the wharf.

The *Hindostan* began boarding prisoners in April 1839. For the last several weeks, the same scene replayed every day. Husbands and lovers, mothers and fathers, aunts and uncles, brothers and sisters, daughters and sons, formed a stark line of silhouettes against the grey sky. Some fought back tears, struggling for stoic control as the nightmare of a loved one awaiting transport materialized before them in the early morning mist. Others wept openly, unable to suppress their grief over what they knew in their hearts was a last good-bye. In these final few minutes together, loved ones drank in every tiny detail so they might remember in the future: dimples around a sister's lips, a chipped front tooth in a mother's half smile, the scent of a lover, the press of a warm body, the last fearful glimpse into the depths of a departing wife's tear-filled eyes.

Because Ludlow was literate, she may have sent letters from New-gate to her older children, Eliza, Ludlow, and John Tedder, and to her own six surviving brothers and sisters—Fanny, William, Elizabeth, Joseph, Mary, and Henry. Mrs. Fry and her volunteers, devoted to comforting prisoners, helped deliver parting messages to those families soon to be torn apart.

In the well-ordered confusion of the transports' departure, small dramas unfolded on the dock. Each individual created a farewell ritual, unique and intensely personal. Some uttered not a word as they stared helplessly into eyes they would never see again. Many pressed a lock of hair into the palms of their relatives, a small loving token of remembrance that preserved the final moments they shared. Ludlow may have exchanged strands of her hair for those of the two daughters she would leave behind. For all social classes, hair from a loved one was treasured like gold and often tucked inside a locket or small tin.

Prisoners left love tokens in many forms. Some used old nails to carve inscriptions into pennies while they awaited transport in New-gate cells. Hundreds of patient taps into the metal imprinted family initials, outlines of a heart, or a message of hope—"until I gain my liberty," "may we live to meet again," "from a friend whose love for you will never end."[1] Defacing a penny and filing off its original design also represented a small act of rebellion against the Crown, encouraging transports to steel themselves for whatever lay ahead.

A woman known only by the initials E. A. left for her father a copper penny, etched with a drawing of her home and her dog. Underneath she chiseled the words "This was once my cottage of peace." The penny's other side decreed her unwelcome fate in exile: "Going out of her cottage for life."[2] Her pocket-sized piece of original art left a tangible memento, as it recorded a piece of her history that would lie undiscovered for many decades.

Transported from London to Van Diemen's Land in 1832, twenty-two-year-old Mary Ann Whitlock gave her aunt a coin before she boarded the transport ship *Hydery*. It was inscribed with the simple words "Adieu, Dear Aunt, Adieu" on one side and her name on the other. Sentenced to fourteen years' exile for stealing a purse, Mary Ann instinctively knew she would never again see her only relative. She wanted nothing more than to be remembered, and her inscription ensured she would. This small token marked her passage more permanently than a tombstone that would later crumble.

Fourteen years before, on the docks where Ludlow stood today, Ann Maloney left behind a large English penny engraved with two doves above two crossed hearts and the initials of her loved one, W. F. The raven-haired beauty with light grey eyes also inscribed the coin with her full name and the message "Tho lost to sight the Memory dear 1825." At age seventeen, she was convicted of shoplifting in London and received a life sentence to Van Diemen's Land. Ludlow would later meet a thirty-one-year-old Ann by the washtubs at the Female Factory.

The Woolwich docks departure platform framed a family portrait that would both haunt and comfort Ludlow in the years to come. The public farewells were soon brought to an end. It was time. Ludlow and Arabella climbed into the small boat waiting below. The coxswain motioned his female cargo onto their seats. Clutching Arabella's hand a little tighter, Ludlow lifted her irons and shuffled toward the back of the skiff. Arabella tried to steady herself on the creaking boards as the boat tilted under the weight of her mother's chains. The worried nine-year-old wondered where her mum was taking her, but Ludlow herself knew very little about their distant destination. Although she had read Barrister Skinner's discarded newspapers, she'd never paid much attention to details about Van Diemen's Land.

Under the guise of the Transportation Act, it was time to dispose of another mother and child. For today, they were together, and that was all that mattered. The launch glided steadily toward the waiting *Hindostan*; the river fell hauntingly silent save for the screaming of the gulls and the sound of oars splashing the water. Arabella clung closely to her mother's sleeve. Ludlow lifted her arm and slipped her precious cargo underneath the chains and next to her breast. Like a mother bear, she grew more protective the instant the skiff bumped up against the gangplank they'd soon scale to board the *Hindostan*. She watched a group of sailors hanging over the rail of the tall-masted ship. Many of them didn't look much older than Arabella. Midshipmen, known as "the young gentlemen," were sent to sea at age twelve or thirteen. Away from home for years at a time, some turned to matrons like Ludlow when they needed comfort from a surrogate mother. Like Agnes McMillan, many of the child sailors were abandoned by their parents and left to fend for themselves.

The *Hindostan* looked serenely elegant as she slumbered, safe and calm in the river, quietly masking her identity as a transport vessel. Once on board, Arabella in tow, Ludlow was ushered by a Navy officer to the smith. As the rivets were removed from her irons, the wily widow wasted no time in assessing the ship's true personality. Tangled ropes, pungent pine tar, open hatches, and confusing passages harkened chaos and unpredictable danger. She would not let her daughter out of sight, not even for a minute. Arabella, on the other hand, studied with fascination the new surroundings, which were causing her mother's brow to crinkle.

This day, a motley crew had blown in from Newgate. On the upper deck, the newest arrivals for transport formed a line in front of Surgeon Superintendent Thomas McDonald. Ann Price, #177 from Limerick, was first, and she didn't look well at all. Her jet-black eyebrows accentuated her sallow complexion and made her appear angry and gaunt.[3] By her knees, her four-year-old daughter, Jane, clung to her mother's shift as a detached McDonald recorded that the twenty-five-year-old had left behind a husband and two older children.[4] Mary Grady, #221, checked in behind her friend and co-conspirator, with whom she'd stolen two sets of stays. She was the smallest of this Newgate contingent at four feet, ten inches tall.[5]

Mary Sullivan, #374, was measured next—four feet, eleven inches tall and forty-six years old, about the same age as Ludlow.[6] She looked much older, however, with her greying hair and protruding front teeth. Thirty-four-year-old #339, Hannah Herbert, appeared aged beyond her years, having lost her front teeth.[7] Decayed or missing teeth were common throughout the general population, but even more so for the poor. Careful not to smear the ink, Surgeon Superintendent McDonald recorded one more perfunctory notation in his oversized black ledger. Yet when forty-eight-year-old Amy Wilson stepped forward, the normally unflappable officer must have caught himself staring. Amy was missing her left eye and had a pink fleshy mole on her left cheek. Poverty had taken its toll on the mother of two, who was being transported for stealing a plate after her husband deserted the family.[8]

With impeccable posture, no disfiguring marks, and a calm demeanor, Ludlow Tedder stood out from her ragged cell mates. Arabella's mother was no fool, already attentive to who made decisions about food, water, and protection aboard the *Hindostan*. Being able to read and write surely accorded her special notice, so Ludlow seized the limelight when it was her turn to be processed by Surgeon Superintendent McDonald. During his examination, he scrutinized the tidy-appearing #151 as she signed her name in a refined cursive hand, unlike the crude X most of the other women entered in the register. He needed a literate and stable matron for his nurse, someone who wouldn't make a deadly mistake when she administered medicine. After all, a surgeon's reputation depended on how many women he delivered alive.

Captain Lamb paced the deck as the women and their children boarded and queued up for the surgeon's examination. Lips pursed in disapproval, he stayed aft, hands clasped behind the small of his back, keeping a sharp lookout for potential troublemakers. Even one woman was considered bad luck on a voyage, and here he was stuck with a full boatload of them, along with their crying children.

Once they passed inspection, Ludlow and Arabella were escorted by an officer across the deck and into an open hatch. Mother and daughter climbed gingerly down the wooden ladder leading to the orlop deck just above the bilge. Once they entered the lowest level, dimly lit by gently swinging candle lamps, they were assigned an open berth. Arabella instinctively hunkered down, tucked her chin close, and pulled her shoulders forward, making it easier to squeeze into the narrow passageway at the bottom of the ship. Ludlow recognized many of the faces on the orlop because most had spent months at Newgate before transfer to the *Hindostan*.

After a meal of salt pork and biscuits topped off with a dose of lime juice, the new prisoners were divided into messes of twelve. Already comfortable with the sensation of movement beneath her boots when the ship swayed, Arabella found joy with her new playmates. Sarah Smith was just a year younger, and the two became fast friends within hours. By suppertime, the nine-year-old knew the names of all the other girls and boys. She'd already spent nearly five months inside Newgate playing with Ann Price's four-year-old daughter, Jane, and now assumed the role of big sister.

When the bells rang for bed call, Arabella was again the little girl ready for comfort from her mother. Ludlow rubbed her back and enfolded her in the woolen cloak she'd brought from London. Arabella was dressed in the hand-sewn flannel clothing and warm hat that Mrs. Fry and her volunteers had delivered for the children on board.

At first, the nine-year-old child couldn't figure out how to position herself comfortably on the narrow bunk, but she managed to squeeze herself into the space between her mother and the scratchy shipboards. Caught between bouts of restless sleep and anxious waking,

Ludlow observed hazy figures in the fetal position, each staking claim to her only private space. Along with captain, surgeon, and crew, the ship now carried 178 women and 18 children.

Some fell ill immediately, right in port, even before the *Hindostan* cast off. Confinement in the ship's bowels, unable to focus on the horizon, proved the worst place for nausea and dizziness. With sheep and chickens on the upper deck and crew one level below, prisoners were housed in an area normally reserved for nonliving cargo. They bunked in near darkness except for slim ribbons of light that filtered through the hatches when they weren't locked tight for bed call.

The urgency in a clanging of bells rousted Ludlow to her feet in a flash. Unaccustomed to the routine *Hindostan* clamor, she instinctively readied to run for safety with Arabella. Blankets in hand for airing on deck, she first helped Arabella into a reeking water closet. With nearly two hundred passengers sharing the two privies, a septic stench soon saturated the air belowdecks. The mother-daughter pair couldn't scurry fast enough to the top deck for morning muster.

Shortly after a breakfast of oatmeal and a dash of sugar, an officer summoned Ludlow to the *Hindostan* infirmary. Surgeon Superintendent McDonald desired an interview with the widow about serving as his nurse. This was the opportunity Ludlow was waiting for, and she embraced it without a breath of hesitation. She and Arabella would benefit from additional rations, extra medicine, and safety from the crew. Without a word, she curtsied deferentially, being careful not to overdo it as the surgeon evaluated her every move.

If the London widow were to pass this test, she needed to convey respect, composure, and, above all, dutiful behavior. Before making Ludlow his assistant, the surgeon would examine the depth of her intelligence, perhaps asking, "What would you bring me for a case of dysentery?" One can only imagine what Ludlow was thinking at this pivotal juncture. Certainly, she was wise enough not to utter the first response that flew into her head: "For you, me Lord? Why, arsenic, of course."

Widow Tedder knew well enough to recognize the potential for elevated status in the ship's hierarchy. A chief nurse commanded a position of power and protection. She would be the one everyone else bribed for medicine and an extra blanket. Payoffs would provide money to purchase provisions and dried meat from the cooks. She and Arabella would have easy access to fresh air on the main deck for the entire journey. Most important, she'd have the comfort of knowing where to find medicine should Arabella fall ill during the long voyage. The picture of obedient politeness, Ludlow opened the cabinet quickly and efficiently, careful not to upset its contents. She examined the glass bottles and dispensers, each with a label penned in black ink.

Employing humor to pull through the worst of times, Ludlow must have lovingly fingered the arsenic bottle, weaving wicked fantasies about the authorities on board. Holding at bay the fomenting anger she felt toward her situation and her captors, she pulled a bright blue bottle from the cabinet and presented it to Mr. McDonald: "Bromide, it says, sir, swallowed with a sip of water, cures the dysentery." Common sense and restraint sealed the deal for Nurse Tedder. Ludlow's literacy was the fortunate break ensuring her safety and, most important, Arabella's. With their homeland casting them adrift, the surgeon superintendent unknowingly offered mother and child a lifeline that ensured survival for this voyage and their future.

Ludlow was savvy enough to know that if she fell from the crew's grace, Arabella was certain to suffer. Every ship left port with barrels of rum stored for the mariners' daily ration, and drunkenness ran rampant among the crew. Like any protective mother, Ludlow grew disgustedly uneasy with the sly glances sailors cast at her young daughter. She knew what was at stake.

Small victories like this, many dependent on sheer luck, often determined who lived and who died. The fabric of her future woven by chance, Ludlow held tight to a very satisfying win in being chosen as the *Hindostan*'s nurse. The benefits offered both mother and daughter a bright ray of hope on the uncertain landscape stretching before them.

Ludlow's Cure

It was May 9, 1839, a day Widow Tedder would never forget. As light broke over the horizon, sailors turned the windlass, and in a few heaves, the anchor broke ground. The *Hindostan* and her cargo sailed steadily east toward the North Sea. Slowly making their way down the Thames, the transports watched passing towns disappear one by one. The sun fell behind them and the moon began to rise before they reached the river's mouth and headed into choppy open waters. Answering the sea's mighty force, the coastal lights disappeared behind the rising waves, and the tenuous cord that connected Ludlow to England finally snapped. Nostalgia gave way to her stern resolve: Survive at any cost.

The *Hindostan* approached good weather as she traveled through the North Atlantic. By the time they reached the Portuguese coast, Nurse Tedder and Arabella fell into a comfortable routine, gaining their sea legs and eating regular meals in the hospital quarters. Because of Ludlow's position, Arabella enjoyed the freedom of playing on deck when the weather permitted. Perhaps a few homesick fathers among the crew found some comfort in her wide-eyed innocence because they would not be seeing their own daughters for another eight or nine months at least.

With her arms resting on the rails, Ludlow watched the endless blue horizon, inhaled a deep breath of fresh sea air, and, for a moment, felt at peace. They were only two weeks into the journey and heading steadily southwest. On board, mother and daughter were better fed than in Newgate. As a result, Arabella gained a little weight. On some voyages, the prisoners' health actually improved if they were given full rations from a relatively honest crew. For transports from the poorest neighborhoods, being fed twice a day more than doubled their previous calorie intake. Surgeon Superintendent John Love, responsible for a large group of children aboard the convict ship *Mellish*, observed: "The general improvement in flesh and appearance was very evident in the whole of them, especially the children amounting to 61 in number, many of whom were puny, delicate and mostly affected with worms."[9]

As Ludlow cast a glance back at her playful, sun-kissed Arabella, a little chuckle escaped from her lips. This was the best job she'd ever had. As a housekeeper, she had barely a moment to herself. Aboard the *Hindostan*, there was hardly anything to do except take care of a few seasick patients and tend to a bit of syphilis. Her shipmates were put to work scouring the decks clean and helping in the galley. When the weather turned stormy and the hatches closed over the orlop deck, the women opened the burlap bags Mrs. Fry left with them and began piecing together hundreds of colored scraps of all shapes and sizes, stitching quilts by candlelight as the waves crashed against the beams.

By the fourth week, the *Hindostan* crossed the Tropic of Cancer into the seas off the west coast of Africa. Nurse Tedder no longer found her job so easy. As the filth belowdecks percolated in the rising heat and humidity, dysentery and a host of tropical diseases ran rampant. As Ludlow was pressed into round-the-clock nursing duty, not a single bed lay empty in the floating infirmary. Earlier in the voyage, prisoners sometimes hid their illness and distress, fearing painful nineteenth-century treatments more than anything else. Symptoms had now grown acute, and Ludlow treated ulcerated tongues, high fevers, dislocated limbs, delirium, diarrhea, and pneumonia. Though primitive, the medical care was more than the transports ever received on the streets of London, Glasgow, and Dublin. Some of the children boarded the ship suffering oozing eye sores from untreated infections. Surgeon Superintendent McDonald and Nurse Tedder gave them the first medical attention of their lives.

Through trial and error, Ludlow soon learned how medicine of her era was an inexact science. The remedies were often worse than the afflictions, causing pain, blisters, and bleeding. Calomel (six parts mercury to one part chloride), laudanum (tincture of opium), and unguent mercuriale (mercury used as a salve for treatment of syphilis and other venereal diseases) killed as many patients as they cured.

Ludlow, opportunely, knew how to temper her nerves as she administered medical treatments that seemed cruelly absurd. Surgeon Superintendent McDonald taught her to apply acid to a patient's skin, burning it to provoke a blister. It was common belief that draining the blister forced out disease, like an unwelcome lodger to be evicted as quickly as possible. Bleeding, purging, and blistering were thought to relieve the body of "morbid" elements. Head shaving was one of the treatments used to reduce fever.[10]

On both land and sea, bloodletting was a widely practiced "cure." Ludlow learned to use lancets to bleed women suffering from fever, indigestion, convulsions, pneumonia, tuberculosis, or insanity. Because nineteenth-century medicine dictated that a patient's blood be removed to affect a cure, some prisoners and crew were weakened toward death in the floating infirmaries. Despite these rather frightening treatments, only one woman died under Mr. McDonald's care.

Forty days into the voyage, on July 28, Ludlow turned forty-six. She still looked much younger than one would expect of a woman who had already lived well beyond the life expectancy for most of Britain's poor. In spite of everything, she'd survived, although she certainly hadn't expected to be off the coast of Africa on her birthday.

By the time the *Hindostan* crossed the equator, Ludlow had witnessed almost every form of physical and mental malady. At the onset of the voyage, women battling alcohol withdrawal suffered tremors and delirium. In desperation, some offered their bodies to the crew in exchange for liquor and a return to hazy comfort. Others defaulted into abstinence, slowly and painfully unmasking both sobriety and the frightening reality of transport.

Captain Lamb would tolerate no troublemakers at sea. Two tiny cells, squeezed under the ship's bow, were reserved for solitary confinement and contained those deemed unruly, regardless of the cause. As their destination drew closer, incidents of panic and hysteria escalated throughout the women's claustrophobic quarters. Sometimes the penetrating pressure of the unknown was too much and drove women over the edge and into madness. Victorian medicine ignored the possibility of treating mental illness, deeming it fake or incurable. Physical restraint by ropes or straitjacket was generally the only remedy prescribed.

Cabin fever, depression, rape by sailors, and outbursts from the mentally ill were conditions for which Surgeon Superintendent McDonald had not been trained. Even if Nurse Tedder wanted to intervene, she had first to consider Arabella and her safety. Heading through the Indian Ocean, the criminally insane were sometimes seen banging their heads against the ship's rail, mimicking the rhythmic pattern of crashing waves.

During the final push eastward through the Indian Ocean, Ludlow witnessed another type of high seas drama when an emigrant ship named the *Cornwall* raised a flag of distress. It had departed from Gravesend, England, on May 12, three days after the *Hindostan*, and had followed the same route around the Cape of Good Hope on its approach to Sydney. Responding to the *Cornwall's* signal, Captain Lamb dispatched a whaleboat with several officers, including Surgeon Superintendent McDonald and perhaps Ludlow, because she was now his competent and trusted nurse.

The *Cornwall's* Captain John Cow asked Mr. McDonald to examine Surgeon Superintendent King, who had fallen ill amid a very rough trip. Under his watch, eighteen passengers had died, most from scarlet fever and rubella. Returning to the *Hindostan*, McDonald "declared Dr. King to be in no serious condition. . . . [He] was very apprehensive however and refused to take the powerful sedative prescribed. He nervously walked the deck all night in the company of the captain and mate. By the next day his 'nervousness' had abated."[11]

Surgeon McDonald also examined the *Cornwall's* emigrants, "whom he pronounced to be in much better state of health than the convicts on board the *Hindostan*."[12] Although he and Nurse Tedder had lost only one patient, many were barely standing. Both women and children were weakened by an array of ailments made worse by poor nutrition and miserably overcrowded conditions, not to mention the "cures."

On Wednesday, September 11, 1839, the *Hindostan* glided into Sullivans Cove and set anchor at the far southeast coast along Van Diemen's Land. With the seasons occurring in reverse from the Northern Hemisphere, the autumnal equinox signaled the beginning of spring, and the air smelled of new blossoms and fresh leaves. This was the same day Agnes McMillan turned nineteen, stuck in Oatlands, more than fifty miles away from Hobart Town at the island's interior. A full year would pass before Agnes would meet Ludlow inside Cascades.

None the worse for wear, Ludlow and Arabella finally landed in Van Diemen's Land 126 days after their journey began. In the eyes of colonists and male convicts, another boatload of "strumpets" had arrived, arousing Hobart Town to a state of pitched anticipation. Bear grease, talc, and witch hazel were brought out from dusty cases and smeared over the men's unwashed bodies. Surely the overeager onlookers were shocked by the appearance of the women, many of whom were pockmarked, missing teeth, and very skinny.

When she first boarded the *Hindostan* in May, Ludlow's gaol report had made note of her "poor connexions," referring to the questionable friends she had made during nearly five months inside Newgate. Back then, the surgeon superintendent had looked unfavorably on the company she kept in prison, because guilt by association followed the women wherever they went. Amy Wilson he labeled "quarrelsome," and both Mary Grady and Ann Price "extremely insolent."[13] But before disembarking, Ludlow's exemplary conduct and her skills as a nurse were recorded by Mr. McDonald.

Anxious to step foot on solid land, Ludlow and her companions felt both relief and trepidation in leaving behind the stench of the ship and the pitch of the sea. Captain Lamb prepared for their departure and delivery. Principal Superintendent of Convicts Josiah Spode and

Muster Master William Thomas Champ were on their way to the *Hindostan* to inspect the cargo and exchange records. In spite of illness and injury, there had been only one death, an excellent record for the journey of twelve thousand nautical miles. Captain Lamb stood proudly on the freshly scrubbed deck alongside Surgeon Superintendent McDonald. Courtly and formal in dress uniforms with polished buttons ablaze in the sun, the two officers exchanged polite congratulations and prepared to greet the small boat being rowed out from the docks. As the proper Englishmen prepared to greet one another, #151 and her daughter, Arabella, lined up for inspection with the rest of the prisoners. The two Tedders had arrived in good health, and the surgeon's kind words ensured Ludlow the best possible assignment at the Female Factory. She had received a stellar recommendation, "the most attentive and best behaved on board doing duty as nurse."[14]

As one mess at a time was ushered onto the main deck, it took two days to complete their inspection. The officers lugged their big black books ashore to complete stacks of paperwork that transferred jurisdiction for the exiled women and children. On Friday afternoon, Surgeon Superintendent McDonald returned with signed documents for London and supplies from Hobart Town. He rewarded his nurse's diligence with a clean bucket of water and fresh milk for Arabella. Ludlow splashed her freckled face and helped her nine-year-old daughter scrub off the heavy grime baked into her skin and hair. Reveling in a generous soaping and a clean towel from the infirmary, she washed and dried her daughter's hair. For the moment, with Arabella by her side, Ludlow held fear at bay and prayed for the best.

White Pinafores

Hindostan passengers still healthy enough to walk were brought ashore and delivered to a waiting contingent of scarlet-coated soldiers for the march along Macquarie Street. Ludlow kept Arabella close at hand as they made their way through the strange sights, sounds, and smells following them uphill to the base of Mt. Wellington.

A soldier ordered the weary transports to silence as they entered the stone enclave deep in the valley of shadows. Once inside, the women and children stood for hours in a long line wrapping around Yard One. While they awaited inspection and processing, an unofficial, albeit persistent, welcoming committee beckoned, bartering for clothing or jewelry in exchange for tobacco, soap, and other forbidden prison luxuries. They appeared one by one from a mysterious passage to whatever lay behind Cascades' inner walls.

The women working in Yard One seemed a strange combination of the defiant and the defeated. Some bore the appearance of caged animals, seemingly tamed yet ready to turn on the captors incapable of extinguishing their raging spirit. Others ambled about at random, evidently terribly out of sorts. The ashen figures moved in slow, deliberate, and strangely silent motion. Ludlow's instincts told her that something was disturbingly amiss. She looked at Arabella and drew her closer still. Mother and daughter eventually inched toward the front of the line and were summoned into a small, dimly lit room.

Matron Hutchinson handed Ludlow a clean Female Factory uniform but offered no clothing for Arabella. Mr. Hutchinson had already perused the thick black volume recording Mrs. Tedder's literacy and good conduct aboard the *Hindostan*. Nurse, cook, housekeeper, and mother, she exceeded the expectations for a petty thief. Towering over the slight widow, the stodgy superintendent informed her that she was assigned to the new prison nursery on Liverpool Street back in the town's center. Nothing was said about Arabella, and Ludlow dared not inquire. As for herself, she had just received the most favorable work assignment a prisoner could expect.

It was nearly half past six by the time all the *Hindostan* transports were processed. Before clanging the supper bell, Deputy Matron Cato assigned Ludlow to a mess of twelve. Arabella was content to follow her mum's lead and dunked her allotment of brown bread into the watery soup. At seven o'clock, Mrs. Hutchinson rang the prison bell for evening chapel, held an hour earlier than during the summer schedule. Mother Tedder took her little girl's hand as they walked toward the modest sanctuary and took a seat before the overstuffed Reverend Bedford. Her first night in the valley, Ludlow prayed for many miracles. As the Southern Cross fell behind Mt. Wellington's black shadow, she draped an arm around Arabella's waist. Before she knew it, mother and child lay snuggled asleep in a hammock that barely cleared the floor under their weight.

Morning muster was at six o'clock in the spring. Ludlow lined up for daily inspection in Yard One while Arabella peeked around from behind her. All shades of green burst across Mt. Wellington, and daffodils danced around its base. Soft pink apple blossoms and cherry trees in shades of dusty rose dotted the hilly farmland Ludlow could smell beyond the prison walls. Most of the women knew little about geography other than that they had been sent "beyond the seas." The reversed seasons were no doubt a source of confusion as they witnessed their first September spring in the Southern Hemisphere.

This time of year, Cascades convict veterans worked an extended morning session from six thirty until eight A.M. The bells rang for a half-hour breakfast break, and then it was off to chapel for morning prayers before the workday began again in earnest. Reverend Bedford and supporters among the colony's elite believed that forced labor redeemed the body's worth, if not the soul's. His captive congregation had little patience for his rather theatrical hissing and spitting from the pulpit. Twice daily, the aptly labeled Holy Willie chastised them for their evil ways and exhorted the virtues of industry for opening a window on redemption.

Widow Tedder's atonement commenced officially after morning chapel. Tapping her foot on the chapel steps, Mrs. Cato impatiently jingled the bell that seemed permanently attached to her palm and summoned #151 to her side. Deputy Matron Cato was charged with escorting prisoners assigned to the Liverpool Street nursery. It was already half past eight; there was not a moment to waste in putting each woman to work. Performing her duty as prison midwife, Mrs. Cato had helped deliver many of the tiny babies now lodged in the new nursery.

Liverpool Street had opened only a year before in response to a newspaper exposé about the atrocious conditions at the Cascades nursery, named the "Valley of the Shadow of Death" by the *Colonial Times*.[15] Inside the Female Factory walls, at least twenty infants died during the first three months of 1838.[16] Authorities had failed to acknowledge that malnutrition and illness had raised the infant mortality rate to four times that of the colony's free settlers. Instead, they blamed the convict mothers, accusing them of deliberately keeping their children near death in order to be with them in the nursery rather than returning to hard labor in Yard Two.

Matron Hutchinson herself understood the devastation of losing a child. She had given birth to twelve children, and six had died in infancy, at least four at the Female Factory.[17] During her nineteen years at Cascades, a severely limited and largely untrained staff helped her manage the perpetually damp, overcrowded prison, where medical care was meager. Not surprisingly, the thinly stretched Mrs. Hutchinson received mixed reviews. Though the prisoners appeared to tolerate her more readily than they did her bureaucratic husband, the press cast her as a villain when it exposed a scandal at the prison.

Public outrage reached a boiling point with the case of Mary Vowles. The Irish lass had freely immigrated to Van Diemen's Land in August 1832, two months later marrying an emancipist. In 1835, working as a servant, she was caught stealing a silver plate in Hobart Town and sentenced to seven years at Cascades. In 1838, the twenty-nine-year-old was charged with using bad language toward another woman and sentenced to six weeks' hard labor at the Female Factory. Appearing before Mr. Hutchinson with her son, Thomas, in her arms, she pleaded to keep the twelve-month-old with her because he was still nursing. Superintendent of Convicts Josiah Spode had already approved the request to keep Thomas with her, but it made no difference. Deputy Matron Cato also implored Mr. Hutchinson not to separate mother from suckling child. Again, he refused.

Five days after her admission to the Female Factory, Mary was allowed to visit her son in the prison nursery. "She did not know her own child, 'it was so sickly looking, and altered so much for the worse!'"[18] A few days later, the nurse sent Mary a message asking for money to buy Thomas sago, a starch derived from palm trees that was mixed with wine to treat ill infants. Upon receiving news of her son's worsening condition, Mary asked Mr. Hutchinson for permission to visit the dying child. When he said no, the frantic mother ran toward the nursery but was detained and sentenced to solitary confinement. Somehow, she managed a message to her husband, who came to Cascades and left with their child. He purchased medicine from a pharmacist, but by now little Thomas was at death's door and soon succumbed.

Little Thomas Vowles was just one of hundreds who suffered the same fate at the nursery. Word began to spread throughout Hobart Town that "the corpses of children had been conveyed secretly out of the Factory, without the slightest regard to ceremony."[19] The *True Colonist* harshly criticized Superintendent Hutchinson's role in Thomas's demise, assailing him for an improper use of authority. Such heartlessness prompted Hobart Town's local newspaper to launch a crusade for change. On May 29, 1838, the *Colonial Times* reported yet another death inside Cascades and called for the resignation of the superintendent's wife.

"Where, again, was the matron, Mrs. Hutchinson, that she did not perceive the gradual decay and drooping of this innocent victim? Is it . . . because Mrs. Hutchinson is so habituated to misery and wretchedness, within the walls of that gloomy prison, that she does not recognize its continual existence? At all events, her removal is certainly requisite, immediately and promptly."[20]

The article went on to beg Governor John Franklin "to ORDER the immediate removal of the children, and not to stand upon any shilly-shally remonstrance as to expense or inconvenience."[21] Despite public outcry about "the perilous and fatal Nursery," the governor's wife, Lady Jane, largely ignored the dying babies.[22] Constructing a botanical garden, a state college, and a museum of natural history modeled after a Greek temple were the tasks she readily performed from an elite distance. Writing her sister during the time of the scandal, the governor's wife revealed her true feelings: "As for doing anything with the women here, in the factory, it seems next to impossible huddled as they all are together, and such impudent creatures, almost all of them. . . . I think the whole system of female transportation . . . so faulty and vicious, that to attempt to deal with the women who are the subjects of it, seems a waste of time and labor.[23]

In this instance, public sentiment held more influence over the governor than did his apathetic wife. After nine years of scandals involving infant deaths, he finally approved the closing of Cascades Nursery in October 1838, motivated by economics rather than altruism. The nursery was relocated to the small Liverpool Street house in Hobart Town. Mindful of both finances and public relations, the Hobart Town coroner had "recommended that a new hospital and nursery be built close to, but outside, the Factory, in order to avoid the necessity of holding an inquest on every death therein. This would minimize administrative expense and avoid 'excit[ing] . . . the Public Mind' through inquests being held on 'ordinary and unavoidable cases.'"[24] According to an act of Parliament, inquests were required only for those who died inside a prison.

Nurse Tedder was about to enter the poorly ventilated little dwelling on Liverpool Street that now held Cascades' tiniest prisoners. It was no place for the faint of heart. Walking down the valley toward the center of town, Arabella held tight to her mother's new prison dress and followed Mrs. Cato's directions to behave herself. This was where proper people lived, and children should be seen and not heard. Strolling by the replicas of English gardens, the ladies of Hobart Town wore black lace dresses embellished with pearl buttons, and white cambric collars and cuffs. Following fashion and imitating the coiffures of Parisians, they swept their hair off the face and styled it into soft curls.[25]

The town was built primarily on a straight grid, its long streets adorned by simple Georgian architecture. Behind the neatly trimmed Hawthorne hedges, private homes and government offices conveyed a gaol-like austerity, with squared bricks and severe edges. Lurking around the corner in the less tasteful side alleys, sly-grog shops enjoyed a booming business. Emancipists, as the freed convicts were known, congregated with sailors, bushrangers, madams, and corrupt government officers. For the most part, the town still tolerated an "anything goes" in a penal colony attitude. Unlicensed pubs abounded, serving homemade liquor, sometimes dangerously laced with laudanum—the same drug used to quiet infants in Britain's slums.

Set amid bawdy houses, taverns, shops, and mansions, the Liverpool Nursery sat at the lower end of the street. Prisoners whose babies were not yet six months old were permitted to nurse their little ones. Some would later be assigned to colonists as wet nurses. Though not nearly as damp as Cascades, the new location was equally crowded, chaotic, and malodorous. A doctor passed through occasionally, but the prisoners themselves were assigned responsibility for fragile babies and scrawny toddlers ranging in age from six months to two years.

Ludlow's hands-on medical training aboard the *Hindostan*, alongside an excellent recommendation from the surgeon superintendent, immediately moved her into the nursery's top spot. Once again, a basic education and literacy led Ludlow to the best assignment among undesirable alternatives. Yet nothing, absolutely nothing, could insulate Ludlow from the harsh and unanticipated reality she was about to face. Back at Cascades for supper, Mrs. Hutchinson asked Widow Tedder to step into her reception room for a private conversation. The matron told Ludlow that there was no place at the Female Factory for Arabella. Her ten-year-old daughter would be transferred to the Queen's Orphanage in Hobart Town within a week.

Typically, mothers were given no warning about their children's removal.[26] But in this case, Mrs. Hutchinson needed a well-trained nurse on her side, and she could ill afford to alienate her. If Ludlow maintained her exemplary behavior, she'd be allowed to make the four-mile walk and visit Arabella once a month, on Sunday. Ludlow listened silently while her heart sank at the prospect of losing another child. Behind her hazel eyes, nearly covered by her mob cap, her mind raced madly ahead, plotting schemes for an escape.

The next six days were a nightmare. The distraught mother decided to shield her darling little girl from the news of their imminent separation until the moment was upon them. Inside the Liverpool Nursery, there was hardly time to think. An overwhelming workload pulled Ludlow through the fear and dread that rose higher every hour. The *Hindostan* had arrived during another outbreak of influenza in the colony. The illness, in particular, targeted the fragile children crammed into the Liverpool Nursery, housing more than fifty women and nearly one hundred children. Within a week, the new nurse witnessed her first death in Van Diemen's Land: Two-year-old Frederick Withely passed away September 17, 1839.

Awakening with a melancholy heart on the following morning, Ludlow lovingly stroked her daughter's grimy cheek, gravely aware of what was about to happen. Heavy footsteps echoed from the far gate toward the women's ward.

It was time to kiss Arabella good-bye. After reassuring her brave child that she would visit whenever the rules permitted, Ludlow watched Mrs. Hutchinson lead her bewildered ten-year-old away. Only seven days after arriving in Van Diemen's Land, her youngest child was admitted to the Queen's Orphanage. Ludlow vowed to get her back, whatever the cost.

Children were separated from their mothers at Cascades for two reasons. First, it was surmised that if a prisoner spent time on parenting, it reduced her hours of productivity and therefore her economic value. Second, separating girls like Arabella from their mothers fell under Britain's master plan for a pure moral pedigree in the expanding colony. Under the guise of protecting children from "the convict stain," the government removed them from their mothers, hoping to prevent corruption of young souls in order to gain strong, healthy, and docile workers.

Children like Arabella were pressed into servitude as soon as they learned to sew a jacket or grew sturdy enough to carry bricks, usually by age thirteen or fourteen. From this day forward, Arabella would belong to the state until her mother received a Ticket of Leave, her passport to freedom. Unlike Agnes McMillan, who had long passed the age of innocence, Arabella was considered young enough to meet Victorian standards for a pure moral canvas.

Young Miss Tedder boarded the orphans' transport cart along with her good chum from the *Hindostan*, eight-year-old Sarah Smith.[27] The two pulled up another young friend, four-year-old Jane Price, and held her between them. Jane's mother, Ann, was confined to a cell on bread and water for insolence to her master, so the two didn't even get to say good-bye. Straining their necks for a last look at their mothers' prison, the three frightened playmates huddled together as the wheels of the cart began creaking away from the factory.

The light cargo jostled down the valley into Hobart Town and then north toward New Town. The tiny cart made steady progress along well-traveled Elizabeth Street, one of the main thoroughfares into the busy little port. Many wagons headed in the opposite direction were loaded with wood, wool, and other products bound for the warehouses by the docks. Several miles outside Hobart Town, the traffic thinned and the prison orphans passed the few homes that constituted New Town's center. Soon a church revealed itself, centered in what appeared to be a large estate surrounded by fences stretching across the rolling hills. As the cart rattled toward the sternly squared stone spire marking the end of the road, it seemed as if the girls would roll right into what looked like a castle.

This was the gate of the Queen's Orphan School, housing youngsters whose parents were deceased or had abandoned them, along with a large contingent of children who had been transported with their mothers. Behind stone walls akin to the Cascades compound, more than four hundred children were fed and warehoused. The nearly even numbers of girls and boys were separated by St. John's parish church in the center of the complex.

The bricks for constructing the orphanage came from the hands of male convicts who labored at Port Arthur and harvested timber from Mt. Wellington. A staff of nine cared for the youngsters, aged two to fourteen.[28] Arabella, Jane Price, and Sarah Smith would follow a routine that mirrored their mothers' at the Female Factory: up by five or six A.M., depending on sunrise; gruel and bread for breakfast; soup and brown bread for supper; in their hammocks by eight P.M.

Mrs. Gazzard, matron for the girls' ward, handed Arabella a uniform, reflecting the fact that the orphanage was run by the Convict Department. Like mother, like daughter. The telltale blue-and-white-patterned dress, sewn in coarse fabric, marked her as the offspring of a convict. A clean white pinafore proclaimed her moral innocence and protected her dress from the chores and work training expected from all but the youngest inmates.

Matron Gazzard examined the young Tedder's hair for lice, then cut short the back of her locks and left the front intact. This odd haircut further branded Arabella the progeny of a sinner, thief, or prostitute. Here, the rules at Cascades were mirrored. If Arabella turned sassy or disobeyed the matron, her tresses would be shorn off, just like those of an adult. Although Arabella and Sarah were old enough for the girls' ward, Jane Price was not. Separated from her temporary guardians, she was brought to the infant branch that housed the little ones, from two to six years old.

Clambering up the stairs to the second-floor dormitory, Mrs. Gazzard assigned Arabella a hammock and handed her two blankets. The young prisoners of the Crown, considered contaminated children, slept in a large room lit by a single lantern hung from the rafters in the roof. Bedding from the orphanage was delivered to the Female Factory for washing in Yard Two, where the disobedient were punished. Once Ann Price was released from her cell, she probably scrubbed the sheets that carried the scent of her own child.

Arabella and the others her age would soon learn how to do laundry for themselves and master the art of knitting, needlework, and other domestic chores. Local settlers hired some of the fully trained girls as servants, kitchen maids, or nurse's assistants. In the plan to lift the convict stain, religious instruction was nearly as important as work apprenticeship. Protestant girls like Arabella attended mandatory morning prayers in the church before breakfast each day. In addition, on Wednesday and Friday mornings, the children divided into Protestant and Roman Catholic classes and were taught separately. For the rest of the day, they sat for religious instruction and examination, rounded off by an evening church service for the Protestants, who represented the majority.[29]

Arabella's surroundings reflected her mother's life in the Female Factory, where everyone followed a rigid schedule. Each minute of her childhood was accounted for and monitored. The only exception was Sunday, after church, when the girls were allowed free time on the open playground. Still, even the strictest rules couldn't stop Arabella, Sarah, and her new mates from managing a bit of girlish fun and stirring up some occasional mischief without being caught.

Like their mothers, the girls at the Queen's Orphanage were deemed less reputable and harder to manage than the boys, demonstrating few of the qualities expected from a restrained and obedient Victorian young miss. In Mrs. Gazzard's judgment, most of her charges had "fallen into improper courses of life."[30]

For the newly streetwise Arabella, witness to her mother's mistakes, being caught at breaking rules was not an option. Wardens who ran the orphanages were attired in grey military-inspired uniforms and carried canes dangling from their fingers. Caning, solitary confinement, or cutting off of hair served as punishment in this prison for children. Fortunately, just a few years before Arabella's arrival, a scandal at the orphanage had cleaned out many staff who were "dismissed for misbehavior, cruelty and stealing provisions to sell for their own gains."[31]

The living conditions themselves inflicted physical punishment on the youngsters. The year Arabella entered the orphanage, the *Colonial Times* recorded the harsh existence characterizing her young life: "The washing places, or lavatories (to use a word more euphonious for the polite and learned ears of our court contemporary) are highly objectionable: they consist of cell-like rooms, paved with flags, with a stone trough in the center, open at both ends, and consequently, extremely cold and comfortless. Indeed, the prevalence of stone pavement, throughout the lower apartments of the building, is, in our humble opinion, highly detrimental to the health of the inmates; in one room, we saw five little fellows, blue and shivering with cold. . . ."[32]

The emotional distance created by the prim and proper language of the *Times* reporter accurately reflected the sentiments of the day toward boys and girls of convict lineage. Because so few staff supervised so many children, the sick were often ignored or treated with callous disregard. With only one fireplace to stave off the cold in the oversized institutional wards, the children often suffered from chilblains, a condition marked by inflamed fingers and toes and caused by the shivering dampness. A school inspector recorded what he saw: "On one occasion in my presence the master gave an order 'Sore hands and feet stand out.' This dismembered several classes, particularly of the younger children. There were 36 with deep red hands or limping feet, formed a double line, and were marched out for the purpose of some remedial treatment."[33]

Managed perhaps more kindly by Mrs. Gazzard since 1833, the orphanage began to hire women who were experienced as teachers. They instructed the children in reading primarily to support the government-mandated religious instruction. The mistresses, as they were called, also taught penmanship and basic arithmetic. Many decades later, the notes Arabella sent to her grandchildren on their birthdays bore the mark of well-practiced and well-learned cursive writing along with perfect spelling and grammar.

No birthdays were celebrated at the orphanage except Queen Victoria's, each year on May 24. On this one observed holiday of the year, coming as winter approached the Southern Hemisphere, "if the weather permits, the teachers take the children out on a day's ramble in the neighbouring country."[34] Unheated classrooms, a playground without equipment and supervision, and the absence of parental attention and care made for an austere childhood, save for the friendships that flourished. Yet a bit of education and the regular, spartan meals were more than what these children's peers and relatives consumed back in the British slums.

Two months after Arabella settled into her routine at the orphanage, another ten-year-old, Catherine Mullins, arrived at its stone entrance. Before long, they were true-blue mates. Together, over the next four and a half years, the girls would mature into optimistic young women, inspired by friendship and monthly visits from their mothers. Every evening, Arabella and Catherine sat down to a meal of soup made with meat and vegetables, "a large piece of coarse, but sweet wheaten bread" and a cup of milk.[35] Before a spoon was lifted, the roomful of children said grace out loud in near unison.

At about the same hour, Ludlow stared into her bowl of broth. Separated from Arabella, a listless #151 resisted swallowing the food she tried to eat. Although she had temporarily lost her youngest child, the Widow Tedder found some solace in devoting loving attention to the tiny babies under her care.

Despite her best efforts, calling upon both maternal instincts and nursing skills, seven more children died before the Christmas holiday. By January, the warm weather that arrived at summer's peak seemed to slow the spread of illness inside the house Ludlow shared with her young charges and their mothers. The Liverpool Street nursery seemed ever more distant from the Keppel Street quarters she had left just one year ago.

Arrivals and Departures

For a year and a half, Ludlow toiled in the nursery alongside head midwife and deputy matron Elizabeth Cato. By now, Ludlow's *Hindostan* friend Ann Price had completed her punishment in the wash yard and was also assigned to Liverpool Street. At least once a month, and when they were granted extra visits for model behavior, together the two mothers walked the hilly four miles from Cascades to New Town for Sunday visits with their daughters.

The women's routine changed abruptly on a foggy autumn morning in April 1841, when Mrs. Cato failed to appear at morning muster. Typically she met Ludlow and Ann immediately after breakfast and issued daily orders for nursery duty. The night before, however, Police Magistrate John Price arrested both of the Catos and charged them with trafficking. During the initial phase of his investigation, Mr. Price confronted the overseer and his wife with the news that he'd seen a letter written by a prisoner, Ellen Watkins, "in which she requests certain articles be sent under cover to Mrs. Cato for her, here accompanied by a fowl for the use of Mrs. Cato."[36] When he requested the Catos turn over both the letter and the chicken, Mrs. Cato responded that "the contents of the letter was too horrible and indecent and that she had thought fit to burn it."[37] Having read the letter himself, Magistrate Price countered her assertion, later noting in his report to Superintendent Josiah Spode: "I must here remark that not an indecent allusion was introduced into that letter."[38] But the excuses were quick and well prepared when Price inquired about the messenger bird. Yes, they were given the fowl for reasons unknown, and "it was a pity it should stink and so I had it plucked."[39]

The two senior officials had contrived a scheme wherein convicts were allowed messages from outside the prison if delivered to Mrs. Cato along with a chicken. It was just the tip of a pervasive and thriving underground economy at Cascades. This relatively small extortion delivered notes between the female prisoners and their paramours in Hobart Town, providing many chickens for the Catos. The overseers and the deputy matron either ate the fowl or traded them for other items available via the illicit marketplace.

For years, the local government ignored the corruption inside Cascades as well as the abuse of prisoners who were mismanaged and mistreated. Word of inhumane conditions reached England and prompted Elizabeth Fry to beg for intervention. Four long years passed before Lady Jane responded to Mrs. Fry's impassioned plea for an investigation into conditions at the Female Factory. In July 1841, shortly after the Catos' indictment, Elizabeth's emissary Miss Kezia Hayter arrived on the *Rajah* and presented Lady Jane with a quilt made by the convict women aboard ship. An embroidered inscription on the fabric rendered it impossible to ignore Fry's mission:

TO THE LADIES
of the
Convict ship Committee
This quilt worked by the Convicts
of the ship Rajah during their voyage
to Van Diemans [sic] Land is presented as a
testimony of the gratitude with which
they remember their exertions for their
welfare while in England and during
their passage and also as a proof that
they have not neglected the Ladies
kind admonitions of being industrious
June 1841[40]

On August 3, 1841, Lady Jane penned a note to Fry, offering an excuse for failing to write sooner: "I had little to tell you respecting the conditions of the female prisoners population here, which . . . would give you any satisfaction to hear, and I shrank from the painful task of being the reporter of evil, and of confessing how little I had personally done. . . ."[41]

The word "evil" was applied liberally to descriptions of the girls and women exiled "beyond the seas." The *Courier* announced the arrival of the *Rajah* in the paper's local news section with this warning:

> The female prisoners brought out in this ship appear to be of much better character than usual; their behavior during the voyage was very good, doubtless in a great degree the result of the indefatigable care which appears to have been exercised both with reference to their morality and physical comfort. The Lieutenant-Governor most judiciously afforded every facility to the inhabitants who had applied for servants, to obtain them direct from the ship; this is a most desirable arrangement, for even an hour's contamination in that receptacle of wickedness, the Factory may prove of lasting evil to the unfortunate creatures who once enter it.[42]

Although the Catos were dismissed from Cascades for their transgressions, there was nowhere to send the increasingly rowdy members of the Flash Mob. The more they were punished, the more unruly and outrageous their rebellion. Five months before Ludlow's arrival, the infamous Ellen Scott was charged with "violently assaulting Mr. Hutchinson with intent to kill or do him some bodily harm."[43] The women at the factory realized they had nothing left to lose as their treatment worsened, and the Mob escalated from simple defiance into all-out war.

Among those involved in the May 6, 1839, riot was Ann Maloney, the Londoner who had left behind a penny for her loved one W. F., engraved with two hearts and two doves. Fourteen years into her life sentence for larceny in a boardinghouse, Ann turned bitter and ornery, her optimism long departed from the days she inscribed the love token inside Newgate Prison. A year after being admitted to Cascades, she attempted escape with a friend named Martha Griffith. While scaling the prison wall, Ann broke her leg, and the constable sentenced both girls to bread and water in solitary confinement. In 1829, Ann had married and was remanded to her husband's oversight for the remainder of her sentence, an escape clause for female convicts. But when the couple was caught running a brothel in Hobart Town, she was returned to Cascades and the company of her Flash Mob mates.

Malnourished, neglected, and increasingly angry women were packed tight behind the stone walls. Seething frustration toward hypocrites like the Reverend Bedford, controller and abuser of many, fueled the Mob's fury. Five others participated in the insurrection directed toward the often-tired, paper-pushing superintendent. Each was charged with insubordination for "forcibly, violently and in a turbulent manner resisting Mr. Hutchinson and refusing to obey his lawful commands."[44] He immediately sentenced Ann Maloney to twelve months at the washtubs and sent Ellen Scott to Launceston for two years' hard labor.

The Hobart Town newspapers printed in-depth stories about the Mob's escapades and included more details in the police report section. In an article about Ellen Scott and her conspirators, the *Colonial Times* wrote:

We have appended to the title of this article, the term *"Flash Mob;"* that this term is technical, is sufficiently obvious; but few of our readers,—few, indeed, of any who possess the ordinary attributes of human nature, can even conjecture the frightful abominations, which are practised by the women, who compose this mob. Of course, we cannot pollute our columns with the disgusting details, which have been conveyed to us; but we may, with propriety, call the notice of the proper Functionaries to a system of vice, immorality, and iniquity, which has tended, mainly, to render the majority of female assigned servants, the annoying and untractable animals, that they are.[45]

Despite these declarations of condemnation, the *Colonial Times* filled many columns with tasty tidbits about the women so often deemed unworthy of its time and attention. Ellen Scott was not alone in providing fodder for gossipmongers. Whisperers were all about town in the shops, gardens, and pubs.

After the departure of the Female Factory's dark heroine, a new cast of colorful characters emerged more vibrant than ever from this theater of unimaginable horrors. Each player took an unspoken oath to torment her captors and stand by her sisters. Like Ellen Scott, Catherine Henrys reached legendary status inside Cascades and across Van Diemen's Land. Twenty-nine, with deep pockmarks across her face, she was transported from Ireland in 1836, the same year as Agnes. She quickly became a master of ingenious escapes, like tunneling her way out of solitary confinement with a sharpened spoon, and using tied blanket strips to scale the stone walls. Tall for her time at five feet, six inches, Catherine sported two tattoos on her right arm and was nicknamed "Jemmy the Rover." During one escapade in 1841, she put on men's trousers, tucked her hair under a boy's cap, and headed into the bush to work as a timber cutter. Before her return to the Female Factory she lived free for a year, chopping down trees with Samuel Dobbs, a freed convict whom she would later marry.[46]

The Flash Mob tended to attract the conspicuously rowdy, but someone literate like Ludlow Tedder would be highly prized for her skills. Her ability to write and deliver messages during her regular pilgrimage from Liverpool Street to Cascades undoubtedly assisted love affairs and contraband smuggling. Such a proper matron was ideal to convey colored scarves and gaudy jewelry for the rebels with a sense of humor and a cause at Cascades.

Ludlow quickly figured out the survival maze inside the prison and how things really worked for those on both sides of the walls. Her regular trek up and down the valley afforded plenty of time to hatch a plan for Arabella's return. For today, it was August 1841 and all of Ludlow's attention was focused on a lovely Scottish redhead and a new baby boy who had been born at the Female Factory. The mother was called Janet Houston, and she had named her son William.[47]

A view of Kilmarnock Cross, East Ayrshire, Scotland, in 1840, Anonymous. Agnes McMillan and Janet Houston were transported for stealing clothing from shops along Kilmarnock Cross in 1836.

"Elizabeth Fry Entering Newgate with Mary Sanderson," Henrietta Ward, 1867

Computer-generated image
of Ludlow Tedder

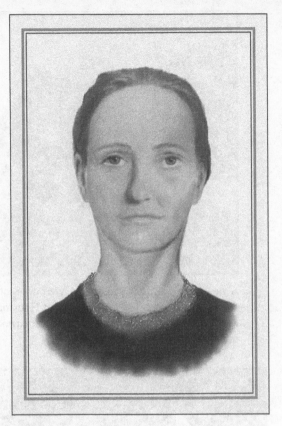

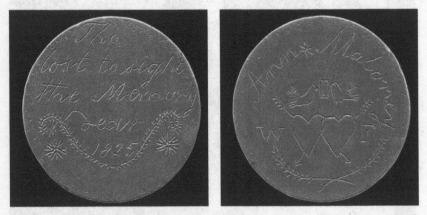

Left: Love Token created by Ann Maloney, 1825
Right: Reverse side of Ann Maloney's Love Token

Rajah Quilt, 1841

"TO THE LADIES
of the
Convict ship Committee

This quilt worked by the Convicts
of the ship Rajah during their voyage
to Van Diemans Land is presented as a
testimony of the gratitude with which
they remember their exertions for their
welfare while in England and during
their passage and also as a proof that
they have not neglected the Ladies
kind admonitions of being industrious
June 1841"

An excerpt from Bridget Mulligan's conduct register from the *Blackfriar*

COURTESY: ARCHIVES OFFICE OF TASMANIA CON41-1-30

"Female factory from Proctor's Quarry," John Skinner Prout, 1844

COURTESY: ALLPORT LIBRARY AND MUSEUM OF FINE ARTS, STATE LIBRARY OF TASMANIA

Remaining walls of Cascades Female Factory, Hobart, Tasmania
COURTESY: DIGNEY FIGNUS

Washtub remains at Cascades Female Factory, Hobart, Tasmania
COURTESY: DIGNEY FIGNUS

"Meal Time, Cascades Female Factory," Peter Gouldthorpe

Solitary cell remains at Cascades Female Factory. Each cell measures approximately four feet by six feet.

"Sawyer's Hut on the River Huon," V.D.L., 1842, William Knight. Agnes McMillan and husband William Roberts settled along the Huon in 1843.

"Swearing Allegiance to the Southern Cross," Charles Alphonse Doudiet, 1854.
Agnes McMillan and her family were witnesses to the Eureka Rebellion.
COURTESY: ART GALLERY OF BALLARAT; PURCHASED WITH THE ASSISTANCE OF MANY DONORS, 1996

Old Lismore 1877, Woodlark Street, Barrie's Buildings, John Dawson Forbes, 1877.
Agnes McMillan died in Lismore on July 24, 1877.

Henry James Laskey and his wife, Hannah, and family. Hannah was Bridget Mulligan's daughter.

Samuel and Fanny Bailey, Janet Houston's son and daughter-in-law
COURTESY: KAYE WILLIAMS

Arabella Tedder Waters Oliver, circa late 1890s

Arabella Tedder's descendants in 1903:

Front Row: from left: Elizabeth Birchmore (daughter), Arabella Birchmore (granddaughter), **Arabella Tedder/Waters/Oliver**, Lavinia Mooney (granddaughter), Arabella Tedder (granddaughter), James Gallagher (bridegroom), Mary Mooney (bride and granddaughter of Arabella), Edith Mooney (granddaughter), William Atkinson (fiancé of granddaughter), Arabella Punton (granddaughter), George Mooney (grandson), Jemima Mooney (daughter, nursing), Charlotte Mooney (granddaughter), Charlotte Punton (daughter), Edith Punton (granddaughter)

Second Row: Jack Mooney, Andrew Mooney, Isaac Tedder (grandsons of Arabella Tedder/Waters/Oliver). The next few people are likely grandchildren of Arabella.

Far right of picture: Patrick Mooney, husband of Jemima and son-in-law of Arabella.

Back Row: Far left, Henry Tedder (son of Arabella); Arabella Ludlow and Sarah Maria (Arabella's eldest two daughters) are more than likely the two women pictured in the middle of this row.

Arabella's youngest son, Isaac John Waters, is probably pictured but not identified in this photo.

COURTESY: ED MOONEY AND GLAD WISHART

Top: Birthday wishes from Arabella to her grandson Jack
Bottom: New Year's card from Arabella to her grandson Jack

Descendants of Ludlow Tedder with the author in 2009:

From left: Matthew Sharpe (great-great-great-great-grandson), Deborah Swiss, Joy Sharpe (GGGGD), Joanne Shannon née Sharpe (GGGGGD), Ty Sinclair (GGGGGS), Keely Millikin (GGGGGGD), Glad Wishart (GGGGD), Stephen Wishart (GGGGGS), Ed Mooney (GGGS), Jenny Millikin née Wishart (GGGGGD), Marlene Leslie (GGGGD), Kristy Finnigan née Leslie (GGGGGD)

Front Row: GGGGG-grandchildren of Ludlow—Matilda Sinclair, Caroline Leslie, Daniel Finnigan, Ryley Millikin

Michele Cullen, Agnes McMillan's great-great-granddaughter, wears a bonnet made for Christina Henri's "Roses from the Heart" installation of 25,000 bonnets, one for each woman transported.
COURTESY: DIGNEY FIGNUS

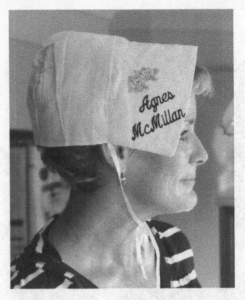

Mary Binks and Gran's Van, a soup kitchen for the homeless and needy in Devonport, Tasmania. Mary is the great-granddaughter of Bridget Mulligan.
COURTESY: SUZANNE BANNON

~ 8 ~

The Yellow C

The Valley of Sorrow

Cradling little William Houston against her grey duffel shift and smiling with contentment, Janet watched her new son grow stronger by the day. It was the end of August 1841. The sun was setting later now, and soon the winds of spring would bring the island back to life. Outside, the temperature drifted toward the fifties, ending a mercifully mild winter. Certainly it was nothing like the freezing nights she'd spent on Goosedubbs Street with Agnes. Still, occasional Antarctic winds blasted and shook the windowpanes facing the front of Liverpool Street. For good measure, Janet sat right next to the warm kitchen stove. Nurse Tedder smiled and offered the new mother a large slice of bread and a cup of tea with sugar, making certain the breast-feeding mothers received their full share of the rations delivered from the cook at Cascades.

The month before, on July 22, Janet had turned twenty-two and on her birthday carried a present, kicking and turning within her swollen belly. She tried to hide her pregnancy, but when she approached full term, doubt no longer lingered about her condition. On August 2, a policeman delivered the winsome Scot to the Factory, "being advanced in pregnancy."[1] Janet held her middle and ambled back to her cell after Reverend Bedford's evening rant. Above the yard, in the clear black sky, a full moon hung suspended.

A few days later, the redheaded lass went into labor and delivered her "currency lad," as colonial-born children were called. "Sterling" children were born in the mother country, the pound sterling being more valuable than colonial currency. As soon as the young mother was able to walk, she and her newborn were sent down the valley to Liverpool Street, where today she stared into the eyes of her little infant. Janet had been born the same year as Nurse Ludlow's dear departed daughter Frances, who passed away at age seven and lay buried in a tiny plot a world away.

The motherly Mrs. Tedder immediately developed a deep affection for the soft-spoken new mother, with her enchanting Scottish brogue and rather wicked sense of humor. Ludlow felt both relieved and gratified to see an infant thrive, especially because she had seen so many perish. Since her first day in the nursery two years before, twenty-four children from Liverpool Street had been hastily laid to rest in St. David's Cemetery near the harbor.

Inside the tiny house where she worked six days a week and often Sundays, Widow Tedder learned many truths about the girls and women who were returned to the Female Factory for what Reverend Bedford proclaimed the sin of adultery. At this time, the adulterer label was attached to every unmarried convict mother, regardless of her circumstances. Many were the victims of rape by a master, a male servant, or a settler. Others carried the child of a lover or common-law husband. Reason mattered not. In the eyes of the Crown, they were all sinners relegated to the same punishment.

Superintendent of Convicts Josiah Spode argued for placing the prisoners in local homes, where, he surmised, the "proper" citizenry would provide role models "both in a moral point of view and in teaching them those useful habits of domestic life."[2] For many among the transported women, assignment to settlers yielded the opposite effect, rendering them angrier and more rebellious as their sentences unfolded.

Most reports of abuse were promptly swept under the rug. Yet the abuse became so widespread that eventually the Crown reluctantly agreed to an Inquiry into Female Convict Prison Discipline, which commenced in 1841. The investigation revealed that recourse for sexual assault was nearly impossible, though a few desperately sought justice after being attacked in their master's care. Grace Heinbury was twenty-six when she arrived in Van Diemen's Land on the convict ship *Atwick*, which anchored on January 24, 1838. The black-haired nursery maid with the dark hazel eyes reported rather matter-of-factly to the committee the horror that soon befell her. During one assignment, she was raped by a man whose wife had unwittingly selected her for their servant. After she reported the attack to the authorities in Hobart Town, the police did nothing. Superintendent Hutchinson promptly assigned her to another household, where she was again assaulted, this time by several male servants. With no recourse via the police to end her abuse, Grace walked off the job. She was punished with six months' hard labor for leaving her assignment, but accepted it as a fair trade.[3] Absconding seemed a reasonable choice. Temporary refuge could usually be found in the safe houses and grog shops tucked into the back alleys and shady streets around Hobart Town.

In caring for the mothers and infants housed on Liverpool Street, Ludlow began to understand the terrible secrets kept by the figures she had first viewed in Yard One two years before. Young women confided in the well-spoken nurse with the soft hazel eyes, who reminded them of their mothers back in Britain. Even if a convict mother wanted to love the child conceived by rape from a master or a male servant, the Female Factory "Rules and Regulations" stifled this natural inclination at every opportunity. The unnatural separation of mother and child caused some to give up entirely, as they sank toward emotional numbness.

A disreputable master could commit the perfect crime with any female under his charge: There were no witnesses and virtually no one to believe the hysterical tale told by a convict maid. There was no way to win. If she ended up pregnant, she was charged an adulterer. Once weaned, her child was taken away and she began a sentence of hard labor in the Crime Class. Police Magistrate John Price admitted that many masters were "totally unfit to be entrusted" with the indentured women "from a perfect disregard to the morality of their female servants."[4]

After her sixth return to Crime Class for misconduct in 1840, Janet avoided attention until she was found pregnant and living with a free man, the suspected father of dear William. When she reported back to the factory on August 2, 1841, Janet knew the punishment she faced. Along with her newborn arrived a sentence of a year's hard labor, six months for "living in a state of adultery with a free man" and an additional six for "being advanced in pregnancy."

The colony's government absolved itself of responsibility for the rising number of unmarried mothers at the Female Factory by making it a crime to give birth to an illegitimate child. Superintendent of Convicts Josiah Spode believed "the regulation was 'the best check . . . of immorality' and that it would 'restrain the promiscuous intercourse of these depraved women.'"[5] His reasoning backfired exponentially. As the number of female transports rose, so, too, did pregnancies among the women, most in their twenties and thirties.

In some cases, a colonist used the system to free a sweetheart from Cascades, requesting her assignment and then setting up household together. Fathers wishing to marry the mother of their child were sometimes denied permission. The lieutenant governor was required to review all marriage requests from 1829 to 1857. If both parties couldn't prove they were legally single and not married to someone else, or failed to pay the exorbitant application fees, their request was denied.[6] Female Factory Superintendent Hutchinson's approval was also required, according to the rules and regulations, which stated: "No Female will be allowed to marry from the 2d. or 3d. Classes, nor, indeed, from the 1st., unless she can obtain a favourable certificate from the Principal Superintendent."[7]

Adding insult to injury, the Reverend Bedford also held veto over betrothed couples. Fancying himself the moral magistrate for Hobart Town, Holy Willie refused to wed convicts who had been married to someone left behind in Britain. It made no difference that there was virtually no chance of ever seeing their first husbands again. Many spouses left behind were already remarried or cohabiting with another woman. Although some preachers applied common sense in such decisions, the ever-unyielding Bedford, himself a well-known adulterer, often refused to marry transported women and men who desired a fresh start.

If not wed to the child's mother, fathers in Van Diemen's Land bore neither blame nor responsibility. The Hobart Town coroner deplored "the fact that unmarried female convicts who became pregnant were punished 'whilst the Father of the child whether he be the Seducer, or paramour, is rarely if ever punished.'"[8]

Despite this double standard, Janet discovered a silver lining when she returned to the Female Factory and especially to Liverpool Street. Shortly after giving birth to baby William at the Cascades infirmary, a stern matron named Mrs. Slea ushered her down the valley to the lying-in room at the nursery. Passing the tiny kitchen on the first floor, Janet spotted a familiar frame standing with her back turned and scrubbing a giant stack of pots. It was a sputtering Agnes, clanging the pans and silverware as the greying water sloshed over her feet and onto the floor. It was the last place Janet expected to see her friend.

Looking forward to the spring in 1841, Janet had much to celebrate. Only a few weeks old, William was already thriving in her loving arms. Kindly Mrs. Tedder offered her valuable guidance on caring for her newborn. Celebrating this happy event with her dear Agnes was bloody good luck indeed, especially because they hadn't seen each other for nearly three years.

The last time had been in summer's heat, shortly before Christmas 1838, when Agnes stood ankle-deep in water hunched over a stone washtub in Yard Two. Janet had returned to Cascades for her fifth offense, one fewer than the feisty Agnes. The slightly less rambunctious of the two, Janet was assigned to the Reverend W. Orton after twice disobeying her first mistress. The incident started on November 4, when the reverend reported his convict maid absent without leave overnight. She got away with only a reprimand, but ten days later she again walked off the job. This time a constable found her in a "disorderly house," a rowdy tavern specializing in strong liquor, gambling, and prostitution. This offense sent Janet back to the prison for a month, picking oakum in solitary confinement.

For the first six days, Overseer Cato passed only bread and water through the grates in her cell door. Upon completion of this latest discipline, Mr. Hutchinson assigned Janet to a different settler. By now, it had become a bit of a game to return to Cascades from a dangerous or dreary placement as quickly as possible. Janet's next position lasted only six days.

Indifferent to the punishment awaiting her, Janet strutted back to the Female Factory that December 20, 1838, where an auspicious surprise awaited her. Agnes, too, had returned to the valley to serve two months at the washtubs for being absent without leave. The two celebrated Hogmanay together as they brought in the new year in 1839. Their reunion was bittersweet because each would be sent her separate way. It would be nearly three years before their paths crossed again, although each returned to the Female Factory at different times. Sent out on four more country assignments, Agnes managed to run away from each. Her fate, however, took a turn for the better when, in 1840, Superintendent Hutchinson dispatched her to the most remote location he could find. While working in Oatlands, located in the middle of nowhere, the twenty-year-old met a dashing older man who captured her heart.

Her most recent spate of trouble involved insolence toward her master. The superintendent had run out of assignment options for the indomitable #253, who was about to turn twenty-one. She'd been sent to work all over Van Diemen's Land, from Richmond fifteen miles north of Hobart Town to the remote Oatlands. Agnes always managed to run away from her master, no matter how distant or isolated the assignment, so a frustrated Hutchinson returned the untamable Scot to a place he could monitor. His wife, as matron, was required to inspect the nursery every day.

Because Agnes had experience as a governess for Mr. Harvey, she was well suited to work at Liverpool Street, although most prisoners who weren't mothers considered it an undesirable assignment. Babies wailed day and night, the stench of diarrhea and vomit invaded every corner, and mothers fought for private space where there was none. The cramped little house was staffed primarily by convict mothers still nursing their infants. In addition to nursing their own child, they also cared for children separated from their mothers and housed in the nursery until transfer to the Queen's Orphanage at age two or three. Agnes's heavy responsibility inside Liverpool Street lightened considerably when she heard Janet's Scottish brogue echo through the front entryway.

The two mates, fully blossomed into womanhood, still found unadulterated joy in recounting the girlish escapades they'd shared. Agnes had picked up a completely new repertoire of rebellious tunes about the regrets and the dreams of a convict maid:

> *I toil each day in greaf [sic] and pain*
> *And sleepless through the night remain*
> *My constant toils are unrepaid*
> *And wretched is the Convict Maid*

Oh could I but once more be free
I'd never again a captive be
But I would seek some honest trade
And never again be a Convict Maid[9]

Sitting inside the Liverpool Street nursery, Agnes excitedly confided in the loyal chum she considered a sister. They'd managed to
survive the first five years of their transport sentence, suffering neither the illnesses nor alcoholism afflicting so many at Cascades. Picking up exactly where they'd left off, the two mates laughed, cursed,
and cried through the stories and adventures they hadn't been able to
share. As Agnes took a turn cuddling William after her kitchen shift
ended, they dared to dream about the promise of their freedom in
1843. Knowing instinctively that this might be their last time together,
Agnes and Janet filled the present with recollections from their past.
Together, they stayed out of trouble, or at least weren't caught by Mr.
Hutchinson.

All went smoothly at Liverpool Street save the death of one toddler in September 1841. The climate remained relatively mild after a
freak snowstorm on September 13. By October, spring unfolded its
arms in earnest as the days grew longer and temperatures climbed
into the sixties. Janet, William, and Agnes spent the next few months
together under Ludlow's watchful eye. The two young women felt
like girls again, and their exuberance lifted the spirits of everyone in
the nursery. It was going to be a bloody good Christmas—and baby
William's first. Agnes could sing the little lad a right fine version of
"Auld Lang Syne." The weather was clear and a balmy seventy degrees for the Scots' Hogmanay toast in 1842. With pubs located
around the corner from the nursery, spirits easily found their way into
the dilapidated kitchen.

As they headed through the warm January summer, Janet could
not hold back the dreadful future that lay ahead. Forced to wean William in early February, precisely six months from the day he was born,

Janet at first refused to leave the nursery. With the onset of six months' hard labor for the crime of unwed pregnancy, she'd be allowed to visit her infant son only once a week. Ludlow tried to comfort the loving mother, reminding her that she could visit William the following Sunday, and Agnes would rock him to sleep once the kitchen was clean and tidy at night. Still inconsolable at being separated from her son, Janet trudged down Liverpool Street, a watchful magistrate at her side.

Janet's Sunday visit never happened. Baby William Houston died on Wednesday, February 9, 1842. Over the next six weeks, Ludlow and Agnes were present at the deaths of six more children, ranging in age from seven to fifteen months. Janet's sweet son must have succumbed to one of the deadly outbreaks that struck the overcrowded little house with neither warning nor recourse. Now it was Agnes's turn to assume the role of protector for the loyal mate who'd always watched out for her. Somehow she persuaded nursery matron Mrs. Slea to allow her to tag along and retrieve Janet from the washtubs at Cascades. It was the worst moment the two childhood friends had ever faced.

Back at Liverpool Street, Nurse Tedder gently washed little William and wrapped him in a layer of off-white muslin. Numb with grief, Janet hurried into the nursery and snuggled her son against her heart one last time before his final passage toward the harbor. Mrs. Slea lined a wooden box with scraps of cloth before she placed the infant inside. Agnes held tight to one arm and Ludlow the other as they helped Janet down Liverpool Street to Harrington, walking the three blocks in silence. Onlookers fell to deferential quiet as they viewed the common sight of a roughly hewn gumwood crate turned tiny makeshift coffin.

As they neared the town's oldest burial grounds at the corner of Harrington and Davey Streets, a summer breeze off the River Derwent spread the essence of eucalyptus over the ragged funeral procession. A bit run-down, St. David's Cemetery was set on a quiet plot surrounded by twisted gum trees, their leafy branches cradling the edges of the burial plots.

Situated near the busy harbor, the cemetery was visible to many passersby who witnessed the two or three prisoner burials nearly every day of the week. So common were Hobart Town funerals that citizens spoke of the rare "maiden day" when not a soul was buried. Hugh Hull, a former Londoner and now government official, observed convict burials about the same time as William's passing: "A few words are mumbled over the body by the purse-proud Clergyman, who as he receives nothing for the business, very soon hurries it over . . . and the hole is not filled up for two days. . . . The thistle takes the place of sweet, lowly flowers which usually bloom in churchyards and there is no one to cut them down. . . ."[10] The occasional goat would slip through a hole in the stone wall and graze over the graves until someone shooed it away.[11]

On a bright and clear February morning between the summer storms, three women wearing the telltale Cascades grey shuffled across the cemetery to St. David's far corner. An unpaid and uninterested minister joined the three prisoners and Mrs. Slea on the lush green near a freshly dug shallow grave. He opened his Bible and began to recite the words he already knew: "Yea, though I walk through the valley of the shadow of death, I will fear no evil. . . ." Janet heard nary a word, as her eyes remained fixed on the smooth grey bark covering her son. "Surely goodness and mercy shall follow me all the days of my life. . . ." Under the scent of blue-green eucalyptus trees, two friends who'd shared so many sorrows watched little William unceremoniously lowered into the ground. Leaning tight against each other, together they shouldered the grief and pondered its senselessness. Janet spent a last moment bidding her firstborn farewell. Just as the small group turned away, they heard the hollow scraping sound of the groundskeeper's shovel as he scattered a few piles of dirt over the tiny coffin.

Yard Two

Other than Agnes's arm draped over her shoulder, the luxury of comfort remained out of Janet's reach. After a last moment with Agnes
and Ludlow at the nursery, the weeping mother was returned to Yard
Two's stone washtubs, where she'd complete her six-month punishment for giving birth to a baby now deceased. As she scrubbed in the
half shadows of Yard Two, a deadened Janet felt neither the stone
scraping her skinny elbows nor the muddy groundwater seeping over
her toes.

Slowly, as summer faded into fall, Janet began to feel again. Numbness wore away and exposed a rage on the edge of eruption. The
grieving mother seethed with fury toward a system that forced early
weaning and placed baby William in the overcrowded infant ward,
where he received insufficient nourishment and little attention. For a
time, she dutifully carried out twelve-hour work assignments, collaps-
ing in her low-slung hammock for fitful sleep. Every night at mandatory chapel, the mourning mother faced Holy Willie, the reverend
who had successfully lobbied for the punishment she now endured
for unwed pregnancy. Janet's emotions certainly ran full bore as she
damned Heaven and the Fates for their cruelty. Above all, she must
have detested the Reverend Bedford from the depths of her soul. On
his recommendation, Superintendent Hutchinson condemned and
punished all pregnant convicts, regardless of the circumstances.[12]

On March 17, five weeks after she'd buried her son, Janet lashed
out against the convict system. Her refusal to leave her hammock and
get to work brought six days back in solitary confinement.

The bloody bastards, what more can they take away?

Godfrey Charles Mundy, a colonel in the British army, toured the
Female Factory and recorded his observations about solitary confinement in the book *Our Antipodes*. At first, he applauded "bread-and-water
discussed in silence and solitude—things that no woman loveth," deem-

ing it "merciful" and "discreet" punishment.[13] But the colonel would later eat his own words when he asked the turnkey to unlock a series of massive doors in the solitary ward. After inspecting two cells where women sat glumly at work, they pried open a third cell door. Mundy described what he saw:

> It looked like the den of a wolf. . . . From the extreme end of the floor I found a pair of bright, flashing eyes fixed on mine. . . . It was a small, slight, and quite young girl—very beautiful in feature and complexion—but it was the fierce beauty of a wild cat! . . . I fear that the pang of pity that shot across my heart when that pretty prisoner was shut again from the light of day, might have found no place there had she been as ugly as the sins that had brought her into trouble. I had no more stomach for solitary cells this day.[14]

Janet's solitary chamber held a mildewed mattress on the floor, a stool, and a bucket for waste. But no punishment could be worse than the loss of her child. The despondent mother quietly curled up against the cold stone, drawing herself into the fetal position.

One week after her release from solitary, up to her elbows in dirty washtub water, a despairing Janet heard the whisper of a familiar voice. A cheeky Agnes had simply walked out of the Liverpool Street nursery and represented herself as a free woman when stopped by a suspicious constable. For this, a magistrate escorted her back to Cascades to begin four months once again in Yard Two. Since the passing of William, whom she'd come to adore like a nephew, she'd seen in rapid succession six more children carried from Liverpool Street to St. David's Cemetery. At an age at which she had good reason to think about a family of her own, Agnes couldn't face another infant death.

Reunited with Janet back in the valley, Agnes tried to cheer her mate, regaling her with tales about the dark-haired dashing prince she'd spotted on the night he galloped through Oatlands on a wild horse. Janet found a bit of comfort in her friend's girlish giggle as she described a freed convict named William Roberts, who sported dark bushy eyebrows and a smile full of mischief. Agnes had fallen deeply in love.

The Glasgow lasses were nearing the end of their seven-year sentences. They probably knew their paths would part as they approached the day each would hold a Certificate of Freedom. There was no sense thinking about Scotland anymore. Those days were over. In spite of the suffering they'd been forced to endure, they found love and a sense of belonging in the colony down under.

For the last decade, their unwavering friendship provided each other with just enough sustenance to endure another year, always holding out hope that the next would be better. The petty theft that transported them to Van Diemen's Land paled in comparison to the crimes they saw nearly every day, which went, for the most part, unpunished. Girls raped by their masters, Holy Willie's hypocrisy, bribes taken by the Catos and others—so much seemed unjust. Angry frustration ebbed and flowed for both Janet and Agnes, though their misconduct was relatively tame compared to the records of many transported with them.

There was all manner of mayhem and insurgency as 1842 unfolded. It began building in 1839, when Ellen Scott and other members of the Flash Mob attempted to throttle Mr. Hutchinson. The night after Janet was released from solitary, just a week before Agnes's latest infraction, the rebels at the top of the valley decided to throw a party. It was precisely the type of disobedience that drove the aging superintendent to tear at his whiskers.

The weather was perfect, mild and dry, and for three weeks not a drop of rain had fallen. Under a bright moon, shortly after eight o'clock on the evening of March 24, Superintendent Hutchinson heard a ruckus coming from one of the wards. He hurried out of his second-floor quarters across the yard to investigate. As he drew closer, the disturbance grew louder. Stopping outside the ward, he peered through the grates and saw a group of prisoners cavorting in a state of wild abandon. Horrified, he waited silently until he could identify at least five of the women who'd joyfully removed their shapeless grey shifts and tossed them in a pile. Singing, cursing, and dancing naked with one another "in imitation of men and women together," they barely noticed the skinny specter of a man whose mouth flapped agape.[15]

Among the bawdy performers were two well-known Flash Mob members who'd assisted with Ellen Scott's 1839 turbulent insubordination. There was raven-haired Eliza Smith and the fierce green-eyed Mary Devereux.[16] Devereux also sported a tattoo, two small blue dots between the finger and thumb of her left hand.[17] Frances Hutchinson from County Kerry, another known troublemaker, displayed the same emblem, along with rings tattooed on her first two fingers.[18] Among the twenty-five thousand women transported, eight other Irish females etched nearly identical blue dots between their fingers.[19] Each encoded a message, perhaps of solidarity or shared heritage, one that could be neither stripped away nor removed by their captors.

This night, each naked dancer received a sentence of either six or twelve months' hard labor for her final curtain call. Mr. Hutchinson, a Methodist minister by training, could tolerate no more of their saucy insurrection and made it a point to separate the five rebels and house them in separate wards. After release from hard labor, Eliza Smith continued her rebellion, thumbing her nose at authorities through foul language and absconding with great regularity. Finally, in February 1845, she was punished once again for misconduct. Only this time, she was dead within the month. The last entry in her conduct record was scribbled haphazardly over other entries: "Died in Factory Launceston, 5 March 1845."[20] She was twenty-seven.

Punishment rarely stopped merriment when it erupted behind the Female Factory walls. In fact, it sometimes encouraged elaborate schemes designed to torment Superintendent Hutchinson and the others in charge. Repeat offenders harbored no fear for what they'd face in the Crime Class, as explained in the *True Colonist* newspaper: "Many women prefer this class to the others, because it is *more lively*!

There is more *fun* there than in the others; and we have been informed, that some of the most sprightly of the ladies divert their companions by acting plays!"[21]

The always simmering readiness for revolution, fueled by absolute disdain toward their captors, persisted throughout the year into winter's long nights. Under the big bright moon of August 23, 1842,[22] the Flash Mob was at it again. Mr. Hutchinson sent his wife to investigate the boisterous sounds of song and dance, undoubtedly fearful of what he might see. The instant Mrs. Hutchinson opened the latch to the crime ward, it fell quiet, and she was unable to tell where the noise had originated. By the time she returned to her residence, the clamor started all over again. Back to the ward she trudged, only to face silent women sitting in their hammocks doing nothing at all. This went on for some time before Mr. Hutchinson made an appearance. In a feeble attempt to end the standoff, he demanded the names of the ringleaders. Without a word, he later reported, the women squatted down, "shouted and clapped their hands, stamped and made noise with their feet and this took place to such an extent that I conscientiously say it was a riot."[23]

Somehow managing to quiet the mob, Mr. Hutchinson left the room, only to be followed by a fresh outburst of clapping and cheering. Tension reached the boiling point, and he called in the town police. The women greeted the officers with a solidarity chant: "We are all alike, we are all alike."[24] The stalemate lasted four hours until the now-crumbling and defeated Ann Maloney turned in the insurgent ringleaders. Her fun and games inside the Female Factory were over, and solidarity was not enough to keep her strong. Although she'd joined Ellen Scott's infamous 1839 revolt and reveled in the wild sisterhood, Ann descended ever deeper into drunkenness and violence as her life sentence endlessly unraveled. The optimistic lass who'd so lovingly inscribed two hearts and two doves on a coin had long since departed.

The sisterhood of rebellious unity was not enough to counteract the darkest side of life inside the Female Factory. Hunger, malnutrition, filth, exhaustion, alcoholism, and a lack of personal space contributed to riots, fistfights, and incidents of sexual assault among the women. All sorts of scandals and uprisings kept the Flash Mob on the lips of many colonists. Lady Jane Franklin, though aloof from the prisoners she had promised Mrs. Fry she would help, bristled at Mob headlines splashed across the newspapers she perused every day.

Earlier in the year, an extension of the Female Factory opened in New Town. Known as the Brickfields Hiring Depot, it became the assignment center for transported women. Lady Franklin wasted no time in launching a campaign to institute harsher penalties for the Crime Class at Brickfields. The *Colonial Times* reported that she had taken over "management of the Female Convict Establishment, in conjunction with a committee of ten other ladies." On the ladies' recommendations, "those in the lowest crime yard are to be employed in breaking stones for the finishing course on the roads, not larger than the yolk of an egg, to be passed through an iron riddle according to Macadam's plan."[25] The newspaper article concluded with a wholehearted endorsement of Lady Jane's approach: "This is delightful. We shall soon hear no more of 'send me to the Factory,' from those heroines, where at present they are engaged in little else than studying how to concoct mischief, and render themselves unworthy the name of WOMAN."[26]

Not surprisingly, Lady Jane informed Mrs. Fry that picking oakum or scrubbing at the washtubs was too easy a punishment for the unwed mothers at Cascades. While Franklin's attitudes toward the transported women grew ever harsher, Elizabeth Fry's views about reform evolved toward a less punitive approach. In 1842, she described her change of heart in a letter to Lady Jane: "With respect to cutting off hair we have not found its effect good in England, for whilst the poor prisoner should be humbled by her faults she should not always carry about it in the view of others the crime she has committed, it hardens and makes them worse than before."[27]

Concerned about the separation of convict mothers from their children, Fry continued: ". . . I am of opinion that it would not be right according to the laws of God and nature not only to preclude the mothers of illegitimates from seeing their children or taking them out when able to maintain them. . . . Of course the mothers of the legitimate children should be very differently treated."[28]

Even Fry, holding tight to her upper middle-class British upbringing, failed to fully understand the plight of transported women who suffered rape or abandonment by the fathers of their children. Yet at sixty-two, she persisted in radical ideas for prison reform that defied rigid Victorian sensibilities. Informed of plans for new prisons in the colony, she made this recommendation to Lady Jane: "I think your Factory capable of great improvement by being made more a house of correction and I think there might be added to it something of house of refuge for hopeful characters that may arrive in the ship or be anxious to improve in the Colony."[29]

Coupling her model behavior aboard the *Hindostan* with exemplary work in the nursery, Arabella's mother personified the "hopeful character" inspiring Fry's optimism. Yet even the perfectly proper and contained Ludlow Tedder would get into trouble. By 1842, the Liverpool Street nursery was packed far beyond capacity. One hundred fifty-three women and children were crammed into a house so dilapidated Mr. Hutchinson feared it might fall down.[30] Superintendent of Convicts Josiah Spode finally approved the opening of a larger nursery inside Dynnyrne House, located in a converted distillery down the rivulet from Cascades.

For three years, the compassionate Nurse Tedder had cared for her little charges as if they were her grandchildren. Ludlow's record had not a single black mark. She took pride in a frequently heartwrenching though rewarding assignment. Shortly before the Liverpool Street quarters were shut down, Ludlow was privy to several incidents her conscience simply wouldn't allow her to condone. Convict worker Ann McCarty was housed in the nursery with her nine-month-old child, from whom she'd soon be separated. At this time, mothers were allowed to nurse their babies for nine months rather than six. In an effort to keep each prisoner productive and out of trouble, Mrs. Slea assigned Ann the care of two children who'd been weaned and whose mothers had been returned to the Female Factory. One of Ludlow's mates from the *Hindostan*, Mary Larney, reported Ann for abusing the two-year-old under her watch.

Bread and Water

Nurse Ludlow found herself in an impossible predicament when called as a witness before the Hobart Town Lower Court. She was well aware that if she informed on a fellow prisoner, she'd be made to pay one way or another. However, if she lied for the woman who abused a child, she'd face Mr. Hutchinson's outrage and lose a plum assignment that allowed occasional visits to Arabella. Mothers sent out to settlers at distant locations rarely saw their children while they lived in the Queen's Orphanage. Ludlow couldn't risk this.

Standing tall before the magistrate, Ludlow refused to lie for Ann McCarty. On June 14, 1842, she offered the following testimony:

> Mary Larney fetched me this morning stating that McCarthy [Mc-Carty] had beaten a child in an improper manner. I went and saw the child. She had beaten it severely across the bottom and back, and it is about 2 years old. . . . She stated that the child had dirtied itself, she gave no other reason. There were marks of the hand across the back and bottom. I have never heard of her doing so before. . . . I also saw her take the child of Marg North out of bed and throw it on the floor not very violently.[31]

Ludlow was returned to Cascades, but not for punishment. Given her experience assisting Surgeon Superintendent McDonald and her fine work in the nursery, Superintendent Hutchinson saw fit to appoint her to work in the Female Factory hospital. Here babies were delivered, the mentally ill restrained, and prisoners with rheumatism and epilepsy admitted.

Ludlow hadn't spent much time inside the Female Factory since her arrival in Van Diemen's Land, but she knew that Ann McCarty was back in the Crime Class, smoldering in anger over the widow who had spoken the truth in court. The levelheaded nurse walked a tightrope every time she strolled through the yards. Her survival (and Arabella's, too) depended on understanding what went on behind the stone walls and using it to her best advantage. She faced her first test within days of her return. Eliza Morgan, a patient missing a front tooth, persuaded the widow to do her a favor.[32] She'd slip Ludlow a few coins in return for the nurse using her position to pick up a bundle in town. Unfortunately, Ludlow failed to realize she was helping a former shipmate of her nemesis, Ann McCarty.

Seizing what appeared to be an opportunity for building the nest egg she'd need to retrieve Arabella and make a fresh start, Ludlow joined the underground subculture at Cascades. Although marriage allowed a woman early release from her sentence and was the fastest way to regain custody of Arabella, it seemed a far-fetched proposition for the forty-nine-year-old widow. Still, Ludlow dared to dream of her future. If she didn't pursue the matrimonial path, she'd have to be prepared. Once free, she'd need lots of money to prove she could provide for Arabella. Currency, in a corrupt and distant colony, bought just about anything, including a daughter. Whatever it took, that was her plan.

Many at the Female Factory surrendered to temptations that offered a lifeline in miserable waters. Convict maids learned the ropes by secretly shadowing their captors and listening for how deals were negotiated and sealed. With her position in the center of Hobart Town, Ludlow certainly understood the fine line that often separated criminal from official.

Both prison constables and their unpaid convict policemen took advantage of profiteering. For a fee, the supervisor turned his back when the convict on his force committed an offense that jeopardized his Ticket of Leave, the probationary period at the end of his sentence. Though the government relied heavily on the police to maintain order in the penal colony, "they used their brief of keeping close surveillance over convicts to cloak dubious and illegal practices that offended the rule of law."[33]

Some constables accepted hush money from sly-grog shops, took convicts off duty to chop their wood and clean their stables, and struck back at those who exposed their breach of public trust. During the year Agnes arrived, *Colonial Times* editors Henry Melville and Gilbert Robertson reported on the Political Association, an organization that addressed police abuse at its first meeting. In retaliation, a police informant lured two of Melville's convict printers to a pub, got them drunk on illegal rum, and then turned them in. The two yokels were sentenced to four months on a chain gang. As expected, without his printers, Melville's ability to produce his newspaper was seriously undermined.[34]

So widespread was this corruption, it sank to the ridiculous in a dog-nabbing racket, in which one dog was used to entrap another. Under the guise of enforcing leash laws, constables seeking a few extra coins found ready targets for extortion and immediate payment:

> In Hobart Town constables allegedly walked down the street, each with a bitch on a lead and a number of ropes with nooses, which they threw around the neck of any dogs that stopped to make acquaintance with the bitches. After thirty minutes, the constables had caught thirteen dogs. Their owners preferred to pay the constables £1 or £2 rather than appear in court, where they could not prove their dogs had been *"seduced"* by the policemen's bitches.[35]

Back at the Female Factory, few risked such blatant graft, but at nightfall the yards came alive with secret bargaining and trade. During daylight hours, boxes made of wood and tin lay safely stashed behind a loose brick or buried next to a washtub. Shortly after evening muster, the goods went up for auction. Tea, sugar, tobacco, pipes, spirits, and fried meat from the kitchen exchanged hands and were quickly consumed or hidden in the unseen corners of Cascades.

Bribing a convict turnkey was an easy transaction. More often than not, she ran an underground business of her own. She'd happily look the other way or leave a door unlatched in exchange for the currency of the day: tobacco, liquor, coins, and even buttons taken from the laundry and prized because prison uniforms had none.[36]

Ludlow's new assignment placed her inside "the nerve centre for illicit commerce."[37] A glimpse into this subculture comes from Eliza Churchill, transported two years after Ludlow for stealing a cloak and a silk umbrella. She spent three weeks in the infirmary at the Launceston Female Factory and offered this testimony before the government's Inquiry into Female Convict Prison Discipline in 1841: "I have seen tobacco constantly brought in and given to the nurse who used to supply the crime class with it. The nurse Mrs. Benson gets money from the prisoners and gives it to Mrs. Littler the sub-matron who gets tobacco & tea & sugar in the town and gives it to the nurse."[38] The thriving smuggling operation that Eliza observed from her hospital bed included creative techniques for transporting the illicit goods, like watching the submatron stuff tobacco inside her corset. Capitalizing on high illiteracy among her patients, the enterprising nurse also charged them for penning letters and even for the paper they used.[39]

For an older convict with few options ahead, Ludlow took a gamble. Just as she never intended to steal silverware from Barrister Skinner, Widow Tedder now swam in a cesspool of corruption, making her choices as a matter of survival. Like the Catos' message-delivery-for-a-chicken scheme, the offer from patient Eliza Morgan seemed too good to resist. Because Mr. Hutchinson trusted Ludlow to procure hospital supplies in town, Eliza innocently asked her to pick up a few goods from a Mr. Smith on Elizabeth Street and smuggle them back into Cascades. In return, Ludlow would pocket a few pennies she could spend on soap for Arabella or save for their future.

If only she had known it was a trap. On June 21, 1842, Ludlow's fate took an abrupt turn for the worse. Constable Goodwin caught her "obtaining goods under false pretenses."[40] She had violated Article 9 of the Female Factory "Rules and Regulations," which stated: "No Officer or Servant of the Establishment shall supply any Female Convict with other provisions or comforts of any kind than those allowed by the Regulations. Neither is any clothing, *nor other articles whatever*, to be delivered to any Convict in the House of Correction."[41]

Though the timing may have been coincidental, Eliza Morgan knew Ann McCarty well from spending nearly four months together aboard the *Westmoreland*. Eliza likely set up Ludlow as payback for testifying against her friend. The court had sentenced the pockmarked Ann to nine months' hard labor, extending the separation from her child. Surely, the two blamed Ludlow. Developing loyalty during their journey across the sea, women who huddled together belowdecks grew protective of their mates, and when push came to shove, they often relied on them for reinforcement inside the harsh Cascades prison.

Loyalty was important to Superintendent Hutchinson as well. He had assigned the sympathetic widow to her second position of great responsibility. By 1842 he had little tolerance for anything that might further tarnish his record, particularly after the recent avalanche of well-publicized scandals involving infant deaths, the Catos' dismissal, and the nefarious Flash Mob. As revealed by testimony under the Inquiry into Female Convict Prison Discipline, the aging Hutchinson actively tried to avoid any contact with the prisoners, preferring his managerial distance.

Sentencing Ludlow to twelve months' hard labor in the solitary working cells, he imposed a punishment quite harsh for a first infraction. Seeing her misconduct as another black mark on his record, he decided to make an example of Ludlow and thereby protect his reputation. Recording his indignation in #151's conduct record, he "confirmed this female was placed in a situation of great trust under promised indulgence of the Principal Superintendent considering her to be a fit subject."[42]

The last person Agnes and Janet expected to see in Crime Class was the crestfallen Ludlow, who walked through the crime yard that morning sporting an unfashionable prison shift emblazoned with large yellow "C"s. The remnants of newly shorn hair peeked from under her mob cap. After all she'd been through over forty-nine years, this minor indignity was the least of her worries.

The formerly impeccably behaved nurse had been thrown to the wolves. Certainly Ann McCarty indulged in spiteful satisfaction watching the widow trudge toward her cell. Like all prison women, Nurse Tedder surely had enemies, but she had also made friends during her time at Liverpool Street. Agnes and Janet knew Ann McCarty from the *Westmoreland*. They may have collaborated to protect Ludlow from further reprisals, but at Cascades they were all in it together, and it was going to be a long chilly winter.

Ludlow had just begun her year of labor inside a solitary working cell. She sat in twilight on her little stool, day after day, pulling apart old rope fibers, with temperatures dipping into the forties. Winter brought long bouts of chilling rain, but the grey days gradually faded away into the lengthening sunlight of early spring.

By the end of August, the two Glasgow maids bid the Female Factory good riddance. Placed back on assignment, they held high aspirations for staying out of trouble. In less than a year, they'd be eligible for Certificates of Freedom. Ludlow received no such reprieve, and her callus-ridden hands continued to work on piles of rope. Summer dragged along like a lazy lizard sunning on a stone. A parade of unfamiliar faces watched the widow wearing large yellow "C"s report without fail to morning muster. Nearly nine months into her punishment, Ludlow heard the sound of a familiar Scottish brogue. As she turned around, her eyes met those of another convict with an impish grin, looking back from across the yard and wearing the same drab shift emblazoned with the familiar C. February 22, 1843, the dauntless #253 was back at the washtubs for another three months' hard labor. So close to the end of her term, if Agnes could avoid a major offense, she'd soon be free.

Ludlow's future was less certain, but at least she'd soon see Arabella. Over the course of her dark-hued isolation, reduced rations of bread and water caused Ludlow's grey uniform to fall farther from her frame. At last, the turnkey unbolted the locks on her cage. Ludlow strode proudly from the half-light of the two-story ward and was summoned to the reception room, where paperwork was already completed for her next assignment. A still-perturbed Mr. Hutchinson would allow just one visit to the Queen's Orphanage, where Arabella, now fourteen, knew nothing of what had happened to her mother and why the Sunday visits stopped so abruptly. Auspiciously, her girlhood chum Catherine Mullins also remained at the orphanage and kept Arabella in good company.

After an all-too-brief visit to the orphanage, Ludlow was transferred by open cart one hundred twenty miles north to the Launceston Female Factory, a new facility constructed in 1834. Although the unusual octagonal configuration looked quite distinct from Cascades' rectangular shapes, little was different inside the prison.

Beginning in 1840, New South Wales would accept no more female convicts. Now all were transported to Van Diemen's Land by order of the Crown. As a result, both Cascades and the Launceston Female Factory were packed beyond capacity. Following the riots and disturbances that plagued 1842, superintendents tried to use the two locations to separate known collaborators, especially Flash Mob members, all to no avail.

Two months after Ludlow's admission, the Crime Class women in Launceston locked out the constables and barricaded themselves inside the prison for more than twenty-four hours. "Only after about 30 prisoners from the men's gaol next door were fetched to assist the constables, was the siege broken."[43] Five months later, simultaneous riots occurred at both female factories, attributable to either remarkable coincidence or crafty planning by the Flash Mob.[44]

Ludlow, however, returned to model conduct. Quietly biding her time, she picked oakum and sometimes scrubbed laundry at the washtubs. Under the Ticket of Leave policy, well-behaved prisoners were released on probation after completing at least four years of their sentence. Under watchful surveillance by local constables, convicts were allowed to work and to marry while serving the rest of their time.

Her excellent behavior yielded a harvest of good news for Widow Tedder in autumn 1844. Launceston Superintendent James Fraser submitted the paperwork for her Ticket of Leave, and Ludlow immediately sent for her daughter. Wasting not a moment, Ludlow must have passed Mr. Fraser every coin she had tucked away from underground trade, first on the *Hindostan* and later in the female factories. Her carefully managed stash paid stagecoach fare from the Queen's Orphanage.[45]

On a crisp April evening in Launceston's center, a dusty stagecoach door flew open, and fifteen-year-old Arabella ran into her mother's open arms. Overhead, black cockatoos squawked a greeting of their own. The reunited pair spoke barely a word as they walked arm in arm along the banks of the Tamar, dotted with wharves, gardens, and lush farmland.

Within weeks of the joyful reunion, Ludlow held her Ticket of Leave. She read aloud the words that justified her early release: "Nearly two thirds of her term of transportation having expired and there being only one offence on record against her."[46] She'd served five years. Though the official document recorded her ten-year conviction delivered at the Old Bailey, the reference to "two thirds" applied more accurately to the seven-year sentence imposed on most transports.

On May 15, 1844, the fresh scent of freedom wafted over a relieved mother and daughter, who began to chart a course for their future. The ever-practical Ludlow Tedder began her search for a new mate.

To survive in the colony, she'd need a partner. Taking full advantage of the nine-to-one ratio of men to women in Van Diemen's Land, she set out to find a healthy younger man. In the end, she had Ann Mc-Carty to thank for this turn of fate. Had she not been punished for helping Eliza Morgan and sent to Launceston, Ludlow wouldn't have met the free settler who captured her heart.

Widower William Manley Chambers managed a farm just outside town and made a good living raising potatoes and sheep. Like Ludlow, he was literate, and seemed not to mind their difference in years. Though well beyond the bloom of maidenhood, Ludlow looked quite young for her age, and surely her wit and wisdom only made her more attractive. Besides, a woman with experience in cooking, housekeeping, and nursing was highly prized in a remote colony. With Ludlow's blessing, William applied for permission to marry Widow Tedder. Astute woman that she was, Ludlow lied about her age on their marriage application, declaring herself forty years old. She was, in fact, fifty-one when she married the thirty-four-year-old farmer on July 29, 1844.

Eight weeks after she walked out of prison, Ludlow donned a simple cotton frock and held William's arm before the altar in Launceston's Holy Trinity Anglican Church. Arabella stood by her mother's side, wearing winter-white magnolias in her hair and holding back tears of happiness and relief.

☞ 9 ☜

Flames of Love

Sleeping Beauty

The year 1844 began like a fairy tale for the trio of convict maids.
Their lives were woven together by the Fates, as they passed through
Liverpool Street and slaved behind the cold stone walls at Cascades.
Now they were free and ready to express themselves on a new canvas
prepared for hope and promise. The future was surely about to call
them in different directions. Though they might never meet again, the
women who walked away from Cascades were to be steadfast mates
for the rest of their lives.

Ludlow Tedder Chambers, the oldest and still vibrant at fifty-one,
contentedly adapted to life around a rustic farm cottage outside Launceston and introduced Arabella to the country roots she'd known as a
young lass in Southminster, England. Now freed from her sentence at
the Female Factory, Janet Houston escaped her recent painful past in
the company of a tall, handsome emancipist. And the spirited Agnes
McMillan, the youngest of the three, had fallen madly in love with

a mysteriously scarred renegade who caught her attention charging through Oatlands on a runaway horse.

Agnes, twenty-three at the time of her release, had certainly scoffed at rules before. She had no trouble dismissing what the *Colonial Times* considered the "Rules and Regulations for Young Ladies" contemplating matrimony:

> *At twenty.*—Consider yourself in some danger of remaining single, and suit your conduct to your circumstances.
>
> *At twenty-one.*—Be less particular than heretofore, for time begins to wane.
>
> *At twenty-two.*—Think seriously of paying a visit to some friend at Madras or Calcutta.
>
> *At twenty-three.*—Marry any body that is not downright intolerable.[1]

At the end of 1839, when Superintendent Hutchinson banished the grey-eyed rebel to the most remote outpost accepting convicts, he inadvertently arranged her introduction to William Watson Roberts. William was a scrappy lad from Manchester, with dark brown eyes and a bit of larceny in his soul. As a young man, he tried his hand at pickpocketing, but had little skill. In 1827, he was arrested for stealing one shilling and sixpence, and three halfpence. Because this was the twenty-two-year-old's second offense, the judge imposed a sentence of fourteen years' transportation to parts beyond the seas. While awaiting exile, William spent eight months aboard the *Dolphin*, a decommissioned warship turned floating prison hulk.

Stripped bare and scrubbed with a stiff brush, the male prisoners were outfitted in coarse grey shirts and breeches and shackled by heavy rings secured by a steel rivet around both ankles. The rings were joined together by heavy chains, making it virtually impossible for a man to run, flee, or swim. Four hundred men ploddingly marched ashore under the watch of guards armed with whips. Now called by their number at five A.M. muster, the convicts, dragging iron balls at their feet, cleaned sewers, dug ditches, and dredged the River Thames. Returned to the ship at dusk, they were fed gruel and meat, then ordered by their taskmasters to clean the old decaying battleship that was their home. The ship slept four men to a bunk in a space seven feet square, and epidemics ravaged the hulks constantly and caused many a man's bones to be dumped in the swampy marshland following a death during the night.

William Roberts managed to survive his stay on the *Dolphin*, but he wouldn't escape unscathed. One of many rampant outbreaks of tuberculosis left a permanent mark. Bearing a bluish-purple mass under his chin, he suffered from scrofula, or "king's evil," a name tied to the medieval belief that a royal's touch offered the cure. His clear complexion was further transformed by another plague common to life on the hulks. Hundreds of angry men in chains, packed together like animals, bred gang warfare, especially terrorizing the youngest boys, some barely twelve. Five feet, five inches tall and never one to back down from a fight, William was quickly rewarded with several deep scars across his forehead "protecting himself from the murderous intentions of low-life troublemakers on board."[2]

The rough-and-ready son of a Manchester coach maker was transferred on March 11, 1828, from the hulk to the transport ship *William Miles*. En route to Van Diemen's Land, seven prisoners died among the 492 on board. Finally, on July 29, 1828, the ship dropped anchor in Sullivans Cove and deposited the brown-eyed Roberts and the rest of the rowdy rabble on the colony's distant shore.

Less than a month after his arrival, William walked off a convict labor crew. He was punished with two days on the tread wheel, a device dubbed "the everlasting staircase" and the "cock-chafer" because "the stiff prison clothes scraped one's groin raw after a few hours on it."[3] Steadying himself against the handrail, he lifted his leg and placed his feet on the rotating steps of the large wheel used to grind wheat. Left, right, left, right, the weight of his footfall caused the creaking mill to slowly revolve while his ankle irons clinked the cadence of his steady, rhythmic pace. Step by heavy step, he worked off his punishment, ten minutes on and five minutes off for up to ten hours each day.

Six weeks later, the strong-willed transport from a gritty industrial town skipped mandatory church muster and was punished with two more days on the giant circular tread wheel in the Hobart Town penitentiary. Colonial society relied heavily on fear to pave the path toward redemption. These devils were to be reformed by the word of God or the kiss of the lash. Extremes of all dimensions ruled an expanding populace caught between medieval practices involving subjugation and torture and rising emancipist sentiments favoring suffrage and freedom.

Great Britain sent prisoners to Botany Bay, Australia, beginning with the First Fleet in 1788. When William arrived forty years later, the ten thousand convicts in Van Diemen's Land were expected to cower and submit to the rule of the master, just as those before them had done. This mission supported the goal of a docile labor class serving at the whim of the wealthy. The cheeky Manchester transport was twice punished with a whipping by leather cat-o'-nine-tails. The first time he'd returned to the barracks one hour late, twelve lashes shredded his bare back that night.

A year later, while working in a road gang, William was taken aside and punished with twenty-five strokes for insolence toward Mr. James Calder, the Surveyor General for Bruny Island. Nine knotted leather strips with lead weights fastened to the end were deliberately designed to rip and tear into the skin, thus prolonging his suffering. Salt, rubbed into the wounds to prevent infection, heightened the pain and the punishment.

His back still bloody from deep lacerations, William was immediately returned to felling huge trees and cutting tracks through dense scrub, as the land was cleared for new roads and settlements. Despite a run-in with Surveyor General Calder, the now experienced ax-man was chosen for a ten-day exploratory trip up the Huon River and its heavily forested, undeveloped, and yet untamed shores.

For the next two years, William's transgressions were minor until he disobeyed direct orders and was sentenced to spend twelve months on a road gang outside the tiny settlement of Oatlands, breaking rocks and hauling them from the quarry. Marked for the Crime Class, he was made to wear the convict arrow of shame. The "pheon," or broad arrow, found its roots in seventeenth-century markings on British property labeled to prevent theft. Petty thieves like William were considered property of the Crown and forced to wear coarse black-and-mustard-yellow "magpie" uniforms. Reinforcing public humiliation with no semblance of subtlety, one trouser leg was yellow and the other black, each emblazoned with three large arrows. His captors had cut back his shoes low on the sides, right at the point where irons would bruise and scrape his shins.

William's sentence dragged on under the threat of the lash and the press of the pulpit. In unwavering attempts to reform convicts through religion, Oatlands' chief magistrate required even Ticket of Leave holders' attendance at church, posting this notice:

Chief Police Magistrate.
POLICE OFFICE, OATLANDS.
District of Oatlands Tickets-of-Leave.
ALL male prisoners holding the above indulgence,
and residing within two miles
from the Court-house, are ordered to attend
church muster in future every Sunday.
Also those residing upwards of two miles,
and not exceeding five miles, are ordered to
attend church muster, the first Sunday in every month.[4]

Benefiting from its location midway between the island's chief ports because of its growing wool trade, Oatlands in 1835 had a free population of 598, plus 695 convicts. It had expanded from twenty dwellings to more than two hundred over the past eight years.[5]

Still, Oatlands remained an outpost marked by contradictory components. The construction of convict-crafted Georgian homes and tree-lined avenues conveyed the superficial appearance of a civilized society. Yet the fringes of town defined its true outlaw flavor. Wide-open country offered fertile ground for marauding bandits who rustled cattle, robbed travelers on the lonely roads between Hobart Town and Launceston, and battled one another in the brutal fashion from which many legends were born.

Notorious bushranger Richard Lemon defined the settlement's early history before its link to other towns, encouraged after a visit by the governor of New South Wales in 1811. Exploring the northern jungles of Van Diemen's Land on horseback, Governor Macquarie proposed a road linking Hobart Town to the settlement he named Oatlands because it looked similar to an area that grew oat crops in his native Scotland.[6]

Until then, Richard Lemon, the leader of the first well-known bushranger gang, had terrorized the area. Between 1806 and 1808, Lemon ran wild and was the namesake for Oatlands' Lemon Springs and Lemon Hill. Living his mocking creed "a short life and a merry one," the ferocious murderer hid in a bark hut along the shores of Lake Tiberias until another ex-convict delivered his head in a sack and collected a bounty from the island's Governor Collins.[7]

Following Lemon's marauding lead, escaped convicts held hostage large tracts of the island's interior, still largely untamed and teeming with indigenous wildlife. Local herdsmen battled with carnivorous marsupials stealing from their flock, including the nocturnal Tasmanian devil and the thylacine (Tasmanian tiger), nicknamed for its stripes.[8]

A different form of wildlife congregated on the fringes of the settlement, outside the order and control of the wardens and the church. Sly-grog shops, "notorious haunts of vice and immorality," opened in secluded shacks and barns in the bush.[9] Inside these treasured haunts, convict women and men re-created the working-class entertainment of their homeland, as they swapped tall tales, smoked tobacco, drank rum, played cards, gambled, and danced with reckless abandon. A lifeline to personal identity and good old-fashioned fun defined the after-dusk subculture from which convict solidarity prospered and dissidence brewed. In remote, predominantly male outposts like Oatlands, bare-knuckle boxing matches and cockfighting also filled the dark recesses of popular underground entertainment, which may have also filled the dark holes in many a lonely heart.[10]

The petite renegade named Agnes McMillan had no trouble adapting to this rustic lifestyle, though she never forgave Superintendent Hutchinson for assigning her to the middle of nowhere. Despite the occasional gunshots and bushranger sightings, it was a rather boring town, with more sheep than settlers. The former street urchin, accustomed to big-city bustle and excitement, found little amusement in this dreary outpost until a certain William Roberts crossed her path.

Twelve years into his sentence, at age thirty-six, after a long day laboring in the summer heat, #510 celebrated his probationary Ticket of Leave in a secret Oatlands grog shop. As he waved the parchment marked January 22, 1840, in front of his mates, beer after beer was passed through his gleeful hands. Perhaps on a dare or merely a celebratory whim, William jumped atop a horse, hooting and hollering his way through the midlands town for all to see. The sleepy citizens who lived securely inside the village's neat orange-brick homes were not in the least amused.

An Oatlands constable pulled the completely inebriated Englishman from his horse and dragged him down Barrack Street through the arched entrance to the old stone gaol. Staggering up the stairs, William stared down at the porous stone steps stained deeply red from blood running down the legs of men who'd been whipped earlier that day.[11] Now that he'd been released from convict status, his sentence was lighter this time, a mere fourteen days in a solitary cell and a fine of five shillings. And the news was about to get better.

On this very night, a spirited Scottish lass must have had a good laugh as she peeked through her master's curtained window and took notice of a dark prince riding wildly through the streets in the bright moonlight. His behavior was comical when compared to the antics of the bushrangers and fugitives who lived in the surrounding woods, where outlaw justice ruled. In this midlands community, a rather clumsy and unexpected courtship ignited between the spirited Agnes and a Ticket of Leave holder with a roguish smile and a wink cast her way.

Fifteen years her senior, William was not the handsome prince of fairy tales. His face featured high, square temples and prominent lips. His unruly black eyebrows nearly met in the center, and he bore the heavy blue mark of the "king's evil" (tuberculosis) on his neck.[12] He had endured the gauntlet of imprisonment, and it was time to settle down and start a family. Nearing the end of his sentence, the lucky expatriate found work as a timber cutter and builder.

William's brassy humor and working-class roots made him a fine match for the bonnie beauty with the Scottish brogue. He taught Agnes to read, to shoot a gun, and to use his well-worn ax. He was skilled, ambitious, and full of adventure and vitality. Like Agnes, he cast off limitations, living with abandon and buoyant good hope. She'd found her wild colonial boy and knew he'd be her mate for life.

Descendants of this well-timed union describe their meeting as fated. William had grown up with a mother and father and lived with them as a young adult, an apprentice at his father's side. For Agnes, his compassion "was her first experience of any love and care in her whole twenty years."[13]

Transported beyond the seas for the temptation of a few coins, the strong and rugged woodsman had survived some of the worst hellholes in the empire. As he worked free in the forest, shirt tied around his waist, Agnes found her eyes drawn to the heavy scar tissue crisscrossing William's back, the signature of the cat-o'-nine-tails. "Old residents speak today of having seen these convicts, in the days of their youth, peel off their shirts to wash, and their backs were cut and marked so that there was not a piece of skin unscarred and scarcely a ridge of the flesh left free of marks of the scourge."[14]

Speaking not a word, the typically gregarious Scot conveyed what she felt for William with a simple touch. She understood his journey and shared his resiliency, yet tears still welled up in her eyes when she placed a gentle palm against the thirty-seven lash scars crossing his back.

With her best intentions now focused on romance and passion, a love-struck Agnes soon found herself climbing the cold stone steps into the Oatlands gaol. She'd been insolent to her master and was to be confined to two weeks in solitary confinement, but her only regret was time away from dear William. Probably aware of the reason for her distraction, Magistrate John Whitefoord put Agnes on the first police cart headed back to Hobart Town. Though a Scotsman himself, he could not be charmed by a familiar brogue.

Over the next three years, the incorrigible Scot stayed in contact with William, twice absconding for the comfort of his arms. Surrendering any opportunity for early release with a Ticket of Leave, Agnes served her entire sentence. Seven years to the day of being found guilty by Ayr's Court of Judiciary, she held Certificate of Freedom #388, dated May 3, 1843. True-blue mate Janet Houston was freed the same day, which was the last time they would see each other.

Head held high, Agnes left Cascades behind her and headed north. Hitching a ride on an Oatlands-bound cart and humming her favorite tunes once again, she felt as though she were looking at the world for the first time. Traveling as a free woman, Agnes breathed in the island's mysterious beauty. Gum trees, their bark stripped stark-white bare in the annual molt, danced over the hills like human skeletons. Decaying eucalyptus appeared like gnarled and twisted fingers trying to scratch their way out of a grave. The wildness of the landscape only excited the wildness of her heart. As she traveled through the interior and approached the outpost, Agnes passed huge groves of bushy honeysuckle shrub, their gigantic yellow cones in full autumn bloom and a welcoming sight that marked the entrance to Oatlands.

William had diverted himself with hard work while he waited for the woman he intended to marry. Convict #253 had finally reclaimed her name and now willingly added William's to hers, though no records indicate an official union. For the next several months, the Robertses saved every penny and plotted their future together. Anxious to make a fresh start and put the past behind them, the determined couple headed south to the Hobart Town docks in the spring of 1843. William's work on Mr. Calder's chain gang ten years earlier had introduced him to the prosperous possibilities for settlement along the Huon River.

These same prospects had not gone unnoticed by the ambitious and entrepreneurial Lady Jane Franklin. Seeing potential in attracting free immigrants with an interest in farming, the governor's wife made an investment she thought wise for the colony's future and her own. In 1838, she purchased 640 acres of fertile land in the Huon Valley, twenty-eight miles southwest of Hobart Town.[15] She subdivided the large tract and sold parcels to God-fearing immigrants who denounced liquor and sin, passed her interview, and met with her approval. Eager tenants, many of the Methodist faith, agreed to her lease-to-buy arrangement, requiring full payment within seven years. In 1843, Her Ladyship left Van Diemen's Land with a tidy profit for land sold at fair value and returned to England following her husband's removal as the colony's governor.

The governor's wife had conducted her business more honestly than certain wealthy landowners who employed a lease-to-buy scheme as a way to avoid the backbreaking work of clearing swamps and felling giant trees. Setting rents that few could afford, these greedy land barons held back eviction notices until after the land was cleared.[16] Instead of paying to have the forests leveled, they collected rent money from hopeful settlers until it ran out. When the owners reclaimed the land, it was more valuable and often resold or used as pasture for sheep or cattle.

During his sixteen years on the island, William Roberts had grown wise to corruption and graft. Carrying coveted skills as a pit-sawyer and carpenter, he'd find honest work crafting durable, seaworm-proof Huon pine into fine sailing vessels for the colony's trade. The water-resistant wood was used on the decks of the empire's finest sailing vessels and was in huge demand. Bringing only what was essential, William and Agnes left Oatlands and headed for the Huon Valley. They may have walked to Hobart Town, then boarded a cart. The former city lad wrapped his ax and sharpening file in canvas sail that would double as a tent. He had a rifle to hunt for food, ammunition, and everything he needed to make a good living. Seated by his side, his smiling common-law bride wore a wool hat and scarf, and a blanket layered over her shawl. Two small possum rugs rested over her lap. They used the fur sides for cool seasons and the reverse for summer.[17]

A cloudless sky looked clearer than ever on this windy September morning. They'd need the lengthening daylight to set up camp and build a permanent shelter before summer's end. Agnes held tight to a tin cup and a cooking pot with some spoons jingling inside. William confidently fingered the coins he'd stashed away for rent and passage up the river. Waterways offered easier travel than overland routes where no roads existed. To reach the Huon River settlement, the freed couple probably took a lighter, a barge headed upriver for a load of timber. Or they might have boarded the forty-ton vessel Lady Franklin had commissioned to service the community now named in her honor.[18] The growing town of Franklin lay twenty-eight miles southwest of Hobart Town, and traveling overland was reserved for only the heartiest of explorers willing to navigate on foot the slippery mountain slopes and confusingly dangerous tangle of forests.

Only the sorrowful ghosts of Aborigines knew the secret paths through sacred ground now on the edge of modern civilization. Once part of Australia's continent, Van Diemen's Land separated from the mainland when sea levels rose during the last major ice age and formed the Bass Strait. Starting in 1803, British rule set in motion a systematic eradication of those deemed to be "savages," the earliest settlers who

had inhabited the island for some forty thousand years. Fifty indigenous tribes with a total population estimated between five thousand
and ten thousand were scattered across Van Diemen's Land when the
English first landed. By the time Agnes arrived, that number had been
reduced to less than two hundred, who lived in exile on Flinders Island
off the northeast coast. Isolated from the rest of the world for about
ten thousand years—the longest known isolation in human history—
the Aboriginal people of Van Diemen's Land were decimated in less
than seventy-five years.

The dense forests of the Huon Valley, first inhabited by the indigenous Nuenonne tribe, was where Agnes and William began to
erase their shared history in Van Diemen's Land. Immigrants who arrived of their own free will voiced an ominously rising prejudice against
an expanding population they needed and despised at the same time.
Comparing the island's beauty to the hideousness of those transported
to its shores against their will, a male settler wrote that "the inhabitants
are like a set of vultures . . . defacing one of the finest countries in the
world."[19] And a female settler similarly observed that the convict, "like
an ugly nose, spoils the face of the country."[20]

As he began to write *On the Origin of Species*, Charles Darwin visited Van Diemen's Land and termed the colony "a festival amongst
the lowest barbarians," writing: ". . . I was disappointed in the state of
society. . . . There are many serious drawbacks to the comforts of a
family, the chief of which perhaps is being surrounded by convict
servants. How thoroughly odious to every feeling, to be waited on by
a man who the day before, perhaps, was flogged, from your representation. The female servants are, of course, much worse: hence children learn the vilest expressions, and it is fortunate, if not equally vile
ideas."[21] Offering less understanding still for Aborigines, he echoed a
sentiment shared by many: that "Van Diemen's Land enjoys the great
advantage of being free from a native population."[22]

An attempt to gloss over the penal colony's past was yet another
cause adopted by Lady Jane Franklin. About the time she purchased

the Huon Valley land, she spearheaded a campaign to change the island's name to Tasmania, a name first printed in an 1808 atlas and
then bandied about in newspapers beginning in 1823.[23]

Following the coast down the River Derwent and passing Bruny
Island, William and Agnes sought a fresh start. Though they were legally free under the terms of the Transportation Act, the heavy chains
of their convict past still rattled ominously against the promise of their
future. Much of the far southeast remained untamed in 1844, though
the island's total population had grown to about fifty-eight thousand.
It was a region greener and wetter than Oatlands and Hobart Town,
fertile for living off the land and water, and for blending into a quiet
wilderness, where the couple could together shed their convict stain
and start afresh.

Agnes found herself in high spirits as they sailed through the magical valley. Enchanted forests carpeted in velvety moss and giant leafy
ferns revealed layers upon layers of deep green density. In the runoff
of spring, streams rushed toward the river, and waterfalls cascaded
over jagged cliffs. Ancient trees of gigantic proportions, some mea-
suring ninety feet in circumference, pushed their lofty crowns toward
a perfectly pristine blue sky.[24]

The river rippled with silver ribbons of light as the bloodred sun
slipped below an endlessly green horizon. Looking north, Agnes spied
a gently muted mountain range aptly named Sleeping Beauty. Remains of a harsh winter lingered in the snow, atop graceful slopes
mirroring the silhouette of a princess who reclines peacefully on her
bed, hair flowing along her side.

Crossing the Tasman Sea, heading upriver, and fighting the current required at least a day and a half from Hobart Town, depending
on the winds and the tides. Buoyant with excitement as they hoisted
their worldly possessions onto their shoulders, the couple was rowed
ashore to a timber camp on the outskirts of Franklin. Traveling with
only what they could carry and the clothes on their backs, William
steadied his wife's arm as they waded through the marshy mudflats

and up the steep hillside banks. The sturdy thirty-nine-year-old knew hundreds of other free men on the island: acquaintances from the hulk in England, the sea voyage, the prison tread wheels, and his sentence to the chain gangs. Even in this remote place, William found familiar faces happy to offer the couple a place at the fire, along with a little rum and cooked eel to welcome their old mate.

Women were still rare in the male-dominated backcountry, so news of the grey-eyed Agnes accompanying her rugged husband ensured plenty of help stringing a canvas awning between trees and settling in that first night. Within the week, William purchased a good saw and paddled upstream to a small riverside plot they'd clear for their future. He gathered kindling wood for a fire and set traps for fish while Agnes prepared supper from the provisions they'd packed from Oatlands. For the time being, they'd sleep in a tent. Using a whetstone, William honed his ax's blade and set to work removing dense tea tree scrub and felling Huon pine.

A simple hut at the river's edge, built from "split timber and clay reinforced with wattle twigs,"[25] seemed a fine spot to raise their brood. The small bulge in Agnes's belly carried a child conceived soon after their reunion in Oatlands. Fresh fish from the river and potatoes from nearby farms offered the twenty-three-year-old and her developing child many a bountiful feast. Crayfish and eels were roasted on an open fire and seasoned with spicy berries from wild pepper plants. Rushing streams provided an abundant supply of crystal-clear water. The water's edge was eerily quiet save for croaking frogs, buzzing mosquitoes, an occasional owl's call, and the sound of the river lapping against the shore. Their new home shielded the couple from the harshness they'd always known and offered a safe place to drift off to a deeply sound sleep. A fine mist embraced this ethereal landscape, as vibrant rain-forest spirits prepared to spring into life.

Sunrise burned off dawn's heavy fog as noisy black currawongs sporting bright yellow eyes swooped clumsily along the river's edge and looked for insects. Fairy wrens and white-bellied sea eagles joined in the chorus. Dragonflies danced on ferns, among the oldest known on earth, many unique to the island. Butterflies displayed brightly colored wings, painted with golden eyes and violet pupils. Large moths, most colored in camouflaging browns and greys and some with surprising additions of soft rosy pink, populated the forests and streams.

While William sawed timber downstream, Agnes explored the woods at their rear boundary. A nearly impenetrable treetop canopy cast a brooding stillness over the spongy rain-forest floor, touched by nary a hint of sunlight. Surrounded by the Huon pine, her closest neighbors were the majestic myrtles and September-flowering sassafras covered in lichen. Smells from the hearth and the smokehouse attracted the occasional curious wallaby or echidna, but Agnes rejoiced in a life simple and free.

Heavy with child and blessedly content, thinking back to Glasgow's stinking streets, the mother-to-be delighted in the fragrance of black peppermint trees. Adding a touch of comfort to the cabin, the couple put up shelves, and William fashioned a table and stools. A rope bed and small crib, crafted with basic tools, added a homey touch to their isolated shack. On a chilly autumn morning in April 1844, Agnes gave birth to a daughter they named Lavinia Louisa; she was joined in 1846 by a brother named after his father. The two were baptized together by a missionary chaplain, who held services inside a modest wooden church built by Lady Jane Franklin. Over the next eight years, Agnes delivered George Henry, Agnes Lavinia, and John Edward. Lavinia and William enrolled in a school that opened in 1848 and helped teach their younger siblings how to read and write.

As the family expanded, the island's economy sank into a depression. Three-quarters of the men in Van Diemen's Land were convicts or ex-convicts, and many could not find work on any part of the island.[26] By 1851, a rising tide of hatred directed toward transports and their offspring swept over the colony, further dividing a society already rife with prejudice. Looking toward the Southern Cross so clear above the Huon Valley, Agnes and William whispered excitedly about news they'd heard about golden opportunities in the nearby colonies of Victoria and New South Wales on Australia's mainland.

Blessings of Abundance

By the time Agnes and William moved from the Huon Forest and set sail for Melbourne, Agnes's old friend Janet Houston had married a highly successful horse breeder and given birth to nine of her eventual twelve children, including two sets of twins. The couple settled in the lovely township of Richmond, first called Sweet Water Hills and located just fifteen miles from Hobart Town.

At first, Janet's union with Robert Bailey was fraught with drama following on the heels of tragedy. Robert, a former convict, was probably the father of the ill-fated baby, William. Despite that relationship, he was not free to wed Janet for more than a decade. When he first set eyes on the redheaded Scot, he was married to another convict maid, a volatile gypsy horse thief who deserted him as soon as she was granted a Ticket of Leave. Divorce not being an option, he did the next best thing, posting a desertion notice in the *Colonial Times* in an attempt to absolve himself of responsibility for his wife's unpredictable behavior:

CAUTION

MARY BOSWELL, Ticket-of-Leave, wife of Robert Bailey, of Richmond, having left her home without cause, he hereby Cautions the Public from giving her credit in his name, as he will not be answerable for any debt she may contract from this date.
ROBERT BAILEY, April 19, 1839[27]

When Janet secured her Certificate of Freedom in 1843, she ran straight into the arms of the tall Englishman with dark grey eyes and thick chestnut hair. At five feet, eight inches tall, he towered above the petite woman, whom he'd met three years earlier. Thirty-six, a full twelve years her senior, Mr. Bailey certainly had his hands full. In a land where there was only one woman for every nine men, Robert found himself with one too many.

Transported in 1820 aboard the *Guildford* after being sentenced to seven years for petty theft, Robert arrived in Van Diemen's Land at the tender age of thirteen. He received his Certificate of Freedom on July 23, 1827, and celebrated by getting roaring drunk and incurring a stiff fine. During his twenties, Robert managed to stay out of trouble except for being accused of stealing a sheep—that is, until he met the fiery Mary Boswell. She arrived aboard the *Harmony* on January 14, 1829. The nineteen-year-old from Birmingham was connected to a gang of gypsy thieves and faced a life sentence for "horse stealing."[28]

As Mary strutted through Hobart Town, the dark-complexioned, dimpled gypsy with deep brown eyes would certainly have turned heads, especially at five feet, four inches, which was tall for that time.[29] She'd endured four miserable months at sea and eight days more anchored in Sullivans Cove, because of the time it took to process the first women who were to be incarcerated at Cascades. In appointing staff for the new prison in 1828, Superintendent of Convicts John Lakeland recommended a staunch Methodist couple, stating:

> The immoral habits and general bad conduct of the female convicts will require all the energy and nerve that any individual may possess to keep them in a proper state of subordination and discipline.[30]

The newly issued rules and regulations for the Female Factory reinforced a strict regime under Esh and Ann Lovell, both former Sunday school teachers. Within a month of Mary Boswell's arrival, the first of many riots erupted at Cascades. It started after a group of sympathetic soldiers tossed cheese, bread, and butter over the stone wall into Yard One. When a prisoner tried to share the bread in the mess hall, an overseer took it away. The women went wild, stomping and clapping until locked down in their cells, where one lit cloth and pine, setting the yard ablaze. Superintendent Lovell shortly erected a fence around the perimeters of Cascades.[31]

Mary, the independent firebrand, had no intention of spending a lifetime under the Crown's stifling rules and regulations. She opted out of her sentence via the fastest escape route from the Female Factory. She got married. Arriving in a wild frontier, the exotic vixen had little trouble finding a spouse, wedding an infatuated Robert Bailey six months after she arrived in Van Diemen's Land. Released to Robert's care to serve out her life sentence, Mary found the loophole to early emancipation less than ideal, bristling at the intent to foster "respectable" women.

After eight years of marriage, Mary earned her Ticket of Leave in 1837, shortening her sentence and reducing government expenses. A year later, her union with Robert turned rocky, and on February 21, 1838, she was recorded "Absent from her husband's premises. Severely reprimanded."[32] By 1840, Mary's Ticket of Leave was revoked, following her arrest for larceny. She faced twelve months' hard labor back at Cascades.

Abandoned by his wife for the past three years, Robert fell in love with Janet Houston. They met on the streets of Hobart Town, and she somehow managed to live on his farm in Richmond for nearly a year. Returned to the Female Factory and carrying a child, she was separated from the dashing Mr. Bailey until the warm autumn day she held Certificate of Freedom #339. Unfortunately, her grand reunion did not go quite as planned.

In 1842, Mary Boswell had absconded from her assignment in a tiny village called Green Ponds (later Kempton), more than twenty miles from Hobart Town. She was returned to her husband, but by March 1843 she left him once again. Two months later, Janet arrived at Robert Bailey's home and by the following year was pregnant with twins. John and James Bailey were born in their parents' cozy stone cottage on May 20, 1845.

Robert prospered breeding horses and developed an upstanding reputation. The *Colonial Times* recommended his farm as one where "good grass and well watered paddocks are provided for mares sent to him."[33] He also invested in land to support their expanding brood. William Houston Bailey was born in May 1847 and named after the little boy Janet had lost five years earlier. Twin girls Rebecca and Betsy arrived in 1848, followed by siblings Robert, Arthur, Mary, Kate, Randolph, Wallace, and Samuel, born last in 1860. Janet finally married Robert on March 3, 1852, at Richmond's United Church of England and Ireland, surrounded by their children and carrying a simple bouquet of wildflowers tied in a ribbon.

A year later, in August 1853, Janet and her family witnessed the official abolition of transportation to Van Diemen's Land. Since 1803, sixty-seven thousand convicts had been shipped to this isolated outpost. Now they made up half its population. The older Bailey children attended the Richmond Primary School, built by prisoners in 1834.[34] Convict labor had built most of the municipal buildings in Hobart Town, and chain gangs had cleared the land for roads that now bustled with settlers and commerce.

Each school-age child was issued a medallion, coined by the Royal Mint in London, commemorating fifty years of European settlement and the close of a penal colony.[35] In both Hobart Town and Launceston, jubilee festivals were orchestrated to erase the lingering stigma associated with freed convicts like Janet Houston and William Bailey. The couple probably avoided the celebration, because the Bailey family, and other emancipists, wanted no more than to blend into the fabric of their small farming community, raise their children, make a living, and attend church on Sundays.

For weeks the newspapers touted the jubilee event as God's answer to their prayers. Finally, on August 10, 1853, the highly anticipated day arrived. At six in the morning, as church bells pealed across the valley, the sleepy town awoke to the rising sun. A thick morning fog quickly retreated from the cliffs hovering over Mt. Wellington— "And then what a lovely prospect was presented! The sun shone in his full strength—the very clouds had taken a holiday, for not one was visible."[36]

When Lieutenant Governor Denison refused to sponsor the jubilee celebration in steadfast allegiance to the economic benefits of transportation, Isaac Wright offered his wool storehouse on the wharf. A brass band serenaded the throng of thousands who pressed into the flag-decorated hall. Schoolchildren marched to the waterfront in groups of five hundred at a time, carrying silk banners at the front of the procession. By half past ten, a giant "Demonstration Cake" weighing 350 pounds, "about fourteen feet in circumference, iced over and most elegantly embellished," was carried into the room by eight bakers and placed on a raised platform.[37] "Loud huzzas" reverberated across the hall as the festivities began.[38]

Celebrants feasted on ham, roast beef, sandwiches, tarts, cake, lemonade, and ginger beer. Special attention was lavished on the children for their role in the colony's future. Girls and boys were outfitted in white clothing, a symbol of untarnished virtue, and the native-born touted their status with light blue ribbons on their left breasts. Henry Hopkins, a Sunday school teacher, addressed the youngsters and implored them to "become true Christians and good and useful citizens."[39] Giant cakes were also delivered to the Queen's Orphan School, though its residents were not awarded the commemorative medallions given to the other schoolchildren.

At noon, ships in the harbor, festooned in bright colors, fired guns into the air. The jubilee's entertainment concluded with bonfires and fireworks, proclaiming "to all the country around that convictism was dead, and that the loyal and respectable portion of the colonists were rejoicing that their beloved Queen had spoken the word of liberation. . . ."[40]

Prayer, in fact, had underpinned the Anti-Transportation League's call for Providence to stop the convict ships from entering the River Derwent. In describing the "Great Demonstration," the *Colonial Times* announced: "In August, 1803, Van Diemen's Land was first occupied 'as a place of exile for the most felonious of felons' from Botany Bay. . . . But the Supreme Governor of the universe had decreed that 'the wickedness of the wicked should come to an end.'"[41]

Yet transportation didn't end for humanitarian reasons. Instead, the British government phased it out after slave labor had served its purpose and free laborers began to fear competition for their jobs. Bitter prejudice about the deep imprint of the convict stain on proper society fueled a rising sentiment to erase the true history of Van Diemen's Land. The clergy, in particular, incited hysteria about homosexuality among male convicts and heightened the urgency to stop the influx of those they considered breeders of vice.

Both the press and the pulpit called for prayer as a means to rescue the colony "from ruin and degradation."[42] In its 1849 Christmas edition, the *Colonial Times* appealed to divine intervention to accomplish what a petition to Queen Victoria, signed by six thousand Hobartians, could not:

> We must petition the throne of Almighty God and pray that the curse be removed; and should all fail, then we must shake off the dust of our feet against our oppressors and depart to place our families where they can form honest associations and earn honest bread.[43]

The Anti-Transportation League of Van Diemen's Land, established by Reverend John West in 1849, led to the formation of the Australasian Anti-Transportation League on the mainland. The gold rush in the Colony of Victoria offered further reason to end forced migration, based on concern that people in Great Britain would commit crimes as a way to reach a continent paved in riches.

Pressure from free settlers in Van Diemen's Land escalated when they threatened to abandon a colony blighted by the "scum and dregs of the offscourings of mankind," as described by William Ullathorne, a Catholic priest who had served in Australia and a leading critic of transportation.[44] Rejecting the possibility of reform and redemption for young mothers like Janet Houston and Agnes McMillan, newspapers on both sides of the world declared: "It is impossible to import the criminal without importing crime."[45] The *Edinburgh Review*, called "the recognized manifesto of the British government" by the *Colonial Times*, asked:

> On what grounds . . . does England assume the singular privilege of establishing colonies to be deluged and drowned with the flood of her own wickedness? What right has any country to turn even a wilderness into a school of sin, to create, even at the antipodes, huge nurseries of depravity, to pollute a young nation from its very birth, and to saturate with its own corruption the sources whence countless generations are to spring?[46]

The *Irish Exile and Freedom's Advocate*, an 1850 emancipist newspaper published in Hobart Town, disputed such claims by purporting that families who lived alongside convicts for twenty years had suffered no "moral contamination."[47] Hoping to encourage acceptance with the help of Christian compassion, emancipists formed the "Society of the Propagation of the Charities, etc., of the Gospels." As it celebrated the strength in their numbers, a Society publication denounced the seeds of bigotry that polluted the pristine island they now called home:

> "They" came to make their fortunes and now "They" rail at you who "They" forced to come. "You" outnumber "Them" by many thousands. . . . Have *you* not made the colony what it is? Has not *your* sweat, in so few years, made this land . . . ? Have not *your* la-

bors given these wandering adventurers at least the position of
settled abodes . . . ?[48]

As tension escalated between the free settlers and the freed convicts, antitransportation advocates displayed their vitriol and solidarity
by pinning blue rosettes on their well-pressed lapels, flooding the
newspapers with lengthy editorials, and hosting public forums about
how to oust the convict population. Their quest for social power rested
precariously on the perceived horrors of a classless society in Van Diemen's Land. John Morgan, the head of the Hobart Town Trades
Union, penned an editorial outlining his concerns about emancipist
"tyranny":

> Presently, we shall have here, not a war of races and colours, but of
> castes and classes. . . . The convict authorities . . . would have us
> adopt the red republican, socialist, levelling principles of revolu-
> tionary France by which all distinctions are abolished.[49]

Now neighbors of those who'd been their masters, emancipated
convicts countered settlers' fears and prejudices by lobbying for their
rights as citizens. While freed convicts strove toward a democratic society, most free settlers were fiercely committed to stifling the voices
of men and women who held Certificates of Freedom. Emancipists
responded with organized solidarity in a town where two of every
three men had arrived on a convict ship. Their influence did not go
unrecognized. By the 1850s, candidates supporting their interests,
some former prisoners, were well represented as aldermen for Hobart
Town.

The deep schism between the two factions festered, refusing to
mend even as they sat side by side at municipal council meetings. Free
settlers remained frustrated by their failure to rid Van Diemen's Land
of "the curse, stain, and peril of convictism."[50] Colonists found it

impossible to bury the legacy left by a penal colony. Women and men who'd been transported with mental disabilities, who defaulted into alcoholic despair, or who couldn't endure unjust cruelty lived and died on the fringes of society. Estimates suggest that about one-third of the female transports never married or had children. "They lived out their lives in lonely exile far from their families and childhood friends. Amongst these were the ones who lived out their final days in the pauper institutions and mental asylums of the colonies, who lived isolated lives in small huts on the edges of towns and villages, or who wandered the colony, homeless and friendless."[51]

Before transportation ceased in Van Diemen's Land, a fresh influx of cheap labor, many Irish refugees from the potato famine, reached its shores. The last convicts to arrive in Van Diemen's Land were not welcomed as cheap labor the way Agnes and Janet were when the *Westmoreland*'s human cargo was paraded through Hobart Town. As antitransportation sentiment rose, each arrival of new convicts met with increased resentment. The last convicts to arrive in Van Diemen's Land were expected to serve their sentences, thus extending the penal practices of the previous fifty years. In April 1853, the final female convict ship, the *Duchess of Northumberland*, anchored off Hobart Town and delivered 216 women. Three women and seven children were lost during the rough voyage. One month later, the *St. Vincent*, the last convict ship destined for Van Diemen's Land, arrived on May 26, 1853, with 207 men on board, having lost seven at sea.

Nearly one-quarter of all transports were Irish: thirty thousand men and nine thousand women. Nearly half were arrested during the famine years, most for larceny. The deep-seated conflict between Ireland and Great Britain escalated with every Irish arrest, particularly when political activists were sentenced to transport.

In 1868, the *Hougoumont*, Britain's last convict ship to Western Australia, transported 279 male prisoners, including a band of 63 Irish political prisoners known as the Fenians. By this time, the Irish constituted about 20 percent of Australia's population. Among their ranks were Irish rebels who had emigrated as free citizens, many of whom played a role in shaping workers' rights and democratic government in the Australian colonies where Agnes McMillan and Ludlow Tedder would settle with their families.

An Gorta Mór: Let Them Eat Grass

While Janet, Agnes, and Ludlow lived out the life of the freed, a new crop of women was targeted for transport half a world away. One was named Bridget Mulligan, from County Cavan. Her passage aboard the *Blackfriar* had everything to do with being born Irish. A writer traveling to Australia in 1847 made this observation about the transported: "A man is banished from Scotland for a great crime, from England for a small one, and from Ireland, morally speaking, for no crime at all."[52]

Bridget's journey to Cascades began in the blackened potato fields of Ireland in 1849. Her brothers—John, Charles, William, and Patrick—had left their homeland for the promise of work in America. The youngest of the clan, Bridget, remained behind with her mother, Catherine, and sister Bessy.

Thousands began to flee the island. The blight escalated tensions between Ireland and England, and nothing could stop the export of grain. Upper society carried on with usual fare. As starving peasants with sunken eyes stepped over decaying corpses, local lords prepared a sumptuous feast for the visiting Queen Victoria and her assemblage of portly aristocrats. While the servants cleared the silver for the next setting of the banquet's twenty-three courses, the lords happily discussed profit from grain exports. Victoria, soon labeled the "Famine Queen" among the Irish, made a personal donation to alleviate suffering but quietly turned down higher contributions from other countries to protect both her pride and the Crown's image.

An Gorta Mór, "The Great Hunger," arose from the blight on

potato crops and worsened in the wake of society's decay. Greedy landlords and a greedier government were the harbingers of famine, together carrying the cruel countenance of inhumanity. Mass evictions in a single year accounted for two hundred fifty thousand Irish left with nowhere to sleep and no way to make a living. Taking advantage of skyrocketing agricultural prices during the Napoleonic War, landlords supplemented their income by leasing small plots, where families built their croft huts and farmed the land. When prices plummeted after the war, landlords aggressively evicted tenants, destroyed their huts, and converted the land into more lucrative livestock grazing. As a final burden, Ireland, normally known for mild winters, experienced abrupt blasts of weather, bringing freezing sleet and snow.

As a black mold crept across the fields, the British government responded with lethal disregard for children, women, and men who lay dying in the dirt with nobody to bury them. Mr. O'Shaughnessy, an assistant barrister who worked in Ireland, pleaded for help before the House of Commons:

> It was quite afflicting to see the state of the children. They were nearly naked, with a few rags upon them; their hair standing on an end from poverty; their eyes sunken; their lips pallid, and nothing but the protruding bones of their little joints visible. I could not help exclaiming as I passed them, "AM I LIVING IN A CIVILIZED COUNTRY AND PART OF THE BRITISH EMPIRE?"[53]

One million perished and at least another million were forced to leave the Emerald Isle for Europe, the United States, and Australia. As one tragedy bled into another, an additional eleven thousand were arrested and readied for transport, as crime escalated among people desperate for survival. A total of 3,687 Irish girls and women were shipped to Van Diemen's Land, most sent after 1840, when transport to New South Wales ceased.[54] The majority of Irish transports were convicted of larceny, many for rustling livestock. Among those convicted for petty theft, more than half had stolen clothing.[55]

For the empire, the Transportation Act was especially helpful in disposing of the Irish, a group supremely disdained throughout England. Illustrations in British newspapers of the day portrayed them as subhuman and simian in nature. Even the open-minded Elizabeth Fry had difficulty, at first, understanding and accepting the Irish she visited in prison. Describing women awaiting transport, she wrote: "The greatest number appeared to me Irish, a very few Scottish; the former are always ignorant, and preserve the peculiarities of their national character, even in this abode of sorrow and captivity. . . ."[56]

So fragile was life on the edge of disaster that entire Irish families chose transport over the likelihood of starvation. For some, exile to Van Diemen's Land was their only chance for remaining a family. Arson was the safest bet. It was an offense guaranteeing immediate transport. Light an oily rag or set a bale of hay on fire. Burn a barn to the ground. Everyone knew there was no way back, yet 242 women from Ireland committed arson, many to escape the famine.[57]

Propelled by love of family, Bridget Butler and daughter Anne Corry, age sixteen, hatched a plan to be reunited with the rest of their kin. Bridget's husband had died, and her children were the only family left in Killard, County Clare. As they looked out the grimy window of a boardinghouse room, rain bore down on what were once green hillsides, now plucked bare by the starving for their evening meal.

On January 11, 1849, armed with red-hot coal in a skillet, Bridget and Anne set fire to Mary Hickey's house, down the lane from the dingy lodging they called home. Mother and daughter prayed they'd be caught, and their prayers were soon answered. Each received a sentence of seven years to Van Diemen's Land.

A year earlier, Anne's sister, Margaret, and her brothers, John and Patrick, had been arrested for stealing a sheep. Margaret was shipped out right away. While her brothers awaited sentencing, Patrick was found dead in Dublin's Smithfield gaol. Not knowing they'd lost Patrick, Bridget and Anne boarded the ship *Australasia* to repeat the journey Margaret had made a year earlier. On March 27, 1849, they escaped the ravages of the potato famine. Every week spent on the *Australasia* brought mother and daughter closer to the chance for survival as a family. Just one day before their ship anchored, Bridget died from dysentery at age sixty, following several days of suffering from griping and purging.[58] Happily, Anne found her sister, Margaret Quealy, who attended Anne's wedding and the baptism of her children.[59]

Many stories were less outwardly dramatic than Bridget Butler's and Anne Corry's, though no less tragic. Bridget Mulligan was another country girl named after Ireland's St. Bridget, a patron saint. Like many, she relied on otherworldly strengths to survive the hard times in County Cavan. Still suffering the famine's aftershocks, Bridget was on her own at twenty-three and shared a small room with her "cara," or best friend, Mary Rennicks.

Just four feet, seven inches tall, with a ruddy complexion covered in freckles,[60] the diminutive lass with a squinting right eye didn't look like a criminal, nor had she intended to become one. But in 1850, she made a big mistake. She and Mary Rennicks stole a one-gallon milk tin, a gown, and a white petticoat from Susan Brady. Each was summoned before the Court of County Cavan in the province of Ulster. Despite no prior record, both Bridget and Mary were sentenced to ten years in "parts beyond the seas."

After Bridget was sent to an island smaller than Ireland, her Roman Catholic religion placed her in a tiny minority. Women from Ireland's western counties also faced a language barrier. Many spoke only Gaelic and did not understand the commands given by their captors.[61] Shipped in the final years of transportation, Bridget benefited from some improvements in shipboard captivity. "Perhaps the most important of these gave each convict a separate sleeping-berth place which could be converted in the daytime into seats and tables."[62]

Although Elizabeth Fry passed away in 1845 at age sixty-five, the work in her final years also eased Bridget's journey on the *Blackfriar*. By 1842, Mrs. Fry had lobbied successfully for the addition of matrons to the all-male ship crew. The *Blackfriar* sailed from Dublin with a cargo of 260 female convicts, 59 children, and 7 free settlers who booked passage on the barque. Though the prisoners were better supervised than those of earlier transports, barbaric medical practices had hardly changed at all. Surgeon Superintendent John Moody treated the insane on board with a straitjacket or a cold bucket of water, later reporting the results of his methods:

> Under the head Hysterical Mania . . . a case is given by no means uncommon in female convict ships and in the Penitentiary in the Colony, caused no doubt in nervous temperaments by the heat of climate, indolent life. . . . Nothing appeared to have a better effect than a shower bath or a few buckets of water thrown over them when first attacked.[63]

Bridget Mulligan's companion, Mary Rennicks, bore the impact of primitive shipboard treatment, arriving in Hobart Town bearing the X mark from blood purging on her right arm. She'd also lost a front tooth.[64] Bridget stayed healthy during the 125 days at sea, and Surgeon Superintendent John Moody recorded her behavior as "very good."[65]

Under a new penal system, convicts did not proceed directly to Cascades but were housed in the Brickfields Hiring Depot, opened as an annex to the Female Factory in 1842. Designed to keep new arrivals isolated from the entrenched Crime Class, especially the Flash Mob, a probation system introduced in 1839 was meant to hasten reform. On paper, it recommended skill training and the opportunity for well-behaved prisoners to earn a small wage, but in bureaucratic reality, progress was held in place.

Arriving two years before transportation ceased in 1853, Bridget faced the full force of prejudice against convict arrivals, more toxic still because she was Irish and because she was Catholic. Lieutenant Governor Denison pleaded for fewer Irish prisoners, declaring: "Their general want of industry, their insubordinate habits, their subservience to their religious instructors, render them particularly unfitted for settlers in a country like this."[66] Denison also lamented the lack of energy for hard labor among those weakened by the potato famine.[67] Rural Irish women, in particular, were ostracized for being "unfitted to engage in domestic service."[68]

Stigmatized by her heritage, her religion, and her country roots, the resourceful Bridget Mulligan took full advantage of the one opportunity for early release from the Female Factory. She managed to shave eight years off her sentence the day she married John Wild, a freed convict from Cheshire, England. At twenty-seven, he'd received a sentence in 1841 of fifteen years for getting into a bar fight and stabbing a "spoon forger." Only five feet, two inches tall, he'd lost some front teeth, his visage was rather sallow,[69] but he was an excellent businessman. Once freed, Mr. Wild opened a store selling tobacco and candles in New Norfolk, located on the banks of the River Derwent twenty-two miles northwest of Hobart Town. He also ran a catering service and sponsored lunches for the New Norfolk regatta and Odd Fellows meetings held in Kensington Park.

Bridget had been sentenced to a New Norfolk family in March 1853, so she was put on a cart and sent north just as the trees were turning colors. Golden poplars had been planted all along the river and displayed themselves in bright autumn yellows. Her romance began with a purchase for her master in Mr. Wild's well-trafficked Charles Street store. The two married in a Catholic Church on July 24, 1853, in the midst of a frosty winter, one month before the official end of transportation to Van Diemen's Land. Bridget gave birth to a daughter named Hannah on November 20, 1855.

Entrepreneurial in spirit, the lass from County Cavan set up a Dutch oven at the back of her husband's store and charged townsfolk a penny to bake their dinners. Hannah grew up inside the family store, learning the business and developing one of her own. When Bridget retired, she took over her mother's oven and, according to descendants, "was remembered for always wearing a snowy white apron."[70] When people came to collect their cooked dinners, she offered a plate of freshly baked scones and expanded her baking empire. With her husband, Henry Laskey, she bought every house on Charles Street, where the two raised nine children in a home named "Tara," after Ireland's mythical seat of power. Hannah became a wealthy woman.

Bridget Mulligan's dear "cara," Mary Rennicks, didn't live long enough to be freed. Shortly after being processed at Brickfields, she struck a fellow prisoner and was sentenced to hard labor. The next year, five months pregnant, she was committed to trial for the "willful murder of a newborn child" under her care at Cascades. Four months later, she delivered her stillborn baby boy inside the Female Factory. This only deepened her anger, and she was soon cited for an incident of insubordination. In February 1856, a highly unusual notation appeared in her conduct record, recognizing "meritorious conduct on the occasion of fire at Brickfields."[71] Two weeks later, the twenty-six-year-old accused murderer, troublemaker, and proclaimed hero died alone inside the stone walls at Cascades, suffering from burns from her selfless actions to save others from the fire.

The year Mary died was the same year Van Diemen's Land was renamed Tasmania, after first explorer Abel Tasman. As many citizens hoped to erase the "convict stain," the women and men who'd suffered forced migration forever changed the complexion of the growing population in Tasmania and New South Wales, becoming the heart and soul of a unique cultural identity.

Bridget received her Certificate of Freedom shortly before the Christmas holidays in December 1862. Like Janet Houston, she lived in Tasmania for the rest of her life. However, when Bridget first arrived on the *Blackfriar* in 1851, people were leaving the island in droves. Nearly eight thousand people, most of them former convicts, had left Van Diemen's Land over the previous three years.[72] Something quite spectacular had been discovered across Bass Strait.

~ 10 ~

Bendigo's Gold

Canvas Town

Gold was discovered in 1851 at Summerhill Creek and Bendigo, two small towns in a new territory on the mainland, the Colony of Victoria. Among those credited as the first to find Bendigo gold were Margaret Kennedy and Julia Farrell, when postings announced that "women were getting quart-pots of gold on Bendigo Creek."[1]

The shape of modern Australia began to take form at the same time the promise of gold electrified imaginations around the world. When news spread of the riches lying just inches beneath the thick scrub, a huge confluence of hopeful and often hapless immigrants headed for Australian shores. For many, Port Phillip and the township of Melbourne was their first destination.

One man, in particular, took credit for starting the gold fever that first swept over the continent and then around the world. Born in Hampshire, England, Edward Hargraves arrived in New South Wales on a merchant marine ship in 1832. He married in Sydney but was unable to earn a living. In 1849, hoping to change his luck, he set off for the California goldfields. While there, Hargraves noticed a striking similarity between the hills surrounding his home in the Macquarie Valley and the claims that were yielding so much gold near Sacramento. Before boarding his ship to return to Australia in 1851, an American digger admonished the British dreamer: "There's no gold in the country you're going to, and if there is, that darned Queen of yours won't let you dig it."[2] The quick-witted response from the egocentric Hargraves became legendary, soon reaching mythic proportions. Answering the American digger, he reportedly removed his hat and struck a well-rehearsed pose of triumphant confrontation, proclaiming: "There's as much gold in the country I am going to as there is in California; and Her Most Gracious Majesty the Queen, God bless her, will make me one of her gold commissioners."[3]

Hargraves's confident statement proved prophetic. Anxious to collect a reward from the government for locating a goldfield, he shortly found the bounty he anticipated and received the commission he sought. The announcement of his discovery in the newspapers started a deluge of enthusiastic, and mostly inexperienced, treasure hunters from adjoining colonies into New South Wales.

A May 1851 news release in the *Bathhurst Free Press* was reprinted in newspapers with broad distribution:

DISCOVERY OF AN EXTENSIVE GOLD FIELD

The existence of gold in the Wellington district has for a long time been an ascertained fact, but public attention has never until now been seriously drawn to the circumstance. . . . Mr. Hargraves states . . . that from the foot of the Big Hill to a considerable distance below Wellington, on the Macquarie, is one vast gold field, that he has actually discovered the precious metal in numberless places, and that indications of its existence are to be seen in every direction. Ophir is the name given to these diggings.

Several samples of fine gold were shown to the company by Mr.

Hargraves, weighing in all about four ounces—the produce, he stated, of three days digging. The amount thus earned by each man he represented to be £2 4s. 8d. per day. . . . From the nature of some of the country explored by him, he is of opinion that gold will be found in mass, and would not be surprised if pieces of 30 or 40 lbs. should be discovered. He had seen no country in California which promised metal in such heavy masses.[4]

With golden visions dancing before their eyes, men deserted farms, crews abandoned their ships, and husbands left wives in a blind rush for the promise of prosperity. Shovels and picks in hand, laborers walked off their jobs, grabbed a wheelbarrow, jumped on a cart, or threw a sack over their shoulders. They streamed out of Victoria to the digging fields in New South Wales to a little patch of ground called Ophir. In hopes of drawing people back to the newly formed Victoria, the colony's governor offered a reward to the first person who found gold in the territory. Within the first month, three claimants presented specimens, vying for the prize. The rush was on. By Christmas 1851, two hundred fifty thousand ounces of gold had been pulled from the Victoria goldfields.[5]

News reached Van Diemen's Land shortly after the initial finds, in a rather unremarkable announcement, buried on page three of the *Colonial Times*, May 23, 1851: "Gold—We understand that Dr. George Bruhn, the celebrated German mineralogist, on his mineralogical excursions from Mount Macedon to the Pyrenees, has been fortunate enough to discover the existence of gold."[6] These initial reports were greeted with skepticism in Hobart Town and Launceston, but more and more stories touting stupendous windfalls began to appear. Word of mouth delivered the news up the Huon River and to campfires around the forests of Franklin. Supper conversations inevitably turned to gold—gold for the taking along a fast road to riches.

In 1852, Ludlow and Arabella Tedder joined the fortune seekers exiting Van Diemen's Land, each in the company of a new husband.

For a few years after her release from the female factories, Ludlow's life had seemed settled. Then suddenly she lost another husband. William Manley Chambers either died or deserted her, most likely the latter. A few years later, a man by his name applied for a Hobart Town liquor license for a pub on Old Wharf called Sailor's Return.[7]

Soon after William's departure, Ludlow met John Atterwell, an ambitious "hawker" who peddled his wares from house to house in Launceston. Still determined to live a full life at fifty-three, she married John on January 20, 1847. A year later, Ludlow had good reason to celebrate the holidays with abandon. On December 21, 1848, ten years after the Old Bailey judge sentenced her into exile for stealing eleven spoons and a bread basket, prisoner #151 held her Certificate of Freedom. The next year, Ludlow became a proud grandmother when nineteen-year-old Arabella gave birth to a son she named Henry James Tedder. The family of four lived together in Launceston. In 1851, Arabella delivered another son called Benjamin Waters, his surname taken from the man she planned to marry, a freed convict from England.

Following news of gold fever, Ludlow's husband, John, and Arabella's fiancé, Isaac Waters, sailed from Launceston to Melbourne aboard the *Shamrock*. Their eyewitness assessment of the diggings was better than imagined, and the two men quickly returned to Launceston, eager to return to Bendigo's goldfields. In the autumn of 1852, Arabella married Isaac, twenty-six years her senior and full of plans for the move to Victoria. Now business partners, John and Isaac sold everything lock, stock, and barrel, booked passage, and headed straight for the diggings. The new bride and groom, their two young sons, Ludlow, and her third husband, John, journeyed across the Bass Strait to try their luck with the thousands of others headed for the shores of Victoria. Torrential rains signaled an inauspicious beginning to their transport aboard the *Sphynx*, a barque about half the size of the *Hindostan*. The journey that typically took one day lapsed into three as the small ship fought heavy seas and driving winds. Carrying thirty-five passengers, the *Sphynx* landed in a flooded Melbourne packed with timber, tobacco, tea, flour, rum, ivory, and apples.[8]

News from the mainland traveled a bit slower to the southern tip of Van Diemen's Land. Agnes and William were preoccupied with four children and another on the way. Even so, by the time Christmas breezes blew through the Huon pines at the close of 1853, they, too, had been bitten by the gold bug. Over the next year, they scrimped and saved for what they'd heard was a costly excursion. Before they left, it was essential that William purchase additional firearms for a dangerous journey and a new and different rough-and-tumble frontier.

Even fare-paying passengers weren't guaranteed access to the diggings because of the ever-festering prejudice against former convicts. The Anti-Transportation League sponsored the Convicts Prevention Act, enacted into law in Victoria in 1852. In an attempt to stop "Vandemonians" from entering the mainland, convicts who held a Ticket of Leave were denied, and only those with Certificates of Freedom allowed. The act added to the challenges of those unable to find work upon release from prison. Bigotry based solely on appearance motivated the law's passage. One lawmaker offered his view of the freed convicts: "Square of jaw, shaggy of eyebrows, low in the forehead, with strongly marked bumps beneath the closely cropped hair, their very appearance was a source of alarm to the respectable citizens."[9]

Before entering Victoria, Agnes and William would have to prove they were unconditionally free and present Certificates of Freedom for #253 and #510. Still, the notion of shedding the past and creating a new future were goals too tempting to resist. In 1854, the plucky couple packed up what they could carry. Baby at her breast, Agnes left Franklin with her family and boarded a small ship destined for Melbourne.

Sitting at the top of Port Phillip Bay at the mouth of the Maribynong River, Melbourne had been chosen as the capital for the new Colony of Victoria. Now, it was the jumping-off point for newly discovered goldfields. When Agnes and William arrived, the harbor was jammed with vessels, many stranded because their crews jumped ship to try their luck in the goldfields.

To the Roberts brood, accustomed to years of living quietly in the wide-open woodlands of the Huon Valley, Melbourne presented a disturbing scene. "Slaughterhouses lined the river—wooden buildings with fenced yards to one side, holding the wretched beasts standing among the decapitated heads of their kind. . . . On the riverside entrails, blood, gore and the stripped carcasses of rotting animals trailed into the river creating a filthy malodorous welcome to the newly arrived immigrant."[10] Even Agnes, who knew well the seamy urban underside from her days as a Glasgow street urchin, must have been horrified by what her little ones were walking into.

The rustic family deposited on the new capital's streets was instantly presented with unanticipated challenges. Compared to the pristine air and water along green rain forests, a city nicknamed "Marvellous Smellbourne" required some getting used to. The roads, though laid out in a well-ordered grid, were largely unfinished and unpaved. When it rained, they turned into impassable bogs and, when dry, into windy dust bowls. Broken bottles, garbage, and decaying animals littered the streets. Carrying everything they owned, the newly arrived couple with five children did their best to navigate a path through the confusion.

The huge influx of gold created a highly inflated economy and drove up prices on everything a family needed. Finding lodging in the city was out of the question for a large group on a tight budget. Upon entering the port, William scanned notices advertising tents for rent just outside the city in Little Adelaide, where temporary shelter could be secured for five shillings a week.

Entering the tent city, Agnes, William, and five wide-eyed children were thrust into a hodgepodge of newcomers speaking in foreign tongues of all flavors. This was the staging area for hopeful miners preparing to fan out across the goldfields. Adventurers from China, France, Italy, Germany, the West Indies, and the Americas joined in the melee caused by gold fever.[11]

A rural family was better prepared than most for the spartan facilities in the temporary village. Agnes and the children were accustomed to hauling water and scrounging wood for a fire. The dirt floor in their riverside cabin was not much different from the dusty ground they laid their blankets on now. Mosquitoes and flies plagued the camp. The worst of their worries, however, were sideward glances from neighboring tents, from those suspicious of Vandemonians.

When night fell on "Canvas Town," a thousand fires sprang to life, and motley human creatures gathered round in a chorus of singing, swearing, and carousing. Armies of dogs barked incessantly, and revolvers crackled everywhere until sunrise brought some semblance of silence.[12] It's doubtful the tight-knit family from Franklin got much sleep their first night under the stars in Little Adelaide.

William easily found employment as a craftsman in the bustling, expanding Melbourne. His expertise in woodcutting, carpentry, and building was in high demand because so many skilled laborers had fled to the goldfields. Reports of incredible finds further fanned the fevered flames.

As people sat around blazing fires in the tent city and digging camps, they told and retold tales of incredible luck. In January 1853, a French sailor unearthed the 132-pound "Sarah Sands" nugget (so named for the ship carrying it back to England). Within sight of Melbourne, he had jumped ship with the rest of its crew and, on a whim, persuaded his mates to lower him on a rope into the first abandoned hole they encountered. A few minutes of working his inexperienced pick, with peals of laughter echoing from his chums aboveground, yielded the unmistakable sound of metal on metal. Leaning into the hole, he spied gleaming yellow just below where previous diggers had given up. As he shoveled deeper, his naïve tenacity paid off. The monster nugget sold for two hundred thousand francs, a hefty profit for two days' work. Word of the lucky Frenchman's find created a frenzied return to this once-abandoned patch of mines. Two more giant chunks were found within a week, "including one nugget weighing 94 lbs and another of 78 lbs."[13]

Melbourne may not have smelled the freshest, but it was anything but boring. While William worked in the city, Agnes and their children settled into life in Canvas Town, a thousand-ring circus teeming with treasure hunters and money-hungry entrepreneurs. Entertainers also found fortune on the fields, though certainly less spectacular than the Frenchman's trove. Jugglers and musicians were showered in gold nuggets if they pleased the right audience or pelted with stones if their performances fell short. The infamous Lola Montes, dubbed "the darling of the diggers,"[14] left California to take Victoria by storm. Traveling across the gold settlements, she performed her "tarantula dance" to packed houses of cheering miners.

Conspicuous consumption and downright madness were symptoms that gold fever had infected another victim. A British woman who visited the Australian goldfields with her digger fiancé recorded in a diary what she heard, saw, and smelled along the way. When riches came fast and furiously, she observed foolishness of outrageous proportions:

> At times, you may see men, half mad, throwing sovereigns, like halfpence, out of their pockets into the streets; and once I saw a digger, who was looking over a large quantity of bank-notes, deliberately tear to pieces and trample in the mud under his feet every soiled or ragged one he came to, swearing all the time at the gold-brokers for "giving him dirty paper money for pure Alexander gold; he wouldn't carry dirt in his pocket; not he thank God!"[15]

With so few women in mining territory, weddings brought more deliriously lavish celebrations. The bride wore a white veil over a gown sewn from satin or velvet and held a silk parasol high over her head. The groom presented his new wife with orange blossoms, exorbitantly expensive and precious for their short supply. He then rented a gaudy carriage that careened through the streets, while the thoroughly inebriated wedding party poured glass after glass of sparkling champagne from a shiny black bottle. Many brides were, in fact, roaming hustlers, willing to create elaborate deception until their husband's money ran out and the next prospect arrived.[16]

The shortage of women among the miners did not go unnoticed by London philanthropist Caroline Chisholm, who journeyed to Australia with her ship captain husband. Devout Christian that she was, Chisholm envisioned that the colony's wild outback could best be tamed by the gentler influence of women, or, as she called them, "God's police."[17] Her work started small, rescuing destitute women from Sydney's streets and driving them in a wagon to farms where they might find employment. So successful was her mission placing "Mrs. Chisholm's Chickens" that she started the Family Colonization Loan Society. It funded passage of fallen women she'd met in London and brought them to the goldfields, where they found work or a husband. Though some reverted to their sinful past, many others married diggers or set up small shops scattered wherever miners set up camp. Some mended clothing or washed laundry for a nugget or two. Others set up "coffee shops," selling unlicensed grog from a washtub.

Amid the mayhem of unlikely unions, drunken men falling over the tents, and new babies crying in the night, the determined William Roberts rose early, walked into the city, and worked every day. Soon a fat sack of coins furnished tools, supplies, and a tent for the newest prospector and his family. In the spring of 1854, the Roberts clan was ready to follow the path of Ludlow's family and head down the trail to try their luck.

Beyond the Black Forest

Nobody but a fool traveled to the goldfields alone. William was a good shot, and his hunting rifle saw plenty of use in Franklin. It hung protectively over his shoulder as he pushed a wheelbarrow piled high with tents, blankets, dishes, pots, and pans. Around his waist, he kept handy a large knife under a leather belt that holstered a revolver, the preferred firearm of the day.

Agnes, youngest child on her hip and leading four-year-old George Henry by the hand, marshaled the other children forward. Though peaceful in many ways, Huon Valley life had strengthened mother Roberts. She'd given birth in the wild, skinned a roo, and learned how to fire a gun. Still, she worried about the latest journey ahead. The safest way for family travel was in a larger group, so William found some new mates to split the expense of bullocks and a dray that would carry their children and their goods. They wouldn't all fit in the wagon, so eight-year-old William walked next to his father for most of the trip. Ten-year-old Lavinia Louisa rode with her younger siblings, now two, four, and six.

Carrying everything they owned, swag bundles strapped to their backs, most parties began the hundred-mile journey from Melbourne to the goldfields well armed and alert. The trail to the diggings was lined in grave danger. Bushrangers routinely preyed on those entering and exiting, some stripping men naked and leaving them tied to a tree to be discovered by another traveler.

Both feared and glorified, daring bushrangers fed folklore and ruled the road. Jack Donahue, among the most famous, was not the typical violent plunderer but a well-dressed rakish Robin Hood. His exploits, robbing the rich to feed the poor, were immortalized in the trail song "The Wild Colonial Boy," Australia's first unofficial national anthem. With thousands of transients spread out across the central plains, it was nearly impossible to tell an honest digger from a lurking villain.

The Roberts party slowly made their way from Melbourne to the goldfields, encountering plenty of reasons to turn their cart around. Depending on the weather, the journey took from three to four weeks over ruts, bogs, and tree stumps. The rough roads they traveled were "littered with the wrecks of expeditions gone wrong, animals that would pull no more simply left to die by the side of the road, goods piled high as merchants waited for relief, or discarded as yet one more traveler sought to lighten his load."[18]

There were many "coffee-shops" and "hotels" at various intervals along the trail. These way stations, often no more than tents themselves, offered refreshment and shelter to the stream of adventurers headed to and from the diggings. In most cases, they were best avoided. Not only were prices highly inflated, but bushrangers gathered intelligence from these haunts. That friendly face across the supper table might well be holding a pistol to a head a few miles down the trail. Travelers were wise to keep to themselves, quickly set up a camp, and post a well-armed guard at night.

The journey's most treacherous passage proceeded through the Black Forest, a thick congregation of dense ironbarks, their trunks still charred from terrible fires.[19] It was the perfect spot for an ambush and notoriously ruled by bushrangers. "Here the trees grow very close together; in some places they are so thickly set that the rear-guard of the escort cannot see the advance guard in the march."[20] William cleaned his revolver, fired a test shot, and returned the dry powder to the safety of his pouch. Agnes mounted the cart and laid the rifle at her feet. Any outlaw who foolishly tested their mettle was in for a fight.

In good weather, the Black Forest danger was cleared in about a day—if a party didn't get lost. Approaching the forest, the road diverged: west to Ballarat or north to Mt. Alexander and Bendigo. Traffic flowed one way or the other depending on rumors of gold strikes, both real and imaginary. Ludlow and her contingent had taken the northern route.

When Ludlow's band pulled into Bendigo in 1852, it was scorched earth like nothing they'd ever seen. As far as the eye could scan, "the trees had been all cut down; it looked like a sandy plain, or one vast unbroken succession of countless gravel pits—the earth was everywhere turned up—men's heads in every direction were popping up and down from their holes. . . . The rattle of the cradle, as it swayed to and fro, the sounds of the pick and shovel, the busy hum of so many thousands, the innumerable tents, the stores with large flags hoisted above them, flags of every shape, color, and nation, from the lion and the unicorn of England to the Russian eagle, the strange yet picturesque costume of the diggers themselves, all contributed to render the scene novel in the extreme."[21]

The tent city stretching before them was a confusing and everchanging metropolis, regulated by strict mining rules and an enforcing army. Before John Atterwell and Isaac Waters staked out a claim, they needed a license, purchased for £1 10s (thirty shillings) for a month's digging right. On the back of their Victoria "Gold Licence," the following rules were printed:

REGULATIONS TO BE OBSERVED BY PERSONS DIGGING FOR GOLD, OR OTHERWISE EMPLOYED AT THE GOLD FIELDS.

1. Every Licenced Person must always have his Licence with him ready to be produced whenever demanded by a Commissioner, or Person acting under instructions otherwise he is liable to be proceeded against as an unlicenced person.
2. Every Person digging for Gold, or occupying Land, without a Licence, is liable by Law to be fined, for the first offence, not

exceeding £5; for the second offence, not exceeding £15, and for a subsequent offence, not exceeding £30.

3. Digging for Gold is not allowed within Ten feet of any Public Road, nor are the Roads to be undermined.

4. Tents or buildings are not to be erected within Twenty feet of each other, or within Twenty feet of any Creek.

5. It is enjoined that all Persons at the Gold Fields maintain and assist in maintaining a due and proper observance of Sundays.[22]

A continual object of contention between the diggers and the commissioner's inspectors, the license later became an instrument of revolt. For the time being, it was a necessary evil and a costly inconvenience. Paid based on the fines they collected, the gun-toting inspectors, or "traps," hounded the miners with carefully orchestrated "licence hunts." Raiding the diggings with military precision, "they stretched out across the gullies and worked their way from one end to the other. A digger caught between the shaft and his tent without his licence in his pocket would be immediately chained like a dog to other unfortunate fellows, and driven back to the Commissioner's Camp to be . . . chained to logs or the trunks of trees, with the excuse, real or pretext, that the lock-ups were full, and often left outside all night and in all weather."[23]

Prospectors were often fined even before they set up camp. Always on the lookout for newcomers, an ornery thug undoubtedly targeted Isaac and John. Arabella and Ludlow attracted attention as well. When the gold rush began, few women were seen near the fields. Sightings of skirts incited whistles and yelping. Diggers dropped tools, and sunburned heads popped out from the mining holes. Apart from diversion, women were also valued as treasure keepers. Prized was the woman willing to carry a man's stash in a money belt at her waist, carefully tucked under a corset or petticoat. Additionally, women weren't charged license fees even if they worked the fields, thus avoiding both fees and nasty collector confrontations.

When she wasn't chasing sons Henry James and Benjamin across the muddy red clay, Arabella helped Isaac dig. Ludlow happily provided grandmotherly care, especially when Arabella was pregnant again in late 1853. Arabella gave birth to her third child in a tent on the Bendigo goldfields. Tossing cloths and towels into boiling water over a campfire, former Nurse Ludlow sterilized what she could and prayed for the best. In the role of midwife, on July 19, 1854, she delivered her newest grandchild, named Arabella Ludlow. There was no room in the hospital because injured miners held priority and filled every bed.[24]

Life around the tents took on a domestic simplicity. Women "baked bread, churned butter, made curtains, bedspreads, rugs, lacework and clothing. They made their own candles, spun their own wool and crocheted . . . whatever it took to make a home in this unforgiving country."[25] They gathered gum leaves to stuff mattresses, stewed mutton, and made simple bread from flour and water.

Everyone looked alike, dressed in moleskin trousers and waterproof boots, and everyone blended in, including the freed convicts. "It was impossible to tell a man's background from his appearance. No one asked any questions and all diggers were, for the time being, of the same class."[26] Each tent, however, took on a unique personality, marked at the entrance by a hanging boot, a billy pot, or a bright piece of cloth. A handy ax-man like William would have built a more elaborate structure from sturdy slabs of timber. A society unto themselves, the tented towns transformed on Sundays when mining was forbidden. The faithful gathered around converted tree stumps used as pulpits by the traveling preachers. By day, the tents were quieter with the men in the fields. But all hell broke loose with their return at night.

Under the Southern Cross

When Agnes and William reached the fork at the Black Forest trail in 1854, they chose the western route, deciding to try their luck in the Ballarat goldfields. There, they would witness an event that shook the continent, a rebellion that many called the birth of Australian democracy: the Eureka Stockade.

Dissension had been brewing for quite some time. In 1851, Governor La Trobe tried to raise licensing fees but rescinded his decision in the wake of the "Great Meeting of the Diggers," in which twelve thousand stood defiantly firm against an increase in fees. When the governor foolishly sent troops to suppress the insurrection, miners stared down the 99th Regiment, forcing their withdrawal when they realized the miners outnumbered them two hundred to one.

The flood of license fees created a bonanza for colonial authorities. In Bendigo alone, permits jumped from six thousand to more than twenty thousand a month by the end of 1852.[27] Soon after their arrival, Ludlow's family watched the tent city's population explode. A torrent of cash filled the coffers of Victoria's newly formed government. Instead of using it for sorely needed improvements in roads, hospitals, and schools, the government betrayed the miners' trust with incompetence and corruption. Fee collection often amounted to little more than thinly disguised extortion for personal gain. When the widely reviled Governor La Trobe was finally removed from office and returned to England in May 1854, one-quarter of the money deposited in the treasury was nowhere to be found.[28]

The goldfields also attracted many who did not hold "Mother England" in high esteem, especially a huge contingent of displaced and mistreated Irish, many of whom were political activists. Chartists—members of a working-class labor movement started in Great Britain—joined freedom-loving Yanks who held no regard for the empire's rules. In addition, a growing number of anarchists and dissenters joined large gatherings at the diggings to promote radical ideas of equality and rights for all. The goldfields lay ripe for firebrands, as the sparks of liberty found easy tinder in the frustrated miners.

Bendigo became a hotbed of dissension. The Anti-Gold Licence Association was formed in 1853, representing twenty-three thousand diggers and their families. Isaac and John likely joined massive rallies where they flew the diggers' flag, depicting the scales of justice and other symbols of democracy. Displaying the flag, leaders presented Governor La Trobe with the Bendigo Petition, stretching ninety feet long and holding five thousand signatures. It demanded reduced mining fees, the right for new colonists to own property, and the elimination of soldiers as fee collectors.

La Trobe ignored the petition, and tensions escalated. Drawing a line in the sand, diggers took matters into their own hands. In united protest, they agreed to pay no more than ten shillings when their licenses came up for renewal in a few days. As a sign of solidarity, miners tied red ribbons to their hats and sent a message to the gold commissioners. The Red Ribbon Rebellion was born, and the "wearing of the ribbon became so common that supplies of red flannel, a popular material used in the making of diggers' shirts, all but dried up."[29]

During the standoff, a few men were arrested when they refused to pay the full license fee. Instantly, diggers armed with pistols, picks, and rifles marched to the Commissioners Camp to set their mates free. Following the miners' unexpected show of force, La Trobe and the legislature quickly capitulated, reducing the license fee to £1 a month, £2 for two months, or £8 a year.[30] The Bendigo association had won a partial victory for all the diggers, but there were still many who were not satisfied.

By the time Agnes and William moved to Ballarat, they found themselves at the flashpoint of an escalating clash between the diggers' movement and Victoria's new governor, Charles Hotham. Miners had cheered his arrival earlier in the year, holding out hope that he'd see things their way. Hotham, however, considered the miners dupes, who were manipulated by foreign agitators, especially the Irish. He also faced a huge deficit and needed license fees to help bring it under control. The miners' initial euphoria over Governor Hotham dissipated quickly.

New to office, Hotham imposed twice-weekly license checks, fueling deeper resentment among the diggers. In Ballarat, their frustration compounded when Scottish miner James Scobie was brutally kicked to death by James Bentley, owner of the Eureka Hotel. Diggers were outraged when Bentley was acquitted after a cursory investigation by a local magistrate known to be corrupt. An angry mob formed and set fire to the Eureka Hotel on October 17, 1854.

An anxious Agnes saw smoke rising above her town. Ever since her family set up camp, a palpable tension ran through the diggings. Scobie's murder had escalated the strife, and now that Bentley was under protection at the Commissioners Camp, the government's collusion against justice seemed all the more apparent. The vastly outnumbered soldiers desperately reinforced the camp's defenses as angry protesters marched through the streets of Ballarat.

The fire at the Eureka Hotel set in motion a flurry of activity, as cooler heads tried to avoid the rising inevitability of bloody confrontation. Within days, miners formed the Diggers Right Society. In November, the hastily formed Ballarat Reform League sent delegates to Melbourne with a new list of demands for diggers' rights. While the delegates awaited the governor's response, a duplicitous Hotham dispatched an additional 450 troops to Ballarat. On Tuesday, November 28, a long line of crimson-jacketed soldiers marched into town. Panicked miners ran in every direction and loaded their guns. Agnes called for her children and gathered them safely inside.

News of the approaching soldiers, bayonets gleaming in the sun, spread like wildfire. The swelling crowd of shocked townsfolk greeted them with pelting stones and shouts of derision. Attempting to block the column's advance, the gathering mob overturned carts. In the confusion, shots were fired and critically wounded the regiment's drummer boy.[31] The soldiers retaliated by drawing their swords. Shots and screams rang out across the hills and gullies surrounding Ballarat, and a bolt of terror tore through a terrified mother of five.

The next day, Wednesday, ten thousand miners met at Bakery Hill. Defying Britain's rule, they raised a new flag for the first time. Three courageous women stitched the blue-and-white flag that represented the Southern Cross, ornamented with white stars against an off-white background. One was a freed convict from Van Diemen's Land named Anastasia Eustes Withers. A dressmaker from London, she was transported for stealing five shawls. Together with a woman also named Anastasia, Anastasia Hayes, and a very pregnant Anne Duke, she left her mark of protest against the rule of the Crown.[32]

Peter Lalor, an upper-class Irish activist and one of the Ballarat Reform League founders, addressed the large, restless crowd. He was perhaps a natural for the role; his brother, James Fintan Lalor, had been involved in the Young Ireland uprising in 1848, and his father served in the British House of Commons. Six-foot-tall, twenty-five-year-old Peter ended his speech with calls for lighting a huge bonfire. Diggers defiantly tossed their licenses into the flames.

It was the last day of the month, November 30, 1854. Governor appointee Robert Rede, Ballarat's Gold Commissioner, knew what had happened the previous night on Bakery Hill. With the backing of additional troops, Rede was confident a show of force would quash the uprising. Knowing that many miners had burned their licenses the night before, he ordered a license hunt with soldiers in full force, provoking more confrontations between diggers and soldiers.

Rede continued the hunt throughout the morning. By noon, he rode to the gravel pits and demanded that diggers present their licenses. Shots were fired, and miners rushed up the gully shouting their outrage. Rede ordered the troops to turn their guns on the gathering mob. Facing the tight line of muskets, they began to disperse.

Later in the day, a large crowd began to congregate on Bakery

Hill. "At a meeting at 4 pm on November 30th, 1854, Peter Lalor stepped up on a tree stump beneath the billowing Southern Cross flag, and into his place in Australian history. The diggers knelt, as one, on the dusty ground, placed their hands over their hearts and chanted together the diggers oath: 'We swear by the Southern Cross to stand truly by each other and defend our rights and our liberties.'"[33]

Lalor later recalled that moment: "I looked around me; I saw brave and honest men, who had come thousands of miles to labor for independence. I knew that hundreds were in great poverty, who would possess wealth and happiness if allowed to cultivate the wilderness which surrounded us. The grievances under which we had long suffered, and the brutal attack of the day, flashed across my mind; and, with the burning feeling of an injured man, I mounted the stump and proclaimed 'Liberty.'"[34]

They were all caught up in it. As much as Agnes wanted to escape with her family, most women on the goldfields knew one another, so Agnes wanted to help if she could. The worried mother watched the freedom fighters piece together their best defenses. For two days straight, a thousand inspired diggers worked to erect a stockade on the Eureka field. "The roughly circular encampment was about an acre in area and barricaded on three sides by a rude construction of pit logs thrown together in a higgledy-piggledy manner. . . ."[35] By Saturday evening, their work was done.

Since the start of the month, there were no new incidents, two days thankfully without bloodshed. Saturday evening as campfires blazed, Agnes put her children to bed with a sigh of relief, looking forward to Sunday's peace. It was not to be so.

At dawn's break on Sunday, December 3, 1854, every available soldier fastened his bayonet and marched toward the thinly manned stockade on Bakery Hill. Their attack was a complete surprise. Drowsy rebels awoke to the sentries' shocked cries, barely grabbing their guns before bullets flew over their heads. The battle was short and fierce. Three hundred soldiers had attacked the stockade, killing twenty-two prospectors and taking one hundred prisoners. Six soldiers lost their lives. A few women joined the rebellion and challenged the troops directly. In an act of defiance and protection, Bridget Hynes and several other women ran onto the battlefield, putting their bodies over the wounded and preventing soldiers bent on revenge from bayoneting them to death.

Nineteen-year-old Bridget Callinan, originally from County Clare, Ireland, helped rescue her two wounded brothers, Patrick and Michael. As the troops began to murder the wounded and burn the hospital tents, Bridget confronted the armed soldiers and created a diversion that allowed her two brothers to escape with the help of her cousins. Michael had received two bullets in his thigh, and Patrick suffered two bayonet wounds.[36]

Just as the tensions came to a head, Agnes's sons William and George Henry were nowhere to be found, out on an errand when the shooting began. Young William later related a "very vivid recollection of the Eureka Stockade riots, and had the unpleasant experience of seeing a man shot down by his and his brother's side at a time they had been sent on a message." Needless to say, the young boys "took to their heels and did not draw breath till they were safely home."[37] Out of her mind with worry when the gunfire ensued, Agnes's frantic screams subsided when she saw her two winded lads running back toward the camp. A battlefield was no place for children.

On this Sunday, even her church was unsafe. Largely made up of Scots, the Presbyterian ministry was harboring a severely wounded Peter Lalor, and women from her congregation were helping to save his life and amputate his shattered arm. Both political hero and hopeless romantic, the insurgent was known for having walked the hundred-mile round-trip journey from Ballarat to Geelong to see his beloved fiancée, Alicia Dunne. With a huge price on his head after the Eureka battle, the fiery Irishman was smuggled from the Presbyterian Church back to Alicia's Geelong home. When amnesty was declared and Lalor's wounds healed, grateful diggers elected him to Victoria's first legislative assembly.

What started as a dispute over licensing fees became a protest for human rights. Within a year, nearly all the miners' demands were met, including suffrage for men, abolition of property requirements for membership in Parliament, equal electoral districts, and the abolition of diggers' licenses. The "Gold Licence" rules were replaced by "a Miner's Right for an annual fee of £1, and an export levy on gold. This Right gave the diggers title deed to their claims, allowing them to establish permanent dwellings, and a permanent sense of community. Commissioners were replaced with mining wardens and military rule was abolished on the goldfields forever."[38]

The Eureka uprising ended with the trial of the century. Charges of treason against the protesters carried a death penalty, but no jury would bring a guilty verdict. Every deliberation brought unexpected acquittals for those taken prisoner. Huge crowds gathered around the courthouse and cheered exultantly. One by one, rebels were acquitted and paraded through the streets, as ten thousand miners carried the exonerated on chairs above their heads. The first of those acquitted was John Joseph, a black American from New York, a man the United States had left to fend for himself after the embassy helped free the four white Americans arrested at the Eureka Rebellion.

A few years after the trial, Agnes, William, and the children headed north with their gold safely hidden in the wee ones' "nappies."[39] Invigorated by newly won freedoms, they raised their tent poles and began mining the fields at Campbell's Creek. By this time, most gold deposits accessible to single prospectors had been harvested, so it was much more difficult to make a go of it alone. Larger deep-shaft mines like the "Hercules," the "New Moon," and the "Deborah" took over the mining fields.[40] Mullock (waste) heaps and towering structures with poppet legs now dominated the skyline across Victoria's central plains. Within a short time, the wandering Roberts contingent packed up and went on the move again. This time, they were hunting for "red gold."

The red cedar forests seemed the ideal place for William to find work, since loggers had founded the community of Lismore. He'd earned the right to buy land, and his family needed a place to call their own. They'd spent too many years living under canvas. It was time for William to put down his pick and sharpen his ax. Huge fortunes were being made from timber stands along the Richmond River, and finding a good tree to fell was certainly easier than searching for a deeply entrenched gold nugget. It would be a long journey up to the Gold Coast, but the children were older now, and the solitude of the rain forest seemed preferable to the strife at the diggings. William purchased a sawmill, and Agnes gave birth to two more children: Caroline in 1858 and Joseph in 1860.

The fervor of gold fever had subsided by Christmas 1869, when Agnes and William sat on the veranda looking out on their grandchildren with pride and delight. Life on the frontier was still rough and the world was changing around them. Agricultural development had taken over the "Big Scrub." The forests had been cleared, and the rich stands of red cedar were nearly depleted. Springing up in their place was a new generation of children who knew nothing of their grandparents' past.

Agnes McMillan's journey had taken her from the murky industrial wasteland along the Glasgow wynds to the subtropical Richmond River Valley, dense with palm trees, leafy ferns, waterfall gorges, and wild orchids. Nestled in a remote timber settlement, with more ducks and black swans than people, the wilderness provided her family with everything they needed. Streams plentiful with eel, cod, bream, lobster, and perch fed a growing brood, which now included seven grandchildren. Wild game from the bush—plover, quail, and scrub turkey—also topped their cedar table, readily adorned with bowls of raspberries and wild bananas. The former street urchin could never have dreamed of the holiday feast that now lay before her. Gone were the days of singing for pennies on the Green or making choices between starving and stealing.

Though she'd followed a separate path and settled more than a thousand miles from her beloved Janet, Agnes never lost sight of the unflinching loyalty that had sustained them through their tumultuous coming of age. The two Scottish lasses had been through it all: the drudgery and filth of the wool mills, the degradation inside Newgate, a terrifying and treacherous sea journey, and finally the prison where Janet suffered the loss of little William. They would still endure tragedy from time to time.

In 1853, the year transportation ended in Van Diemen's Land, there was little triumph for Janet. Within ten days in October, she lost two sons, eight-year-old James and three-year-old Arthur, victims of scarlet fever. By Christmas 1869, the now-greying redhead had given birth thirteen times, buried three children, witnessed the marriage of her two oldest sons, and welcomed into the world at least one grandchild. Her son William celebrated his heritage when he and his wife, Dinah, christened eleven of their twelve children with the middle name Freeman. With a touch of humor and perhaps a bit of irreverence toward British rule, they named their ninth child Charles Napoleon (Warrior) Bailey.

Ludlow, too, had relied on an unshakable bond, hers between mother and daughter. It had carried them from a Christmas inside Newgate Prison through their journey to a land "beyond the seas." Though she'd been forced to suffer a five-year separation from Arabella in Van Diemen's Land, Ludlow now heard the sound of laughter, from three generations, echo through the ironbark forest in Sandhurst, Victoria. Mother and child had arrived in Van Diemen's Land with nothing, but by 1869, both owned property in a thriving township stirring with commerce from banks, hotels, watchmakers, grocers, music halls, and a bowling alley.[41] After the miners' rights were won, Arabella's husband, Isaac, continued to work the diggings, while his expanded family settled down in a quiet country cottage just outside

Bendigo proper. With Ludlow by her side, Arabella gave birth to five more children: four girls and a boy.

At age thirty-seven, Arabella became a widow in 1867, when Isaac passed away at age sixty-three. Twelve years later, she wed a widower named John Oliver. Her grandchildren, like many in Sandhurst, still found specks of gold in the dirt after a hard rainfall. Arabella lived to age eighty-eight, enjoying life as the matriarch of four generations and remembered in her 1918 obituary as "a well known and highly esteemed resident of the Golden Square district."[42]

Pursuing ordinary lives twelve thousand miles from their homeland, Arabella, Ludlow, Agnes, and Janet helped shape an emerging culture with traits born of their extraordinary past. With iron wills forged in a crucible of greed, injustice, punishment, and prejudice, these survivors refused to be broken. When transportation ended, convict women and men constituted about 40 percent of Australia's English-speaking population.

Bold women sent to a wild land against their will—Agnes McMillan, Janet Houston, Ludlow Tedder, and twenty-five thousand others—wove the rich tapestry for a nation's future. Whether Irish, English, or Scottish, it didn't matter where they were from or why they were transported. The winds of change had blown away much of the past. Under the Southern Cross, healing had begun. They were all Australians now.

Agnes McMillan

Description List
(*Westmoreland*, AOT CON 19-1-14 p. 438)

POLICE NUMBER	
NAME	Agnes Mackmillan [name misspelled in record]
TRADE	house servant
HEIGHT	5' 1¼" (without shoes)
AGE	17
COMPLEXION	fresh
HEAD	long
HAIR	light brown
WHISKERS	
VISAGE	oval
FOREHEAD	medium height
EYEBROWS	light brown
EYES	grey
NOSE	medium length
MOUTH	medium width
CHIN	medium length
NATIVE PLACE	Glasgow
REMARKS	none

Transcription provided by Female Factory Research Group

Conduct Record

POLICE NO. 253

Millan Mc Agnes

Westmoreland   3 December 1836
Ayr Court of Justiciary   3rd May 1836   *7 years*

Transported for theft, habit, repute and previous convictions.
Gaol Report: twice before convicted, bad character, single.
Stated this Offence: robbing a shop; tried with Houstan on board,
    [previous convictions] once for Housebreaking 18 months, once 60
    days for theft; 3 years on the town; single. Surgeon's Report: bad.

22 March 1837 (Donahoo) Absent without leave & insolent – Crime
    Class 3 months & not again assigned in Town (PS*)
3 November 1837 (Parker) Disobedience of orders – 2 months Crime
    Class (HBT) Hobart vide Lieutenant Governor's decision 11
    November 1837
8 September 1838 (Sweet) Refusing to return to her service – cell 10
    days on bread & water & returned to her service (PS)
28 September 1838 (Harvey) Out after hours – cell on bread & water
    6 days & returned to her service (PS)
8 October 1838 (Harvey) Absent without leave & taking 2 young
    children with her – Crime Class 1 month, first 6 days on bread &
    water (PS)
7 December 1838 (Palmer) Absenting herself without leave – hard
    labour at the wash tub for 2 months sleeping in a cell at night (PS)
25 February 1839 (Evans) Absenting herself without leave – 7 days
    cells on bread & water (RCG)
3 April 1839 (Ross) Absent without leave – returned to Government &
    not to be assigned in any township (WHB)
17 June 1839 (Amos) Absent without leave – 2 months in the Crime
    Class, Female House of Correction Hobart & recommended to be
    assigned in the Interior (BB & JH)
13 October 1840 (Walker) Insolence – 14 days solitary confinement (JW)
30 March 1842 (Nursery Liverpool Street) Absent without leave and
    representing herself to be free – 4 months hard labour in the
    House of Correction (WG)

22 February 1843 (McDonald) Absent 2 nights and a day without
leave – 3 months at the wash tub (PS)

Free Certificate No. 388 1843

2.4.39 Richmond office 28.7.40 Richmond 4.8.40 Oatlands office
24.4.43 Police Superintendent

*These are the initials of the sentencing magistrate, which in this case is the
Principal Superintendent. Agnes was imprisoned at Cascades Female Factory
on each occasion.

Transcription provided by Female Factory Research Group. Reference: AOT,
CON40-1-8 p. 9

Description List
(*William Miles*, AOT CON 18-1-21 p. 76)

POLICE NUMBER	510
NAME	William Roberts [Agnes McMillan's husband]
TRADE	Coach Maker and painter Birmingham
HEIGHT	5' 5½" (without shoes)
AGE	24
COMPLEXION	fresh
HEAD	small oval flat top
HAIR	brown
WHISKERS	scarcely any
VISAGE	small broad oval
FOREHEAD	high square temples
EYEBROWS	dark bushy nearly meet
EYES	dark brown
NOSE	small and straight full at the bridge
MOUTH	small—lips prominent
CHIN	small and pointed
REMARKS	scar on right temple—scar on left temple high up—mark of Scrophula [*sic*] left side under chin

Janet Houston

Description List
(*Westmoreland*, AOT CON 19/1/14 p. 415)

POLICE NUMBER

NAME ·   Houston, Janet

TRADE   house Servant

HEIGHT   5' ¾" (without shoes)

AGE   17

COMPLEXION   fresh

HEAD   round

HAIR   red

WHISKERS

VISAGE   oval

FOREHEAD   high

EYEBROWS   light brown

EYES   hazel

NOSE   M. L. (medium length)

MOUTH ·   wide

CHIN   M. L. (medium length)

NATIVE PLACE   Glasgow

REMARKS

Conduct Record

POLICE NO. 284

Houstan Janet
[name misspelled in record]

Westmoreland 3 Dec 1836
Ayr Court of Justiciary 3 May 1836   *7 years*

Transported for Theft habit repute and previous conviction. Gaol
report, bad character before convicted twice. Single Stated this
offence, Theft stealing money at Ayr, 4 times convicted for Theft,
60 days twice, 6 months twice, four years on the Town, single,
Surgeon's report, orderly

Aug. 12, 1837 Mrs. Ray/disobedience of orders. Cell on bread and
water 3 days returned to service / P.S.

July 24, 1838 Ray /Insolence to her Mistress. returned to the factory
for country assignment / P.S.

Nov 7, 1838 Rev W. Orton / Absent all night without leave Rep@ /
W.G. (Rev Joseph Orton is Chairman of the district, Institute of
Wesleyan Ministers)

Nov 14, 1838 Orton/ Absent all night without leave and found in a
disorderly house Sentence – working cells for one month, first six
days on bread and water thru assignment in country/ P.S.

Dec 20, 1838 Ratcliffe / Disorderly conduct

March 23, 1840 Misconduct

Aug 2nd, 1841 Misconduct living in a state of adultery with a free man /
being advanced in pregnancy / 12 Months Labor Female House of
Correction

March 17, 1842 Misconduct 6 days of solitary

May 3, 1843 – Free Certificate #339

Reference: AOT, CON 40-1-6 p. 9

Ludlow Tedder

Description List
(*Hindostan*, AOT CON 19/1/13 p. 299)

POLICE NUMBER

NAME	Ludlow Tedder
TRADE	cook & house Servant
HEIGHT	5' 2" (without shoes)
AGE	47
COMPLEXION	dark
HEAD	round
HAIR	dark brown
WHISKERS	
VISAGE	long
FOREHEAD	high
EYEBROWS	brown
EYES	hazel
NOSE	
MOUTH	medium
CHIN	
NATIVE PLACE	Essex
REMARKS	freckled

Transcription provided by Female Factory Research Group.

Conduct Record

POLICE NO. 151

Tedder Ludlow

Hindostan   11 September 1839
Central Criminal Court   17 December 1838*   *10 years*

Transported for larceny. Gaol Report: poor connexions. Surgeon's
Report: the most attentive & best behaved on board doing duty as
nurse; widow & 5 children. Stated this Offence: stealing plate from
my master Mr F Kenneth, Keppel Street on Banister; widow & 5
children.

---

22 June 1842 (Nursery, Liverpool Street) Misconduct in taking advantage of her situation as nurse in the Hospital at the House of
Correction to obtain articles & money for the purpose of clandes-
tinely delivering the same to "Eliza Morgan," a prisoner of the
crown then in confinement, the articles having been obtained
from Mr Smith in Elizabeth Street – 12 months hard labour in the
House of Correction and to be placed in the separate working
cells until the Lieutenant Governor shall be pleased to consider her
case (PS)

Confirmed this female was placed in a situation of great trust under
promised indulgence of the Principal Superintendent considering
her to be a fit subject, to be placed under this sentence to separate
confinement vide Lieutenant Governor's decision 23 June 1842.

Ticket of Leave 15 May 1844

Conditional Pardon for Australian Colonies recommended
27 May 1845

Approved 22nd May 1846

Certificate of Freedom 21 December 1848

28.4.42 Principal Superintendent office 25.6.42 Principal
Superintendent office 8.6.43 Superintendent 13/2/44 Morven
29.2.44 Principal Superintendent 8/3/45 Launceston

---

* Transcription provided by Female Factory Research Group. Reference: AOT,
CON 40-1-10 p. 113; trial recorded 19 December in the Old Bailey records

Bridget Mulligan

Description List
(*Blackfriar*, AOT CON 19/1/9)

POLICE NUMBER

NAME   Bridget Mulligan

TRADE

HEIGHT

AGE

COMPLEXION   ruddy

HEAD   large

HAIR   brown

WHISKERS

VISAGE   round

FOREHEAD   low

EYEBROWS   brown

EYES   blue

NOSE   medium

MOUTH   medium

CHIN   medium

NATIVE PLACE

MARKS   squints right eye, freckled and slightly pockmarked, bled left arm

Transcription provided by Female Factory Research Group.

Conduct Record

POLICE NO. 1231

1 MARCH 1855 NEW NORFOLK

Mulligan Bridget

Tried Co. Cavan   *1 March 1850*
Embarked   *10 years*

Arrived 29 May 1851

Roman Catholic   *neither read nor write*

Transported for having stolen goods in possession. Gaol Report: never convicted before, very good, single. Stated this Offence: receiving a milk can prosecutor unknown at Cavan. Single. Surgeon's Report: very good.

Services: 5 June 1851 Brickfields Hiring Depot; 17 October 1851 House of Correction*; 10 November 1851 Brickfields Hiring Depot; 30 January 1852 H Martyn, Battery Point; 20 August 1852 Brickfields Hiring Depot; 11 September 1852 John Gill, Davey Street; 15 October 1852 House of Correction; 12 November 1852 J Bandall, New Norfolk; 18 March 1853 Mr Charles Menzie, New Norfolk; 12 July 1853 J Randall, New Norfolk

Offences & Sentences

  3 January 1854 Marriage with George Jones approved.[†]

  Ticket of Leave 1 May 1855

  Ticket of Leave revoked 15 March 1859 absent &

Certificate of Freedom to self 1 December 1862.

---

*This was Cascades Female Factory, sometimes referred to as the House of Correction.

[†]This is an error on the part of the authorities—even though Bridget Mulligan is listed on the Permissions to Marry index as marrying George Jones, this was in fact Biddy Mehan, also transported on the *Blackfriar*.

Transcription provided by Female Factory Research Group. Reference: AOT, CON 41/1/30 *Blackfriar*

Description List
(Tortise 19 Feb 1842, AOT CON 18-1-30 p. 80)

POLICE NUMBER

NAME	Wild, John (Bridget Mulligan's husband)
TRADE	laborer
HEIGHT	5' 2" (without shoes)
AGE	27
COMPLEXION	sallow
HEAD	oval
HAIR	brown
WHISKERS	ditto
VISAGE	oval
FOREHEAD	medium
EYEBROWS	black
EYES	grey
NOSE	long
MOUTH	large
CHIN	ditto
NATIVE PLACE	Cheshire
REMARKS	lost some of front teeth

Rules and Regulations for the Management of the House of Correction for Females

HOBART TOWN COURIER
Saturday 10 October 1829, page 4

Rules And Regulations

(The regulations for the management of the House of Correction for females being in themselves so excellent, and so many of our readers having expressed a desire that they should be printed in the *Courier*, we have determined, though they occupy a very large share of our Journal of this week, to give them at large.)

1. A House of Correction having been erected for the reception of Female Convicts, and for the punishment and reformation of female offenders, the following rules and regulations are to be observed for the due management of the establishment,

2. The Principal Superintendent of convicts being a magistrate, is charged with the general direction of the house of correction. He is to visit it daily for the purpose of hearing and determining offences committed within the walls, of seeing that all the records hereinafter described are correctly kept, of examining minutely into the state of the establishment, and of issuing instructions in writing, to the superintendent upon all such matters as requite his interference.

3. He is to countersign all requisitions, examine the accounts, (and certify that he has so done) as well of the articles supplied for the use of the establishment, as of those manufactured by the women, and he is to transmit such reports and returns as shall place the Lieutenant Governor in possession of the requisite information as to the increase or decrease of crime amongst the female convicts, the quantity of work performed, the general state of the establishment, and most especially the expense of the institution.

4. He is to submit, for the more efficient control, or for the reformation of the females, such measures as he may be enabled from time to time to sug-

gest from his own observations, or from the information of the superintendent; and on the Lieutenant Governor's sanction being notified to him by
the Colonial Secretary, he is to record the instruction in order that it may
thenceforth be observed as a standing regulation of the establishment.

5. Cleanliness, quietness, regularity, submission and industry are inserted
in the general regulations, as being expected by the government to be observed throughout the establishment, and therefore they are to be uninter-
ruptedly enforced by the principal superintendent, and he is to allow no
excuse whatever in justification of the slightest occasional departure from
the strict observance of all these essential points which are required un-
varyingly to characterise [sic] the house of correction.

6. With all the attention that can be bestowed, the establishment must
necessarily be a heavy charge up on the government, and the most scrupu-
lous attention to economy is therefore expected to pervade the whole system of the establishment.

7. It is alone by frequently visiting the different classes, and by constantly
inspecting the treatment, the food, and the employment of the women,
that the principal superintendent can conscientiously satisfy himself, or
faithfully assure the government, that they are neither allowed improper
indulgences, nor subject to unnecessary harshness, and that the rules and
regulations for the management of the establishment, and for the punishment and reformation of the female offenders, are duly observed and punctually enforced in every department.

8. For the management of the establishment, the following officers are or
will be appointed—a superintendent, a matron, an overseer and task mistress for the crime class, a porter, a clerk and two constables.

The Superintendent—He is intrusted [sic] with the immediate management of the establishment, under the directions of the principal superintendent of convicts, and held responsible for the safe custody of the women,
and for the strict observance of the rules and regulations for the house of
correction.

Every article within the walls is also intrusted [sic] to his charge, and he
is responsible that the public property is carefully preserved and accounted for.

He is to communicate to the subordinate officers, in writing, such instructions as he may receive from the principal superintendent, and to see that they are duly carried into effect.

He is to keep a regular journal, noting in it all occurrences of importance, especially cases of misconduct, and the measures thereupon adopted. This book is to be submitted to the principal superintendent whenever he visits the establishment.

Before breakfast every morning, and after supper every evening, he is to read to all the classes assembled in the chapel, a portion of Scripture, accompanied by a short prayer; if the chaplain should be present, this duty will of course be performed by him.

He is to inspect all the rooms and yards of the building after the women have proceeded to their morning's labour, and see that they are kept in order, and perfectly clean throughout the day.

He is from time to time during the day to visit all the classes while at work, to satisfy himself that quietness is observed, that idleness is not permitted by the task women, and that in every way good order is strictly maintained.

He is to inspect the provisions when issued to the cooks, and again when divided into messes, and to be present during dinner for the purpose of preventing any irregularity.

He is to give instructions daily to the overseer of the crime class, and through the matron to the several task women respecting the employment of the convicts under their charge; and at the close of the day, is to require from each a report of the manner in which the work has been performed, and of the general conduct of each class, and comparing them with his own personal observations during the day, is to note the result in his journal.

He is, with the assistance of some of the well-conducted task women, to devote a portion of every alternate evening during the week to the instruction of such women as may be inclined to learn, and on Sundays he is to cause such as cannot read to be assembled and instructed.

He is to inspect all articles of provisions when furnished for the use of the establishment, and to satisfy himself that they are wholesome, and supplied according to the terms of contract. When any of an unwholesome or inferior quality are supplied, he is to reject them, reporting the circumstance to the principal superintendent.

He is empowered to confine any female in a solitary cell, for disobedience of orders, neglect of duty, or other improper conduct, for a period not exceeding 24 hours, but he is to enter the full particulars of each case in his journal, and to report the same to the principal superintendent, on his visiting the establishment.

He is to visit the females confined in the cells every morning, to satisfy himself that they are in health, and that their punishment is duly enforced. Should any female, while confined in a cell, represent herself to be sick, he is to report the same to the medical officer when he visits the establishment, and, immediately, if the case be urgent, remove her to the hospital yard.

He shall be allowed a clerk for the regular keeping of the undermentioned books:

1. A victualling book according to the scale of rations allowed the establishment, (in the form furnished by the commissariat).

2. A register in which shall be entered the names of the females as they shall be received into the establishment, with the date of entry, and the day on which they shall be assigned or discharged, (Form A).

3. An alphabetical book which shall contain the names of all females received into the establishment, their offences, general conduct, description, temper and habits during their confinement, (B).

4. A record of all offences committed within the walls, distinguishing the cases adjudged by the principal superintendent, from the minor offences disposed of by himself.

5. A book in which shall be entered the receipt and expenditure of all articles furnished for the employment of the females, and which shall exhibit their daily employment, the proceeds of their labour, and the value and appropriation of the articles manufactured.

6. The convicts' private property book, in which all articles received shall be entered, and their mode of disposal recorded.

7. A book in which shall be inserted these regulations, together with such additional regulations as shall from time to time be issued for the government of the establishment.

8. A memorandum book containing a journal of daily occurrences, in which any directions given by the principal superintendent are to be inserted.

He is to furnish the following returns weekly to the principal superintendent, who will certify as to their accuracy, and transmit them through the Colonial Secretary for the information of the Lieutenant Governor.

1. The weekly state of each class, the mode of employment, the number admitted, and the number discharged.

2. Return of offences within the walls, by whom adjudged, nature and extent of the punishment.

3. Enumeration of the articles manufactured, or work performed by the females, and how disposed of.

4. A list of those females who shall be assignable, exhibiting their names, ship, date of arrival, the service from which they are received, date of entrance into the establishment, the description of work they are capable of performing, together with the particulars of their conduct, character and habits, as far as they can be ascertained.

He shall note in his journal his own absence and that of the matron, whenever either of them may have occasion to leave the establishment.

The Matron—The matron shall superintend such part of the employment of the women as falls within the province of a female, and shall attend to such matters as could not be properly performed by the superintendent, and shall generally assist him in the care and control of the establishment.

She is to give instructions to the task women about the employment of the females, and shall receive from them the articles manufactured.

She is to inspect the females in their separate wards at the morning muster, and shall see that they are clean and properly dressed.

She is to visit the sleeping rooms daily, and see that they are kept perfectly clean and in order by the wardswomen.

She is to visit constantly throughout the day, the hospital, nursery and kitchen yards, and to superintend and give directions in all that is going forward in either, most watchfully observing that in every thing extreme cleanliness, and order, and industry, and economy prevail.

Overseer and Task Mistress of the Crime Class—The overseer is to superintend the crime class at their several occupations, keep an account of all the implements and tools required for their employment, on occasions when the superintendent is necessarily absent, he is to act his deputy, and in the general management of the establishment, shall render the superintendent such assistance as he may require, conforming himself to his instructions. The women confined in the cells are most especially under his charge, he is to visit them at least morning and evening to watch them whilst they are alternately permitted to be in the cell yard, to issue to them their daily allowance of bread and water, to cause the cells to be cleaned in his presence, and to take especial care that no person whatever is allowed to hold conversation with the convicts under confinement.

The task mistress of the crime class is to assist the overseer in all his duties, and on her vigilance and unremitting attention the order and general improvement of the women greatly depends.

Minute instructions for the direction of this class will be prepared and signed by the principal superintendent, and having been approved by the Lieutenant Governor, are to be affixed in some conspicuous part of the yard, and even the slightest deviation is on no account to be allowed or passed by without the severest animadversion.

The Porter—The porter is to keep a book (form C), in which he shall enter the name of every individual who comes into or goes out of the establishment, with the exact hour of such entry and departure, and he is not to suffer any person attached to the establishment to leave it without a written order from the superintendent, which he is also to enter in his book.

He is not to permit any person to enter the inner door of the establishment, except the members of the executive and legislative councils, magistrates, chaplains, and medical attendants, without the written authority of the principal superintendent.

He is to keep an account of all articles as they are supplied for the use of the establishment, and of such as may be taken away.

When any articles shall be delivered at the establishment, he is to give notice thereof to the superintendent or matron, who is to attend for the purpose of receiving them.

He is to ring the bell at such times as are required by the rules and regulations of the establishment, and as the season varies the stated boors will be notified on a board fixed in the lodge, under the hand of the principal superintendent.

Constables—Two constables are to be attached to the establishment, one of whom shall be constantly on duty, and they shall act as messengers.

They are not to be permitted to enter the inner gate, unless their aid should be required in quelling any riot or disturbance, nor are they to speak to or converse with any female confined within the walls of the establishment. More detailed instructions will be issued to them by the principal superintendent, task women, and wards women.

For each class a task woman is to be selected, of approved conduct. She is to have the immediate superintendence of the women in her class. She is to see that they rise at the proper hour in the morning as the first bell rings, that their persons are washed, their bedding properly made up, and that they are in readiness for the inspection of the superintendent and matron at the general muster, when they shall proceed to the performance of their several duties.

In case of any irregularity, neglect of duty, or disobedience of orders by the women under their charge, the task women are immediately to report the circumstance to the superintendent or matron.

One wards woman is to be allotted to each sleeping room; her duty will be to superintend the care of all the bedding and utensils which belong to her room and to see that the apartment is kept in proper order.

Female Convicts—No female convict shall be received into the establishment (excepting such as may be placed there on their arrival from England) without the written authority or warrant of a magistrate, stating the offence of which she has been guilty, and her sentence, if any shall have been passed.

Every female brought to the establishment shall be placed in the reception room until she shall have been examined by the surgeon, she shall then be bathed, washed and dressed in the clothing of the establishment; and if incarcerated for any offence she shall have her hair cut short. The clothes which she shall have brought with her shall be burned if foul or unfit to be preserved, but if otherwise they shall be washed and kept for her benefit on her discharge from the establishment. All articles so kept shall, in the presence of the female, be entered in the "Private property book," be made up into a parcel, numbered, and marked with the name of the female to whom it belongs, and shall be kept in a place appropriated for that purpose, and shall be delivered up to her on her discharge from the establishment.

The females are to be placed in three distinct classes, which shall on no account be suffered to communicate with each other.

The first class shall consist of those women who may be placed in the establishment on their arrival from England, without any complaint from the surgeon superintendent,—of those who are returned from service with good characters,—and of those who have undergone at least three months' probation in the second, after their sentence in the third class has expired. The women of this class alone shall be considered assignable, and shall be sent to service when proper situations can be obtained.

The second class shall consist of females who have been guilty of minor offences, and of those who by their improved conduct merit removal from the crime class.

The third or crime class shall consist of those females who shall have been transported a second time, or who shall have been guilty of misconduct on their passage to the colony,—of those who shall have been convicted of offences before the Supreme Court, who shall have been sent in under the sentence of a magistrate, or who shall have been guilty of offences within the walls,—they shall never be removed from the 3rd to the 1st class.

The dress of the females shall be made of cheap and coarse materials, and shall consist of a cotton or stuff gown or petticoat, a jacket and apron, with a common straw bonnet of strong texture, and the classes shall be distinguished as follows, viz:

The first class shall wear the dress without any distinguishing mark.

The second class by a large yellow C on the left sleeve of the jacket.

The third class by a large yellow C in the centre of the back of the jacket, one on the right sleeve, and another on the back part of the petticoat.

Each female is to be furnished with clean linen every week, viz: 2 aprons, 2 shifts, 2 caps, 2 handkerchiefs, and 2 pair stockings.

The first class shall be employed as cooks, task women, hospital attendants, or in such other manner as shall be directed by the principal superintendent.

The second class shall be employed in making clothes for the establishment, in getting up linen, or in such other manner as shall be directed by the principal superintendent.

The third class shall be employed in washing for the establishment, for the orphan schools, penitentiary, in carding wool, spinning, or in such other manner as shall be directed by the principal superintendent.

The hours of labour shall be as follows:

	1st. Nov. to end of Feb.	Mar. Apl. Sept, and Oct.	May, June, July, and August.
Muster....	½ past 5	Six	Seven
Labour....	Six	½ past 6	
Breakfast....	Eight	Eight	Eight
Prayer & Labour	½ past 8	½ past 8	½ past 8
Dinner....	Twelve	Twelve	Twelve
Labour....	Sunset	Sunset	Sunset
Eveng. Meal	½ past 7	½ past 6	½ past 6
Prayers....	Eight	Seven	Seven

The diet of the several classes shall be as follows:
Breakfast: ¼ lb. bread and a pint of gruel.
Dinner: ½ lb. bread and a pint of soup.
¼ lb. bread and pint of soup.

The soup to be made in the proportion of 25 lbs. of meat to every 100 quarts of soup, and to be thickened with vegetables and peas, or barley, as may be most convenient.

Ox or sheep heads may be used advantageously for making the soup.

The females in each class are to be formed into messes consisting of twelve each,—the best conducted woman is to be named overseer of her mess, and to be responsible for the conduct of the other eleven. Each mess is to sleep in the same room, and their hammocks are to be slung together.

Females guilty of disobedience of orders, neglect of work, profane, obscene, or abusive language, insubordination, or other turbulent or disorderly or disrespectful conduct, shall be punished by the superintendent with close confinement in a dark or other cell, until her case shall be brought under the consideration of the principal superintendent.

Hospital and Nursery—The internal economy of the hospital and nursery yards will be regulated by the medical attendant, who will accordingly frame a code of regulations which, when approved by the Lieutenant Governor, are to be strictly observed by the individuals intrusted [sic] with the duties of these yards. The medical officer is punctually to attend the establishment every morning, whether there are or are not any sick women.

General Regulations.

1. None of the inferior officers shall absent themselves from the establishment without first obtaining the superintendent's authority.

2. No officer belonging to the establishment shall be permitted to receive under any pretence whatever any gratuity or present, either pecuniary or otherwise from persons with whom the government shall have contracted for the supply of any article for the establishment, or from persons who may visit the establishment, or have any work performed in it,—in plain language, no persons employed in the establishment are, either directly or indirectly; to receive any gratuity or reward whatever beyond the salary and allowance granted by the government.

3. No female who shall have been returned from service for misconduct, shall be allowed to be again assigned until she shall have undergone a pro-

bation of not less than three months in the second class; in cases of frequent misconduct in previous service not less than six months, and in all cases of dishonesty not less than twelve.

4. The conduct of the task women, wards women and overseer, will be considered when they apply for any indulgence.

5. The testimony of the superintendent as to the character of any female applicant for indulgence, who has been placed in the house of correction, will be indispensable before her application can be considered.

6. No female will be allowed to marry from the second or third classes, nor indeed from the first unless she can obtain a favourable certificate from the principal superintendent.

7. Every female, except such as may be exempted by a certificate from the medical attendant, will be required to attend prayers both morning and evening, and divine service whenever performed in the chapel.

8. One bible, together with such books as the chaplain may recommend, will be allowed to each mess, of which the task woman of the class shall have charge, and for the preservation of which she shall be held accountable.

9. No officer or servant of the establishment shall supply any female convict with other provisions or comforts of any kind than those allowed by the regulations. Neither is any clothing, nor other articles whatever, to be permitted to be delivered to any convict in the House of Correction, nor are any letters or notes to be given them unless the same shall have been first opened and perused by the superintendent, by whom they will be destroyed if they be not from relatives or approved friends, and of a proper character and tendency.

Any person, connected with the establishment who shall disobey the orders contained in this regulation, if free shall be immediately dismissed, and if a convict shall be severely punished under the sentence of the principal superintendent.

10. No fires are to be allowed but such as are sanctioned by the principal superintendent, and he is to define the supply of fuel for the superintendent, free overseer, porter, constables and others, according to the general regulations of the government.

11. No poultry, pigeons, or pigs shall be kept within the walls of the establishment, nor is smoking on any account to be allowed.

12. It is to be distinctly explained by the principal superintendent to all the free officers employed within the establishment, and by the superintendent to all the female convicts on their admission that the utmost cleanliness, the greatest quietness, perfect regularity, and entire submission are laid down as fundamental laws of the establishment; and according to the degree of offending against any of them, punishment of some kind is invariably to follow. If these be observed, patient industry will appear, and reformation of character must be the result.

13. The Rev. Mr. Norman will superintend the religious instruction of the establishment occasionally during the week, and will perform divine service at least once every Sunday, and the resident superintendent will at all times give facility to any arrangement proposed by the chaplain for the more convenient assembly of the women, provided such arrangements do not militate against the established regulations of the House of Correction.

14. A general inspection of the establishment shall be made on the first Tuesday in every month by a committee, which shall be appointed by the Lieut. Governor, when a general return of the receipts and expenditure shall be furnished, together with a report exhibiting the number of females received and discharged during the preceding month, and a particular statement of their conduct, and the quantity of work performed. The observations of the committee, or of any authorized visitor will be entered in a book kept open for that purpose.—(D).

By His Excellency's command, J. BURNETT.
Colonial Secretary's Office, Jan. 1, 1829.

COLONIAL TIMES
Friday 4 March 1831, page 4

Rules and Regulations for Young Ladies

At fifteen.—Affect vivacity, and line your bonnets with pink. If in company with an agreeable gentleman, hold your breath long enough to blush when he speaks to you, and incline your eyes downwards when giving an answer.

At sixteen.—Seem to have a high spirit, but show the most unbounded submission to the opinion of the favoured [*sic*] one. You may now (when in conversation) look in a gentleman's face, but be cautious that the eyebrows are kept well arched. Affect a great liking for little babies, and get the credit of being an excellent nurse.

At seventeen.—Read the news of literature and fashion, and form your opinion of the follies of the day, upon their mode. Condemn a taste for public amusements, and talk of the happiness of retirement, and of domestic life. Simper "nimming pimming," to put your lips in pretty shape, and kiss children before gentlemen, that they may look and envy. Wear frocks as low as the fashion will allow, but still leave much to conjecture.

At eighteen.—Look out seriously for a husband, and be everywhere upon your best behaviour [*sic*], taking great care not to smell of bread and butter.

At nineteen.—Go to routs and parties, but avoid general flirting. Dress fashionably, but with great neatness and propriety. Wear no flowers in your hair, but let the curls have an appearance of simple negligence.

At twenty.—Consider yourself in some danger of remaining single, and suit your conduct to your circumstances.

At twenty-one.—Be less particular than heretofore, for time begins to wane.

At twenty-two.—Think seriously of paying a visit to some friend at Madras or Calcutta.

At twenty-three.—Marry any body that is not downright intolerable.

At twenty-four.—You cease to be a young lady, and must manage as well as you can.

COLONIAL TIMES
Tuesday 10 March 1840, page 4

Female Factory—The Flash Mob!

On more than one occasion, as our readers may recollect, have we directed the attention of the proper authorities, to the laxity of discipline, which is practised at the Female House of Correction, near this town. Did nothing further result from this heedlessness, than a winking at certain harmless pastimes, indulged in by the inmates, we should not again bring forward the subject, thus prominently; but information has reached us of so flagrant and revolting a character, that we cannot, under any consideration, remain silent.

We have appended to the title of this article, the term "Flash Mob"; that this term is technical, is sufficiently obvious; but few of our readers,—few, indeed, of any who possess the ordinary attributes of human nature, can even conjecture the frightful abominations, which are practised by the women, who compose this mob. Of course, we cannot pollute our columns with the disgusting details, which have been conveyed to us; but we may, with propriety, call the notice of the proper Functionaries to a system of vice, immorality, and iniquity, which has tended, mainly, to render the majority of female assigned servants, the annoying and untractable animals, that they are.

The Flash Mob at the Factory consists, as it would seem, of a certain number of women, who, by a simple process of initiation, are admitted into a series of unhallowed mysteries, similar, in many respects, to those which are described by Goethe, in his unrivalled Drama of Faust, as occurring, on particular occasions, amongst the supposed supernatural inhabitants of the Hartz Mountains. Like those abominable Saturnalia, they are performed in the dark and silent hour of night, but, unlike those, they are performed in solitude and secrecy, amongst only the duly initiated. With the fiendish fondness for sin, every effort, both in the Factory, and out of it, is made by these wretches, to acquire proselytes to their infamous practices; and, it has come to our knowledge, within these few days, that a simple minded girl, who had been in one and the same service, since she left the ship,—a period of nearly six months,— very narrowly escaped seduction (we can use no stronger term) by a well known, and most accomplished member of this unholy sisterhood.

This practice constitutes one of the rules of the "order;" and we need not waste many words to show how perniciously it must act upon the "new hands," exposed to its influence. Another rule is, that, should any member be assigned, she must return to the Factory, so soon as she has obtained (we need not say by what means) a sufficient sum of money to enable herself and her companion to procure such indulgences, as the Factory can supply,—or, rather, as can be supplied by certain individuals, connected with the Factory. This sufficiently accounts for the contempt, which the majority of female prisoners entertain for the Factory, while it shows, also, why the solitary cell is considered the worst punishment.

Presuming that neither the Superintendent of the Female House of Correction, nor the Matron, can be cognizant of these things, we have thus publicly directed their attention to them; while we cannot but remark, that, their want of knowledge can only originate in direct and palpable negligence. In more than one sense, is this place deserving of the title of the "Valley of the Shadow of Death;" and in reflecting upon, what we can vouch to be true we do not, know, whether horror of indignation prevails most in our mind. Good God! When we consider that these wretches in human form, are scattered through the Colony, and admitted into the houses of respectable families, coming into hourly association with their sons, and daughters, we shudder, at the consequences, and cannot forbear asking the question: "Are there no means of preventing all this?" Is the Superintendent of the Female House of Correction (!) afraid of these harpies? Or is he too indolent or too good-natured to trouble himself about the matter? We cannot think that either is the case; for we believe Mr. Hutchinson to be a righteous man, and not likely to tolerate such rank abomination. If he be ignorant of the practices to which we have referred, we will willingly afford him all the information, that we possess. In concluding this painful subject, we may observe, that a favorite resort of this Flash Mob, when any of its members are out of the Factory, is the Canteen of a Sunday afternoon, and the Military Barracks of a Sunday night, where comfortable quarters may be procured until the morning! The whole system of Female Prison Discipline is bad and rotten at the very core, tending only to vice, immorality, and the most disgusting licentiousness.

NOTES

Introduction

1 Thomas Johnston, *The History of the Working Classes of Scotland* (Yorkshire, UK: EP Publishing, 1974), 319.

2 Susanna Corder, *Life of Elizabeth Fry: Compiled from Her Journal, as Edited by Her Daughters, and from Various Other Sources* (Philadelphia: Henry Longstreth, 1853), 251, 312; Abraham Harvey, 2nd Officer, "Reminiscences of the Voyage of the *Garland Grove 2*," Archives of Tasmania, NS816; Frances J. Woodward, *Portrait of Jane: A Life of Lady Franklin* (London: Hodder & Stoughton, 1951), 143.

Chapter 1: The Grey-Eyed Girl

1 Scottish Record Office. High Court of Justiciary Processes, Reference JC26.

2 T. M. Devine, *The Scottish Nation* (New York: Viking Press, 1999), 334.

3 Christopher Hibbert, *Queen Victoria: A Personal History* (Cambridge, MA: Da Capo Press, 2000), 12.

4 Janet R. Glover, *The Story of Scotland* (New York: Roy Publishers, 1960), 320.

5 Heather Shore, *Artful Dodgers: Youth and Crime in Early 19th-Century London* (Woodbridge, UK: Boydell Press, 1999), 49.

6 E. P. Thompson, *The Making of the English Working Class* (New York: Vintage Books, 1966), 267.

7 Thomas Johnston, *The History of the Working Classes of Scotland* (Yorkshire, UK: EP Publishing, 1974), 295.

8   L. A. Selby-Bigge, ed., *British Moralists: Being Selections from Writers Principally of the Eighteenth Century*, Volume I (New York: Dover Publications, 1965), 394.

9   T. R. Malthus, *An Essay on the Principle of Population; or, A View of its Past and Present Effects on Human Happiness with an Inquiry into our Prospects Respecting the Future Removal or Mitigation of the Evils which it Occasions* (London: Ward, Lock and Co., 1890), 579.

10 Glover, *The Story of Scotland*, 257.

11 Johnston, *The History of the Working Classes of Scotland*, 294.

12 W. Hamish Fraser and Irene Maver, eds., *Glasgow Volume II: 1830 to 1912* (Manchester, UK: Manchester University Press, 1996), 361.

13 Ibid., 362.

14 Johnston, *The History of the Working Classes of Scotland*, 319.

15 R. A. Cage, ed., *The Working Class in Glasgow, 1750–1914* (London: Croom Helm, 1987), 42.

16 Johnston, *The History of the Working Classes of Scotland*, 203.

17 Ibid., 273.

18 Ibid., 318.

19 Douglas A. Galbi, "Through Eyes in the Storm: Aspects of the Personal History of Women Workers in the Industrial Revolution," prepublication draft, *Social History*, Vol. 21, No. 2 (May 1996), 142–159; http://www.galbithink.org/eyes.pdf, 17.

20 Johnston, *The History of the Working Classes of Scotland*, 319.

21 Ibid.

22 "Child Labour, Factory Workers: Robert Blincoe," http://www.spartacus.school net.co.uk/IRblincoe.htm.

23 Excerpt from *A Memoir of Robert Blincoe* (1828) by John Brown, http://www.spartacus.schoolnet.co.uk/IRblincoe.htm.

24 Ibid.

25 Johnston, *The History of the Working Classes of Scotland*, 322.

26 Samuel Fielden, excerpt from *Autobiography of Samuel Fielden* (1887), http://www.spartacus.schoolnet.co.uk/IRpunishments.htm.

27 "Child Labour, Sarah Carpenter," http://www.spartacus.schoolnet.co.uk/IRpunishments.htm.

28 "Child Labour, Samuel Davy," http://www.spartacus.schoolnet.co.uk/IRpunishments.htm.

Chapter 2: Crown of Thieves

1   Charles Dickens, *Sketches by Boz* (London: Everyone's Library, 1968), 241.

2   Heather Shore, *Artful Dodgers: Youth and Crime in Early 19th-Century London* (Woodbridge, UK: Boydell Press, 1999), 7.

3   Henry Mayhew and Others, *The London Underworld in the Victorian Period: Authen-*

tic First-Person Accounts by Beggars, Thieves and Prostitutes (Mineola, NY: Dover Publications, 2005), 122.

4 Alasdair Cameron, "Popular Entertainment in Nineteenth-Century Glasgow: Background and Context for the Waggle o' the Kilt Exhibition," *A Companion to an Exhibition Drawn from the Scottish Theatre Archive and Featuring the Jimmy Logan Collection, Held in the Upper Hall, Hunterian Museum, 7th December 1992–20th February 1993*, http://www.arts.gla.ac.uk/SESLL/STELLA/STARN/crit/WAGGLE/popular.htm.

5 John MacGibbon, *Going Abroad* (Wellington, New Zealand: Ngaio Press, 1997), 43.

6 Ibid.

7 "Glasgow Broadside Ballads: Cheap Print and Popular Song Culture in Nineteenth-Century Scotland," Special Collections Department, Library, University of Glasgow, Scotland, http://special.lib.gla.ac.uk/teach/ballads/.

8 MacGibbon, *Going Abroad*, 43–44.

9 Archibald R. Adamson, *Rambles Round Kilmarnock* (T. Bibliobazaar; first published in 1875), 137.

10 Archibald M'Kay, *The History of Kilmarnock* (BiblioLife; first published in 1848), 11.

11 Scottish Record Office, Reference JC26/671.

12 "Kilmarnock with the Villages of Riccarton and Kilmaurs Ayrshire," Directory, 1837, by Pigot & Co., http://www.maybole.org/history/Archives/1837directory/kilmarnock.htm.

13 Ibid.

14 Scottish Record Office, Reference JC26/671.

15 Mayhew, *The London Underworld in the Victorian Period*, 118–119.

16 Scottish Record Office, Reference JC26/671.

17 Ibid.

18 Ibid.

19 M'Kay, *The History of Kilmarnock*, 170.

20 *The Green Guide to Scotland* (Watford, Herts, UK: Michelin Travel Publications, 2000), 72.

21 Ayrshire Roots Towns, "Ayr: The Burgh of Newton, The Parish of St Quivox, & Monktown with Prestwick," Ayrshire Directory, 1837, by Pigot & Co., http://www.ayrshireroots.com/Towns/Ayr/Ayr%201837.htm.

22 Rob Close, *Ayrshire and Arran: An Illustrated Architectural Guide* (Edinburgh: Royal Incorporation of Architects in Scotland, 1992), 22.

23 South Ayrshire Council, "County Buildings," http://www.south-ayrshire.gov.uk/maps/countybuildings/.

24 Scottish Record Office, Reference JC26/671.

25 Donald A. Low, *The Regency Underworld* (Stroud, UK: Sutton Publishing, 2005), 68.

26 Corder, *Life of Elizabeth Fry*, 301.

27   Scottish Record Office, Reference JC26/671.

28   Ibid.

29   Ibid.

30   Ibid.

31   Lennox, Lord William Pitt, *Coaching, with Anecdotes of the Road* (London: Hurst & Blackett, Publishers, 1876), 94.

32   Tony Rayner, *Female Factory, Female Convicts* (Dover, Australia: Esperance Press, 2004), 34.

33   Michael Paterson, *Voices from Dickens' London* (Cincinnati, OH: David & Charles, 2007), 255.

Chapter 3: The Angel of Newgate

1   John Kent, *Elizabeth Fry* (London: B. T. Batsford, 1962), 99–100.

2   Janet Whitney, *Elizabeth Fry* (London: Guild Books, 1947), 135.

3   Ibid.

4   Ibid.

5   Ibid.

6   Susanna Corder, *Life of Elizabeth Fry: Compiled from Her Journal, as Edited by Her Daughters, and from Various Other Sources* (Philadelphia: Henry Longstreth, 1853), 244.

7   Whitney, *Elizabeth Fry*, 110.

8   Stephen Halliday, *Newgate: London's Prototype of Hell* (Stroud, UK: Sutton Publishing, 2007), v.

9   Georgina King Lewis, *Elizabeth Fry* (London: Headley Brothers, 1912), 102.

10   Corder, *Life of Elizabeth Fry*, 289.

11   *Memoir of the Life of Elizabeth Fry, with Extracts from her Journal and Letters, Edited by Two of her Daughters, Vol. I* (Philadelphia: J. W. Moore, 1847), 225.

12   Corder, *Life of Elizabeth Fry*, 238.

13   Whitney, *Elizabeth Fry*, 178.

14   J. C. Long, *George III: The Story of a Complex Man* (New York: Little, Brown, 1960), 96.

15   Whitney, *Elizabeth Fry*, 179.

16   Clive Emsley, *Crime and Society in England, 1750–1900* (Harlow, UK: Pearson Education, 2005), 74–75.

17   Nicolas Bentley, *The Victorian Scene* (London: G. Weidenfeld & Nicolson, 1968), 105.

18   Whitney, *Elizabeth Fry*, 178.

19   Ibid.

20   Ibid.

21   Ibid.

22 *Memoir of the Life of Elizabeth Fry*, 327.

23 Corder, *Life of Elizabeth Fry*, 262.

24 *Memoir of the Life of Elizabeth Fry*, 327.

25 Abraham Harvey, 2nd Officer, "Reminiscences of the Voyage of the *Garland Grove 2*," Archives of Tasmania, NS816.

Chapter 4: Sweet Sixteen

1   Stephen Halliday, *Newgate: London's Prototype of Hell* (Stroud, UK: Sutton Publishing, 2007), 238.

2   Kay Daniels, *Convict Women* (Sydney: Allen & Unwin, 1998), 81.

3   Jean Hatton, *Betsy: The Dramatic Biography of Prison Reformer Elizabeth Fry* (Oxford, UK: Monarch Books, 2005), 272.

4   Bernard O'Donnell, *The Old Bailey and Its Trials* (London: Clerke & Cockeran Publishers Limited, 1950), 136.

5   Ibid.

6   Halliday, *Newgate*, 239.

7   John Kent, *Elizabeth Fry* (London: B. T. Batsford, 1962), 125.

8   Halliday, *Newgate*, 59.

9   Arthur Griffiths, *The Chronicles of Newgate* (New York: Dorset Press, 1987), 412.

10 Ibid., 105.

11 Philip Priestley, *Victorian Prison Lives* (London: Methuen, 1985), 5.

12 Frank Lewis, "The Cost of Convict Transportation: Britain to Australia, 1796–1810," *Economic History Review*, Series 2, Vol. 41, No. 4 (1988), 521.

13 Dennis Bardens, *Elizabeth Fry: Britain's Second Lady on the Five-Pound Note* (London: Chanadon Publications, 2004), 55.

14 Description List: Agnes McMillan, Archives of Tasmania, CON 19/1/14, 438.

15 Charles Bateson, *The Convict Ships, 1787–1868* (North Sydney: Library of Australian History, 1985), 65.

16 Abraham Harvey, 2nd Officer, "Reminiscences of the Voyage of the *Garland Grove 2*," Archives of Tasmania, NS816.

17 Bateson, *The Convict Ships, 1787–1868*, 66.

18 Ibid., 66.

19 James Ellis, Surgeon Superintendent, "Surgeon's Report *Westmoreland*," AJCP ADM 101/74, Archives of Tasmania, Reel 3212.

20 Phillip Tardif, *Notorious Strumpets and Dangerous Girls* (North Ryde, Australia: Angus & Robertson Publishers, 1990), 12.

21 William H. Render, *Through Prison Bars: The Lives and Labours of John Howard & Elizabeth Fry* (London: S. W. Partridge, 1894), 110.

22 Conduct Record, Agnes McMillan, Archives of Tasmania, CON 40/1/8, 9; Conduct Record, Janet Houston, Archives of Tasmania, CON 40/1/6, 9.

23 Elizabeth Fry, *Observations on the Visiting, Superintendence, and Government of Female Prisoners* (London: John & Arthur Arch, 1827), 37–38; Tony Rayner, *Female Factory, Female Convicts* (Dover, Australia: Esperance Press, 2004), 47.

24 J. R. Roberts, Surgeon Superintendent, "Journal of His Majesty's Convict Ship *Royal Admiral*, between the 23rd day of February, 1842 and 14th day of October, 1842," transcription courtesy of Port Arthur Historic Site for Female Factory Research Group.

25 Allan M. Grocott, *Convicts, Clergymen and Churches: Attitudes of Convicts and Ex-Convicts towards the Churches and Clergy in New South Wales from 1788 to 1851* (Sydney: Sydney University Press, 1980), 56.

26 "Convict Maid," Australian Folk Songs, from Butterss & Webby, *Penguin Book of Australian Ballads*, http://folkstream.com/026.html.

27 Ellis, "Surgeon's Report *Westmoreland*."

28 Frank Murcot Bladen, ed., "Letter from a Female Convict, 29th March 1791," *Historical Records of New South Wales, Vol. 2* (Sydney: Charles Potter, Government Printer, 1893), 779.

29 Bateson, *The Convict Ships, 1787–1868*, 250.

30 Ellis, "Surgeon's Report *Westmoreland*."

31 Conduct Record, Agnes McMillan, Archives of Tasmania, CON 40/1/8, 9.

32 Ibid.

33 Conduct Record, Janet Houston, Archives of Tasmania, CON 40/1/6, 9.

34 Bateson, *The Convict Ships, 1787–1868*, 76.

35 Ibid.

36 Ellis, "Surgeon's Report *Westmoreland*."

37 Harvey, "Reminiscences."

38 Ellis, "Surgeon's Report *Westmoreland*."

39 Ibid.

40 Hyland, Jeanette E., *Maids, Masters and Magistrates* (Blackmans Bay, Australia: Clan Hogarth Publishing, 2007), 15.

Chapter 5: More Sinned Against Than Sinning

1 *Hobart Town Courier*, "Trade and Shipping," Friday, 9 December 1836, 3.

2 James Ellis, Surgeon Superintendent, "Surgeon's Report *Westmoreland*," AJCP ADM 101/74, Archives of Tasmania, Reel 3212.

3 Linus W. Miller, *Notes of an Exile to Van Diemen's Land* (New York: Johnson Reprint Corporation, 1968; first published in 1846), 260.

4 Margaret C. Dillon, "Convict Labour and Colonial Society in the Campbell Town Police District: 1820–1839," unpublished doctoral thesis (University of Tasmania, 2008), 179.

5 Description List: Janet Houston, Archives of Tasmania, CON 19/1/14, 415.

6 *Hobart Town Courier*, Friday, 23 December 1836, 2.

7   Charles Wooley and Michael Tatlow, *A Walk in Old Hobart* (Walk Guides Australia, 2007), 4.

8   John West, *The History of Tasmania* (London: Angus & Robertson Publishers, 1971; first published in 1852), 342.

9   Alan Villiers, *Vanished Fleets* (Oxford, UK: Scribner's, 1974), 145–146.

10 Phillip Tardif, *Notorious Strumpets and Dangerous Girls* (North Ryde, Australia: Angus & Robertson Publishers, 1990), 18.

11 West, *The History of Tasmania*, 47.

12 Peter Bolger, *Hobart Town* (Canberra: Australian National University Press, 1973), 17.

13 Ibid., 60.

14 Ibid., 36.

15 Sir William Molesworth, *Report from the Select Committee of the House of Commons on Transportation; Together with a Letter from the Archbishop of Dublin on the Same Subject, and Notes by Sir William Molesworth, Bart., Chairman of the Committee 1838* (Adelaide: Libraries Board of South Australia, 1967), 36.

16 *Colonial Times* (Hobart, Australia), Friday, 23 March 1827, 4.

17 Kay Daniels, *Convict Women* (Sydney: Allen & Unwin, 1998), 86.

18 Henry Melville, *The History of Van Diemen's Land* (Sydney: Horwitz-Grahame, 1965), 161.

19 Bolger, *Hobart Town*, 59.

20 Hyland, Jeanette E., *Maids, Masters and Magistrates* (Blackmans Bay, Australia: Clan Hogarth Publishing, 2007), 24.

21 Wooley and Tatlow, *A Walk in Old Hobart*, 82.

22 Hyland, *Maids, Masters and Magistrates*, 24.

23 Joy Damousi, *Depraved and Disorderly: Female Convicts, Sexuality and Gender in Colonial Australia* (Cambridge, UK: Cambridge University Press, 1997), 51.

24 *Hobart Town Courier*, "Rules and Regulations," Saturday, 10 October 1829, 4.

25 Ibid.

26 Ibid.

27 Ibid.

28 Hyland, *Maids, Masters and Magistrates*, 126.

29 *Hobart Town Courier*, Friday, 30 December 1836, 2.

30 *Hobart Town Courier*, Friday, 13 January 1837, 2.

31 Miller, *Notes of an Exile to Van Diemen's Land*, 266–267.

32 Frances J. Woodward, *Portrait of Jane: A Life of Lady Franklin* (London: Hodder & Stoughton, 1951), 143.

33 Thomas Timpson, *Memoirs of Mrs. Elizabeth Fry* (Elibron Classics; first published in 1847), 150.

34 Ibid., 158.

35 Conduct Record, Agnes McMillan, Archives of Tasmania, CON 40/1/8, 9.

36   Ibid.

37   West, *The History of Tasmania*, 254.

38   Conduct Record, Ellen Scott, Archives of Tasmania, CON 40/1/9.

39   Damousi, *Depraved and Disorderly*, 59.

40   Miller, *Notes of an Exile to Van Diemen's Land*, 262.

41   *Colonial Times* (Hobart, Australia), Tuesday, 10 March 1840, 4.

42   Daniels, *Convict Women*, 140.

43   Damousi, *Depraved and Disorderly*, 61.

44   Conduct Record, Agnes McMillan, Archives of Tasmania, CON 40/1/8, 9.

Chapter 6: Ludlow's Choice

1   Daniel Pool, *What Jane Austen Ate and Charles Dickens Knew* (New York: Simon &
     Schuster, 1993), 30.

2   Eliza Lynn Linton, "On the Side of the Maids," *Cornhill Magazine*, Vol. 29, No. 171
     (1874), 304.

3   Pool, *What Jane Austen Ate*, 30.

4   Ibid., 252.

5   Judith Flanders, *Inside the Victorian Home* (New York: W. W. Norton, 2006), 371.

6   Charles Dickens, *Sketches by Boz* (London: Everyone's Library, 1968), 164.

7   Ellen W. Darwin, "Domestic Service," *Nineteenth Century*, Vol. 39, No. 162 (August
     1890), 290.

8   Sally Mitchell, ed., *Victorian Britain: An Encyclopedia* (New York: Garland Publish-
     ing, 1988), 706.

9   Linton, "On the Side of the Maids," 304.

10   Bobbie Kalman, *Victorian Christmas* (New York: Crabtree Publishing, 1997), 6.

11   Sian Rees, *The Floating Brothel* (New York: Hyperion Press, 2002), 37.

12   Ibid., 24.

13   The Old Bailey Online: The Proceedings of the Old Bailey, 1674–1913, "History
     of the Old Bailey Courthouse," http://www.oldbaileyonline.org//static/The-
     old-bailey.jsp.

14   Rees, *The Floating Brothel*, 25.

15   Proceedings of the Old Bailey Central Criminal Court, Sessions Paper, held on
     Monday, 17 December 1838, Reference Number: t18381217-301, http://www
     .oldbaileyonline.org//browse.jsp?id=def1-301-18381217&div=t18381217-301.

16   Ibid.

17   The Old Bailey Online: The Proceedings of the Old Bailey, 1674–1913, "Trial Pro-
     cedures: How Trials Were Conducted at the Old Bailey," http://www.old
     baileyonline.org/static/Trial-procedures.jsp.

18   Proceedings of the Old Bailey Central Criminal Court, Sessions Paper, held on
     Monday, 17 December 1838, Reference Number: t18381217-301, http://www
     .oldbaileyonline.org//browse.jsp?id=def1-301-18381217&div=t18381217-301.

19 Henry Mayhew with William S. Gilbert, *London Characters: Illustrations of the Humour, Pathos, and Peculiarities* (London: Chatto & Windus, 1881), 216.

20 Ibid., 213.

21 Clive Emsley, *Crime and Society in England, 1750–1900* (Harlow, UK: Pearson Education, 2005), 201.

22 Proceedings of the Old Bailey Central Criminal Court, Sessions Paper, held on Monday, 17 December 1838, Reference Number: t18381217-350, http://www.oldbaileyonline.org//browse.jsp?id=def1-350-18381217&div=t18381217-350.

23 Proceedings of the Old Bailey Central Criminal Court, Sessions Paper, held on Monday, 17 December 1838, Reference Number: t18381217-330, http://www.oldbaileyonline.org/browse.jsp?id=def1-330-18381217&div=t18381217-330.

24 The Old Bailey Online: The Proceedings of the Old Bailey, 1674–1913, "Punishments at the Old Bailey," http://www.oldbaileyonline.org/static/Punishment.jsp.

25 Mayhew, *London Characters*, 204.

26 Heather Shore, *Artful Dodgers: Youth and Crime in Early 19th-Century London* (Woodbridge, UK: Boydell Press, 1999), 134.

27 Proceedings of the Old Bailey Central Criminal Court, Sessions Paper, held on Monday, 17 December 1838, Reference Number: t18381217-417, http://www.oldbaileyonline.org/browse.jsp?id=def1-417-18381217&div=t18381217-417.

28 Proceedings of the Old Bailey Central Criminal Court, Sessions Paper, held on Monday, 17 December 1838, Reference Number: t18381217-269, http://www.oldbaileyonline.org//browse.jsp?id=def1-269-18381217&div=t18381217-269.

29 Proceedings of the Old Bailey Central Criminal Court, Sessions Paper, held on Monday, 17 December 1838, Reference Number: t18381217-333, http://www.oldbaileyonline.org/browse.jsp?id=def1-333-18381217&div=t18381217-333.

30 Proceedings of the Old Bailey Central Criminal Court, Sessions Paper, held on Monday, 17 December 1838, Reference Number: t18381217-333, http://www.oldbaileyonline.org/browse.jsp?id=def1-300-18381217&div=t18381217-300.

31 Gay Hendriksen, Dr. Carol Liston, and Dr. Trudy Cowley, *Women Transported: Life in Australia's Convict Female Factories* (Parramatta, Australia: Parramatta Heritage Centre), 18.

32 Ibid.

Chapter 7: Liverpool Street

1 Michele Field and Timothy Millett, eds., *Convict Love Tokens* (Kent Town, Australia: Wakefield Press, 1998), 13–14.

2 Ibid., 4.

3 Description List: Ann Price, Archives of Tasmania, CON 19/1/13, 296.

4 Ibid., 141.

5 Description List: Mary Grady, Archives of Tasmania, CON 19/1/13, 261.

6 Description List: Mary Sullivan, Archives of Tasmania, CON 19/1/13, 306.

7   Description List: Hannah Herbert, Archives of Tasmania, CON 19/1/13, 265.

8   Description List: Amy Wilson, Archives of Tasmania, CON 19/1/13, 321.

9   John Love, Surgeon Superintendent, "Surgeon's Report *Mellish*," ADM 101/53, Archives of Tasmania, Reel 3204.

10   Patrick Howard, *To Hell or to Hobart* (Kenthurst, Australia: Kangaroo Press, 1993), 124.

11   Malcolm Ronan, *Up and Down the River: The Butlers from Benenden* (Melbourne, Australia: Macron Publishing, 1998), 14.

12   Ibid.

13   Conduct Record, Amy Wilson, Archives of Tasmania, CON 40/1/10, 175; Conduct Record, Mary Grady, Archives of Tasmania, CON 40/1/4, 177; Conduct Record, Ann Price, Archives of Tasmania, CON 40/1/8, 141.

14   Conduct Record, Ludlow Tedder, Archives of Tasmania, CON 40/1/10, 113.

15   *Colonial Times* (Hobart, Australia), Tuesday, 10 March 1840, 4.

16   Joan C. Brown, *Poverty Is Not a Crime: Social Services in Tasmania, 1803–1900* (Hobart, Australia: Tasmanian Historical Research Association, 1972), 63.

17   Kay Daniels, *Convict Women* (Sydney: Allen & Unwin, 1998), 124.

18   *Colonial Times* (Hobart, Australia), "Fatality of the Factory Nursery Repeated!" Tuesday, 29 May 1838, 4.

19   *Colonial Times* (Hobart, Australia), "Coroners Inquest: Inspection of the Female Factory," Tuesday, 3 April 1838, 6.

20   *Colonial Times*, "Fatality of the Factory Nursery Repeated!"

21   Ibid.

22   Ibid.

23   George Mackaness, *Some Private Correspondence of Sir John and Lady Jane Franklin (Tasmania, 1837–1845), Part I* (Sydney: D. S. Ford Printers, 1947), 37–38.

24   Rebecca Kippen, "'And the Mortality Frightful': Infant and Child Mortality in the Convict Nurseries of Van Diemen's Land," paper for Research School of Social Sciences, Australian National University, 5.

25   *Hobart Town Courier*, "Fashions for March," Friday, 23 July 1841, 4.

26   Brown, *Poverty Is Not a Crime*, 27.

27   Joyce Purtscher, *Children in Queen's Orphanage Hobart Town, 1828–1863* (New Town, Australia: Irene Schaffer, 1993).

28   Joyce Purtscher, "Queen's Orphanage Hobart Town, 1828–1879," paper presented to Female Factory Research Group, November 2007, 2, 8.

29   Ibid., 9.

30   Ibid., 12.

31   Ibid., 1.

32   Brown, *Poverty Is Not a Crime*, 67.

33   Purtscher, "Queen's Orphanage Hobart Town, 1828–1879," 7.

34   Ibid., 4.

35   Ibid., 6.

36   John Price, Letter to Josiah Spode, Principal Superintendent of Convicts, March 19, 1841, Archives of Tasmania, Colonial Secretary's Office 5/1/282/7406.

37   Ibid.

38   Ibid.

39   Ibid.

40   Margaret Rolfe, *Australian Quilt Heritage* (Rushcutters Bay, Australia: J. B. Fairfax Press, 1998), 19.

41   Mackaness, *Some Private Correspondence of Sir John and Lady Jane Franklin*, 22.

42   *Hobart Town Courier*, Friday, 30 July 1841, 3.

43   Supplementary Conduct Record, Ellen Scott, Archives of Tasmania, CON 32/1/1, 309.

44   Female Factory Research Group, *Convict Lives: Women at Cascades Female Factory* (Hobart, Australia: Research Tasmania, 2009), 68.

45   *Colonial Times* (Hobart, Australia), Tuesday, 10 March 1840, 4.

46   Female Factory Research Group, *Convict Lives*, 52, 55.

47   Female Factory Research Group, "Infant Deaths at Hobart Nurseries" (name misspelled as William Hoaston), http://www.femalefactory.com.au/FFRG/nurseries.htm.

Chapter 8: The Yellow C

1   Conduct Record, Janet Houston, Archives of Tasmania, CON 40/1/6, 9.

2   Joy Damousi, *Depraved and Disorderly: Female Convicts, Sexuality and Gender in Colonial Australia* (Cambridge, UK: Cambridge University Press, 1997), 109.

3   Damousi, *Depraved and Disorderly*, 91.

4   Ibid.

5   Rebecca Kippen, "'And the Mortality Frightful': Infant and Child Mortality in the Convict Nurseries of Van Diemen's Land," paper for Research School of Social Sciences, Australian National University, 4.

6   Kippen, "'And the Mortality Frightful,'" 4.

7   *Hobart Town Courier*, "Rules and Regulations," Saturday, 10 October 1829, 4.

8   Kippen, "'And the Mortality Frightful,'" 5.

9   "Convict Maid," Australian Folk Songs, from Butterss & Webby, *Penguin Book of Australian Ballads*, http://folkstream.com/026.html.

10   Hyland, Jeanette E., *Maids, Masters and Magistrates* (Blackmans Bay, Australia: Clan Hogarth Publishing, 2007), 18.

11   *Colonial Times* (Hobart, Australia), Tuesday, 7 April 1846, 3.

12   James Boyce, *Van Diemen's Land* (Melbourne, Australia: Black, 2009), 179.

13   Lt. Colonel Godfrey Charles Mundy, *Our Antipodes: or, Residence and Rambles in the Australasian Colonies, with a Glimpse of the Goldfields* (London: Richard Bentley, 1855), 501.

14   *Hobart Town Courier*, "Rules and Regulations."

15   Damousi, *Depraved and Disorderly*, 60.

16   Description List: Eliza Smith, Archives of Tasmania, CON 19/1/12, 247.

17   Description List: Mary Devereux, Archives of Tasmania, CON 19/1/13, 511.

18   Description List: Frances Hutchinson, Archives of Tasmania, CON 19/1/14, 17.

19   David Kent, "Decorative Bodies: The Significance of Convicts' Tattoos," *Journal of Australian Studies*, No. 53 (1 June 1997), 79.

20   Conduct Record, Eliza Smith, Archives of Tasmania, CON 40/1/10, 14.

21   Damousi, *Depraved and Disorderly*, 61.

22   *Colonial Times* (Hobart, Australia), "Calendar for the Ensuing Week," Tuesday, 16 August 1842, 2.

23   Damousi, *Depraved and Disorderly*, 60.

24   Ibid., 61.

25   *Colonial Times* (Hobart, Australia), "The Factory," Tuesday, 1 February 1842, 2.

26   Ibid.

27   George Mackaness, *Some Private Correspondence of Sir John and Lady Jane Franklin (Tasmania, 1837–1845), Part II* (Sydney: D. S. Ford Printers, 1947), 51.

28   Ibid.

29   Ibid.

30   Kippen, "'And the Mortality Frightful,'" 7.

31   Ludlow Tedder, Testimony before the Principal Superintendent, Tuesday, 14 June 1842, Archives of Tasmania, AC 480/1/1.

32   Description List: Eliza Morgan, Archives of Tasmania, CON 19/1/14, 235.

33   Stefan Petrow, "Policing in a Penal Colony: Governor Arthur's Police System in Van Diemen's Land, 1826–1836," *Law and History Review*, Vol. 18, No. 2 (Summer 2000), http://www.historycooperative.org/journals/lhr/18.2/petrow.html (18 October 2009).

34   Ibid.

35   Ibid.

36   Eleanor Conlin Casella, "To Watch or Restrain: Female Convict Prisons in 19th-Century Tasmania," *International Journal of Historical Archaeology*, Vol. 5, No. 1 (2001), 61.

37   Lucy Frost and Hamish Maxwell-Stewart, *Chain Letters: Narrating Convict Lives* (Carlton South, Australia: Melbourne University Press, 2001), 81.

38   Ibid.

39   Ibid., 82.

40   Hobart Court of Petty Sessions May–November 1842, Tuesday, 21 June 1842, Archives of Tasmania, LC 247/1/11, 154.

41   *Hobart Town Courier*, "Rules and Regulations," Saturday, 10 October 1829, 4.

42   Conduct Record, Ludlow Tedder, Archives of Tasmania, CON 40/1/10, 113.

43   Gay Hendriksen, Dr. Carol Liston, and Dr. Trudy Cowley, *Women Transported: Life*

in Australia's Convict Female Factories (Parramatta, Australia: Parramatta Heritage Centre), 65.

44 Ibid., 62.

45 Queen's Asylum, Register of Children Admitted and Discharged from the Male and Female Orphan School, 1828–1863, SWD28, 13.

46 Ticket of Leave, Ludlow Tedder, New South Wales and Tasmania, Australia, Convict Pardons 1834–1859, http://search.ancestrylibrary.com/search/db.aspx?dbid=1184.

Chapter 9: Flames of Love

1 *Colonial Times* (Hobart, Australia), "Rules and Regulations for Young Ladies," Friday, 4 March 1831, 4.

2 Phil Cullen (Agnes McMillan's great-grandson-in-law), Agnes McMillan family history.

3 Robert Hughes, *The Fatal Shore* (New York: Alfred A. Knopf, 1987), 454.

4 *Hobart Town Courier*, Friday, 14 September 1838, 2.

5 Brad Williams, Heritage Project Officer, Southern Midlands Council, *Oatlands Gaol Conservation Management Plan 2006*, 17, http://www.southernmidlands.tas.gov.au/webdata/resources/files/OatlandsGaol_CMP_compressed.pdf.

6 Anna Gurnhill, "Oatlands Supreme Court House and Collections Access and Interpretation Plan," *People and Place*, Vol. 2 (March 2007), 3, http://www.southernmidlands.tas.gov.au/webdata/resources/files/OatlandsCourt_House_Interps_Plan_Volume_2.pdf.

7 K. R. Von Stieglitz, *A History of Oatlands and Jericho* (Launceston, Australia: Telegraph Printery, 1960), 14.

8 Ibid., 71.

9 Bruce Hindmarsh, "Beer and Fighting: Some Aspects of Male Convict Leisure in Rural Van Diemen's Land, 1820–40," *Journal of Australian Studies*, Vol. 63 (1 December 1999), 153.

10 Ibid., 154–156.

11 Vera Fisher, *Oatlands Heritage Walk One*, Municipality of Oatlands, 8.

12 Description List: William Roberts, Archives of Tasmania, CON 18/1/21, 76.

13 Phil Cullen, Agnes McMillan family history.

14 Alan Villiers, *Vanished Fleets* (Oxford, UK: Scribner's, 1974), 62.

15 Ken McGoogan, *Lady Franklin's Revenge* (London: Bantam Books, 2007), 251.

16 James Boyce, *Van Diemen's Land* (Melbourne, Australia: Black, 2009), 232.

17 Von Stieglitz, *A History of Oatlands and Jericho*, 71.

18 McGoogan, *Lady Franklin's Revenge*, 233.

19 Boyce, *Van Diemen's Land*, 157.

20 Ibid.

21 Charles Darwin, *A Naturalist's Voyage: Journal of Researches into the Natural History*

and Geology of the Countries Visited during the Voyage of H.M.S. 'Beagle' Round the World (London: John Murray, 1889), 531.

22   Ibid., 534.

23   Boyce, *Van Diemen's Land*, 158.

24   John West, *The History of Tasmania* (London: Angus & Robertson Publishers, 1971; first published in 1852), 543.

25   Charles Wooley and Michael Tatlow, *A Walk in Old Launceston* (Battery Point, Tasmania: Walk Guides Australia, 2007), 26.

26   Boyce, *Van Diemen's Land*, 224–225.

27   *Colonial Times* (Hobart, Australia), Tuesday, 23 April 1839, 1.

28   Phillip Tardif, *Notorious Strumpets and Dangerous Girls* (North Ryde, Australia: Angus & Robertson Publishers, 1990), 1476.

29   Ibid.

30   Tony Rayner, *Female Factory, Female Convicts* (Dover, Australia: Esperance Press, 2004), 126–127.

31   Gay Hendriksen, Dr. Carol Liston, and Dr. Trudy Cowley, *Women Transported: Life in Australia's Convict Female Factories* (Parramatta, Australia: Parramatta Heritage Centre), 61–62.

32   Tardif, *Notorious Strumpets and Dangerous Girls*, 1477.

33   *Colonial Times* (Hobart, Australia), Friday, 25 September 1846, 4.

34   Richmond Primary School website, Department of Education, Tasmania, http://www.richmond.tased.edu.au/School/Principal/Principal.htm.

35   Michael Tatlow, Charles Wooley, and Peter Mercer, *A Tour of Old Tasmania* (Battery Point, Tasmania: Walk Guides Australia, 2008), 100.

36   *Colonial Times* (Hobart, Australia), "Great Demonstration—Jubilee—Cessation of Transportation," Thursday, 11 August 1853, 2.

37   Ibid.

38   Ibid.

39   *Colonial Times* (Hobart, Australia), "Great Demonstration."

40   Ibid.

41   Ibid.

42   *Colonial Times* (Hobart, Australia), "The Jubilee," Tuesday, 9 August 1853, 2.

43   *Colonial Times* (Hobart, Australia), "Abolition of Transportation—Free Institutions—Slanderous Despatches," Tuesday, 25 December 1849, 2.

44   Boyce, *Van Diemen's Land*, 236.

45   *Colonial Times*, "Abolition of Transportation."

46   Ibid.

47   Peter Bolger, *Hobart Town* (Canberra: Australian National University Press, 1973), 52.

48   Ibid.

49   Ibid., 50.

50   *Colonial Times* (Hobart, Australia), "Jubilee—10th August," Saturday, 6 August 1853, 2.

51   Rayner, *Female Factory, Female Convicts*, 186.

52   L. L. Robson, *The Convict Settlers of Australia* (Carlton, Australia: Melbourne University Press, 1965), 10.

53   *Ballina Chronicle*, "Condition of the Poor," Mayo, Ireland, Wednesday, 6 June 1849.

54   John Williams, *Ordered to the Island* (Darlinghurst, Australia: Crossing Press, 1994), 14.

55   Ibid., 7.

56   Susanna Corder, *Life of Elizabeth Fry: Compiled from Her Journal, as Edited by Her Daughters, and from Various Other Sources* (Philadelphia: Henry Longstreth, 1853), 255.

57   Williams, *Ordered to the Island*, 8.

58   Trudy Mae Cowley, *A Drift of Derwent Ducks* (Hobart, Australia: Research Tasmania, 2005), 105.

59   Ibid., 247.

60   Description List: Bridget Mulligan, Archives of Tasmania, CON 19/1/9.

61   Cowley, *A Drift of Derwent Ducks*, 99.

62   Charles Bateson, *The Convict Ships, 1787–1868* (North Sydney: Library of Australian History, 1985), 73.

63   John Moody, Surgeon Superintendent, "Surgeon's Report *Blackfriar*," ADM 101/12, Archives of Tasmania, Reel 3189.

64   Conduct Record, Bridget Mulligan, Archives of Tasmania, CON 41/1/30.

65   Description List: Mary Rennicks, Archives of Tasmania, CON 19/1/9,160.

66   Patrick Howard, *To Hell or to Hobart* (Kenthurst, Australia: Kangaroo Press, 1993), 154.

67   Williams, *Ordered to the Island*, 113.

68   Boyce, *Van Diemen's Land*, 226.

69   Description List: John Wild, Archives of Tasmania, CON 18/1/30, 80.

70   Mary Binks (Bridget Mulligan's great-granddaughter), Bridget Mulligan family history.

71   Conduct Record, Mary Rennicks, Archives of Tasmania, CON 41/1/30, 222.

72   Boyce, *Van Diemen's Land*, 250.

Chapter 10: Bendigo's Gold

1   Geoff Hocking, *Gold: A Pictorial History of the Australian Goldrush* (Rowville, Australia: Five Mile Press, 2006), 50.

2   Hocking, *Gold*, 34.

3   Ibid.

4   *Maitland Mercury & Hunter River General Advertiser* (New South Wales, Australia), "Discovery of an Extensive Gold Field," Saturday, 17 May 1851, 4.

5   Hocking, *Gold*, 45.

6   *Colonial Times* (Hobart, Australia), Friday, 23 May 1851, 3.

7   William Manley Chambers, "Licensee—Sailor's Return," Archives of Tasmania, *Hobart Town Gazette*, 5 August 1850, 29 September 1850, 30 September 1851.

8   *Argus* (Melbourne, Australia), "Shipping Intelligence," Thursday, 27 May 1852, 4.

9   Judith O'Neill, *Transported to Van Diemen's Land* (Cambridge, UK: Cambridge University Press, 1977), 32.

10   Hocking, *Gold*, 76–77.

11   Ibid., 129.

12   Ellen Clacy, *A Lady's Visit to the Gold Diggings of Australia in 1852 to 1853* (Kessinger Publishing), 8.

13   Hocking, *Gold*, 101–103.

14   Ibid., 120.

15   Clacy, *A Lady's Visit*, 12.

16   Hocking, *Gold*, 114.

17   Ibid., 73.

18   Ibid., 85.

19   Frank Cusack, *Bendigo: A History* (Kangaroo Flat, Australia: Bendigo Modern Press, 2006), 32.

20   Clacy, *A Lady's Visit*, 25.

21   Ibid., 33.

22   Ibid., 28.

23   Hocking, *Gold*, 122.

24   Laurel Johnson, *Women of Eureka* (Ballarat, Australia: Historic Montrose Cottage and Eureka Museum, 1995), 8.

25   Ibid., 6.

26   O'Neill, *Transported to Van Diemen's Land*, 36.

27   Hocking, *Gold*, 132.

28   Ibid., 137.

29   Ibid., 136.

30   Ibid.

31   Ibid., 142.

32   Cathryn Game, ed., *We Swear by the Southern Cross: Investigations of Eureka and Its Legacy to Australia's Democracy* (Carlton, Australia: Curriculum Corporation, 2004), 57.

33   Hocking, *Gold*, 146.

34   *Argus* (Melbourne, Australia), "To the Colonists of Victoria," Tuesday, 10 April 1855, 7.

35   Hocking, *Gold*, 146.

36   Johnson, *Women of Eureka*, 22.

37   *Ballina Beacon*, "The Passing of a Pioneer: Mr. William Roberts," Monday, 29 July 1935.

38 Hocking, *Gold*, 155.

39 Glenda Manwaring, *At the Crossroads: The History of the Wilsons Ridges/Wollong-bar/Alphadale Cemetery and St. Pauls Church* (Daisy Hill, Australia: Glenda Manwaring, 1996).

40 Hocking, *Gold*, 13.

41 Cusack, *Bendigo: A History*, 71–73.

42 *Bendigo Advertiser*, Arabella Oliver, obituary, Tuesday, 3 September 1918.

BIBLIOGRAPHY

Primary Sources

Argus (Melbourne, Australia). Wednesday, 26 May 1852, 4.

Argus (Melbourne, Australia). "Shipping Intelligence." Thursday, 27 May 1852, 4.

Argus (Melbourne, Australia). "To the Colonists of Victoria." Tuesday, 10 April 1855, 7.

Ballina Beacon. "The Passing of a Pioneer: Mr. William Roberts." Monday, 29 July 1935.

Ballina Chronicle. "Condition of the Poor." Mayo, Ireland. Wednesday, 6 June 1849.

Bendigo Advertiser. Arabella Oliver, obituary. Tuesday, 3 September 1918.

Binks, Mary (Bridget Mulligan's great-granddaughter). Bridget Mulligan family history.

Bowan, John C., Surgeon Superintendent. "Surgeon's Report *Cadet.*" ADM 101/15, Archives of Tasmania, Reel 3191.

Buxton, Thomas Fowell. *An Inquiry Whether Crime and Misery Are Produced or Prevented by Our Present System of Prison Discipline.* London: John & Arthur Arch, 1818.

Chambers, William Manley. "Licensee—Sailor's Return." Archives of Tasmania, *Hobart Town Gazette,* 5 August 1850, 29 September 1850, 30 September 1851.

Colonial Times (Hobart, Australia). "Rules and Regulations for Young Ladies." Friday, 23 March 1827, 4.

Colonial Times (Hobart, Australia). Friday, 4 March 1831, 4.

Colonial Times (Hobart, Australia). "Female Factory—Nursing Infants." Tuesday, 20 March 1838, 4.

Colonial Times (Hobart, Australia). Friday, 30 March 1838, 2.

Colonial Times (Hobart, Australia). "Coroner's Inquest: Inspection of the Female Factory." Tuesday, 3 April 1838, 6.

Colonial Times (Hobart, Australia). "Fatality of the Factory Nursery Repeated!" Tuesday, 29 May 1838, 4.

Colonial Times (Hobart, Australia). Tuesday, 23 April 1839, 1.

Colonial Times (Hobart, Australia). "Female Factory—The Flash Mob!" Tuesday, 10 March 1840, 4.

Colonial Times (Hobart, Australia). "Hobart Town Police Report." Tuesday, 12 May 1840, 7.

Colonial Times (Hobart, Australia). "Meteorological Observations." Tuesday, 10 August 1841, 2.

Colonial Times (Hobart, Australia). "Meteorological Observations." Tuesday, 31 August 1841, 3.

Colonial Times (Hobart, Australia). "Meteorological Observations." Tuesday, 23 November 1841, 2.

Colonial Times (Hobart, Australia). "The Factory." Tuesday, 1 February 1842, 2.

Colonial Times (Hobart, Australia). "Meteorological Observations." Tuesday, 8 February 1842, 2.

Colonial Times (Hobart, Australia). "Meteorological Observations." Tuesday, 15 February 1842, 2.

Colonial Times (Hobart, Australia). "Meteorological Observations." Tuesday, 1 March 1842, 2.

Colonial Times (Hobart, Australia). "Meteorological Observations." Tuesday, 8 March 1842, 2.

Colonial Times (Hobart, Australia). "Meteorological Observations." Tuesday, 22 March 1842, 2.

Colonial Times (Hobart, Australia). "Meteorological Observations." Tuesday, 29 March 1842, 2.

Colonial Times (Hobart, Australia). "Calendar for the Ensuing Week." Tuesday, 16 August 1842, 2.

Colonial Times (Hobart, Australia). Tuesday, 7 April 1846, 3.

Colonial Times (Hobart, Australia). Friday, 25 September 1846, 4.

Colonial Times (Hobart, Australia). "The Irish in 1749 and 1847." Friday, 26 November 1847, 3.

Colonial Times (Hobart, Australia). "Abolition of Transportation—Free Institutions—Slanderous Despatches." Tuesday, 25 December 1849, 2.

Colonial Times (Hobart, Australia). Friday, 23 May 1851, 3.

Colonial Times (Hobart, Australia). "Demonstration and Jubilee." Thursday, 4 August 1853, 2.

Colonial Times (Hobart, Australia). "Jubilee—10th August." Saturday, 6 August 1853, 2.

Colonial Times (Hobart, Australia). "The Jubilee." Tuesday, 9 August 1853, 2.

Colonial Times (Hobart, Australia). "Great Demonstration—Jubilee—Cessation of Transportation." Thursday, 11 August 1853, 2.

Conduct Record, Anastasia Eustes. Archives of Tasmania, CON 41/1/4, 51.

Conduct Record, Mary Grady. Archives of Tasmania, CON 40/1/4, 177.

Conduct Record, Janet Houston. Archives of Tasmania, CON 40/1/6, 9.

Conduct Record, Agnes McMillan. Archives of Tasmania, CON 40/1/8, 9.

Conduct Record, Bridget Mulligan. Archives of Tasmania, CON 41/1/30.

Conduct Record, Ann Price. Archives of Tasmania, CON 40/1/8, 141.

Conduct Record, Mary Rennicks. Archives of Tasmania, CON 41/1/30, 222.

Conduct Record, Ellen Scott. Archives of Tasmania, CON 40/1/9, 78.

Conduct Record, Ludlow Tedder. Archives of Tasmania, CON 40/1/10, 113.

Conduct Record, Amy Wilson. Archives of Tasmania, CON 40/1/10, 175.

Cullen, Phil (Agnes McMillan's great-grandson-in-law). Agnes McMillan family history.

Darwin, Charles. *A Naturalist's Voyage: Journal of Researches into the Natural History and Geology of the Countries Visited during the Voyage of H.M.S. 'Beagle' Round the World.* London: John Murray, 1889.

Description List: Mary Devereux. Archives of Tasmania, CON 19/1/13, 511.

Description List: Mary Grady. Archives of Tasmania, CON 19/1/13, 261.

Description List: Hannah Herbert. Archives of Tasmania, CON 19/1/13, 265.

Description List: Janet Houston. Archives of Tasmania, CON 19/1/14, 415.

Description List: Frances Hutchinson. Archives of Tasmania, CON 19/1/14, 17.

Description List: Agnes McMillan. Archives of Tasmania, CON 19/1/14, 438.

Description List: Eliza Morgan. Archives of Tasmania, CON 19/1/14, 235.

Description List: Bridget Mulligan. Archives of Tasmania, CON 19/1/9.

Description List: Ann Price. Archives of Tasmania, CON 19/1/13, 296.

Description List: Mary Rennicks. Archives of Tasmania, CON 19/1/9, 160.

Description List: William Roberts. Archives of Tasmania, CON 18/1/21, 76.

Description List: Eliza Smith. Archives of Tasmania, CON 19/1/12, 247.

Description List: Mary Sullivan. Archives of Tasmania, CON 19/1/13, 306.

Description List: John Wild. Archives of Tasmania, CON 18/1/30, 80.

Description List: Amy Wilson. Archives of Tasmania, CON 19/1/13, 321.

Ellis, James, Surgeon Superintendent. "Surgeon's Report *Westmoreland*." AJCP, ADM 101/74, Archives of Tasmania, Reel 3212.

Fry, Elizabeth. *A Brief Memoir of Elizabeth Fry.* Philadelphia: Association of Friends for the Diffusion of Religious and Useful Knowledge, 1858.

Fry, Elizabeth. *Observations on the Visiting, Superintendence, and Government of Female Prisoners.* London: John & Arthur Arch, 1827.

Guide to the Public Records of Tasmania: Colonial Secretary's Office, Governor's Office, Convict Department. Hobart, Australia: Tasmanian Historical Research Association, 1868.

Harvey, Abraham, 2nd Officer. "Reminiscences of the Voyage of the *Garland Grove 2*." Archives of Tasmania, NS816.

Hobart Court of Petty Sessions May–November 1842. Tuesday, 21 June 1842, Archives of Tasmania, LC 247/1/11, 154.

Hobart Town Courier. "Rules and Regulations." Saturday, 10 October 1829, 4.

Hobart Town Courier. Friday, 2 December 1836, 2; Friday, 9 December 1836, 2.

Hobart Town Courier. "Swallows." Friday, 9 December 1836, 2.

Hobart Town Courier. "Trade and Shipping." Friday, 9 December 1836, 3.

Hobart Town Courier. Friday, 23 December 1836, 2.

Hobart Town Courier. Friday, 30 December 1836, 2.

Hobart Town Courier. Friday, 6 January 1837, 2.

Hobart Town Courier. Friday, 13 January 1837, 2.

Hobart Town Courier. Friday, 14 September 1838, 2.

Hobart Town Courier. "Fashions for March." Friday, 23 July 1841, 4.

Hobart Town Courier. Friday, 30 July 1841, 3.

Hobart Town Courier. "Despatches Relative to the System of Prison Discipline." Friday, 16 February 1844, 4.

Hobart Town Courier and Van Diemen's Land Gazette. Friday, 5 May 1843, 4.

Hocking, Geoff. *Gold: A Pictorial History of the Australian Goldrush.* Rowville, Australia: Five Mile Press, 2006.

Love, John, Surgeon Superintendent. "Surgeon's Report *Mellish*." ADM 101/53, Archives of Tasmania, Reel 3204.

Mackay, Samuel, Surgeon Superintendent. "General Remarks, Sick List, *Waverly* 1842."

Maitland Mercury & Hunter River General Advertiser (New South Wales, Australia). "Discovery of an Extensive Gold Field." Saturday, 17 May 1851, 4.

Mercury Supplement. "Expatriated: A Tale of the Early Days of the Colony." Saturday, 5 June 1886, 28.

Millar, Andrew, Surgeon Superintendent. "Surgeon's Remarks from HMS *Anson* on her Journey to Hobart 1843/4."

Moody, John, Surgeon Superintendent. "Surgeon's Report *Blackfriar*." ADM 101/12, Archives of Tasmania, Reel 3189.

National Archives of Ireland, Transportation of Female Convicts.

Price, John. Letter to Josiah Spode, Principal Superintendent of Convicts, March 19, 1841. Archives of Tasmania, Colonial Secretary's Office 5/1/282/7406.

Proceedings of the Old Bailey Central Criminal Court, Sessions Paper. Held on Monday, 17 December 1838. Reference Number: t18381217-269. http://www.oldbailey online.org//browse.jsp?id=def1-269-18381217&div=t18381217-269.

Proceedings of the Old Bailey Central Criminal Court, Sessions Paper. Held on Monday, 17 December 1838. Reference Number: t18381217-300. http://www.oldbailey online.org/browse.jsp?id=def1-300-18381217&div=t18381217-300.

Proceedings of the Old Bailey Central Criminal Court, Sessions Paper. Held on Monday, 17 December 1838. Reference Number: t18381217-301. http://www.oldbailey online.org//browse.jsp?id=def1-301-18381217&div=t18381217-301.

Proceedings of the Old Bailey Central Criminal Court, Sessions Paper. Held on Monday, 17 December 1838. Reference Number: t18381217-330. http://www.oldbaileyonline.org/browse.jsp?id=def1-330-18381217&div=t18381217-330.

Proceedings of the Old Bailey Central Criminal Court, Sessions Paper. Held on Monday, 17 December 1838. Reference Number: t18381217-333. http://www.oldbaileyonline.org/browse.jsp?id=def1-333-18381217&div=t18381217-333.

Proceedings of the Old Bailey Central Criminal Court, Sessions Paper. Held on Monday, 17 December 1838. Reference Number: t18381217-350. http://www.oldbaileyonline.org//browse.jsp?id=def1-350-18381217&div=t18381217-350.

Proceedings of the Old Bailey Central Criminal Court, Sessions Paper. Held on Monday, 17 December 1838. Reference Number: t18381217-417. http://www.oldbaileyonline.org/browse.jsp?id=def1-417-18381217&div=t18381217-417.

Queen's Asylum. Register of Children Admitted and Discharged from the Male and Female Orphan School, 1828–1863. SWD28, 13.

Report from the Select Committee of the House of Commons on Transportation. London: Henry Hooper, 1838.

Roberts, J. R., Surgeon Superintendent. "Journal of His Majesty's Convict Ship *Royal Admiral,* between the 23rd day of February, 1842 and 14th day of October, 1842." Transcription courtesy of Port Arthur Historic Site for Female Factory Research Group.

Scottish Record Office. High Court of Justiciary Processes. Reference JC26.

Scottish Record Office. Reference JC26/671.

Supplementary Conduct Record, Ellen Scott. Archives of Tasmania, CON 32/1/1, 309.

Tasmanian Bicentenary Rajah Quilt Project Curator's Guide. Hobart, Australia: Female Factory Historic Site Board, 2004.

Tedder, Ludlow. Testimony before the Principal Superintendent. Tuesday, 14 June 1842. Archives of Tasmania, AC 480/1/1.

Thomson, David, Surgeon Superintendent. "Surgeon's Journal of the Female Convict Ship *New Grove* between 24th November 1834 and 1st April 1835."

Ticket of Leave, Ludlow Tedder, New South Wales and Tasmania, Australia, Convict Pardons 1834–1859. http://search.ancestrylibrary.com/search/db.aspx?dbid=1184.

Wilson, John, Surgeon Superintendent. "General Remarks, Surgeon's Log, Female Convict Ship *Emma Eugenia.*"

Secondary Sources

Adamson, Archibald R. *Rambles Round Kilmarnock.* Bibliobazaar. First published in 1875.

Alexander, Alison. *Obliged to Submit: Wives and Mistresses of Colonial Governors.* Dynnyrne, Tasmania: Montpelier Press, 1999.

Aspin, Chris. *The Woolen Industry.* Buckinghamshire, UK: Shire Publications, 2000.

Ayrshire Roots Towns. "Ayr: The Burgh of Newton, The Parish of St Quivox, & Monk-

town with Prestwick." *Ayrshire Directory, 1837*, by Pigot & Co. http://www
.ayrshireroots.com/Towns/Ayr/Ayr%201837.htm.

Bardens, Dennis. *Elizabeth Fry: Britain's Second Lady on the Five-Pound Note*. London: Chanadon Publications, 2004.

Bateson, Charles. *The Convict Ships, 1787–1868*. North Sydney: Library of Australian History, 1985.

Bentley, Nicolas. *The Victorian Scene*. London: G. Weidenfeld & Nicolson, 1968.

Bladen, Frank Murcot, ed. "Letter from a Female Convict, 29th March 1791." *Historical Records of New South Wales, Vol. 2*. Sydney: Charles Potter, Government Printer, 1893.

Bogle, Michael. *Convicts: Transportation to Australia*. Sydney: Historic Houses Trust of New South Wales, 2008.

Bolger, Peter. *Hobart Town*. Canberra: Australian National University Press, 1973.

Boyce, James. *Van Diemen's Land*. Melbourne, Australia: Black, 2009.

Brand, Ian. *Sarah Island*. Launceston, Australia: Regal Publications, 1984.

Brown, Joan C. *Poverty Is Not a Crime: Social Services in Tasmania, 1803–1900*. Hobart, Australia: Tasmanian Historical Research Association, 1972.

Brown, John. Excerpt from *A Memoir of Robert Blincoe*. 1828. http://www.spartacus .schoolnet.co.uk/IRblincoe.htm.

Bryant, Mary. *A Long Way Home: The Life and Adventures of the Convict Mary Bryant*. Chichester, UK: John Wiley & Sons, 2005.

Cage, R. A., ed. *The Working Class in Glasgow, 1750–1914*. London: Croom Helm, 1987.

Cameron, Alasdair. "Popular Entertainment in Nineteenth Century Glasgow: Background and Context for the Waggle o' the Kilt Exhibition." *A Companion to an Exhibition Drawn from the Scottish Theatre Archive and Featuring the Jimmy Logan Collection, Held in the Upper Hall, Hunterian Museum, 7th December 1992–20th February 1993*. http://www.arts.gla.ac.uk/SESLL/STELLA/STARN/crit/WAGGLE/popu lar.htm.

Cameron, Mary, ed. *A Guide to Flowers & Plants of Tasmania*. Sydney: New Holland Publishers, 2002.

Casella, Eleanor Conlin. "To Watch or Restrain: Female Convict Prisons in 19th-Century Tasmania." *International Journal of Historical Archaeology*, Vol. 5, No. 1 (2001), 45–72.

"Child Labour, Factory Workers: Robert Blincoe." http://www.spartacus.schoolnet .co.uk/IRblincoe.htm.

"Child Labour, Samuel Davy." http://www.spartacus.schoolnet.co.uk/IRpunishments .htm.

"Child Labour, Sarah Carpenter." http://www.spartacus.schoolnet.co.uk/IR punishments.htm.

Clacy, Ellen. *A Lady's Visit to the Gold Diggings of Australia in 1852 to 1853*. Kessinger Publishing.

Clark, Anna. *The Struggle for the Breeches: Gender and the Making of the British Working Class.* Berkeley: University of California Press, 1995.

Clarke, Patricia, and Dale Spender, eds. *Life Lines: Australian Women's Letters and Diaries, 1788–1840.* North Sydney, Australia: Allen & Unwin, 1992.

Close, Rob. *Ayrshire and Arran: An Illustrated Architectural Guide.* Edinburgh: Royal Incorporation of Architects in Scotland, 1992.

"Convict Maid." Australian Folk Songs, from Butterss & Webby, *Penguin Book of Australian Ballads.* http://folkstream.com/026.html.

Cook, Thomas. *The Exile's Lamentations.* North Sydney: Library of Australian History, 1978.

Corder, Susanna. *Life of Elizabeth Fry: Compiled from Her Journal, as Edited by Her Daughters, and from Various Other Sources.* Philadelphia: Henry Longstreth, 1853.

Cowley, Trudy Mae. *A Drift of Derwent Ducks.* Hobart, Australia: Research Tasmania, 2005.

Crooke, Robert. *The Convict.* Hobart, Australia: University of Tasmania Library, 1958.

Cunnington, C. Willett. *English Women's Clothing in the Nineteenth Century.* New York: Dover Publications, 1990.

Cusack, Frank. *Bendigo: A History.* Kangaroo Flat, Australia: Bendigo Modern Press, 2006.

Daley, Louise Tiffany. *Men and a River: Richmond River District, 1828–1895.* Carlton, Australia: Melbourne University Press, 1968.

Damousi, Joy. *Depraved and Disorderly: Female Convicts, Sexuality and Gender in Colonial Australia.* Cambridge, UK: Cambridge University Press, 1997.

Daniels, Kay. *Convict Women.* Sydney: Allen & Unwin, 1998.

Darwin, Ellen W. "Domestic Service." *Nineteenth Century,* Vol. 39, No. 162 (August 1890), 286–296.

Dawes, Frank. *Not in Front of the Servants: A True Portrait of English Upstairs/Downstairs Life.* New York: Taplinger Publishing, 1973.

Devine, T. M. *The Scottish Nation.* New York: Viking Press, 1999.

Dickens, Charles. *Sketches by Boz.* London: Everyone's Library, 1968.

Dillon, Margaret C. "Convict Labour and Colonial Society in the Campbell Town Police District: 1820–1839." Unpublished doctoral thesis, University of Tasmania, 2008. http://www.convicthistory.com.

Dixson, Miriam. *The Real Matilda.* Middlesex, UK: Penguin Books, 1976.

Donaldson, Gordon. *Mackie's Short History of Scotland.* New York: Frederick A. Praeger, 1962.

Dore, Gustave, and Blanchard Jerrold. *London: A Pilgrimage.* London: Grant, 1872.

Dreen, Edith. *Great Women of the Christian Faith.* New York: Harper & Brothers, 1959.

Duckworth, Jeannie. *Fagin's Children: Criminal Children in Victorian England.* London: Hambledon & London, 2002.

Duffield, Ian, and James Bradley. *Representing Convicts: New Perspectives on Convict Forced Labour Migration*. London: Leicester University Press, 1997.

Eisler, Benita, ed. *The Lowell Offering: Writings by New England Mill Women (1840–1845)*. New York: Harper Colophon Books, 1977.

Emsley, Clive. *Crime and Society in England, 1750–1900*. Harlow, UK: Pearson Education, 2005.

Evans, L., and P. Nicholls. *Convicts & Colonial Society, 1788–1853*. North Melbourne, Australia: Cassell Australia, 1976.

Female Factory Research Group. *Convict Lives: Women at Cascades Female Factory*. Hobart, Australia: Research Tasmania, 2009.

Female Factory Research Group. "Infant Deaths at Hobart Nurseries." http://www.femalefactory.com.au/FFRG/nurseries.htm.

Ferguson, William. *Scotland: 1689 to the Present*. New York: Frederick A. Praeger, 1968.

Field, Michele, and Timothy Millett, eds. *Convict Love Tokens*. Kent Town, Australia: Wakefield Press, 1998.

Fielden, Samuel. Excerpt from *Autobiography of Samuel Fielden*. 1887. http://www.spartacus.schoolnet.co.uk/IRpunishments.htm.

Fisher, Vera. *Oatlands Heritage Walk One*. Municipality of Oatlands.

Fitzpatrick, Kathleen. *Sir John Franklin in Tasmania, 1837–1843*. Melbourne, Australia: Melbourne University Press, 1949.

Flanders, Judith. *Inside the Victorian Home*. New York: W. W. Norton, 2006.

Fraser, W. Hamish, and Irene Maver, eds. *Glasgow Volume II: 1830 to 1912*. Manchester, UK: Manchester University Press, 1996.

Fraser, W. Hamish, and R. J. Morris. *People and Society in Scotland*. Edinburgh: John Donald, 2000.

Frost, Lucy. *A Face in the Glass: The Journal and Life of Annie Baxter Dawbin*. Port Melbourne, Australia: William Heinemann Australia, 1992.

Frost, Lucy, and Hamish Maxwell-Stewart. *Chain Letters: Narrating Convict Lives*. Carlton South, Australia: Melbourne University Press, 2001.

Fuchs, Rachel G. *Gender and Poverty in Nineteenth-Century Europe*. New York: Cambridge University Press, 2005.

Galbi, Douglas A. "Through Eyes in the Storm: Aspects of the Personal History of Women Workers in the Industrial Revolution," prepublication draft, *Social History*, Vol. 21, No. 2 (May 1996), 142–159. http://www.galbithink.org/eyes.pdf.

Game, Cathryn, ed. *We Swear by the Southern Cross: Investigations of Eureka and Its Legacy to Australia's Democracy*. Carlton South, Australia: Curriculum Corporation, 2004.

"Glasgow Broadside Ballads: Cheap Print and Popular Song Culture in Nineteenth-Century Scotland." Special Collections Department, Library, University of Glasgow, Scotland. http://special.lib.gla.ac.uk/teach/ballads/.

Glover, Janet R. *The Story of Scotland*. New York: Roy Publishers, 1960.

Gold, Geoffrey. *Eureka: Rebellion beneath the Southern Cross.* Adelaide, Australia: Rigby, 1977.

Goodrick, Joan. *Life in Old Van Diemens Land.* Adelaide, Australia: Rigby, 1977.

The Green Guide to Scotland. Watford, Herts, UK: Michelin Travel Publications, 2000.

Griffiths, Arthur. *The Chronicles of Newgate.* New York: Dorset Press, 1987.

Grocott, Allan M. *Convicts, Clergymen and Churches: Attitudes of Convicts and Ex-Convicts towards the Churches and Clergy in New South Wales from 1788 to 1851.* Sydney: Sydney University Press, 1980.

Gurnhill, Anna. "Oatlands Supreme Court House and Collections Access and Interpretation Plan." *People and Place*, Vol. 2 (March 2007), 3. http://www.southernmid lands.tas.gov.au/webdata/resources/files/Oatlands Court_House_Interps_Plan_ Volume_2.pdf.

Halliday, Stephen. *Newgate: London's Prototype of Hell.* Stroud, UK: Sutton Publishing, 2007.

Hanson, Harry. *The Coaching Life: The Heyday of the Stagecoach in Britain.* Manchester, UK: Manchester University Press, 1984.

Harvey, W. *London Scenes and London People.* London: W. H. Collingridge, City Press, 1863.

Hatton, Jean. *Betsy: The Dramatic Biography of Prison Reformer Elizabeth Fry.* Oxford, UK: Monarch Books, 2005.

Henderson, W. O., and W. H. Chaloner, eds. *The Condition of the Working Class in England.* Stanford, CA: Stanford University Press, 1958.

Hendriksen, Gay, Dr. Carol Liston, and Dr. Trudy Cowley. *Women Transported: Life in Australia's Convict Female Factories.* Parramatta, Australia: Parramatta Heritage Centre, 2008.

Hibbert, Christopher. *Queen Victoria: A Personal History.* Cambridge, MA: Da Capo Press, 2000.

Hindmarsh, Bruce. "Beer and Fighting: Some Aspects of Male Convict Leisure in Rural Van Diemen's Land, 1820–40." *Journal of Australian Studies*, Vol. 63 (1 December 1999), 150–156, 203–205.

Howard, Patrick. *To Hell or to Hobart.* Kenthurst, Australia: Kangaroo Press, 1993.

Hughes, Robert. *The Fatal Shore.* New York: Alfred A. Knopf, 1987.

Hyland, Jeanette E. *Maids, Masters and Magistrates.* Blackmans Bay, Australia: Clan Hogarth Publishing, 2007.

Irvine, Nance, ed. *Dear Cousin: The Reibey Letters.* Sydney: Hale & Iremonger, 1992.

Johnson, Laurel. *Women of Eureka.* Ballarat, Australia: Historic Montrose Cottage and Eureka Museum, 1995.

Johnston, Thomas. *The History of the Working Classes of Scotland.* Yorkshire, UK: EP Publishing, 1974.

Kalman, Bobbie. *Victorian Christmas.* New York: Crabtree Publishing, 1997.

Kent, David. "Decorative Bodies: The Significance of Convicts' Tattoos." *Journal of Australian Studies*, No. 53 (1 June 1997), 78–85.

Kent, John. *Elizabeth Fry*. London: B. T. Batsford, 1962.

"Kilmarnock with the villages of Riccarton and Kilmaurs Ayrshire." Directory, 1837, by Pigot & Co. http://www.maybole.org/history/Archives/1837directory/kilmarnock.htm.

Kippen, Rebecca. "'And the Mortality Frightful': Infant and Child Mortality in the Convict Nurseries of Van Diemen's Land." Paper for Research School of Social Sciences, Australian National University, 2005.

Lennox, Lord William Pitt. *Coaching, with Anecdotes of the Road*. London: Hurst & Blackett, Publishers, 1876.

Lewis, Frank. "The Cost of Convict Transportation: Britain to Australia, 1796–1810." *Economic History Review*, Series 2, Vol. 41, No. 4 (1988), 507–524.

Lewis, Georgina King. *Elizabeth Fry*. London: Headley Brothers, 1912.

Linklater, Eric. *The Survival of Scotland*. Garden City, NY: Doubleday, 1968.

Linton, Eliza Lynn. "On the Side of the Maids." *Cornhill Magazine*, Vol. 29, No. 171 (1874), 298–307.

Long, J. C. *George III: The Story of a Complex Man*. New York: Little, Brown, 1960.

Low, Donald A. *The Regency Underworld*. Stroud, UK: Sutton Publishing, 2005.

MacGibbon, John. *Going Abroad*. Wellington, New Zealand: Ngaio Press, 1997.

Mackaness, George, ed. *The History of Van Diemen's Land*. Sydney: Horwitz-Grahame, 1965.

Mackaness, George. *Some Private Correspondence of Sir John and Lady Jane Franklin (Tasmania, 1837–1845), Part I*. Sydney: D. S. Ford Printers, 1947.

Mackaness, George. *Some Private Correspondence of Sir John and Lady Jane Franklin (Tasmania, 1837–1845), Part II*. Sydney: D. S. Ford Printers, 1947.

Mackay, George. *History of Bendigo*. Bendigo, Australia: Lerk & McClure, 2000.

Manwaring, Glenda. *At the Crossroads: The History of the Wilsons Ridges/Wollongbar/Alphadale Cemetery and St. Pauls Church*. Daisy Hill, Australia: Glenda Manwaring, 1996.

May, Allyson N. *The Bar and the Old Bailey, 1750–1850*. Chapel Hill: University of North Carolina Press, 2003.

Mayhew, Henry. *London Labour and the London Poor*. London, England: Penguin Books, 1985.

Mayhew, Henry, and Others. *The London Underworld in the Victorian Period: Authentic First-Person Accounts by Beggars, Thieves and Prostitutes*. Mineola, NY: Dover Publications, 2005.

Mayhew, Henry, with William S. Gilbert. *London Characters: Illustrations of the Humour, Pathos, and Peculiarities*. London: Chatto & Windus, 1881.

McCrone, David, Stephen Kendrick, and Pat Straw, eds. *The Making of Scotland: Nation, Culture & Social Change*. Edinburgh: Edinburgh University Press, 1989.

McGoogan, Ken. *Lady Franklin's Revenge*. London: Bantam Books, 2007.

Melville, Henry. *The History of Van Diemen's Land*. Sydney: Horwitz-Grahame, 1965.

Memoir of the Life of Elizabeth Fry, with Extracts from her Journal and Letters, Edited by Two of Her Daughters, Vol. I. Philadelphia: J. W. Moore, 1847.

Miller, Linus W. *Notes of an Exile to Van Diemen's Land*. New York: Johnson Reprint Corporation, 1968. First published in 1846.

Mitchell, Sally. *Daily Life in Victorian England*. Westport, CT: Greenwood Press, 1996.

Mitchell, Sally, ed. *Victorian Britain: An Encyclopedia*. New York: Garland Publishing, 1988.

M'Kay, Archibald. *The History of Kilmarnock*. BiblioLife. First published in 1848.

Molesworth, Sir William. *Report from the Select Committee of the House of Commons on Transportation; Together with a Letter from the Archbishop of Dublin on the Same Subject, and Notes by Sir William Molesworth, Bart., Chairman of the Committee 1838*. Adelaide: Libraries Board of South Australia, 1967.

Mullins, Marcia, ed. *Town and Country Journal on the Richmond*. Lismore, Australia: Richmond River Historical Society, 2001.

Mundy, Lt. Colonel Godfrey Charles. *Our Antipodes: or, Residence and Rambles in the Australasian Colonies, with a Glimpse of the Goldfields*. London: Richard Bentley, 1855.

Murphy, Theresa. *The Old Bailey: Eight Centuries of Crime, Cruelty and Corruption*. Edinburgh: Mainstream Publishing, 2003.

Murray, Venetia. *An Elegant Madness: High Society in Regency England*. New York: Viking Press, 1999.

Nead, Lynda. *Myths of Sexuality: Representations of Women in Victorian Britain*. Oxford, UK: Basil Blackwell, 1988.

Nicholas, Stephen. *Convict Workers*. Cambridge, UK: Cambridge University Press, 1988.

O'Donnell, Bernard. *The Old Bailey and Its Trials*. London: Clerke & Cockeran Publishers, 1950.

O'Farrell, Patrick. *The Irish in Australia*. Notre Dame, IN: University of Notre Dame Press, 1989.

The Old Bailey Online: The Proceedings of the Old Bailey, 1674–1913, "History of the Old Bailey Courthouse." http://www.oldbaileyonline.org//static/The-old-bailey.jsp.

The Old Bailey Online: The Proceedings of the Old Bailey, 1674–1913, "Punishments at the Old Bailey." http://www.oldbaileyonline.org/static/Punishment.jsp.

The Old Bailey Online: The Proceedings of the Old Bailey, 1674–1913, "Trial Procedures: How Trials Were Conducted at the Old Bailey." http://www.oldbaileyonline.org/static/Trial-procedures.jsp.

O'Neill, Judith. *Transported to Van Diemen's Land*. Cambridge, UK: Cambridge University Press, 1977.

Oxley, Deborah. *Convict Maids*. Cambridge, UK: Cambridge University Press, 1996.

Paterson, Michael. *Voices from Dickens' London*. Cincinnati, OH: David & Charles, 2007.

Pearn, John Hemsley. *In the Capacity of a Surgeon: A Biography of Walter Scott, Surgeon and Australian Colonist, and First Civilian of Queensland.* Brisbane, Australia: University of Queensland, 1988.

Petrow, Stefan. "Policing in a Penal Colony: Governor Arthur's Police System in Van Diemen's Land, 1826–1836." *Law and History Review,* Vol. 18, No. 2, 351–395, 2000.

Picard, Liza. *Victorian London: The Tale of a City, 1840–1870.* New York: St. Martin's Griffin, 2005.

Pinchbeck, Ivy. *Women Workers and the Industrial Revolution, 1750–1850.* New York: F. S. Crofts, 1930.

Poirteir, Cathal, ed. *The Great Irish Famine.* Dublin: Mercier Press, 1995.

Pool, Daniel. *What Jane Austen Ate and Charles Dickens Knew.* New York: Simon & Schuster, 1993.

Pridmore, Walter B. *Van Diemen's Land to Tasmania, 1642–1856.* China: Everbest, 2008.

Priestley, Philip. *Victorian Prison Lives.* London: Methuen, 1985.

Purtscher, Joyce. *Children in Queen's Orphanage Hobart Town, 1828–1863.* New Town, Australia: Irene Schaffer, 1993.

Purtscher, Joyce. "Queen's Orphanage Hobart Town, 1828–1879." Paper presented to Female Factory Research Group, November 2007.

Rae, Janet. *The Quilts of the British Isles.* New York: E. P. Dutton, 1987.

Rayner, Tony. *Female Factory, Female Convicts.* Dover, Australia: Esperance Press, 2004.

Reakes, Janet. *How to Trace Your Convict Ancestors.* Sydney: Hale & Iremonger, 1987.

Reece, Bob, ed. *Irish Convict Lives.* Darlinghurst, Australia: Crossing Press, 1993.

Reece, Bob. *Irish Convicts.* Dublin: University College, 1989.

Rees, Sian. *The Floating Brothel.* New York: Hyperion Press, 2002.

Reid, Kirsty. *Gender, Crime and Empire: Convicts, Settlers and the State in Early Colonial Australia.* Manchester, UK: Manchester University Press, 2007.

Render, William H. *Through Prison Bars: The Lives and Labours of John Howard & Elizabeth Fry.* London: S. W. Partridge, 1894.

Richmond Primary School website, Department of Education, Tasmania. http://www.richmond.tased.edu.au/School/Principal/Principal.htm.

Robinson, Portia. *The Women of Botany Bay.* Victoria, Australia: Penguin Books Australia, 1988.

Robson, L. L. *The Convict Settlers of Australia.* Carlton, Australia: Melbourne University Press, 1965.

Rolfe, Margaret. *Australian Quilt Heritage.* Rushcutters Bay, Australia: J. B. Fairfax Press, 1998.

Ronan, Malcolm. *Up and Down the River: The Butlers from Benenden.* Melbourne, Australia: Macron Publishing, 1998.

Russell, Penny. "'Her Excellency': Lady Franklin, Female Convicts and the Problem of Authority in Van Diemen's Land." *Journal of Australian Studies* (1 June 1997).

Ryan, Lyndall. "Abduction and Multiple Killings of Aborigines in Tasmania: 1804–

1835." Visiting Fellow, Genocide Studies Program, Yale University, and Honorary Conjoint Professor School of Humanities and Social Sciences, Faculty of Education & Arts, University of Newcastle Ourimbah Campus, New South Wales, Australia.

Selby-Bigge, L. A., ed. *British Moralists: Being Selections from Writers Principally of the Eighteenth Century,* Volume I. New York: Dover Publications, 1965.

Selden, Bernice. *The Mill Girls.* New York: Atheneum Books, 1983.

Shaw, A. G. L. *Convicts and the Colonies: A Study of Penal Transportation from Great Britain and Ireland to Australia and Other Parts of the British Empire.* Dublin: The Irish Historical Press, 1998.

Shore, Heather. *Artful Dodgers: Youth and Crime in Early 19th-Century London.* Woodbridge, UK: Boydell Press, 1999.

Smith, Coultman. *Shadow over Tasmania.* Hobart, Australia: J. Walch & Sons, 1941.

South Ayrshire Council. "County Buildings." http://www.south-ayrshire.gov.uk/maps/countybuildings/.

Summers, Anne. *Damned Whores and God's Police.* Victoria, Australia: Penguin Books, 1975.

Tardif, Phillip. *Notorious Strumpets and Dangerous Girls.* North Ryde, Australia: Angus & Robertson Publishers, 1990.

Tatlow, Michael, Charles Wooley, and Peter Mercer. *A Tour of Old Tasmania.* Battery Point, Tasmania: Walk Guides Australia, 2008.

Thomas, Donald. *The Victorian Underworld.* New York: New York University Press, 1998.

Thompson, E. P. *The Making of the English Working Class.* New York: Vintage Books, 1966.

Timpson, Thomas. *Memoirs of Mrs. Elizabeth Fry.* Elibron Classics. First published in 1847.

Vallone, Lynne. *Becoming Victoria.* New Haven, CT: Yale University Press, 2001.

Villiers, Alan. *Vanished Fleets.* Oxford, UK: Scribner's, 1974.

Von Stieglitz, K. R. *A History of Oatlands and Jericho.* Launceston, Australia: Telegraph Printery, 1960.

Weeding, J. S. *A History of Oatlands.* New Norfolk, Australia: Derwent Printery, 1988.

West, John. *The History of Tasmania.* London: Angus & Robertson Publishers, 1971. First published in 1852.

Whitlock, Gillian, and Gail Reekie, eds. *Uncertain Beginnings.* St. Lucia, Australia: University of Queensland Press, 1993.

Whitney, Janet. *Elizabeth Fry.* London: Guild Books, 1947.

Williams, Brad, Heritage Project Officer, Southern Midlands Council. *Oatlands Gaol Conservation Management Plan 2006.* http://www.southernmidlands.tas.gov.au/webdata/resources/files/Oatlands_Gaol_CMP_compressed.pdf.

Williams, John. "Irish Female Convicts and Tasmania." *Labour History,* No. 44 (May 1993), 1–17.

Williams, John. *Ordered to the Island*. Darlinghurst, Australia: Crossing Press, 1994.

Williamson, Kristin. *Women on the Rocks*. Lucia, Australia: University of Queensland Press, 2003.

Wilson, A. N. *The Victorians*. New York: W. W. Norton, 2003.

Windschuttle, Elizabeth, ed. *Women, Class, and History*. Melbourne, Australia: Fontana Books, 1980.

Woodward, Frances J. *Portrait of Jane: A Life of Lady Franklin*. London: Hodder & Stoughton, 1951.

Woodward, Nicholas. "Transportation Convictions during the Great Irish Famine." *Journal of Interdisciplinary History*, Vol. 37, No. 1 (Summer 2006), 59–87.

Wooley, Charles, and Michael Tatlow. *A Walk in Old Hobart*. Battery Point, Tasmania: Walk Guides Australia, 2007.

Wooley, Charles, and Michael Tatlow. *A Walk in Old Launceston*. Battery Point, Tasmania: Walk Guides Australia, 2007.

Yancey, Diane. *Life in Charles Dickens's England*. San Diego, CA: Lucent Books, 1999.

INDEX